The Cambridge Companion to
Modern Irish Culture

This Companion provides an authoritative introduction to the
historical, social and stylistic complexities of modern Irish culture.
Readers will be introduced to Irish culture in its widest sense and
helped to find their way through the cultural and theoretical debates
that inform our understanding of modern Ireland. The volume
combines cultural breadth and historical depth, supported by a
chronology of Irish history and arts. A wide selection of essays on a rich
variety of Irish cultural forms and practices are complemented by a
series of in-depth analyses of key themes in Irish cultural politics. The
range of topics covered will enable a comprehensive understanding of
Irish culture, while the authors gathered here – all acknowledged
experts in their fields – provide stimulating new essays that together
amount to an invaluable guide to the shaping of modern Ireland.

JOE CLEARY is senior lecturer in English Literature at the National
University of Ireland, Maynooth, and has been Visiting Professor at
Notre Dame University. He has published several essays and book
chapters on modernisation, colonialism and twentieth-century Irish
culture, and a book, *Literature, Partition and the Nation State: Culture and
Conflict in Ireland, Israel and Palestine* (Cambridge, 2002).

CLAIRE CONNOLLY is a senior lecturer in English Literature and
Cultural Criticism at Cardiff University, and has been Visiting Associate
Professor of Irish Studies at Boston College. She edited the critical
anthology, *Theorizing Ireland*, as well as a number of scholarly editions of
nineteenth-century Irish novels, including two volumes of the *Tales and
Novels of Maria Edgeworth* and (with Stephen Copley) Sydney Owenson's
The Wild Irish Girl.

Cambridge Companions to Culture

The Cambridge Companion to Modern German Culture
Edited by EVA KOLINSKY *and* WILFRIED VAN DER WILL

The Cambridge Companion to Modern Russian Culture
Edited by NICHOLAS RZHEVSKY

The Cambridge Companion to Modern Spanish Culture
Edited by DAVID T. GIES

The Cambridge Companion to Modern Italian Culture
Edited by ZYGMUNT G. BARAŃSKI *and* REBECCA J. WEST

The Cambridge Companion to Modern French Culture
Edited by NICHOLAS HEWITT

The Cambridge Companion to Modern Latin American Culture
Edited by JOHN KING

The Cambridge Companion to Modern Irish Culture
Edited by JOE CLEARY *and* CLAIRE CONNOLLY

The Cambridge Companion to
Modern Irish Culture

Edited by
JOE CLEARY AND CLAIRE CONNOLLY

CAMBRIDGE
UNIVERSITY PRESS

CAMBRIDGE UNIVERSITY PRESS
Cambridge, New York, Melbourne, Madrid, Cape Town, Singapore, São Paulo

Cambridge University Press
The Edinburgh Building, Cambridge CB2 2RU, UK

Published in the United States of America by Cambridge University Press, New York

www.cambridge.org
Information on this title: www.cambridge.org/9780521820097

First published 2005

A catalogue record for this publication is available from the British Library

Library of Congress Cataloguing in Publication data
The Cambridge companion to modern Irish culture/edited by Joe Cleary and Claire Cannolly.
 p. cm. – (Cambridge companions to culture)
Includes bibliographical references and index.
ISBN 0 521 82009 X – ISBN 0 521 52629 9 (pbk.)
1. Ireland – Civilization – 20th century – Handbooks, manuals, etc. 2. Ireland –
Civilization – 19th century – Handbooks, manuals, etc. I. Cleary, Joe (Joseph N.)
II. Connolly, Claire. III. Series.
DA959.1.C35 2004
941.508 – dc22 2004052682

ISBN-13 978-0-521-82009-7 hardback
ISBN-10 0-521-82009-X hardback

ISBN-13 978-0-521-52629-6 paperback
ISBN-10 0-521-52629-9 paperback

Transferred to digital printing 2006

Contents

Illustrations

Contributors

ALAN BAIRNER is Reader in the Sociology of Sport at Loughborough University. He is the author of *Sport, Nationalism, and Globalization: European and North American Perspectives*, the co-author of *Sport, Sectarianism and Society in a Divided Ireland* and co-editor of *Sport in Divided Societies*. He has advised the Sports Council for Northern Ireland and the Irish Football Association on community relations issues and was a member of the ministerial advisory panel set up in 2001 to examine the future of soccer in Northern Ireland.

HUGH CAMPBELL is College Lecturer at the School of Architecture, University College Dublin, where he teaches the history and theory of architecture as well as working in the design studio. He has published numerous essays on modern architecture and urban history. His doctoral research was on the politics of urban development in nineteenth-century Dublin, and he is currently researching the relationship between urban consciousness and architecture.

JOE CLEARY is Senior Lecturer in English Literature at the National University of Ireland, Maynooth, and has been Visiting Professor at Notre Dame University. He has published several essays and book chapters on modernisation, colonialism and twentieth-century Irish culture, and a book, *Literature, Partition and the Nation-State: Culture and Conflict in Ireland, Israel and Palestine* (Cambridge, 2002).

CLAIRE CONNOLLY is Senior Lecturer in English Literature and Cultural Criticism at Cardiff University, and has been Visiting Associate Professor of Irish Studies at Boston College. She edited the critical anthology, *Theorizing Ireland*, as well as a number of scholarly editions of nineteenth-century Irish novels, including two volumes of the *Tales and Novels of Maria Edgeworth* and (with Stephen Copley) Sydney Owenson's *The Wild Irish Girl*.

FINTAN CULLEN teaches Art History at the University of Nottingham. His most recent publication is *The Irish Face: Redefining the Irish Portrait*, published by the National Portrait Gallery, London (2000). In 2005 he is co-curating an exhibition with Roy Foster at the National Portrait Gallery, entitled 'Conquering England: Ireland in the Victorian Metropolis'.

LUKE GIBBONS is the Keough Family Professor of Irish Studies at the University of Notre Dame. His publications include *Edmund Burke and Ireland: Aesthetics, Politics and the Colonial Sublime*; *Gaelic Gothic: Race, Colonization and Irish Culture*; *The Quiet Man*; *Transformations in Irish Culture* and (with Kevin Rockett and John Hill) *Cinema and Ireland*.

MARY J. HICKMAN is Professor of Irish Studies and Sociology at London Metropolitan University. Her publications include *Religion, Class and Identity* and (as editor with Avtar Brah and Mairtin Mac an Ghaill) *Thinking Identities: Ethnicity, Racism and Culture* and *Global Futures: Migration, Environment and Globalization* (1999). She and Bronwen Walter co-authored *Discrimination and the Irish Community in Britain* for the Commission for Racial Equality (1997). Professor Hickman has served on the Irish government's Task Force on Policy Regarding Emigrants (2001–2) and is currently writing a book about the Irish diaspora.

TOM INGLIS is Associate Professor of Sociology at University College Dublin. He has written extensively on religion in Ireland, particularly the influence of the Catholic Church on Irish culture and society. He is author of *Moral Monopoly: The Catholic Church in Modern Irish Society*; *Lessons in Irish Sexuality*; and *Truth, Power and Lies: Modern Irish Society and the Case of the Kerry Babies*.

ALVIN JACKSON is Professor of Modern British and Irish History at the University of Edinburgh. He has been Professor of Modern Irish History at Queen's University, Belfast, John Burns Visiting Professor at Boston College and a British Academy Research Reader. His recent books include *Home Rule: An Irish History* (2003) and *Ireland 1798–1998: Politics and War* (2004).

SIOBHÁN KILFEATHER teaches in the English Department at Queen's University, Belfast. She has edited *The Field Day Anthology of Irish Writing: Irish Women's Writing and Traditions* and the Pickering and Chatto edition of Maria Edgeworth's *Belinda*. She has published a number of influential essays on Irish women's writing, particularly in the eighteenth and nineteenth centuries and is currently writing a book on *Rhetorics of Atrocity in Romantic Ireland*.

CHRISTOPHER MORASH is author of *A History of Irish Theatre: 1601–2000*, winner of the Theatre Book Prize, 2002. His earlier work includes *Writing the Irish Famine* and many articles on Irish cultural history. He is currently Director of Media Studies at National University of Ireland, Maynooth.

EMER NOLAN is a Lecturer in English at the National University of Ireland, Maynooth. She is the author of *Joyce and Nationalism*, a study of Joyce's politics and Irish modernism.

BERNARD O'DONOGHUE teaches Medieval English at Wadham College, Oxford. He has written a study of Seamus Heaney's language, as well as an anthology of medieval European love poetry. His first book of poems was *Poaching Rights* and he has published four collections with Chatto & Windus, of which the most recent is *Outliving*.

LIAM O'DOWD is Professor of Sociology and Director of the Centre for International Borders Research at Queen's University, Belfast. He has published extensively on the political sociology and economy of Northern Ireland, on Irish intellectuals and on changing state borders.

DIARMUID Ó GIOLLÁIN is Senior Lecturer in Folklore at the National University of Ireland, Cork, and author of *Locating Irish Folklore: Tradition, Modernity, Identity*. He has published essays on ethnology; popular religion; historical tradition; and Irish, Nordic, Estonian and Latin American (particularly Brazilian) popular culture and research traditions.

LILLIS Ó LAOIRE is Lecturer in Irish Language and Literature, Department of Languages and Cultural Studies, University of Limerick, and Visiting Assistant Professor at Loyola Marymount University, Los Angeles. A noted traditional singer, he is also director of Ionad na nAmhrán, a centre for the study and performance of traditional song at the Irish World Music Centre, University of Limerick. His book, *On A Rock in the Middle of the Ocean: Songs and Singers in Tory Island*, will be published in 2005.

GEARÓID Ó TUATHAIGH is Professor of History at the National
University of Ireland, Galway. He is the author of *Ireland Before the Famine 1798–1848* and many influential essays on nineteenth-century history and the Irish language.

PÁDRAIGÍN RIGGS is Senior Lecturer in the Department of Modern Irish at the National University of Ireland, Cork. She is the author of *Donncha Ó Céileachair: Anailís Stíleach*; *Pádraic Ó Conaire: Deoraí* and the editor of *Dáibhí O Bruadair: His Historical and Literary Context* and (with B. Ó Conchúir and S. Ó Coileáin) *Saoi na hÉigse*. She is currently preparing an edition of the writings of Pádraic Ó Conaire for the Irish Texts Society.

NORMAN VANCE is Professor of English and Director of the Humanities Graduate Research Centre at the University of Sussex. He has published widely on Victorian and Irish literature: his books include *The Victorians and Ancient Rome*, *Irish Literature: a Social History* and *Irish Literature since 1800*.

KEVIN WHELAN is the inaugural Michael J. Smurfit Director of the University of Notre Dame's Keough Centre in Dublin. He has been a Visiting Professor at New York University, Boston College and Concordia University. Among his books are *Nations and Nationalisms in the Eighteenth Century*, *The Tree of Liberty*, *The Atlas of the Irish Rural Landscape* and *1798: A Bicentenary Perspective*.

Preface

Ireland is a small island that has made large claims on world interest. To some, it will be best known for its eventful history of conquest and settlement, dispossession and diaspora, repression and rebellion, land agitation and famine. Its independence struggle triggered the beginning of the end of an empire, but issued domestically in partition, civil war and new state repressions – a turbulent history, then, the bitter intensity of which has been most recently evident in the quarter-century-long conflict in Northern Ireland usually termed the 'Troubles'.

Despite this, Ireland has long nurtured a romantic rural self-image calculated to appeal to those in flight from the complexities of the modern world. History fades against its much-sung landscape of rocky coastlines, rolling grasslands, misted mountain ranges, boglands and moor. In one of the many paradoxes of modern Irish culture, the country has come to represent both the romantic pleasures of solitude and seclusion and traditional virtues of conversation, sociability and tight-knit communities. Ever since the mid nineteenth century, when Belfast became one of the world's major industrial centres, that rural image became associated more with the southern than with the northern part of the island, and indeed it was not until the census of 1966 that the urban population of the Irish Republic was first recorded as having exceeded the rural. Today, the old rural national image is on the wane and the country currently likes to represent itself as a thriving, energetic, cosmopolitan place, a vibrant multicultural hub of postindustrial, information-age entrepreneurial activity. The revels of the comely maidens dancing at the crossroads of the local townsland now are ended or linger only as national kitsch; the country prefers instead a corporate quick-step on a global crossroads between Boston, Bermuda and Berlin.

For many people, of course, Ireland's claim to attention will reside primarily in an extraordinarily sustained tradition of literature and letters distinguished by Bishop Berkeley and Jonathan Swift, Oliver Goldsmith and Edmund Burke, Thomas Moore and Maria Edgeworth, Oscar Wilde and George Bernard Shaw, James Joyce and W. B. Yeats, Sean O'Casey and Samuel Beckett, Louis MacNeice and Seamus Heaney, Elizabeth Bowen and John McGahern. Classical music traditions weigh lightly compared to those of other Western European nationalities such as the Germans or Italians, and yet the Irish are no less famous for their love of music and song. The country's traditional airs, *sean nós* singing, ballad treasuries and folk-music revivals have exerted influence across the globe, either in their own right or as stimulus to other musical cultures. Ireland's own cultural traditions have drawn heavily on popular song and the lyric inheritance. In contemporary times, Ireland's accomplishments in popular music especially have won a global audience that will compare in reach with that which its writers have already achieved.

The small population of the island itself must be set, moreover, against an extensive Irish diaspora that stretches from the Americas to the Antipodes and all across the far-flung territories of what was, until relatively recent decades, the British Empire. Some of the great cities of modern times, Manchester, New York, Liverpool, Boston, Glasgow, Toronto or Melbourne, to name but a few, have modern Irish histories and heritages as varied and interesting as those of Dublin or Belfast. By virtue, then, of its tempestuous history, which generated this far-flung diaspora, and which inspired its sometimes extraordinary achievements in literature and the other arts, Ireland attests in a whole complex of ways to the manner in which supposedly minor or peripheral societies can have an impact on the world as significant as that of countries more commonly considered major and metropolitan.

This volume aims to offer its readers a useful overview of modern Irish culture as it has changed and developed from 1800 to 2000. Beginning with a century of frequently calamitous change that followed the United Irishmen's rebellion in 1798 and Ireland's integration into the United Kingdom consequent to the Act of Union in 1800, the volume concludes with another period of rather dramatic social transformation ushered in by the economic boom in the Republic of Ireland usually known as the 'Celtic Tiger' and by the concurrent 'peace process' in Northern Ireland that has proceeded since the Good Friday Agreement of 1998. A country with so disputed a history has inevitably generated much scholarly controversy and today Ireland as subject is of interest to academics and students concerned with issues as diverse as nation-building and globalisation, colonialism and postcolonialism, sexuality and religion, modernism and regional cultures, migration studies and ethnic conflict.

The topics engaged here have been selected with an eye to the interests of both the general reader and the more specialised student of the culture, and while the volume cannot over a two-century stretch claim to comprehensiveness, the individual chapters, all written by distinguished authorities in the field, offer lucid, accessible surveys that are also scholarly, searching and provocative. Some of the chapters lean towards a chronological or narrative account of their matter, dealing with the more significant episodes or contours of development in the area in question; others are more conceptual in format, opting for an approach that evaluates the major controversies that have shaped scholarship in their subject areas. The volume as a whole offers its readers, we believe, an attractively varied account of the manifold social forces, domestic and international, that have gone into the making of Irish culture over the past two hundred years.

Contemporary commentators remind us that the word 'culture' is at once too slack to serve specialist analysis and too rigid to be greatly useful. In its broader anthropological definitions, culture can refer to the 'whole way of life' of a group of people, or to the state of intellectual development of a complete society; in its more restrictive usages, it is narrowly identified with processes of self-cultivation and mental refinement and associated with certain valued artistic and intellectual activities. Whereas 'culture' broadly defined risks becoming co-extensive with society such that any capacity to distinguish between what is and is not deemed cultural activity collapses, in its narrower versions the term can connote forms of practice so rarefied as to be almost totally unconnected to the everyday lives of the vast majority of people in any society.

The present volume can hardly escape the conceptual dilemmas that attend to our contemporary usage of the word, but it does try to steer its way between the more all-inclusive and the more specialised notions of 'culture' as adroitly as possible. The volume opens with an introductory essay designed to give readers a solid foundation in the historical and conceptual frameworks necessary to understand modern Irish culture. In critically surveying the different ways in which Ireland's relationship to the modern and to modernity has been elaborated over the past two centuries, the introductory chapter serves to ground and position what follows. The chapters in Part I, 'Cultural politics', then move on to deal with defining historical events (such as the Act of Union or the Great Famine) or with broader social movements and political and cultural practices (such as unionism, republicanism, religion, language change, migration and feminism) that have significantly conditioned the texture of Irish culture understood in the extended sense of the whole way of life of a people. Part II, 'Cultural practices and cultural forms', deals with culture in the more restricted aesthetic sense that refers to the arts and social recreation, but does so in a way that makes space alongside what are conventionally deemed the 'high' or 'fine' arts for more popular pursuits such as sports, cinema or folklore as well. Ireland's exceptional achievements in the literary arts are reflected in the weighting of the volume, but one of the attractions of the present collection will be, we hope, that developments in the various 'popular' and 'fine' arts can be surveyed here directly alongside each other such that the diversity and the inter-weave of modern Irish cultural production can more readily be appreciated. In so far as has been possible within the remit of these short essays, the volume attempts to deal with modern Irish culture as it extends not only across two centuries but also across two languages and indeed across the two states that emerged when the island was partitioned in the early nineteen twenties. Recognising that some of the most exciting and controversial developments in Irish cultural history begin at Holyhead, Larne or Shannon, the chapter on migration deals with the Irish abroad, primarily with their modern histories in Britain and the United States, but also in Australia, New Zealand and Canada.

We hope to have assembled here a volume useful to those wishing to understand the contradictory, contested elements that went into the making of the past two centuries of modern Irish culture. Should those wishing to renovate and innovate within that culture as we move into the new century ahead also find some stimulus in its pages, we would be especially pleased.

Acknowledgements

The editors would like express their gratitude to our authors for their patience and good humour and to Ray Ryan, literature editor at Cambridge University Press, who commissioned the project. Deep-felt thanks to the following for advice, assistance and encouragement: Jacqueline Belanger, Chris Evans, Kevin Kenny, Tim Killick, Andrew Lane, Liam Lanigan, Jane Moore, Conor McCarthy, Emer Nolan, Matthew Stout and Kevin Whelan. Our special gratitude to Paul and to Gemma and Conor, companions who sustained us during our work on 'the Companion'.

Chronology

Year	Irish cultural and intellectual events	Irish history	International cultural and intellectual events	International history
1789	Charlotte Brooke, *Reliques of Irish Poetry*		Noah Webster, *Dissertations on the English Language*	Outbreak of the first French Revolution; first cotton factory established in Manchester
1795		Orange Order founded; Act for the establishment of a Catholic seminary at Maynooth		Dutch surrender of Ceylon to British; Warren Hastings acquitted of corruption; building of the Bank of England begins (finished 1827)
1796	Edward Bunting, *A General Collection of the Ancient Music of Ireland*			British capture Elba; Chinese authorities forbid the import of opium
1798	Regina Maria Roche, *Clermont*	United Irishmen's Rebellion	William Wordsworth and Samuel Coleridge, *Lyrical Ballads* (1798–1800); Thomas Malthus, *Essay on the Principle of Population*; Charles Brockden Brown, *Wieland*	Napoleon invades Egypt
1800	Maria Edgeworth, *Castle Rackrent*	Act of Union passed	Robert Burns, *The Poems of Robert Burns* (4 vols)	British occupy Malta

1803		Robert Emmet Rebellion		
1804				Haiti (Saint-Dominique) becomes first independent black country
1806	Sydney Owenson (Lady Morgan), *The Wild Irish Girl*		Walter Scott, *Ballads and Lyrical Pieces*	Britain reoccupies the Cape of Good Hope
1807	Gaelic Society of Dublin founded		G. W. F. Hegel, *The Phenomenology of Spirit*	British abolition of the slave trade; Sierra Leone and Gambia become British colonies
1808	Thomas Moore, *Irish Melodies* (−1834); Charles Maturin, *The Wild Irish Boy*; Elizabeth Hamilton, *The Cottagers of Glenburnie*	Edmund Rice founds Christian Brothers	William Blake, *Milton*	United States prohibits the import of slaves from Africa
1811	Kildare Place Society founded; Sydney Owenson, *The Missionary*		Jane Austen, *Sense and Sensibility*	British troops occupy Java; Luddite riots in northern England
1812	Charles Maturin, *The Milesian Chief*; Maria Edgeworth, *The Absentee*		P. B. Shelley, *An Address to the Irish People*; Lord Byron, *Childe Harold's Pilgrimage*; Jane West, *The Loyalists*	United States declares war on Britain; last major outbreak of bubonic plague in Europe

(cont.)

Year	Irish cultural and intellectual events	Irish history	International cultural and intellectual events	International history
1813		Catholic relief bill introduced by Grattan in the House of Commons	Jane Austen, *Pride and Prejudice*	The monopoly on Indian trade of the East India company ended; Paraguay becomes first independent republic in South America; Simón Bolívar titled 'the Liberator' in Venezuela
1814	Maria Edgeworth, *Patronage*	Belfast Academical Institution opened	Walter Scott, *Waverley*; Jane Austen, *Mansfield Park*	British invade Washington
1815	William Drennan, *Fugitive Pieces in Verse and Prose*		Jane Austen, *Emma*; S. T. Coleridge, *Christabel* and *Kubla Khan*	Battle of Waterloo and defeat of Napoleon; Congress of Vienna
1817	Thomas Moore, *Lallah Rookh*; Maria Edgeworth, *Ormond*	Famine and typhoid fever epidemic	S. T. Coleridge, *Biographia Literaria*; James Mill, *The History of British India*; John Keats, *Poems*	Venezeulan independence confirmed; First Seminole War begins in the United States (–1818)
1818	Sydney Owenson, *Florence Macarthy*		William Blake, *Jerusalem*; John Keats, *Endymion*; Walter Scott, *Rob Roy*; Mary Shelley, *Frankenstein*	British defeat the Maratha Empire in India to secure the Gangetic plain; Chile declares independence
1820	Charles Maturin, *Melmoth the Wanderer*	Accession of George IV; death of Henry Grattan	Thomas Malthus, *Principles of Political Economy*; P. B. Shelley, *Prometheus Unbound*	

1823	Royal Hibernian Academy (of Art) founded	Catholic Association founded	James Fenimore Cooper, *The Pioneers*	The Monroe Doctrine prevents new European colonial settlements in Western hemisphere
1824	Thomas Moore, *Memoirs of Captain Rock*; T. C. Croker, *Researches in the South of Ireland*		James Hogg, *Private Memoirs and Confessions of a Justified Sinner*	British invasion of Upper Burma (–1826)
1825	William Thompson and Anne Wheeler, *An Appeal of One Half of the Human Race, Women, against the Pretensions of the Other half, Men, to Retain them in Political....Slavery*; J. and M. Banim, *Tales of the O'Hara Family* (–1826); T. C. Croker, *Fairy Legends and Traditions of the South of Ireland*	Ordnance Survey commences (–1841)	Alessandro Manzoni, *The Betrothed* (–1827); William Hazlitt, *The Spirit of the Age*	John Franklin begins Arctic explorations to find a north-west passage to Asia and the Pacific; Upper Peru establishes itself as Bolivia
1826	John Banim, *The Boyne Water*		James Fenimore Cooper, *The Last of the Mohicans*; William Hazlitt, *The Plain Speaker*	
1829	Gerald Griffin, *The Collegians*	Catholic Emancipation	Walter Scott, *Waverley Novels*, 48 vols. (–1833)	
1830	William Carleton, *Traits and Stories of the Irish Peasantry*, 1st series	Accession of William IV	Stendhal, *The Red and the Black*; Founding of Royal Geographic Society in London	Sati abolished in Bengal

(cont.)

Year	Irish cultural and intellectual events	Irish history	International cultural and intellectual events	International history
1831	James Hardiman (ed.), *Irish Minstrelsy*; Thomas Moore, *The Life and Death of Lord Edward Fitzgerald*	State-directed system of National Education introduced	Edgar Allan Poe, *Poems*	Mazzini founds Young Italy movement; Jamaican slave revolt; Darwin voyages on HMS *Beagle* to South America, New Zealand and Australia
1832	John Banim, *The Denounced; or, the Last Baron of Crana*	Cholera outbreak in Belfast and Dublin spreads across country	P. B. Shelley, *The Masque of Anarchy*; Robert Southey, *Essays, Moral and Political*	Great Reform Act passed by British parliament
1833	*Dublin University Magazine* founded (–187?); Jonah Barrington, *Rise and Fall of the Irish Nation*; George Petrie, *Essay on the Round Towers of Ireland*		Charles Lamb, *The Last Essays of Elia*; Alexsandr Pushkin, *Eugene Onegin*	Abolition of slavery throughout the British Empire; American Anti-Slavery Society founded
1837	S. Mahony, *Reliques of Father Prout*	Death of William IV; Victoria succeeds to British throne	Ralph Waldo Emerson, 'The American Scholar'; Nathaniel Hawthorne, *Twice-Told Tales*	Accession of Queen Victoria; revolts in Lower and Upper Canada
1839	T. C. Croker, *Popular Songs of Ireland*	The Custody of Infants Act		
1840	Thomas Moore, *The Poetical Works of Thomas Moore* (10 vols.) (–1841)	Daniel O'Connell's Repeal Association established	Robert Browning, *Sordello*	Treaty of Waitangi establishes British control over New Zealand

1841	Frederic William Burton, *The Aran Fisherman's Drowned Child*	Daniel O'Connell elected lord mayor of Dublin	Thomas Carlyle, *On Heroes, Hero-Worship and the Heroic in History*; Ralph Waldo Emerson, *Essays, First Series*	New Zealand recognised as a British colony; British proclaim sovereignty over Hong Kong
1842	*The Nation* founded (–1896); R. R. Madden, *Lives and Times of the United Irishmen*, 7 vols. (–1846)	College of All Hallows established to educate Catholic missionaries	Death of Stendhal; Giuseppi Verdi, *Nabucco*	Treaty of Nanking ends Opium War, confirming the cession of Hong Kong to Britain
1843	W. M. Thackeray, *Irish Sketchbook*	Monster repeal meetings in Trim and Tara; Clontarf meeting proclaimed	Thomas Carlyle, *Past and Present*; Søren Kierkegaard, *Either/Or*; John Ruskin, *Modern Painters*	Maori revolts against British settlement in New Zealand
1844	Queen's University of Ireland (colleges in Cork, Galway and Belfast) opened; T. C. Croker, *The Keen in the South of Ireland*		Søren Kierkegaard, *The Concept of Dread*; Dumas père, *The Three Musketeers*; Ralph Waldo Emerson, *Essays; Second Series*	
1845	Charles Gavan Duffy, *The Ballad Poetry of Ireland*	The Great Famine (–1848)	Friedrich Engels, *The Condition of the Working Class in England*; Benjamin Disraeli, *Sybil; or, The Two Nations*; Edgar Allan Poe, *The Raven and Other Poems*; Domingo F. Sarmineto, *Facundo*; Richard Wagner, *Tannhäuser*	First British–Sikh War in India; USA annexes Texas

(cont.)

Year	Irish cultural and intellectual events	Irish history	International cultural and intellectual events	International history
1846	James Clarence Mangan, 'Siberia' and 'The Dark Rosaleen'; Thomas Davis, *Literary and Historical Essays* and *The Poems of Thomas Davis*		Honoré de Balzac, *Cousin Bette*; Herman Melville, *Typee*	Treaty of Lahore ends First Sikh War; Seventh Kaffir War begins in South Africa; Repeal of the Corn Laws ends protectionism; Mexican War (–1848)
1847	Anthony Trollope, *The Macdermots of Ballycloran*	Daniel O'Connell dies in Genoa	Emily Brontë, *Wuthering Heights*; Charlotte Brontë, *Jane Eyre*; Herman Melville, *Omoo*	Liberia declared a settlement territory for freed slaves, though under US protection
1848	J. O'Donovan (ed.), *Annals of the Four Masters* (1848–51); William Carleton, *The Emigrants of Ahadarra*	Young Ireland Rising	Karl Marx and Friedrich Engels, *The Communist Manifesto*; J. S. Mill, *Principles of Political Economy*; Elizabeth Gaskell, *Mary Barton*; W. M. Thackeray, *Vanity Fair*; Charles Dickens, *Dombey and Son*;	Revolutions across Europe; Californian gold rush
1849	James Clarence Mangan, *The Poets and Poetry of Munster*		Herman Melville, *Redburn*; Robert Browning, *Poems*	British annex Punjab
1850		Irish Tenant League founded	Alfred Tennyson, *In Memoriam*; Charles Dickens, *David Copperfield*; Nathaniel Hawthorne, *The Scarlet Letter*; Richard Wagner, *Lohengrin*; Death of Balzac	

1851	Society for the Preservation and Publication of the Melodies of Ireland founded	Ecclesiastical Titles act	Herman Melville, *Moby Dick*; Giuseppe Verdi, *Rigoletto*	Great Exhibition opens in Crystal Palace, London
1852	William Wilde, *Irish Popular Superstitions*		Harriet Beecher Stowe, *Uncle Tom's Cabin*	The South Africa Republic (the Transvaal) established
1854	John Mitchel, *Jail Journal*	Catholic University founded	Ernest Renan, 'La poésie des races Celtiques'; Henry David Thoreau, *Walden*	Crimean War (–1856)
1855	George Petrie, *The Petrie Collection of the Ancient Music of Ireland*, vol. I	Emmet Monument Association formed by Michael Doheny and John O'Mahony in New York	Richard Burton, *Pilgrimage to Mecca*	Britain begins war against Persia
1856	Irish Academy of Music founded			Natal established as a Crown Colony
1857	John Elliot Cairnes, *The Character and Logical Method of Political Economy*	Sectarian rioting in Belfast	Gustave Flaubert, *Madame Bovary*; Anthony Trollope, *Barchester Towers*	Great Indian Rebellion, known as the Mutiny, begins
1858		Irish Republican Brotherhood founded		Government of India Act places sovereignty over India in hands of British monarch
1859	*Poems of James Clarence Mangan* (Introduction by John Mitchel)	Religious revival in Ulster; Fenian Brotherhood founded in New York; First number of *Irish Times*	Charles Darwin, *On the Origin of Species*; George Eliot, *Adam Bede*; Alfred Tennyson, *Idylls of the King*; Samuel Smiles, *Self-Help*; John Stuart Mill, *On Liberty*	Work on the Suez canal begins

(cont.)

Year	Irish cultural and intellectual events	Irish history	International cultural and intellectual events	International history
1860	Dion Boucicault, *The Colleen Bawn*	Adair evictions at Derryveagh, Co. Donegal	Nathaniel Hawthorne, *The Marble Faun*	Outbreak of the Second Maori War (–1863); Treaty of Peking signed; Garibaldi's expedition to Sicily
1861	John Mitchel, *The Last Conquest of Ireland (Perhaps)*; Edmund Falconer, *Peep O'Day*		Ivan Turgenev, *Fathers and Sons*; Charles Dickens, *Great Expectations*	American Civil War breaks out; Vittorio Emanuel II becomes king of united Italy
1864	National Gallery of Ireland opened; Samuel Ferguson, *Lays of the Western Gael*; Sheridan Le Fanu, *Uncle Silas*; John Elliot Cairnes, *The Slave Power*	Contagious Diseases Act; foundation stone laid for John Henry Foley's statue to O'Connell	Fyodor Dostoyevsky, *Notes from Underground*	
1867	Meeting in Belfast of National Association for the Promotion of Social Science	Fenian Rising	Karl Marx, *Das Kapital I*; Matthew Arnold, *On the Study of Celtic Literature*; Henrik Ibsen, *Peer Gynt*; Emile Zola, *Thérèse Raquin*	First Vatican Council (–1870); British North American Act establishes the Dominion of Canada; diamonds discovered in South Africa
1869		Disestablishment of the Church of Ireland; Ladies National Association for the Repeal of the Contagious Disease Act formed in London (branches opened in Ireland by 1871)	Gustave Flaubert, *A Sentimental Education*; John Stuart Mill, *On the Subjection of Women*	Opening of the Suez Canal

Year				
		launched in Dublin; Gladstone's First Land Act; first public suffrage meeting in Dublin; Married Women's Property Act	*the Irish Land Question*; Charles Dickens, *The Mystery of Edwin Drood*; *Revue Celtique* founded	The Commune; official foundation of Second German Reich, Otto von Bismarck in office as chancellor
1871	Gaiety Theatre opens	Fenian invasion of Canada	Edward Taylor, *Primitive Culture*; Charles Darwin, *The Descent of Man*; Giuseppi Verdi's *Aïda* performed in Cairo	
1872	Samuel Ferguson, *Congal: An Epic Poem*; Charles Lever, *Lord Kilgobbin*; Nathaniel Hone, *Old Woman Gathering Sticks* (c. 1872)		Friedrich Nietzsche, *The Birth of Tragedy*; Jules Verne, *Around The World in Eighty Days*	
1873	Charles Kickham, *Knocknagow*	Home Rule League founded	Leo Tolstoy, *Anna Karenina* (–1877)	Asante Expedition leads to the creation of the Gold Coast as Crown Colony (–1874); famine in Bengal
1874	Dion Boucicault, *The Shaughraun*	59 Home Rule MP's Returned in General Election	First Impressionist exhibition held in Paris; Modest Mussorgsky, *Boris Gudanov*; Richard Wagner, *Der Ring des Nibelungen*	
1876	Society for the Preservation of the Irish Language founded	Dublin Women's Suffrage Association founded		Queen Victoria proclaimed empress of India; Battle of the Little Bighorn

(cont.)

Year	Irish cultural and intellectual events	Irish history	International cultural and intellectual events	International history
1877	Dublin Metropolitan School of Art established; Margaret Anna Cusack, *A History of the Irish Nation*; Annie Besant, *The Gospel of Atheism*	Parnell elected president of Home Rule Confederation of Great Britian and Ireland; Michael Davitt released from Dartmoor; Society of African Missions founded	Henry James, *The Europeans*	Revolt of Chief Joseph of the Nez Perce; famine in Bengal; Britain annexes the Transvaal
1878	Standish O'Grady, *History of Ireland: The Heroic Period*		Friedrich Nietzsche, *Human, All Too Human*	Paris World Exposition; Gold Standard established in Europe
1879	Standish O'Grady, *Early Bardic Literature, Ireland*	National Land League founded; campaign to extend Royal University Act to women	Henrik Ibsen, *A Doll's House*; Henry James, *Daisy Miller*	The British–Zulu War; *La Marseillaise* becomes French national anthem; Spanish prime minister frees all Cuban slaves
1883	Anthony Trollope, *The Land Leaguers*; Rosa Mulholland, *The Wild Birds of Kileevy*; Charlotte Riddell, *A Struggle for Fame*		Friedrich Nietzsche, *Thus Spake Zarathustra* (–1892); J. R. Seeley, *The Expansion of England*; R. L. Stevenson, *Treasure Island*; Olive Schreiner, *The Story of an African Farm*; Guy de Maupussant, *A Life*	
1884	Gaelic Athletic Association founded	Fenian dynamite campaign in Great Britain	Joris-Karl Huysmans, *A rebours*; Mark Twain, *Huckleberry Finn*; G. A. Henty, *With Clive in India*	Convention in London confirms independence of Transvaal; Germany occupies South West Africa

Year				
1886	George Moore, *A Drama in Muslin*; Emily Lawless, *Hurrish*; Standish O'Grady, *Toryism and the Tory Democracy*; Rosa Mulholland, *Marcella Grace*	Contagious Diseases Act repealed; Gladstone presents Home Rule Bill to House of Commons	Friedrich Nietzsche, *Beyond Good and Evil*; Henry James, *The Bostonians* and *The Princess Casamassima*; R. L. Stevenson, *Dr Jekyll and Mr Hyde*	Britain annexes Upper Burma; opening of Statue of Liberty in New York
1888	W. B. Yeats, *Fairy and Folk Tales of the Irish Peasantry*; *Poems and Ballads of Young Ireland*; John Kells Ingram, *A History of Political Economy*; Oscar Wilde, *The Happy Prince and other Stories*		First International Folklore Congress held in Paris; August Strindberg, *Miss Julie*; Henry James, *The Aspern Papers*	Brazil abolishes slavery
1889	W. B. Yeats, *The Wanderings of Oisin*	Pigott forgeries, attempting to blacken the reputation of Charles Stewart Parnell, exposed		Cecil Rhodes launches the British South Africa Company; Eiffel Tower completed
1890	Belfast City Art Gallery opened; Jeremiah Curtin, *Myths and Folklore of Ireland*; Douglas Hyde, *Beside the Fire*; T. W. Rolleston, ed., *Prose Writings of Thomas Davis*	Fall of Parnell, split in the Irish Parliamentary Party; Opening of National Library and of Science and Art Museum	J. G. Frazer, *The Golden Bough*; Henrik Ibsen, *Hedda Gabler*; Emily Dickinson, *Poems*; Peter Tchaikovsky, *Queen of Spades*	The dismissal of Bismarck; Eritrea becomes Italian colony; US Bureau of Census declares the American frontier closed

(cont.)

Year	Irish cultural and intellectual events	Irish history	International cultural and intellectual events	International history
1891	Oscar Wilde, *The Picture of Dorian Gray* and *The Soul of Man under Socialism*; George Bernard Shaw, *The Quintessence of Ibsenism*	Death of Parnell: John Redmond becomes leader of the Parnellites	Thomas Hardy, *Tess of the d'Urbervilles*; José Martí, 'Our America'; Paul Gaugin goes to live in Tahiti; Sherlock Holmes stories begin in *Strand* magazine	Franco-Russian Entente
1892	National Literary Society founded; W. B. Yeats and Lady Gregory, *Countess Cathleen*; W. E. H. Lecky, *A History of Ireland in the Eighteenth Century*, 4 vols.; Douglas Hyde, 'On the Necessity for De-Anglicising Ireland'	Ulster Convention in Belfast; Belfast Labour Party (first Irish labour party) formed	A. Conan Doyle, *The Adventures of Sherlock Holmes*; Rudyard Kipling, *Barrack-Room Ballads*	Keir Hardie becomes first British Labour MP; First Pan-Slav conference held at Cracow
1893	Gaelic League founded; Oscar Wilde, *Salomé*; W. B. Yeats, *The Celtic Twilight*; Douglas Hyde, *Love Songs of Connacht*; George Moore, *The Strike at Arlingford*	Gladstone introduces Second Home Rule Bill; disturbances in Belfast; Home Rule Bill passes in House of Commons; Trades Union Congress meets in Belfast	William Morris, *Socialism: Its Growth and Outcome*	World Exhibition in Chicago; Natal granted responsible self-government; Swaziland annexed by the Transvaal
1894	Sommerville and Ross, *The Real Charlotte*; George Moore, *Esther Waters*; Jeremiah Curtin, *Hero-Tales of Ireland*	Horace Plunkett founds Irish Agricultural Organisation Society; first Irish Trade Union Congress	Claude Debussy, *L'Après-midi d'un Faune*; Gustav Mahler, *Resurrection Symphony*	The conviction of Dreyfus for treason; Alfred Webb, MP for Waterford West, elected president of Indian National

Year				
	Gaelic Literature; Oscar Wilde, *The Importance of Being Ernest*; John Kells Ingram, *A History of Slavery and Serfdom*		Lumière Brothers; Thomas Hardy, *Jude the Obscure* and *The Wessex Novels* (16 vols. –1896); Joseph Conrad, *Almayer's Folly*; H. G. Wells, *The Time Machine*; Marie Corelli, *The Sorrows of Satan*	Transvaal Republic; Guglielmo Marconi invents telegraphy; Roentgen's discovery of X-rays; The trial of Oscar Wilde
1896	Kuno Meyer founds *Zeitschrift für Celtische Philologie*; Sommerville and Ross, *Some Experiences of an Irish R. M.*	Irish Socialist Republican Party founded, secretary James Connolly	Anton Chekhov, *The Seagull*	Italian forces defeated by Abyssinians at Adowa; Kitchener begins reconquest of Sudan; Klondike gold rush commences in Canada
1897	Irish Literary Theatre founded; Bram Stoker, *Dracula*: George Sigerson, *Bards of the Gael and Gall*; Oscar Wilde, *De Profundis* (published 1905)	First Irish céilí held at Bloomsbury Hall in London	Rudyard Kipling, 'Recessional'; James, *What Maisie Knew*; Mary Kingsley, *Travels in West Africa*	Queen Victoria's Diamond Jubilee; widespread famine in India; First Zionist Congress launches the Basle Programme to resettle Jewish people in Palestine; World Zionist Organisation established
1898	Oscar Wilde, *The Ballad of Reading Gaol*	Local government vote granted to women	Emile Zola, 'J'Accuse'; Thomas Hardy, *Wessex Poems*; Henry James, *The Turn of the Screw*	Kitchener fights Battle of Omdurman against the Mahdists to avenge Gordon; the Fashoda Incident; the Curies discover radium and plutonium

(cont.)

Year	Irish cultural and intellectual events	Irish history	International cultural and intellectual events	International history
1899	Douglas Hyde, *A Literary History of Ireland*; W. B. Yeats, *The Wind Among the Reeds*; F. N. Finck, *Die araner Mundart*; *The Countess Cathleen* staged	Catholic Truth Society of Ireland founded	Joseph Conrad, *Heart of Darkness*; Rudyard Kipling, 'The White Man's Burden'; Anton Chekhov, *Uncle Vanya*; Leo Tolstoy, *Resurrection*; Thorstein Veblen, *Theory of the Leisure Class*	Outbreak of the Boer War (–1902)
1900	First number of D. P. Moran's *The Leader*; Alice Milligan, *The Last of the Fianna*	Cumann na nGaedheal founded (later becomes Sinn Féin); first meeting of Inghinidhe na hÉireann	Joseph Conrad, *Lord Jim*; Sigmund Freud, *The Interpretation of Dreams*; Giacomo Puccini, *Tosca*	Nigeria becomes a British Protectorate; 'Boxer Rebellion' in China
1901	Lady Gregory (ed.), *Ideals in Ireland*; Canon Sheehan, *Luke Delmege*	Queen Victoria succeeded by Edward VII	August Strindberg, *Dance of Death*; Anton Chekov, *Three Sisters*; Rudyard Kipling, *Kim*	Australian Federation established; death of Queen Victoria
1902	W. B. Yeats, *Cathleen ni Houlihan*; Lady Gregory, *Cuchulain of Muirthemne*; John B. Yeats, *George Moore*	Emergence of Ulster branch of Irish Literary Theatre	André Gide, *The Immoralist*; J. A. Hobson, *Imperialism*; Euclides da Cunha, *Rebellion in the Backlands*	The South African War ends; death of Cecil Rhodes

1903	Irish National Theatre Society founded; *An Túr Gloine* founded; J. M. Synge, *In the Shadow of the Glen*; Lady Gregory, *Poets and Dreamers*; George Moore, *The Untilled Field*	Wyndham's Land Act	Rabindranath Tagore, *Binodini*; W. E. B. Du Bois, *The Souls of Black Folk*; Henry James, *The Ambassadors*; *The Great Train Robbery* (film)	Emily Pankhurst founds the Women's Social and Political Movement; first airborne flight by the Wright Brothers
1904	Abbey Theatre opens; Michael Davitt, *The Fall of Feudalism in Ireland*; J. M. Synge, *Riders to the Sea*; Peadar Ó Laoighre, *Séadna*; George Bernard Shaw, *John Bull's Other Island*		Joesph Conrad, *Nostromo*; Anton Chekhov, *The Cherry Orchard*; Giacomo Puccini *Madame Butterfly*	Beginning of Russo-Japanese War; second wave of Jewish immigration to Palestine; Jews demand exclusive use of Jewish labour in Jewish colonies; Panama Canal opened
1905	D. P. Moran, *The Philosophy of Irish Ireland*; George Moore, *The Lake*; J. M. Synge, *The Well of the Saints*; G. B. Shaw, *Man and Superman*	Elaboration of Sinn Féin policy by Griffith	Henry James, *The Golden Bowl*; Richard Strauss, *Salomè*	Curzon initiates Partition of Bengal; Swadeshi movement formed in India
1907	J. M. Synge, *The Playboy of the Western World* (riots at Abbey Theatre production); Patrick Pearse, *Íosagán agus Scéalta Eile*; James O'Neill, *The Dance Music of Ireland*	Sinn Féin League established	Pablo Picasso, *Les Demoiselles d'Avignon*; August Strindberg, *The Ghost Sonata*; Cubist exhibition in Paris and *Blue Rose* exhibition in Moscow	Pius X issues *Ne Temere* decree on mixed marriages; the self-governing (white) colonies declared Dominions

(cont.)

Year	Irish cultural and intellectual events	Irish history	International cultural and intellectual events	International history
1908	The Cuala Press founded (–1987); Hugh Lane opens Dublin Municipal Gallery of Modern Art; Rosa Mulholland, *Mary O'Murrough*	Irish Transport and General Workers' Union established; Irish Women's Franchise League founded	Gertrude Stein, *Three Lives*; Ezra Pound, *A Lume Spento*; Robert Baden-Powell, *Scouting for Boys*	Young Turks revolution in Istanbul
1909	Rudolf Thurneysen, *Handbuch des Altirischen* (2 vols.); T. W. Rolleston, *Sea Spray*; P. W. Joyce, *Old Irish Folk Music and Songs*		H. G. Wells, *Tono-Bungay*; Ezra Pound, *Personae*	
1910	James Connolly, *Labour in Irish History*; Padraic Ó Conaire, *Deoraíocht*		Igor Stravinsky, *The Firebird*; E. M. Forster, *Howards End*	Mexican Revolution begins
1911	Kuno Meyer, *Selections from Ancient Irish Poetry*; George Moore, *Hail and Farewell* (3 vols. –1914); St. John Ervine, *Mixed Marriage*; T. W. Rolleston, *Myths and Legends of the Celtic Race*	Irish Vigilance Association founded; statue to Charles Stewart Parnell by Augustus St Gaudens unveiled; Oliver Sheppard's figure of Cú Chulainn located in the GPO; Maynooth Mission to China established	George Lukács, *Soul and Form*; G. K. Chesterton, *The Innocence of Father Brown*; Joseph Conrad, *Under Western Eyes*	First flight across the United States; international crisis at Agadir
1912	James Stephens, *The Chawoman's Daughter*; G. B. Shaw, *Pygmalion*; Lady Gregory, *Irish Folk History Plays*	Third Home Rule Bill; Ulster Solemn League and Covenant signed; sinking of the *Titanic*	Rabindranath Tagore, *Gitanjali*; Arnold Schönberg, *Pierrot Lunaire*	Formation of the South African Native National Congress (later the African National Congress); beginning of the Balkan Wars

Year				
1913		Lockout of unionised workers in Dublin; Ulster Volunteer Force and Irish Volunteers founded; Third Home Rule Bill passed in House of Commons but defeated in Lords	Albert Einstein, *Theory of Relativity*; Marcel Proust, *A La Recherche du Temps Perdu* (begins); Thomas Mann, *Death in Venice*; D. H. Lawrence, *Sons and Lovers*; Igor Stravinsky, *The Rite of Spring*; Edmund Husserl, *Phenomenology*; Tagore wins Nobel Prize for Literature	Violent suffragette demonstrations in Britain; war in the Balkans
1914	James Joyce, *Dubliners*; W. B. Yeats, *Responsibilities*; James Stephens, *The Demi-Gods*; Padraic Ó Conaire, *An Chéad Chloch*	Cumann na mBan founded; the Curragh Incident	Founding of *Blast*	World War I (–1918) commences
1915	Peadar Ó Laoighre, *Mo Sgéal Féin*		Virginia Woolf, *The Voyage Out*; D. H. Lawrence, *The Rainbow*; D. W. Griffith, *The Birth of a Nation*	Armenian genocide begins (–1916); British conquest of Mesopotamia
1916	James Joyce, *A Portrait of the Artist as a Young Man*; Sean Keating, *Men of the West*	Easter Rising	Ferdinand de Saussure, *Course in General Linguistics*; D. W. Griffith, *Intolerance*	Battle of the Somme

(cont.)

Year	Irish cultural and intellectual events	Irish history	International cultural and intellectual events	International history
1917	W. B. Yeats, *The Wild Swans at Coole*		V. I. Lenin, *Imperialism: The Highest Stage of Capitalism*; T. S. Eliot, *Prufrock and other Observations*; Sigmund Freud, *Introduction to Psychoanalysis*	Bolshevik Revolution; Balfour Declaration confirms British support for a Jewish national home in Palestine
1918	James Joyce, *Exiles*	Sinn Féin victory in general election; franchise granted to women over 30; Countess Markievicz elected first woman to Dáil Eireann	Bertold Brecht, *Baal*; Gerard Manley Hopkins, *Poems* (posthum.); Lytton Strachey, *Eminent Victorians*	The Allies and Germany sign Armistice on 11 November; women age 30 get the vote in Britain; start of Russian Civil War (–1920)
1919		Irish War of Independence commences (–1921)	Thomas Hardy, *Collected Poems*; Bauhaus founded at Weimar by Walter Gropius	Peace Conference in Versailles creates the League of Nations; Amritsar Massacre; division of the Austro-Hungarian Empire
1920	W. B. Yeats, *Michael Robartes and the Dancer*; Lady Gregory, *Visions and Beliefs of the West of Ireland* (2 vols.); G. B. Shaw, *Heartbreak House*	First enrolments of 'Black and Tans'; 'Bloody Sunday'; Government of Ireland Act passed to provide Ireland with separate parliaments in Dublin and Belfast	Ezra Pound, *Hugh Selwyn Mauberly*; Georg Lukács, *Theory of the Novel*; Eugene O'Neill, *Emperor Jones*	Britain given Mandate over Iraq, Transjordan, Palestine; Women in the United States achieve the vote; Chinese Communist Party founded; Kemal Atatürk abolishes Ottoman sultanate
1921		Anglo-Irish Treaty; Northern Ireland Parliament opened by George V	D. H. Lawrence, *Women in Love*; Luigi Pirandello, *Six Characters in Search of an Author*; Picasso,	Non-Cooperation Movement begins in India led by Gandhi (–1922); New Economic Policy

Year				
	…En Gàm, established of Irish Free State confirms partition; Irish Civil War begins (–1923)		Ludwig Wittgenstein, *Tractatus Logico-Philosophicus*	…the BBC; Britain recognises 'independence' of the Kingdom of Egypt but maintains control of foreign policy
1923	Sean O' Casey, *The Shadow of a Gunman*; W. B. Yeats receives the Nobel Prize	Irish Free State joins League of Nations; Cumann na nGaedheal founded; Censorship of Films Act introduced	Georg Lukács, *History and Class Consciousness*; Bertrand Russell, *The Prospects of Industrial Civilisation*	Escalation of post-war inflation and collapse of German currency
1924	Sean O'Casey, *Juno and the Paycock*	First meeting, in London, of Irish Boundary Commission	Thomas Mann, *The Magic Mountain*; E. M. Forster, *A Passage to India*; André Breton, 'The Surrealist Manifesto'	Zinoviev letter published; first minority Labour government in Britain; Gandhi fasts against Hindu–Muslim riots; death of Lenin
1925	G. B. Shaw receives the Nobel Prize; An Gúm established; Daniel Corkery, *The Hidden Ireland*; Austin Clarke, *The Cattle Drive in Connaught*; Liam O'Flaherty, *The Informer*	Boundary Commission powers revoked	Adolf Hitler, *Mein Kampf*; Franz Kafka, *The Trial*; F. Scott Fitzgerald, *The Great Gatsby*; Virginia Woolf, *Mrs. Dalloway*; Alban Berg, *Wozzeck*	Locarno Conference; John Logie Baird transmits first televised image
1926	Sean O' Casey, *The Plough and the Stars*; Eimar O'Duffy, *King Goshawk and the Birds*	Fianna Fáil founded; birth of Ian Paisley	D. H. Lawrence, *The Plumed Serpent*; Ernest Hemingway, *The Sun Also Rises*; T. E. Lawrence, *Seven Pillars of Wisdom*	Imperial Conference defines Dominion status and allows Dominions to opt out of treaties signed by the United Kingdom

(cont.)

Year	Irish cultural and intellectual events	Irish history	International cultural and intellectual events	International history
1927	*An Taibhdhearc* Irish-language theatre founded	Kevin Higgins assassinated	Martin Heidegger, *Being and Time*; Virginia Woolf, *To the Lighthouse*	
1928	W. B. Yeats, *The Tower*; Sean O'Casey, *The Silver Tassie*; first production by the Gate Theatre Company: *Peer Gynt*; An Taibhdhearc opens with Mícheál MacLiammóir's *Diarmuid agus Gráinne*	Irish Manuscripts Commission founded	Bertold Brecht and Kurt Weill, *The Threepenny Opera*; D. H. Lawrence, *Lady Chatterley's Lover*; Federico García Lorca, *The Gypsy Ballads*; Sergei Eisenstein, *October*	Start of first Soviet Five Year Plan; Antonio Gramsci sentenced to 20 years by Italian Special Tribunal
1929	Elizabeth Bowen, *The Last September*; Tomás Ó Criomhthainn, *An t-Oileánach*; Austin Clarke, *Pilgrimage and other Poems*	Censorship of Publications Act passed in the Irish Free State; Proportional Representation abolished for parliamentary elections in Northern Ireland	William Faulkner, *The Sound and the Fury*; Ernest Hemingway, *A Farewell to Arms*; Virginia Woolf, *A Room of One's Own*; Alfred Döblin, *Berlin Alexanderplatz*; Rómulo Gallegos, *Doña Barbara*; M. M. Bakhtin, *Problems of Dostoevsky's Poetics*	The Wall Street Crash heralds start of world economic crisis and the Great Depression
1930	Gate Theatre moves to premises in buildings at Rotunda Hospital; Irish Folklore Institute founded	Irish Free State elected to the council of the League of Nations; first Free State censorship board appointed	Sigmund Freud, *Civilisation and its Discontents*; Robert Musil, *The Man Without Qualities* (–1943); T. S. Eliot, *Ash Wednesday*; William Faulkner, *As I Lay Dying*	France begins building Maginot Line; Amy Johnson flies from London to Australia in nineteen and a half days

	Anglo-Irish Literature; Frank O'Connor, *Guests of the Nation*; Teresa Deevey, *A Disciple*	issued	*Becomes Electra*; Hermann Broch, *The Sleepwalkers*	Britain abandons the gold standard; Statute of Westminster recognises constitutional equality of the the Dominions with Britain
1932	Austin Clarke, *The Bright Temptation*; Sean O'Faolain, *Midsummer Night Madness and Other Stories*	International Eucharistic Congress; Army Comrades Association (Blueshirts) founded; Northern Ireland parliament buildings at Stormont formally opened	Joseph Roth, *The Radetzky March*; Aldous Huxley, *Brave New World*; Bertold Brecht, *The Mother*; Louis-Ferdinand Céline, *Voyage to the End of the Night*	Indian National Congress declared illegal and Gandhi arrested; Iraq becomes independent
1934	Samuel Beckett, *More Pricks than Kicks*; Robert Flaherty, *Man of Aran*; Kate O'Brien, *The Ante-Room*	Anglo-Irish 'cattle and coal' agreement	T. S. Eliot, *After Strange Gods*; Agatha Christie, *Murder on the Orient Express*	Hitler installs himself as president of the German Reich and takes title of 'Führer'; Chinese Communists' 'Long March' begins
1935	Irish Folklore Commission established; Teresa Deevey, *The King of Spain's Daughter*	The Dance Halls Act, designed to regulate Irish dance by clergy, police and judiciary, enacted	T. S. Eliot, *Murder in the Cathedral*; Elias Canetti, *Auto-da-Fé*	Italian invasion of Abyssinia; Nuremberg Race laws introduced in Germany
1936	Peig Sayers, *Peig*; Kate O'Brien, *Mary Lavelle*; Teresa Deevey, *Katie Roche*; Austin Clarke, *The Singing-Men at Cashel*; Joyce Cary, *The African Witch*	Left-wing Irish unit under Frank Ryan joins republican government forces in Spain	Dylan Thomas, *Twenty-five Poems*; Margaret Mitchell, *Gone With the Wind*; Charles Chaplin, *Modern Times*	Spanish Civil War breaks out; Great Arab Revolt breaks out against British rule in Palestine

(cont.)

Year	Irish cultural and intellectual events	Irish history	International cultural and intellectual events	International history
1937	Conrad Arensberg, *The Irish Countryman*	New constitution approved by Dáil; Medical Missionaries of Mary established	Georg Lukács, *The Historical Novel*	
1938	W. B. Yeats, *Purgatory*; Samuel Beckett, *Murphy*; Séan O Faoláin, *King of the Beggars*; *Irish Historical Studies* founded		Jean-Paul Sartre, *La Nausée*; C. L. R. James, *The Black Jacobins*; Bertold Brecht, *Life of Galileo*;	Munich crisis over German claims to the Sudetenland; Franco begins Catalonian offensive in Spanish Civil War; Cárdenas nationalises the oil business in Mexico
1939	James Joyce, *Finnegans Wake*; Flann O'Brien, *At-Swim-Two-Birds*; Louis MacNeice, *Autumn Journal*; Joyce Cary, *Mister Johnson*	Death of W. B. Yeats; De Valera announces Free state policy of neutrality	George Antonius, *The Arab Awakening*; Thomas Mann, *Lotte in Weimar*; Bertold Brecht, *Mother Courage and Her Children*; John Steinbeck, *The Grapes of Wrath*; Aimé Césaire, *Cahier d'un retour au pays natal*	World War II (–1945) begins after the Nazi occupation of Poland
1940	*The Bell* (–1954) founded by Sean O'Faoláin; Ulster Group Theatre formed; W. B. Yeats, *Last Poems and Plays*; Conrad Arensberg and Solon Kimball, *Family and Community in Ireland*		Ernest Hemingway, *For Whom the Bell Tolls*; W. H. Auden, *Another Time*	Fall of France to German forces
1941	Flann O'Brien, *An Béal Bocht*; Kate O'Brien, *The Land of Spices*	Death of James Joyce	W. H. Auden, *New Year Letter*	Japanese attack Pearl Harbor; United States enters World

1942	Patrick Kavanagh, *The Great Hunger*; Sean O'Casey, *Red Roses for Me*; Emyr Estan Evans, *Irish Heritage*		Albert Camus, *L'Etranger* and *The Myth of Sisyphus*; T. S. Eliot, *Little Gidding*	Enrico Fermi splits the atom in the US; Quit India movement leads to violent confrontation between Indian National Congress and the British Raj
1943	Arts Council established in Northern Ireland		J. P. Sartre, *Being and Nothingness*	
1945		Congress of Irish Trade Unions formed; Sean T. O'Kelly succeeds Douglas Hyde as president of Éire	Hermann Broch, *The Death of Virgil*; George Orwell, *Animal Farm*	World War II comes to an end after unconditional surrender of German High Command and atomic bombing of Hiroshima and Nagasaki
1947		Roman Catholic bishops express disapproval of the clauses in the Health Act having to do with mother and child services	Theodor Adorno and Max Horkheimer, *The Dialectic of Enlightenment*; Malcolm Lowry, *Under the Volcano*; Thomas Mann, *Dr. Faustus*	Partition of India; independence of India and Pakistan
1948	Patrick Kavanagh, *Tarry Flynn*; Francis Stuart, *The Pillar of Cloud*; John Hewitt, *No Rebel Word*; Séan O Faoláin, *The Short Story*	Irish Republic declared	Alon Paton, *Cry, the Beloved Country*; Jean-Paul Sartre, *Black Orpheus*; Graham Greene, *The Heart of the Matter*; T. S. Eliot, *Notes Towards the Definition of Culture*; F. R. Leavis, *The Great Tradition*	Partition of Palestine and the creation of the state of Israel; Ceylon achieves independence; Gandhi assassinated; Marshall Plan for reconstruction of Europe initiated

(cont.)

Year	Irish cultural and intellectual events	Irish history	International cultural and intellectual events	International history
1949	Mairtín Ó'Cadhain, *Cré na Cille*; Louis MacNeice, *Collected Poems*; Joseph Campbell, *The Hero with a Thousand Faces*; Francis Stuart, *Redemption*	Éire formally becomes a Republic	Simone de Beauvoir, *The Second Sex*; Theodor Adorno, *Philosophy of Modern Music*; Naguib Mahfouz, *The Beginning and the End*; Miguel Angel Ásturias, *Men of Maize*; Alejo Carpentier, *The Kingdom of this World*; Arthur Miller, *Death of a Salesman*; George Orwell, *1984*	People's Republic of China declared; National Government in South Africa implements apartheid
1951	Arts Council founded in the Irish Republic; Lyric Players Theatre founded in Belfast; *Comhaltas Ceoltóirí Éireann* mount first annual Fleadh Cheoil; Dolmen Press founded; Samuel Beckett, *Malone Dies* (in French); Sam Hanna Bell, *December Bride*	Dr Noel Browne resigns as minister of health over 'mother and child scheme'	J. D. Salinger, *Catcher in the Rye*	
1952	John Ford, *The Quiet Man*		Flannery O'Connor, *Wise Blood*	Mau Mau rebellion begins in Kenya
1953	Samuel Beckett, *En attendant Godot* (French production; Irish premiere 1955) and *Watt*; Alfred Chester Beatty Library opened	Establishment of Pike Theatre	Alejo Carpentier, *The Lost Steps*; James Baldwin, *Go Tell it on the Mountain*; Roland Barthes, *Writing Degree Zero*	Egyptian republic proclaimed; death of Joseph Stalin; end of the Korean War

1955	Samuel Beckett, *Molloy*; Austin Clarke, *Ancient Lights*; J. P. Dunleavy, *The Ginger Man*; Brian Moore, *The Lonely Passion of Judith Hearne*; *Ulster Folklife* journal founded	Irish Republic joins United Nations	Vladimir Nabokov, *Lolita*; Claude Lévi-Strauss, *Tristes Tropiques*	Bandung Conference; Messina conference plans creation of European Economic Community
1956	Thomas Kinsella, *Poems*; Brendan Behan, *The Quare Fellow*; Louis le Brocquy's *A Family* wins a Venice Biennale prize	IRA 'border campaign' begins	Eugene O'Neill, *Long Day's Journey into Night*; Albert Camus, *The Fall*; Allen Ginsberg, *Howl*; Alejo Carpentier, *The Lost Steps*	Suez Crisis; Hungarian uprising crushed by Soviet troops; Fidel Castro lands in Cuba to overthrow the Batista dictatorship; independence of Sudan
1957	Samuel Beckett, *Endgame* (in French); Emyr Estan Evans, *Irish Folk Ways*; *Threshold* established	Boycott of Protestants at Fethard-on-Sea, Co. Wexford, begins	Camus wins Nobel Prize; Jack Kerouac, *On the Road*; Northrop Frye, *Anatomy of Criticism*	Founding of the Common Market; independence of Malaya and Ghana
1958	Samuel Beckett, *Krapp's Last Tape*; Thomas Kinsella, *Another September*; Brendan Behan, *Borstal Boy*	First Programme for Economic Expansion introduced	Chinua Achebe, *Things Fall Apart*; Giuseppe Tomasi di Lampedusa, *The Leopard*; Harold Pinter, *The Birthday Party*; Raymond Williams, *Culture and Society*	King Feisal overthrown in Baghdad; United Arab Republic founded by merger of Syria and Egypt
1959	Seán Ó Riada, *Mise Eire*; John B. Keane, *Sive*	Eamon de Valera elected President of Irish Republic	Günter Grass, *The Tin Drum*; Robert Lowell, *Life Studies*	Fidel Castro assumes power in Cuba

(cont.)

Year	Irish cultural and intellectual events	Irish history	International cultural and intellectual events	International history
1960	Edna O'Brien, *The Country Girls*; Sam Thompson's *Over the Bridge* produced		Harold Pinter, *The Caretaker*	Independence of Nigeria and Cyprus; Harold Macmillan's 'wind of change' speech in Cape Town
1961	Samuel Beckett, *The Beckett Trilogy*; Tom Murphy, *A Whistle in the Dark*	Republic of Ireland applies for membership of EEC; television service of Radio Éireann begins transmission	Frantz Fanon, *The Wretched of the Earth*; V. S. Naipual, *A House for Mr Biswas*	Bay of Pigs invasion; Cuban Missile Crisis; Berlin Wall erected; Yuri Gagarin is first man in space
1962	Samuel Beckett, *Happy Days*; Frank O'Connor, *The Lonely Voice*; Máire MacNeill, *The Festival of Lughnasa*		Carlos Fuentes, *The Death of Artemio Cruz*; Lawrence Durrell, *The Alexandrian Quartet*	Independence of Algeria, Jamaica, Trinidad and Uganda.
1963	Seán Ó Riada, *Nomos. No. 2*; John McGahern, *The Barracks*; Louis MacNeice, *The Burning Perch*; Seán Ó'Súilleabháin and Reidar Christinasen, *Types of the Irish Folktale*	Second Programme of Economic Expansion published	Ghassan Kanafani, *Men in the Sun*; Thomas Pynchon, *V*; E. P. Thompson, *The Making of the English Working Class*	Martin Luther King, 'I have a dream' speech; assassination of J. F. Kennedy; Kenya gains independence
1964	Flann O'Brien, *The Dalkey Archive*; Brian Friel, *Philadelphia, Here I Come!*; Patrick Kavanagh, *Collected Poems*	Ulster Folk Museum opened at Cultra, Co. Down	Sartre refuses Nobel Prize for Literature; Philip Larkin, *The Whitsun Weddings*	States of Tanzania and Zambia established; PLO established

1965	John McGahern, *The Dark*	Sean Lemass visits Terence O'Neill in Belfast	Sylvia Plath, *Ariel*; Harold Pinter, *The Homecoming*; Mikhail Bakhtin, *Rabelais and his World*	US–Vietnam War begins (–1975) when President Lyndon Johnson commits US forces to defence of Southern Vietnam
1966	New Abbey Theatre opens; Seamus Heaney, *Death of a Naturalist*; Austin Clarke, *Mnemosyne Lay in the Dust*; Samuel Beckett, *Eh Joe*	Easter Rising 50th anniversary commemorations; UVF founded; Nelson's Pillar destroyed in Dublin	Hans Blumenberg, *The Legitimacy of the Modern Age*; Thomas Pynchon, *The Crying of Lot 49*; Marguerite Duras, *The Vice-Consul*	Guyana, Lesotho, Botswana and Barbados gain independence; Cultural Revolution begins in China
1967	Seoirse Bodley, *Configurations for Orchestra*; Eavan Boland, *New Territory*	Northern Ireland Civil Rights Association founded	Jacques Derrida, *Of Grammatology*; Gabriel García Márquez, *One Hundred Years of Solitude*; Ngugi Wa Thiongo, *A Grain of Wheat*; V. S. Naipaul, *The Mimic Men*	Six-Day Arab–Israeli war; British withdrawal from Aden
1968	Lyric Theatre opens in Belfast; Thomas Kinsella, *Nightwalker*; Tom Murphy, *Famine*; Derek Mahon, *Night-Crossing*; Críostóir Ó Floinn, *Aggiornamento*; Brian Friel, *Lovers*	Civil Rights marches begin; People's Democracy formed; clashes between civil rights marchers and police in Derry; 'Troubles' commence	John Updike, *Couples*; W. H. Auden, *Selected Poems*	Student insurrection and worker general strike in France; 'Prague Spring' uprising; Martin Luther King assassinated; Paul VI issues *Humanae vitae* condemning artificial contraception

(cont.)

Year	Irish cultural and intellectual events	Irish history	International cultural and intellectual events	International history
1969	Samuel Beckett receives the Nobel Prize; James Plunkett, *Strumpet City*; Thomas Kinsella, *The Táin*; Maurice Leitch, *Poor Lazarus*	People's Democracy march from Belfast to Derry ambushed by militant Protestants; British troops move into Derry; Terence O'Neill resigns as Prime Minister in Northern Ireland; UVF bomb explodes at RTÉ Headquarters, Dublin	John Berryman, *The Dream Songs*; Ernesto Cardenal, *Homage to the American Indians*	Apollo 11 moon landing; De Gaulle resigns
1970	J. G. Farrell, *Troubles*; Osborn Bergin, *Irish Bardic Poetry*; *Irish University Review* (journal) established; Gallery Press founded; David Lean, *Ryan's Daughter*	Social Democratic and Labour Party (SDLP) founded; split between 'Officials' and 'Provos' at Sinn Féin convention	Theodor Adorno, *Aesthetic Theory*; Mahmoud Darwish, *A Lover from Palestine*	Independence of Fiji; Nigerian Civil War ends
1971	Seán O'Riordáin, *Línte Limbo*; Oisin Kelly's *The Children of Lir* unveiled in Garden of Remembrance; Thomas MacGreevy, *Collected Poems*; Mary Lavin, *Collected Stories*; Francis Stuart, *Black List, Section H*; Tom Murphy, *The Morning After Optimism*; John Boyd, *The*	UDA emerges in Belfast; GAA ban on 'foreign' sports rescinded; internment without trial introduced in Northern Ireland; Women's Liberation Movement begins activities in Dublin		Civil War in Pakistan; third Indo–Pakistan War; Independent State of Bangladesh established

1972	Radio na Gaeltachta established; John Montague, *The Rough Field*; Seoirse Bodley, *The Narrow Road to the Deep North*	'Bloody Sunday', 13 civilians killed in Derry by British Army	Italo Calvino, *Invisible Cities*	
1973	John Banville, *Birchwood*; Paul Muldoon, *New Weather*; Brian Friel, *The Freedom of the City*; Conor Cruise O'Brien, *States of Ireland*	Republic of Ireland joins EEC along with UK and Denmark; Sunningdale Conference; removal of Marriage Ban in Civil Service and Local Authorities	Raymond Williams, *The Country and the City*; Roland Barthes, *The Pleasure of the Text*; Thomas Pynchon, *Gravity's Rainbow*; Aleksandr Solzhenitsyn, *The Gulag Archipelago* (3 vols., –1975);	Oil-Producing countries in Persian Gulf increase price of oil; world economic recession; military coup in Chile deposes Salvador Allende, the first popularly elected socialist president in the Western hemisphere; Yom Kippur War
1974	David Thomson, *Woodbrook*	Ulster Workers' Council declares General Strike	Augusto Roa Bastos, *I the Supreme*	Military coup in Lisbon ends Portuguese rule in Africa
1975	Druid Theatre Company established; Seamus Heaney, *North*; Derek Mahon, *The Snow-Party*; Bob Quinn, *Caoineadh Airt Uí Laoire*	Death of Eamon de Valera	Gabriel García Márquez, *The Autumn of the Patriarch*	General Franco dies, democracy restored in Spain
1976	John Banville, *Doctor Copernicus*; Antony Cronin, *Dead as Doornails*; Tom Murphy, *The Sanctuary Lamp*	Irish Architectural Archive and Heritage Trust established	Wole Soyinka, *Death and the King's Horseman*; Alex Haley, *Roots*; Manuel Puig, *Kiss of the Spider Woman*; Michel Foucault, *The History of Sexuality*	'Dirty War' (–1983) ravages Argentina under military dictatorship

(cont.)

Year	Irish cultural and intellectual events	Irish history	International cultural and intellectual events	International history
1977	*The Crane Bag* founded (–1988)		Ngugi Wa Thiongo, *Petals of Blood*	President Sadat of Egypt addresses Israeli Knesset
1978		High Court declares Wood Quay a national monument Well Woman Clinic opens in Dublin	Edward Said, *Orientalism*	Israel undertakes limited invasion of Lebanon and occupies a strip of the southern part of that country in Operation Litani; Egyptian–Israeli peace talks at Camp David
1979	Brian Friel, *Faith Healer*; John McGahern, *The Pornographer*; Seamus Heaney, *Field Work*; Derek Mahon, *Poems, 1962–1978*	Pope John Paul II visits Ireland		Ayatollah Khomeini takes over in Iran; Idi Amin overthrown in Uganda; Sandinistas overthrow Samoza regime in Nicaragua
1980	Field Day Theatre Company established; Brian Friel, *Translations*	Republican prisoner hunger strikes begin in Maze Prison	Death of Roland Barthes and J.-P. Sartre; J. M. Coetzee, *Waiting for the Barbarians*	Solidarity campaign begins in Poland; independence of Zimbabwe under majority rule; Iran–Iraq war begins (–1988)
1981	Terence Brown, *Ireland: A Social and Cultural History*; John Banville, *Kepler*; Seán Ó Tuama and Thomas Kinsella, *An Duanaire 1600–1900: Poems of the Dispossessed*; Nuala Ní Dhomhnaill, *An Dealg Droighin*; Derek Mahon, *Courtyards in Delft*; Pat Murphy and John	Bobby Sands hunger strike begins; Sands and nine other strikers die	Fredric Jameson, *The Political Unconscious*; Salman Rushdie, *Midnight's Children*; Mario Vargas Llosa, *The War of the End of the World*; Nadine Gordimer, *July's People*	AIDS syndrome identified; Sadat assassinated in Cairo

			Saul Bellow, *The Dean's December*	Israel invades Lebanon; Falklands War
1982	Eavan Boland, *Night Feed*; John Banville, *The Newton Letter*; Neil Jordan, *Angel*			
1983	Charabanc Theatre Company founded; Tom Murphy, *The Gigli Concert*; Paul Muldoon, *Quoof*; Bob Quinn, *Atlantean*	Referendum to amend the constitution to prevent the possibility of laws permitting abortion carried	Salman Rushdie, *Shame* Terry Eagleton, *Literary Theory*	United States invades Grenada; Tamil revolt in Sri Lanka
1984	Attic Press founded; UCD Women's Studies Forum established; Pat Murphy, *Anne Devlin*		Marguerite Duras, *The Lover* Martin Amis, *Money*	Anglo-Chinese Hong Kong Agreement
1985	Frank McGuinness, *Observe the Sons of Ulster Marching Towards the Somme*; Tom Murphy, *Bailegangaire*	Anglo-Irish Agreement signed	Cormac McCarthy, *Blood Meridian*	Mikhail Gorbachev comes to power in the Soviet Union; Israel withdraws from northern Lebanon
1986	Seamus Deane, *Celtic Revivals*; John Hewitt, *Freehold*; Paul Muldoon, *Selected Poems, 1968–83*; Thomas Kilroy, *Double Cross*	Divorce Referendum confirms ban on divorce	Richard Ford, *The Sportswriter*	World's worst nuclear accident at Chernobyl
1988	Roddy Doyle, *The Commitments*; Brian Friel, *Making History*; Medbh McGuckian, *On Ballycastle Beach*	Gibralter Three assassinated by SAS	Salman Rushdie, *The Satanic Verses*; Tony Morrison, *Beloved*; J. M. Coetzee, *White Writing*; Peter Carey, *Oscar and Lucinda*	PLO recognises the state of Israel at Algiers Conference; Soviet withdrawal from Afghanistan

(cont.)

Year	Irish cultural and intellectual events	Irish history	International cultural and intellectual events	International history
1989	Ciaran Carson, *Belfast Confetti*; Jim Sheridan, *My Left Foot*	Guildford Four released	Martin Amis, *London Fields*	Fall of the Berlin Wall; disintegration of Communist bloc in Eastern Europe
1990	Eavan Boland, *Outside History*; Brian Friel, *Dancing at Lughnasa*; John McGahern, *Amongst Women*; Thaddeus O'Sullivan, *December Bride*; Jim Sheridan, *The Field*; Paul Durcan, *Daddy, Daddy*	Mary Robinson elected first woman president of Ireland	Hanif Kureishi, *The Buddha of Suburbia*	German reunification; Nelson Mandela freed, De Klerk government begins to dismantle apartheid; free elections annulled in Burma and military dictatorship installed
1991	*Field Day Anthology of Irish Writing*, vols. I–III	Birmingham Six released	Derek Walcott, *Omeros*; Ariel Dorfman, *Death and the Maiden*; Nadine Gordimer wins Nobel Prize	Soviet Union dissolved, Russian Federation established; First Gulf War
1992	Gerald Barry, *Sextet* (–1993) and *Piano Quartet*; Patrick McCabe, *The Butcher Boy*; Nuala Ní Dhomhnaill, *Pharaoh's Daughter*; Glenn Patterson, *Fat Lad*; Neil Jordan, *The Crying Game*	'X' case; Abortion Information and Right to Travel referenda passed; Maastricht Treaty approved	Derek Walcott wins Nobel Prize	Civil war in Algeria begins; war in Yugoslavia begins (–1995)
1993	Frank McGuinness, *Someone Who'll Watch Over Me*; Roddy Doyle, *Paddy Clarke, Ha Ha Ha*	Homosexuality decriminalised	Edward Said, *Culture and Imperialism*; Toni Morrison wins Nobel Prize	Maastricht Agreement comes into force; Oslo Agreement signed between Israel and the

Year				
1994	Paul Muldoon, *The Annals of Chile*; Marina Carr, *The Mai*; Edna O'Brien, *The House of Splendid Isolation*; Emma Donoghue, *Stir-fry*; Dermot Healy, *A Goat's Song*	IRA and Loyalist paramilitary ceasefires		Civil war and massacre in Rwanda; first South African democratic general election won by ANC; uprising in Chiapas, Mexico, over lack of land reform
1995	Teilifís na Gaeltachta established; Seamus Heaney awarded Nobel Prize; Declan Kiberd, *Inventing Ireland*; Roger Doyle, *Under the Green Time*	Divorce referendum passed; major confrontation in Drumcree	Salman Rushdie, *The Moor's Last Sigh*; Simon Schama, *Landscape and Memory*	EEC becomes European Union; Quebec narrowly votes against independence
1996	Seamus Deane, *Reading in the Dark*; Martin McDonagh, *The Beauty Queen of Leenane*; Frank McCourt, *Angela's Ashes*; Marina Carr, *Portia Coughlan*; Neil Jordan, *Michael Collins*	IRA bombs in London and Manchester	Harold Pinter, *Ashes to Ashes*; Rohinton Mistry, *A Fine Balance*	Taliban take control in Afghanistan
1997	John Banville, *The Untouchable*; Frank McGuinness, *Mutabilitie*		Ian McEwan, *Enduring Love*	Hong Kong is returned by United Kingdom to China
1998	Neil Jordan, *The Butcher Boy*; Tom Collins, *Bogwoman*; Seamus Heaney, *Open Ground*	Good Friday Agreement	Nadine Gordimer, *The House Gun*; Alan Warner, *The Sopranos*	Former Chilean dictator, Augusto Pinochet, detained in London

(cont.)

Year	Irish cultural and intellectual events	Irish history	International cultural and intellectual events	International history
1999	Angela Bourke, *The Burning of Bridget Cleary*; Roddy Doyle, *A Star Called Henry*; Glenn Patterson, *The International*; Éilís Ní Dhuibhne, *The Dancers Dancing*	Northern Irish Assembly meets for the first time – suspended; Republic of Ireland joins single European currency; Flood Tribunal begins, investigating political corruption in the Republic		East Timor Votes for independence from Indonesia; NATO forces bomb Serbia; conflict in Chechyna intensifies
2000	RTÉ screens documentary 'States of Fear', exposing decades of clerical abuse and state collusion in involuntary adoption; government announces a programme of response and retribution	Northern Irish Assembly revived		Global Warming conference fails in Hague; DNA Human Genome Sequencing project well advanced; Israel withdraws from south Lebanon; Second Intafada begins in Palestinian occupied territories

Ireland

Land over 300m OD

N

0   50 miles
0   80 km

DONEGAL
Derry
DERRY
ANTRIM
Belfast
TYRONE
FERMANAGH
ARMAGH
DOWN
SLIGO
MONAGHAN
LEITRIM
CAVAN
MAYO
ROSCOMMON
LONGFORD
LOUTH
MEATH
WESTMEATH
GALWAY
Galway
OFFALY
DUBLIN
Dublin
KILDARE
LAOIS
WICKLOW
CLARE
CARLOW
Limerick
TIPPERARY
KILKENNY
LIMERICK
WEXFORD
KERRY
Waterford
WATERFORD
CORK
Cork

JOE CLEARY

1
_____

Introduction: Ireland and modernity

The aim of this *Companion* is to introduce readers to modern Irish
culture in all its complexity and variety. Before moving into detailed cultural analysis, however, the opening chapter invites readers to consider
the historical and theoretical meanings of our framing concept: modern
Ireland. What does modernity mean for Ireland? How can we conceptualise the modern culture of a country and a people with two languages,
divided since the early twentieth century into two states? Officially incorporated into the United Kingdom with the Act of Union in 1800, Ireland
in the nineteenth century was a constituent element of a sprawling
empire of global reach. Union with Britain survives into the twenty-first
century in the shape of the political border dividing Northern Ireland
from the Republic. And yet the long history of Irish migration and diaspora means that even the divided island – the basic geopolitical unit –
cannot be taken for granted as the sole sphere of modern Irish culture.

The nowadays much-debated terms terms 'modern' or 'modernity'
also require consideration. For a long time, these words were associated with the radical intellectual iconoclasm of the Enlightenment
and with the transformational dynamism of capitalism. The revolutionary utopianism of feminism, socialism and communism sprang from
such quintessentially Enlightenment beliefs as human rights and global
justice and equality: all such claims expressed in terms of a cry for the
optimal extension of the modern. At the start of the new millennium,
however, calls for the extension of modernisation are more likely to hin-
der than to abet campaigns for social justice or the dream of a better world
beyond capitalism. As Oskar Lafontaine remarks: 'If you try to figure
what the people called "modernizers" today understand by "modernity",
you find that it is little else than economic and social adaptation to the

supposed constraints of the global market.' The term thus becomes a 'code for turning down alternatives to capitalism', signifying little more than a long goodbye to the more utopian hopes once invested in the radical Enlightenment project of modernity.[1]

While even the most cursory survey of the vast body of writing about the 'modern' will reveal the vicissitudes of that term, our starting premise here is that in Ireland the meanings of 'modernisation' and 'modernity' – terms now come to crisis point in metropolitan social theory – have actually been an object of intellectual and cultural controversy for some considerable period. Ireland's long colonial connection to a British state thought to be the exemplary incarnation of modernity has meant that the historically subordinate country's relationship to 'the modern' has always been much vexed, much disputed. Irish intellectuals and cultural commentators have over the centuries returned time and again to questions as to whether Ireland was a modern society at all, whether the modern was to be equated with progress or its obverse (and if the former, with the progress of what and for whom), whether the agencies that had apparently generated or stymied the modern were largely external or internal to Irish society, and so forth. These conundrums were never simply the preserve of academics and intellectuals; the issue as to how to articulate the relationship between Ireland and the modern has also constituted an abiding stimulus or tonic to Irish cultural activity in literature, in cinema, in music and in the visual and other arts. In short, a complex, contested history of claim and counter-claim means that in an Irish context the term 'modernity' is stripped of its semblance of obviousness: its meanings have been consistently interrogated. For this reason alone, it will be worth our while at the outset of this volume to dwell briefly on some of the matters provoked by these debates.

Beginnings and endings

Conceptions of the 'modern' or of 'modernity' typically connote an epochal rupture with the 'pre-modern' or the 'non-modern', the latter then conceived of as the pre-history of that modernity. As Fredric Jameson describes it, this separation of the past and present operates 'by way of a powerful act of disassociation whereby the present seals off its past from itself and ejects it; an act without which neither present nor past truly exist, the past not yet fully constituted, the present still living on within the force field of a past not yet over and done with.'[2] The ascription of modernity, in short, always requires setting a date and positing a beginning. When, then, does modern Ireland begin and end?

Historical conceptions of Irish modernity are typically derived largely from standard European versions or metanarratives. Western modernity is conventionally ascribed to an inventory of inaugural ruptures of the following kind: the Protestant Reformation and the development of novel modes of consciousness, discipline and enterprise; the emergence of capitalism and the gradual dissolution of the feudal mode of production with its characteristic forms of authority, land tenure and labour; the conquest of the Americas and the expansion of the European terrestrial and maritime empires across the globe; the conception of a sovereign and self-reflexive human subjectivity as one of the cardinal features of modernity.

Taking its cues from these wider paradigms of Western modernity, the emergence of 'modern Ireland' is conventionally ascribed in Irish historiography to the sixteenth and seventeenth centuries: the inception of that modernity is attributed (in a manner chronologically congruent with inaugural events of European modernity generally) to the Tudor and Stuart colonisations of the island, conquests viewed either as part of the larger theatre of struggle between European Reformation and Counter-Reformation or as a component of the westward drive of imperial expansion: its corollary was the inception of a centuries-long attempt to render Ireland amenable to the imperatives of English and later transnational capital. Whichever of these narratives is accepted, the inception of Irish modernity is invariably associated with British dominance on the island and with the termination of the older Gaelic civilisation instigated by these sixteenth- and seventeenth-century intrusions. Modernity and modernisation, as conceived in this historiographical enterprise, come entirely from 'above' and 'without', rather than from 'within' or 'below': modernity is a gift of colonial or religious conquest mediated primarily through an expanding British state (and the ruling élites that promoted the remit of that state in Ireland) rather than through any efforts by the pre-existing Gaelic society to modernise itself by its own exertions and on its own terms. Modernisation in such accounts is coterminous with the Anglicisation of the island: Gaelic culture by that same move is aligned with the medieval, with the pre-modern, the archaic and the maladapted; with all those things whose inevitable fate it was to be vanquished by modernity.

It is also conventional in Western historiography to distinguish a later, more mature and fully fledged modernity from this incipient or early version. In this later instance, inaugural moments typically include the French Revolution and the European Enlightenment that prepared and accompanied it; the development of industrial capitalism, and its accompanying technological revolutions; the emergence of the modern bureaucratic state and its modes of disciplinary and instrumental reason; the elaboration initially in the Americas and then in Europe of anti-colonial and official state nationalisms; the dissemination of Darwinian evolutionism and the secular natural and social sciences and the consequent crisis of religious conceptions of human history; the formation of modern bourgeois subjectivity and sexuality. The advent of Irish modernity in this later 'mature' sense is typically ascribed to some time between the end of the eighteenth and the mid nineteenth centuries, with the United Irish Rebellion of 1798, the Act of Union in 1800, Catholic Emancipation in 1829 or the Great Famine in the late 1840s variously offered as decisive watersheds in that wider transition.

The Irish transition from an 'early' to a more 'mature' or 'advanced' modernity is again conventionally situated in terms of a wider Euro-American context: contributing forces include the influence of the American and French Revolutions on the development of Irish republicanism; the impact of the British industrial revolution on Irish economic subordination and underdevelopment; the emergence of the 'second', eastward-looking British Empire, and the technological dominance of the Anglo-American industrial world with its gravitational effects on Irish migration and diaspora from the nineteenth century onwards; the ideological 'wars' between clerical and secular forces that raged across the European continent throughout the nineteenth century even as in Ireland the Catholic church, after two centuries of suppression, established a moral monopoly over Irish society designed to shelter the island from the icy blasts of continental secularism.

Irish modernity in this second 'mature' phase, as in its 'early' phase, can quite clearly be tracked to a larger concatenation of social, political, technological and cultural forces that made Western modernity generally. The emphasis on democratisation and citizenship in this second moment brings a significant new element to the narrative; this later modernisation drive is more closely associated with upheavals from below or originating within the emergent middle classes rather than with the colonial officials and settlers newly arrived from Britain deemed the emissaries of the modern in the earlier period. In an Irish context, this drive towards democratisation and citizenship can be identified with either the revolutionary and militant republicanism of the United Irishmen, who insisted that a viable Irish polity could be created only by abolishing the congealed sectarian social structures and mentalities that were the invidious legacy of the plantations, or with a constitutional nationalism that aspired to democratise Irish society electorally via the political mobilisation of the Irish masses (in the campaigns first for Catholic Emancipation and then the Repeal of the Union led by Catholic politician Daniel O'Connell), or with the start of public lobbying for the rights of women from the mid nineteenth century onwards.

Readers of the volume may wish to pause here and consider what is at stake in explanations such as those offered above, which seek to make Ireland comprehensible in terms of wider European and Atlantic developments. The normalising power of such explanations has made them powerfully attractive; they allow us to construe Ireland as a reasonably typical instance of universalising Western European and North American patterns. Nevertheless, any account that describes Irish modernisation primarily in terms of local reactions to wider tendencies leaves itself vulnerable to the objection that in such accounts modernity is always one-way traffic, with the modern invariably disseminated outwards from a given centre – England, France, Europe or America – to the retarded margins. In such paradigms, marginal cultures (like Ireland), reduced to the status of the recipients of modernity, can only progress to the extent that they imitate the centre; it becomes impossible to imagine any alternative future to that already prescribed by the centre; the marginal culture's destiny is to emulate; it does not inaugurate, initiate or invent.

A counter-version suggests that modernity, however, is not a one-way process issuing from metropole to benighted periphery; the circuits of the modern have always been more latticed and labyrinthine than simplistic diffusion models of the kind just described allow. In an Irish context, the United Irishmen, for instance, though certainly adherents to the universal ideals of the Enlightenment, were not simply the crude importers of American or French republicanism. The Address of the United Irishmen to the Scottish Convention of 1793 boldly asserts: 'We will not buy or borrow liberty from America or France, but manufacture it ourselves, and work it up with those materials which the hearts of Irishmen furnish them with at home.'[3] Working with these domestic materials, the United Irishmen sought to reformulate the intellectual heritage of republicanism to take account not only of the hitherto despised Catholicism of the Irish masses, but also of the equally despised Gaelic culture of the island. Whereas American and French republicans were fiercely hostile to North American Indian or to Breton and Basque cultures respectively, viewing them only as barbaric impediments to progress that ought to be wholly extirpated, the United Irishmen, chastened by Ireland's colonial experience, refused to regard either Catholicism or the vernacular culture of the masses as insuperably opposed to national advancement. Without surrendering their Enlightenment principles, they also repudiated the stadialist conceptions of history and the cultural hierarchies endorsed by the Scottish Enlightenment; in so refusing, there is a real case to suggest that the United Irishmen opened fertile new intellectual territory for rethinking the relationship between the Enlightenment and specific cultures. In Ireland, in other words, the Enlightenment attitude to tradition was developed in more complex ways than in the European mainstream. After the defeat of 1798, Irish republicans forced overseas were also to become important agents for the transmission of republican ideals in Scotland, England, the United States and Australia; hence the effects of the Irish experience made themselves felt not only at home but also much farther afield. Viewed from such a standpoint, peripheries cease to be regarded essentially as passive consumers of ideas of the modern; at certain pivotal moments in their histories, at least, they can function as sites of 'alternative enlightenment' where ideas of the modern are intellectually tested, creatively extended, radicalised and transformed, and indeed transferred eventually to the metropolitan centre.

Secondly, one might want to question not just the geographical but also the chronological parameters of conventional narratives of the modern. In such accounts, metropolitan societies are typically identified with a more advanced temporality and with a more fully modern consciousness than peripheral ones, but assumptions of this kind have also come under increasing interrogation in recent decades. Alternative accounts of modernity would argue that it was the oppressed peoples of the world, whether African slaves or colonised peoples, who were in fact the first to endure the accelerated processes of social transformation and cultural hybridisation, the violent uprootings and diasporic migrations, now routinely deemed typical characteristics of modernity and indeed globalisation. This alternative model of modernity contends, in other words, that it was the peripheries and their peoples that first endured, and with least shelter or state protection, a massive assault on their inherited traditions – the melting of all that had appeared culturally solid in the smelter of imperial conquest and assimilation. Their traumatic experience of cultural convulsion and dislocation only became the substance of everyday life in metropolitan places much later.[4]

Where diffusionist models, then, typically conceive of peripheries as fastnesses of tradition prised out of their retarded pre-modern mentalities reluctantly and belatedly, this alternative view takes the cataclysmic contact between centre and periphery or coloniser and colonised as its starting point, and concludes that as a result of that encounter the peripheral masses had no alternative but to acquire a modernised consciousness at least as early as and indeed often well in advance of their metropolitan counterparts. This model compels a re-thinking of the Irish situation since Ireland can be considered an exemplary nursery of exilic consciousness. For those who migrated into the country as colonial settlers in the early modern period, Ireland was and was not home; the very fact that the settlers referred to themselves as New English, Anglo-Irish or British implies an outlander mentality, which claims allegiance to the centre but does so self-consciously from the frontiers of a radical otherness. Alongside this exilic consciousness of the inward migrant, a persistent pattern of outwards migration can also be observed: this extends from the flight of the native nobility (or 'Wild Geese') in the aftermath of the Williamite conquest, to the Catholic clergy under the Penal Laws, to the Irish poor compelled to emigrate to Britain and America in the post-Famine period. Hence Ireland did not have to await – as is too frequently assumed – the arrival of industrialisation or technological modernity to undergo that traumatic sense of breakneck modernisation, of rapid cultural transformation and psychic alienation – the shock of the new – conventionally regarded as a constitutive or exemplary experience of the modern. In Ireland, modernisation via colonisation preceded modernisation via industrialisation; colonisation was at least as devastating and destructive to any idea of stable organic society or to the continuity of tradition as the latter would ever be.

Anomalies of the modern

The array of competing temporal and spatial coordinates considered thus far should suggest some of the challenges involved in plotting the development of Irish modernity. In this section, we consider the ways in which Irish culture presents a challenge to the normative Western models of development previously outlined. While Irish historiography comports quite comfortably in many respects with standard accounts of Western modernity, the country's history has in other fundamental respects proved stubbornly recalcitrant to these same metanarratives. In the early modern period, Ireland was indeed, as mentioned earlier, one of the bitter theatres of war between European Reformationist and Counter-Reformationist forces. Yet the increasingly centralised and successful British state never secured the mass conversion of the Gaelic and Old English populations to Protestantism, despite this having been an ostensible objective of the various plantations. Whether in its 'early' or 'later' stages of modernity, therefore, Ireland, unlike neighbouring peripheries such as Scotland or Wales, remained a largely Catholic country. As the country's Gaelic culture and language receded, and as its ties with both England and the United States intensified through emigration and trade during the nineteenth and twentieth centuries especially, Ireland's Catholicism became increasingly one of the essential markers of its distinctiveness, something which set it apart in the overwhelmingly Protestant and Anglophone world it increasingly inhabited.

The distinction between Catholic and Protestant on the island – one of the enduring axes of Irish socio-cultural division – was from the outset complicated by issues of class, cultural capital and national or state allegiance. It was also susceptible, however, to codings in terms of a wider international 'civilisational' conflict between the pre-modern and the modern: one in which Protestantism was commonly equated with the enterprise, rationality, materialism and liberalism of the modern, Catholicism with the traditionalism, superstition and dogmatic 'Gothic' authoritarianism of the pre-modern. The temporalities and values of the modern and the pre-modern, in other words, have routinely been mapped in Ireland not only onto the topography of the country (the modern identified with the urban, the industrial northeast, and the eastern seaboard; tradition or the pre-modern with the country, with agriculture, the West and the islands), but onto the island's religious or sectarian denominations as well. From this standpoint, the minority Protestants were the exemplary bearers of Irish modernity, the Catholic masses remaining trapped in everything from which the modern had heroically detached itself.

If its Catholicism was one of the things that seemed to render Ireland anomalous, its capitalist development was another matter perceived as strangely aberrant. Political economists over the last two centuries have consistently remarked upon the many ways in which Ireland can be seen to depart from those pathways to capitalist development regarded as normal in the Western world. Thus in the nineteenth century Ireland's population doubled from somewhere near 4 million in 1800 to over 8 million by the 1840s. This remarkable demographic expansion was not accompanied by wholesale industrialisation along the lines of England, Scotland or Wales. It issued, rather, in the devastation of the Great Famine – a drastic reduction of population to market rather than expansion of market to population and the last great subsistence crisis of its kind in Western Europe – which left 1 million dead and another 2 million forced into emigration, and setting in motion patterns of demographic decline well out of kilter with Western European patterns generally. Even after independence, the country still remained largely a dependent agricultural economy until well into the 1970s, primarily a supplier of cheap food to Britain, and its levels of emigration still remained by far the highest in the entire 'British Isles' region.

In Ireland, therefore, the lived experience of modernisation meant something quite different to what it did to its near neighbours in Europe where modernity was associated with domestic innovation, industrial trailblazing, national aggrandisement and even global pre-eminence. From the Elizabethan period on, political modernisation in Ireland meant a diminishment rather than an extension of political sovereignty. Incorporation into the United Kingdom with the Union of 1800 did not usher in the economic prosperity promised. For peoples such as the English, the Spanish, the French or the Germans, modernity brought about a dramatic elevation, indeed globalisation, of their national cultures and vernaculars; for the Irish, modernity issued in the wholesale collapse or destruction of Gaelic culture. All of this generated a heightened intellectual scepticism about the equation of either political or economic modernisation with progress; in the period after the Great Famine, the country proved a fertile breeding-ground for unorthodox economic theories of development, uneven development and underdevelopment as political economists grappled with the question as to whether Ireland had failed political economy or whether political economy had failed Ireland.[5]

Irish modernity has thus in one way and another come to seem to many as puzzlingly eccentric and strange, its history enigmatically at odds with the standard vectors of modernisation that Western European core countries apparently exemplify: a largely Catholic enclave within a Protestant British state; a chronically underdeveloped economy situated cheek by jowl alongside the most industrially developed European economy; a 'feudal' or 'semi-feudal' redoubt that was nonetheless after 1800 an integral part of the most advanced Western liberal democracy; an overwhelmingly rural and, across all denominations, devoutly religious society until virtually the end of the twentieth century in a supposedly increasingly secular and urban Western world. In the circumstances, theories, histories and sociologies of Irish modernity frequently turn into extended deliberations on Ireland's deficient modernisation, anxious ruminations on the ways in which Irish society has remained an uncanny site of the 'pre-modern' or the 'non-modern', despite its geographic location astride the very highway of Euro-American modernity.

There was an important flip side, however, to the obsession with Ireland's deficient or perennially laggard modernity. For those who were disenchanted with modernity – those disposed to view the modern not as coeval with progress but rather as the tyranny of civilisation over instinct, of reason over imagination, of smokestack and asphalt sterility over green hills and natural spontaneity, of bourgeois materialism and anomie over the vital organic community of the folk – Ireland's supposed deficiencies could be trans-valued and recreated as its greatest resource. From this perspective, Ireland acquired an aura of mystery and romance, an association with the archaic and the antique. The country was construed as a sublime periphery to the European mainstream, a place that was out of the world, beyond the world, an alternative to the world. Viewed thus, Ireland becomes almost wholly identified with 'tradition', the latter conceived from this perspective, however, in a positive sense; not as a lamentable obstacle to progress (as 'tradition' is typically construed in modernisation discourses) but as a repository of all those values lost or about to be lost in the destructive maelstrom of 'progress'.

From the nineteenth century onwards, Ireland acquired a refurbished reputation as a national culture distinguished by its supposed antipathy to the modern. Irish culture (like that of Scotland in the same period) became a significant site for the elaboration of a European Romanticism that represented both a reaction against and a radicalising extension of the European Enlightenment. The Romantic reaction against the abstract universalism of the Enlightenment, a reaction that disputed the equation of tradition with ignorance and which advanced the idea that all cultures had their own intrinsic inherited value, issued in complex ways in Ireland. On the one hand, the celebration of local cultures over abstract universalism served as warrant to defend Irish culture against the assumed superiority of its English counterpart. On the other hand, in an increasingly Anglophone Ireland, attempts to define Irish national culture were invariably plagued by anxieties about what constituted the basis for that culture and whether it should find its 'natural' vernacular expression in the Irish or in the English tongue. The appeal to tradition and the vernacular had real attraction for Irish cultural nationalists, but in a country where deep tradition or cultural continuity had been severely mauled by a turbulent history, where discontinuity (except for its Catholicism) was always easier to discern than continuity, the appeal to 'tradition' would recurrently prove maddeningly difficult.

Long before twentieth-century critiques of orthodox ideas of Western modernity and modernisation were issued in theories of uneven development or dependency theory, or before the various post-modern or post-colonial challenges to Eurocentric grand narratives were articulated, Ireland had served as an intellectual laboratory where the idea of the modern was subjected to a variety of Romantic interrogations. Irish Romanticism was stimulated by antiquarian investigations into the country's bardic past. This Romanticism sometimes developed cultural nationalist overtones with a distinctly separatist accent, but could also be appropriated to a conservative Irish Ascendancy agenda that aimed to establish a moderate cultural nationalism that would work within the Union. The appeal of the Gaelic world in this latter structure of feeling was that that world could be represented as defiantly aristocratic and patriarchal; antithetical in spirit to everything that smacked of the modern, the materialistic and the masses; its civilisational shipwreck could be read as tragedy because it seemed prophetic of the ways in which the heroic spirit of the past was destined to be crushed by the base and levelling spirit of modern democracy. An Ascendancy appropriation of things Gaelic might also allow, however, for a liberal cultural nationalist rapprochement between the Irish élites of Gaelic and Anglo ancestry and hence serve as the basis for a refurbished Irish national identity that would safeguard both from the condescensions of the English. In its various Celticist, unionist, nationalist, Catholic and other guises, this conception of Ireland as a welcome antithesis to a debilitated modern world would undergo an ongoing series of mutations and transformations across the last two centuries.

The most formidable and ambitious legatee to this Romantic tradition was Ireland's most distinguished poet, W. B. Yeats. The intellectual lineages of Yeats's cultivation of things Gaelic are a curious synthesis of varieties of unionism, cultural nationalism and Celticism. During the Irish Revival in the late nineteenth century, the cultural nationalist note was ascendant as Yeats tried to conjure into being a new Ireland that would blend the simplicity and responsiveness to the supernatural and the esoteric that he associated with the West of Ireland peasantry and the elegant refinement he identified with the Anglo-Irish Ascendancy. As it became increasingly apparent that the new Ireland emerging out of the national independence struggle would be that of the Irish Catholic middle classes, Yeats's work took on a more aggressively anti-democratic temper, railing against the way in which an elevated Protestant aristocracy is brought low by betrayal and degeneration from within (especially by its women who married outside of their proper lineage and class) and from without by a philistine populace instinctively destructive of everything refined and superior.

In his late work, this fierce antagonism to everything modern, Christian, bourgeois and democratic acquires a cosmopolitan scope and accent: as Yeats peers into the long historical future, the Irish are cast in racial terms as a venerable aristocratic people, 'that ancient sect', temperamentally hostile to the 'filthy modern tide' of twentieth-century society. At this stage, his imagined Ireland was destined to do spiritual warfare against an unholy trinity of British materialism, middle-class mass culture and orthodox Christianity that had rendered the modern world ugly, and accordingly in desperate need of a cleansing renewal that would come about only by a civilisational crisis of apocalyptic magnitude. However much its cadences may change across his career, the Ireland that Yeats values is consistently associated with the pre-modern; crucially, the country's hostility to modernity, its pre-modern temperament, are something not to be lamented but celebrated because, for Yeats, to be archaic is to possess that sense of fullness, human plenitude, mystery and possibility that a modern secular society has supposedly abandoned.[6]

While Yeats's anti-Christian bent and sexual libertarianism were patently at odds with the values of the Catholic church, that church shared a conception of Ireland as an enclave of the wholesomely pre-modern that was formally at least oddly similar to that of Yeats. In the Roman Catholic conception of things, Ireland represented an island of exceptional piety and devotion – 'an island of saints and scholars' that had fortunately escaped the general corruption of the secular modern world. In the Catholic hierarchy's view, their innate peasant virtue and devotion to Rome, which centuries of persecution had only hardened, had equipped the Irish with a unique destiny to convert the non-European continents and to lead a decadent Western world back to its lost spiritual values. It is not without irony that this conception of an Irish 'spiritual empire' that would overlap with and help to improve its British 'materialist' counterpart owed much of its inspiration to an Englishman and convert to Catholicism, Cardinal John Henry Newman, who served as Rector of the then newly established Catholic University of Ireland in the years 1854–58.

In sum, Yeats forged from the raw materials of Irish Romanticism an esoteric vision of a sufficiently powerful aesthetic quality to make him one of the twentieth century's most influential poets; the Catholic church forged from a like conception of anti-modern Ireland a vigorous missionary movement of world-wide ambition, the institutional fingers of which were to reach for much of the twentieth century across every continent. As remarked earlier, in orthodox modernisation discourses, Irish Catholics and Protestants were habitually positioned *vis-à-vis* each other as the pre-modern to the modern. As the examples of Yeats and the Irish Catholic church variously attest, in the Protestant and Catholic traditions alike, however, it was the identification of Ireland with the pre-modern or with the defiantly anti-modern that yielded the most audacious and indeed extravagant visions of national destiny.

Embracing and interrogating the modern

Yeats's aristocratic-aesthetic vision of Ireland survived independence only by an act of obdurate poetic will; the Catholic church's ascetic vision approximated the official nationalist ideology elaborated by the new southern state until the 1960s. The economic arthritis, escalating emigration levels, censorious crassness and general sense of social torpor that prevailed from the 1930s until the 1960s was eventually, however, to torpedo that vision; its discrediting prepared the way for the modernisation drive that has prevailed ever since. In the decades immediately after independence, the state's official policy was to build up domestic industry behind a protective wall of tariff barriers; when that failed, the First Programme for Economic Expansion, launched by Taoiseach Seán

Lemass in 1958, removed import restrictions and introduced fiscal incentives to encourage multinational corporate investment (conceived of as the new motor for economic and social change). At the same time, the state sought incorporation into the European Economic Community, membership of which was eventually attained by both the Irish Republic and the United Kingdom of Great Britain and Northern Ireland in 1973.

The results of this latest modernisation drive have been mixed; increased industrialisation and rising employment levels in the sixties were succeeded by a quarter-of-a-century-long recession from the seventies to the mid-nineties (manifesting itself in the form of massive international debt, constantly rising unemployment, and emigration levels that recalled those of the fifties). Since then the southern economy has undergone the rather dramatic recovery generally termed the 'Celtic Tiger'. Despite its mixed fortunes, however, that modernisation drive has secured general support from across the broad political spectrum in Ireland, partly due to a lack of a discernible global alternative, partly because economic modernisation was so successfully conscripted as the new national *raison d'être*. The goal of Irish nationalism during the independence campaign had been to create an Ireland that would be culturally distinctive, independent and free; since the 1960s, the revised national agenda of the Irish Republic has been to create an Ireland that would simply be economically and socially 'modern', a vague term now typically identified as a process of general convergence with other Western societies. This kind of *volte face*, from the aspiration for a revived national culture that would be distinct and exceptional to a more contemporary aspiration to be normal and unexceptional, is a common enough feature of national post-independence narratives everywhere. Even in societies less divided than Ireland, such adjustment is rarely achieved, however, without considerable difficulty.

Does contemporary Ireland still remain an appropriate site for tracking the ambiguities of the modern? Or have the successes of the move towards modernisation marginalised dissent? It must be acknowledged that the economic modernisation programme, and the attendant neo-liberalisation, Europeanisation and Americanisation (sometimes mistakenly termed 'globalisation') of Irish society have enjoyed considerable intellectual and popular support. The most audible opposition to this social agenda was a conservative Catholic backlash, which mobilised considerable opposition to various forms of social liberalisation – especially on divorce, sexuality and abortion – for a period in the eighties, only then to dramatically collapse in the nineties when the economic boom arrived to vindicate the modernisation programme, and a litany of highly publicised clerical sex and physical abuse scandals discredited the authority of the Catholic hierarchy that had earlier given a lead to such campaigns.

Nevertheless, two identifiable contemporary sources of counter-cultural critique deserve mention here. One of these counter-cultures, Irish feminism, has, like international feminism generally, maintained a rather ambiguous relationship to the concept of the modern and modernity. Discourses of the modern since the Enlightenment endorsed a pervasive cultural equation of the modern with the male: modernity is equated with rationalism and masculinity, tradition with the irrational and femininity. Depending on whether the writer enthusiastically espoused a narrative of progress or regarded the modern world in baleful terms, femininity represented – rather as with Ireland itself – either a primitive state of arrested development or an organic condition of pre-modern wholeness untouched by the malign contradictions and existential alienations of the modern age. Nevertheless, women's struggles for emancipation are complexly interconnected with modernisation as well; phenomena typically considered 'modern' (urbanisation, industrialisation, secularisation, modern technology and mass education) have undoubtedly improved the basic conditions of women's everyday lives. Moreover, if conventional discourses of the modern aligned women with the dead weight of tradition, feminism frequently overturned such assumptions by constructing women themselves as one of the avant-gardes of the modern. Emblematic figures such as the late nineteenth-century New Woman, the early twentieth-century suffragette, the sexually liberated woman of the 1960s or the self-assertive professional woman of recent decades have all been represented in their day by feminists as exemplary figures at the forefront of social change; in such discourses, modern women epitomise the 'shock of the new', refusing the dead weight of the past to pioneer new futures – men, by contrast, are associated with a regressive attachment to outmoded tradition.[7]

Given the oppressive nature of the Irish state as it developed after independence, and the pervasive equation of women with tradition in Irish nationalist and clericalist culture, it was virtually inevitable perhaps that

Irish feminism would largely endorse modernisation theory. Because Ireland was construed as an oppressively traditional society, modernisation by convergence with 'the Western world' was viewed by contrast as an emancipatory process that would liberate Irish women. Irish liberal feminism especially has tacitly espoused this vision of contemporary Ireland, insisting only that the promised emancipations of the modern must equally be extended to women as well as to men. Modernisation theories and 'second wave' Irish feminism are not only historically coincident with each other, both gaining momentum in the 1960s and 1970s, but they also share a structure of feeling in which contemporary Ireland is viewed as a 'traditional' society now undergoing an exhilarating liberation from the past.

Indeed, the degree to which modernisation and feminist discourses had become intertwined with each other since the sixties was dramatically illustrated in the election of Mary Robinson as the first woman president of the Republic of Ireland in 1990. Obviously a progressive development by any measure and a notable watershed in gender politics, Robinson's success was almost universally construed as a climacteric victory of 'modern' over 'traditional' Ireland, of 'post-nationalist' over 'nationalist' Ireland, of 'liberal and secular' over 'conservative and clerical' Ireland. Though she had stood as a Labour candidate, and hence was also the first left-wing candidate ever to achieve such office, it was never suggested that Robinson's electoral success represented a victory of socialist or even radical social democratic over capitalist or neoliberal Ireland. Clearly it did not represent anything remotely of the kind. Within the restrictive terms espoused by modernisation discourse, questions of property relations, of class, of how and to whom the benefits of modernisation are to be distributed, of whether modernisation on Western lines is even sustainable or at what cost to whom, are effaced. (Robinson herself has often courageously addressed such matters, but this is not the issue here; the point is, rather, that her presidency was socially constructed in terms of a victory of the 'modern' over the 'traditional' in ways that equated the 'modern' with unambiguous progress.) When, in other words, such simplistic dichotomies organise public perception, it suffices to show that the 'modern' is at last superseding the 'traditional' to assure the public that the country must be uniformly moving in the right direction. In an important sense, Robinson's election attested to the capacity of Irish feminists to appropriate modernisation discourse for liberal feminist social ends. It needs to be asked, however, whether the purveyors of modernisation discourses hadn't even more successfully annexed feminism to *their* own ends as well by making Robinson into a feminised symbol of the supposedly socially progressive character of the brave new corporate Ireland that had become the darling of transnational capital.

Given the imbrication of liberal feminist and modernisation discourses in Ireland, the most sustained critique of the current modernisation orthodoxy has stemmed from the Field Day enterprise. This enterprise initially commenced as the Field Day Theatre Company, a Derry-based but touring company that began its life with a staging of Brian Friel's play *Translations* in 1980. Today, the enterprise continues mainly in the form of the Field Day *Critical Conditions* publications series, which has featured work by a number of distinguished contemporary cultural theorists. Drawing on an eclectic – apparently discordant – variety of intellectual resources that includes the Frankfurt School, post-colonialism, critical theory, and memory theory, and much less vigorously on feminist theory, the Field Day enterprise has generated new ways of thinking about much that is conventionally dismissed merely as 'tradition' or 'regressive' in Irish culture. It has also questioned sweeping evaluations of the modern as an inevitably liberating phenomenon, pointing to the unevenness of its manifestations. The contributors to this series have developed no concerted or systemic theoretical critique of Irish modernisation: they do not have a shared methodological agenda, such as the South Asian Subaltern Studies historians had at the inception of their enterprise, for example. Nevertheless, the tenor of the series as a whole expresses a critical scepticism with regard to liberal teleologies of progress of a kind that is distinctly out of step with the dominant intellectual, political and popular cultural consensus in Ireland. For that reason, the works in question are worthy of our attention.

The single most sustained critique of modernisation discourse has been developed by Seamus Deane, the leading intellectual presence of the Field Day enterprise since the mid-1980s, in a series of books extending from *Celtic Revivals: Essays in Modern Irish Literature* (1985) to *Strange Country: Modernity and Nationhood in Irish Writing Since 1790* (1997).[8] In these and other works, Deane has meticulously inventoried the promiscuous changes which Irish writing – literary, political, intellectual – has rung on the relationship between Irishness and modernity across two centuries. Charting the tectonic shifts of such discourses through a

range of (chiefly male) writers – from Edmund Burke through Matthew
Arnold and Ernest Renan and thence through Yeats to Joyce and Beckett
and up to the contemporary historians – Deane's achievement has
been to show how different conceptions of Ireland and modernity have
infected, whetted, dogged and quickened each other throughout that
period. In these books, he has tracked the conundrums of Ireland as
a place both within and without the modern – as a haven from the
modern or a site haunted by the non-modern, as a place about to sacrifice
everything of value in order to succumb to the bland homogeneity of the
(post-)modern or, alternatively, as an island finally prepared to shake off
the dogmatic slumber of tradition and courageously to wake to the challenges of the modern. On these conundrums of Ireland and the modern,
he has demonstrated, an entire national literature has battened, revisiting the vicissitudes of that problematic monotonously, occasionally with
extraordinary brilliance.

To inventory a condition is not to escape it; on the contrary, it may
simply confirm one's utter incapacity to overcome it. Deane's work –
especially *Strange Country* – has elicited frustration from Irish critics –
feminist, revisionist, Marxist and republican – because it offered so
little alternative to the intellectual condition it inventories. It could be
argued in Deane's defence that his caution about going beyond the apor-
ias of Irish modernity is a direct consequence of his recognition that any
ambition towards radical transcendence reenacts the habitual temporal
structures and conceptual imperatives of modernity itself. To assume,
in other words, that with one concerted intellectual heave we could
entirely escape the modern conceptualisations of history that we now
recognise as problematical would be to reinscribe the hubristic mentality
of Western modernity that is partially the object of critique. In his inventories of the narrative models deployed to represent the relationship
between Ireland and the modern, Deane's work insists that we become
more self-conscious and self-critical about how we use these models even
if we can rarely discard them altogether.

One of the things that the Field Day and feminist critiques have in
common is that both seek to displace the bourgeois male subject as
the privileged subject of history, a move that reopens but leaves unresolved the question of what Irish modernity has meant for women and
other subaltern groups. The vagaries of Irish history being what they are,
however, the conception of Irish modernity generally, and of its recent

modernisation drive more particularly, shared by these two intellectual formations diverge more often than they converge. Irish feminism is a broad social movement with an ambiguous relationship to modernisation discourses in which it has a considerable investment. Field Day, though it may have had more expansive ambitions in the 1980s, has essentially remained an intellectual coterie; the complexity of its take on Irish modernity has as yet in any case scarcely impinged on Irish public or popular cultural discourses. Irish feminism, one might be tempted to say, has a strong constituency but a weak critique of modernisation discourse; Field Day has a stronger intellectual critique, but a considerably more limited constituency or institutional reach.[9]

Today, however, when the bankruptcy of the tradition–modernity opposition is widely acknowledged in academic circles, when the very word 'modernity' is deemed by many to have outlived its conceptual utility, when the option of regarding peoples or practices that do not conform to our idea of the modern as simply 'backward' is no longer viable, the once-easier distinctions between modern and traditional, the premodern and the modern, have come under sustained and unprecedented pressure. New lexicons (critical traditionalism, alternative modernities, alternative enlightenments, the subaltern, the post-modern, the non-modern, radical memory) are symptomatic both of an erosion of the older complacencies of the modern as well as an acknowledgement that the term 'modernity' (with its connotations of the human capacity to develop, to democratise and to emancipate itself) cannot simply be junked either.

Accordingly, in contemporary Irish scholarship, evolutionist and stadial conceptions of history contend with more recent models that start with the assumption that there can be no clear-cut dividing line between past and present; in these models, every present is non-synchronous, a coeval mix of radically disjunct temporalities. They assume that all our 'nows' (whether at the level of the individual or the collective subject) represent a continuous process of anticipated futures and reconstructed pasts lived in traumatic relay with each other. Hence this volume has to contend not only with the practical pressures of compressing the events of two centuries of Irish social and cultural history into compact chapters; it must also negotiate the complex task of finding narrative forms adequate to a moment in which older ways of conceptualising the modern have lost their unwarranted, often arrogant assurance, but at a time when public faith in the possibility of a more emancipated future has also weakened dramatically. Which is to say, the more we deconstruct the flawed promises of the modern, the more we discover that we still need to sustain some of those promises as well.

Notes

1. Oskar Lafontaine, *Das Herz schlägt links* (Munich: Econ, 1999), cited in Fredric Jameson, *A Singular Modernity: Essay on the Ontology of the Present* (London: Verso, 2002), p. 9; Christopher Prendergast, 'Codeword Modernity', *New Left Review* 24 (November/December 2003), 95–111, 95.
2. Fredric Jameson, *A Singular Modernity: Essay on the Ontology of the Present* (London: Verso, 2002), p. 25.
3. Luke Gibbons, 'Alternative Enlightenments: The United Irishmen, Cultural Diversity and the Republic of Letters' in Mary Cullen (ed.), *1798: 200 Years of Resonance* (Dublin: Irish Reporter Publications, 1998), pp. 119–27, 119.
4. Paul Gilroy, *The Black Atlantic and Double Consciousness* (Cambridge, MA: Harvard University Press, 1993).
5. Thomas Boylan and Timothy Foley, *Political Economy and Colonial Ireland* (London: Routledge, 1992).
6. Seamus Deane, *Strange Country: Modernity and Nationhood in Irish Writing since 1790* (Oxford: Clarendon Press, 1997), p. 153.
7. For an extended discussion, see Rita Felski, *The Gender of Modernity* (Cambridge, MA: Harvard University Press, 1995).
8. Seamus Deane, *Celtic Revivals: Essays in Modern Irish Literature* (London: Faber, 1985) and *Strange Country: Modernity and Nationhood in Irish Writing since 1790* (Oxford: Clarendon Press, 1997).
9. The 1990s have seen a number of important publications that work across concerns associated with Field Day and also with Irish feminism. Hence the distinction drawn here between these bodies of work is of broad schematic value only and the intellectual field is considerably more complex. Examples of crossover works of this kind include: Claire Wills, *Improprieties: Politics and Sexuality in Northern Irish Poetry* (Oxford: Clarendon Press, 1993); Emer Nolan, *James Joyce and Irish Nationalism* (London: Routledge, 1995); Marjorie Howes, *Yeats's Nations: Gender, Class and Nationhood* (Cambridge: Cambridge University Press, 1996); and Elizabeth Butler Cullingford, *Ireland's Others: Ethnicity and Gender in Irish Literature and Popular Culture* (Cork: Cork University Press/Field Day Critical Conditions Series, 2001).

Further reading

Terence Brown, *Ireland: A Social and Cultural History, 1922–1985*, 2nd edition (London: Fontana Press, 1985)
Clare Carroll and Patricia King (eds.), *Ireland and Postcolonial Theory* (Cork: Cork University Press, 2003)
Linda Connolly, *The Irish Women's Movement: From Revolution to Devolution* (Basingstoke: Palgrave, 2001)

Seamus Deane, *Strange Country: Modernity and Nationhood in Irish Writing since 1790* (Oxford: Clarendon Press, 1997)

J. J. Lee, *The Modernisation of Irish Society, 1848–1914* (Dublin: Gill and Macmillan, 1973)

David Lloyd, *Anomalous States: Irish Writing and the Postcolonial Moment* (Durham, NC: Duke University Press, 1993)

Conor McCarthy, *Modernisation: Crisis and Culture in Ireland, 1969–1992* (Dublin: Four Courts, 2000)

I

Cultural politics

2
_____

The survival of the Union

I

The constitutional union of 1800 was an extreme political formula. It was pursued with ruthless energy; it ultimately disappointed its architects. Yet the Union provided a constitutional framework for Ireland for 120 years, and has survived in a truncated form within Northern Ireland since 1920. The Belfast Agreement of 1998, which is sometimes viewed as a 'renegotiation' of the Union, has brought into focus the issue of its survival. More than ever, there is a need to understand not only why the original Union failed in 1920–21, but also how and why it lasted for over a century. More than ever there is a need to illuminate some of the explanations for the survival of the British state in nineteenth-century century Ireland and beyond.

Yet even though the Union was a central feature of political life in the nineteenth century modern Irish historians have somehow evaded the question of its survival. At one level the reason for this is not hard to locate: modern Irish political historiography remains dominated by the Home Rule and revolutionary era; and it is hard to escape the impression that a good deal of Irish history writing has, as its ultimate destination, the political settlements of the early 1920s, when the Irish Free State and Northern Ireland were each established. Of course this is an entirely unexceptional emphasis, given the enormous and lasting significance which the revolutionary and Ulster Unionist movements possessed. It is also entirely reasonable that Irish historians should emphasise the ultimate failure of the Union in the twenty-six counties. But it is possible that this reasonableness has created a paradox – that many Irish historians have effectively dedicated themselves to explaining the death of a settlement which (whatever the quality of its life) clung on for a remarkable length of time. The Union and its government were widely unpopular, were sometimes actively oppressive, and were periodically challenged; but they also survived, and Irish people worked around them, or accommodated themselves to them, or (in the case of the Unionists) became active supporters. We know why the Union ultimately failed the Irish people, and how it died; we need to begin to explain more directly why it survived for as long as it did.

The political history of nineteenth-century Ireland remains by and large an historiography of resistance and crisis. As in other European countries which have successfully struggled for their independence, so in Ireland there remains a fascination with the processes of liberation, and (equally) an understated or embarrassed or unwritten history of collaboration, compromise and political inertia. Thus, we have a reasonably sophisticated understanding of why Presbyterian radicals and Catholic Defenders took up arms in 1798; but we still have only a very crude notion of the countervailing pressures which nudged Irish people in the nineteenth century into the ranks of the Royal Irish Constabulary or the British army.

Irish political historiography tends naturally to be the story of the minority who were politically active; it offers little space for the quietist majority – those who, while holding doubtless sincere political convictions, lived out undemonstrative lives against the backdrop of revolution and war. The experience of the Northern Ireland troubles suggests that, while there was much bloodiness and pain, many were only indirectly touched, and accommodated themselves to the various political and military crises which characterised the 'Long War'. We need a vision of Irish political history which recognises the extremes of human experience – extreme suffering, extreme heroism, extreme skill – but can also give appropriate weight to low-key but everyday experiences, the unheroic or passive. Many politically aware men and women nurtured their ideals in private and clung on to the framework of normal lives. Without understanding such lives, the survival of the Union remains difficult to comprehend.

Equally, Irish historians have a hawk-like eye for political movement, and a magpie-like fascination for the tinsel of radical or extreme politics. They are keen on watersheds and revolutions; and they tend to be more preoccupied by the hard men and women of Irish politics than by centrists or conciliationists. Yet emphases such as these are achieved only at a cost. We know a lot about the various crises of nineteenth-century and early twentieth-century Irish politics, but less about sustained and gradual political change. We know about advanced or radical politics in the period, but we know much less about moderate or centrist themes. For example, while much lip-service is paid to peace-making in modern Ireland, there is no sustained history of consensual politics on the island – of the efforts by centrist politicians of one kind or another to reconcile the nationalist and unionist traditions. For so long as Irish political historiography is skewed in these ways, then certain historical questions become exceedingly difficult to formulate, let alone to answer.

For these different reasons the Union, that controversial old spectre, has experienced two deaths. It was extinguished by Irish revolutionaries in the war of 1919–21. But it has also been effectively throttled by Irish historians, who have been beguiled by other more radical and exciting issues and personalities.

II

The Union and its mode of passage were a focus of controversy throughout the nineteenth century, with many of Ireland's later ills being traced back, with a crisp historicist logic, to this great Fall. The old Irish parliament (augmented in 1782) was, in nineteenth-century nationalist rhetoric, a prelapsarian golden age. For unionists, the same parliament was as corrupt and parochial as the Home Rulers who sought to restore an assembly to Dublin.

In some respects it is easy to exaggerate the loss of the parliament. Irish parliamentary life did not, of course, die in 1800, but instead was transplanted to Westminster where many of the leading figures of the old Irish Commons found new seats and new prominence. And, just as it is easy to exaggerate the extent of Ireland's parliamentary independence in the years before the Union, so it is easy to exaggerate the impact of its loss.

It is also possible to exaggerate the economic consequences of Union. Despite 'free trade' and 'legislative independence', Ireland's economy had in fact grown more intertwined with that of Britain in the later eighteenth century: the Union did not, therefore, create British economic ascendancy in Ireland, nor is it regarded as the single most important influence over the early nineteenth-century Irish economy. The Napoleonic wars were a much more substantial influence, stimulating Irish agriculture, the provisions trade and some Irish manufactures over the years spanning the Union debate. Equally, the wars brought higher levels of taxation and a quadrupling of the Irish national debt in the period 1801–16.

But the critical aspect of the Act of Union in the early nineteenth century was not what it did, but what it failed to do. The architects of the Union, and particularly Prime Minister William Pitt, had conceived the measure as a means of extending and reinforcing the state, and – more widely – of consolidating the government of the empire. But this vision was worthless if the Union did not accommodate the Irish people, or if it was passed over the heads of a resentful majority. British and imperial stability in 1800 required a Union; this, in turn, demanded a measure of civil equality or 'emancipation' for Catholics. The support of leading Catholics for the Union was crucial, therefore, and it was won, not through any specific promises or assurances from the government, but rather (as Patrick Geoghegan has suggested) 'by making it implicitly understood that emancipation would follow union at some point'.[1]

Catholic hopes were duly raised, and then crushed with equal celerity. Political opposition to emancipation was led by Lord Loughborough, the lord chancellor, who seems to have briefed the king, George III, on the sly: but there were certainly other obstacles to movement on the issue, such as William Pitt's flagging health, division and disintegration within his ministry, and alternative political challenges at this crucial juncture in the war against France. A bare majority of British ministers favoured emancipation; but the combination of the dissidents and the king proved to be decisive. Catholic hopes of an inclusivist Union were smashed together with Pitt's government at the end of January 1801.

The implications of this are hard to exaggerate. The Union which was formulated on 1 January 1801 was, not (as Pitt had envisaged) between Britain and Ireland, but rather between Britain and the Irish Protestant élite. The failure of emancipation meant that Catholics were not immediately incorporated into the new polity or its institutions. More than this, however, the Union looked like another painful example of English perfidy; for, while (as has been said) no firm promises were ever given, hints were cast and expectations fanned. To a people who were already susceptible to the notion of English treachery, the Union looked like sharp practice. It would take nearly thirty years for emancipation to be enacted; and, even then, victory came only because an angry Catholic democracy effectively extorted relief from reluctant Tory ministers. This fatal and protracted delay ensured that Pitt's Union, rather than providing a great buttress to the empire, looked instead like a mine within its walls.

The Union was an audacious political stroke which, from the start, was riven with ambiguity and disappointed expectations. It was designed for British and imperial purposes, and it was sold to the Irish using patronage and arguments which concerned, and sometimes scandalised, contemporaries. Catholics in contact with the government thought that the Union would bring relief; many Protestants were persuaded until a very late stage that the Union would serve to bolster the ascendancy interest. Building a parliamentary majority for the Union meant applying outrageously large sums from the secret service fund, and abandoning any pretence of accountability, to say nothing of legality. Catholics felt deceived and exposed – promised a place in the sun, they were consigned lastingly to the shade of the Union.

III

Logically, given this tragic and complex nativity, the Union of Great Britain and Ireland might well have been an immediate and complete failure. In fact, one of the great paradoxes of modern Irish history is that (against all the odds) the Union provided a lasting, if clearly vitiated, constitutional settlement. It remained in place until the early 1920s and beyond. Ulster Unionists have argued (particularly at the time of the Belfast Agreement) that the Union enjoyed an afterlife: they have seen the survival of Northern Ireland within the United Kingdom as the last vestige of Pitt's constitutional surgery, and have argued that Northern Ireland's position within the United Kingdom depends still upon the Union of 1801. Certainly if longevity is a measure of success, then the Union settlement can scarcely be written off.

Though there is a temptation to see the Union as an expression of political modernisation in nineteenth-century Ireland, it might be argued that it depended for its survival on the pre-modern and localised condition of much of Irish politics at this time. It is perhaps the case that for most Irish people through much of certainly the early and mid-nineteenth century wider political struggles mattered less than local issues and a passive, or resigned, acceptance of the constitutional status quo. Theo Hoppen has suggested that the focus and structure of popular Irish politics in the middle years of the nineteenth century was the local as much as the national arena; and that 'limited goals and local priorities' were at least as significant for most Irish people at this time as universal causes. In his classic study *Elections, Politics and Society in Ireland, 1832–1885* (1984), Hoppen has argued that 'the more the detailed workings of individual political communities in Ireland were examined [by him] the more striking and important seemed the gap between local realities and the rhetoric of national politics . . . Irish politics . . . were often profoundly localist in both content and style'.[2] It is certainly the case that the vision of liberation purveyed by militant separatists commanded relatively little active support through much of the century – rebellions in 1803 and 1848 were small affairs, and were suppressed with comparatively little official effort. The Irish Republican Brotherhood, or Fenian movement, which was founded in 1858, recruited an impressive following in the early and mid 1860s; but some historians (such as Vincent Comerford) have daringly suggested that this popularity was based upon the local, social and recreational appeal of the movement as much as upon proactive militancy. Certainly the Fenian rising of 1867 mobilised only a small fraction of the IRB's numbers, with much less than 20 per cent of the total membership turning out.[3]

Constitutional national endeavours had clearly very great success in recruiting support. But often they also had an ambiguous or pragmatic relationship with the Union. It is worth stressing that the Union survived at least partly because some leading national politicians often pursued relatively flexible, accommodationist political strategies. Daniel O'Connell, for example, united much of Catholic Ireland behind the campaign for Catholic emancipation (1823–29), creating a national organisation, politicising Irish people and imbuing them with a sense of their history and purpose. But O'Connell's was a richly inventive political intelligence and he devoted the middle section of his career to making the Union work for Irish Catholics: his priorities in the 1830s (for example) seem quite clear, with a sustained and explicit effort to mould the structure of the Union government in Ireland along more popular, Catholic, lines. He famously defined this strategy in 1836 when he claimed that 'the people of Ireland are ready to become a portion of the Empire . . . they are ready to become a kind of West Briton if made so in benefits and justice; but if not we are Irishmen again'.

It ultimately became clear to O'Connell that Irish Catholics would not quickly emerge as a 'kind of West Briton' in terms of 'benefits and justice'. But this did not prevent later national leaders (like the Independent Irish Party in the 1850s or Isaac Butt in the 1870s or John Redmond) pursuing pragmatic and gradualist strategies. It is also very far from saying that the Union was a wholly static phenomenon. The Union of 1800 was in fact a moderately adaptable political settlement which permitted some subsequent political movement, and which could be adjusted to accommodate a degree of political challenge.

Indeed, the strength of the Union lay not in its moral rigour, but rather in its capacity for reinvention. The Union was originally defined by Pitt in inclusivist terms, was redefined as an instrument of Protestant ascendancy, and was used to expand Catholic and farmer rights after the 1830s. It was used against itself in terms of the Irish Church Act of 1870 (this disestablished the Church of Ireland, and thereby abolished the United State Church which had been created under the Union settlement). The Union was ultimately 'greened' at the end of the nineteenth century in preparation for Home Rule – that is to say, redefined in a manner more accessible to nationalists. In 1810 the Union remained an instrument of Protestant ascendancy; in the last quarter of the nineteenth century it can be seen as the mechanism by which successive British governments undertook social experiments of a much more radical design than they would ever have countenanced in England.

It should be said at the outset that there are obvious dangers in pushing this argument too far. While a panoramic view of the Union reveals its varieties and fluidity, particular episodes (and above all the Great Famine of 1845–51, discussed in chapter 8) illustrate the considerable potential for ideological rigidity. Recent scholarship has tended to confirm the limitations of British relief policy during the Famine, as well as the profound failure of imagination and humanity within Whitehall and Westminster. The rigidities of *laissez-faire* liberalism have traditionally been stressed; more recent scholars tend to underline the providentialist outlook of senior British officials, who were sometimes characterised by a narrow form of evangelical religious outlook. There is little doubt that this case has power; nor can there be any doubt that perceptions of official neglect or malevolence fuelled the militant nationalism of the later nineteenth century.

Still, the failure of the British government during the Famine years is all the more problematic because the Union could be, and was, used as a framework within which fundamental and otherwise untouchable issues such as property rights might be addressed. It has been suggested (by the Trinity historian, W. E. Vaughan) that the Union facilitated the revolution in landed proprietorship which occurred in the late nineteenth century; Vaughan has speculated that an Irish parliament, containing a strong local propertied element, would have baulked at the kinds of social and contractual change which Westminster was willing to pursue in Ireland.[4] The Union certainly did not preclude types of advanced reform, particularly in the area of land tenure, which the British parliament was not prepared at this time to countenance in an English context.

The malleability of the Union as a political instrument is particularly evident in the nature of British policy in Ireland from the late 1860s onwards as Irish national politics attained a greater force and coherence. Though Gladstone claimed that he was not responding to violence, the Fenian movement clearly indirectly inspired a succession of popular reforms (such as the disestablishment of the Church of Ireland) during his first administration (1868–74). His second administration (1880–85) was characterised by an intermixing of significant reforms (such as the land act of 1881) and severe policing measures.

Gladstone's conversion to Home Rule in 1885–86 illustrates other essential truths about the possibilities and limitations of the Union government. It indicates that the government was susceptible to the pressure of Irish popular opinion, and that – like some great engineering work – there was at least a theoretical degree of 'give' within its structures. Gladstone was prepared to restore a subordinate Irish parliament in the interests of preserving what he saw as the essence of the Union settlement: the supremacy of Westminster, the security of the realm and the viability of the United Kingdom. His efforts towards Home Rule failed in 1886 and again in 1893. But this should not divert from the fact that he represents a significant tradition of pragmatic constitutional thought which has been prepared to jettison the traditional forms of Union in order to preserve a measure of its substance.

It might be said, following on from this, that Gladstone's vision of the Union has had a lasting, if frequently neglected, relevance. Gladstone invested reform of the union with a strong Providentialist tone. He devised a constitutional proposition which still has an importance – the paradox that a union between Britain and Ireland could best be sustained through the creation of a devolved government in Ireland. He also defined, through Home Rule, a form of variable geometry for the government of the United Kingdom. In all of these senses Gladstone's vision of union seems to have left a greater impact upon contemporary politicians than some (at least) would care to acknowledge. Moreover, his commitment to Home Rule, however ineffectual, helped to encourage an accommodation between Irish nationalism and the United Kingdom parliament which lasted until the eve of the revolution; the mere promise of Home Rule kept Irish nationalists at Westminster for thirty-five years.

Home Rule was one positive strategy through which British Liberals sought to retain a constitutional linkage with Ireland. British Conservatives and Unionists (who were in power for seventeen of the twenty years between 1886 and 1905) attempted to retain the Union in a more direct and uncomplicated way than this; but they, too, were prepared to demonstrate a degree of adaptability both in terms of attitudes and institutions. For much of their period in office the Tories pursued 'constructive Unionist' measures which were designed to address a variety of popular Irish grievances, particularly (though not exclusively) in the area of land: land purchase was one of the central themes of this legislation. Local government in Ireland was partially democratised through legislation passed in 1898. By the last years of their period in office some Tories were inching towards the possibility of creating both a form of devolved administration as well as a university controlled by Irish Catholics.

It should be said immediately that these reforms have sometimes been seen as sporadic and half-baked, the product of parliamentary opportunism as much as philosophical conviction. On the other hand, the pendulum of interpretation has swung away from narrowly high-political explanations towards an interpretation of late Victorian and Edwardian Toryism (for example, in the work of Ewan Green) which gives greater scope to ideology and intellect. In fact, it has always been quite clear that the Tory commitment to land purchase was deep-seated, and went beyond issues of political pragmatism. Land purchase was for long seen as a means of creating a settled peasant proprietorship in Ireland that would have no interest in social revolution, and that would eventually be accommodated within the Union.

But the survival of the Union was not solely a matter of localism, nationalist pragmatism, reformism or political malleability – the Union was also bolstered by cultural and economic mechanisms, and by the armed forces and bureaucratic resources of the British state. The Union created a single currency and trade area for the United Kingdom. The Union coincided with the age of mass production, with an expansion of advertising and of consumerism and with ever-swifter modes of transportation and communication. There was an inflow into Ireland of printed materials and other goods bearing British patriotic imagery or slogans. Attention has traditionally focused upon direct British state intervention in cultural questions (such as the role of the new National School system of the 1830s in promoting the English language). But there is an argument for suggesting that British manufacturing supremacy, together with the free market, was at least as important as this as an anglicising influence in nineteenth-century Ireland. And, while historians have traditionally linked advances in transportation and communication to the growth of popular nationalism, it might also be considered that railways, steamships and the electric telegraph facilitated the spread of British influences, and the consolidation of British government in Ireland. Moreover, improved transportation facilitated British rule in a cruder sense than this, for it permitted the swifter movement of troops and police.

The Union was also bolstered by other agencies and mechanisms, including even perhaps the British army and British royalty. The British royal family were frequent visitors to the island, and on the whole these occasions reinforced or exposed some complex ties with the crown. Queen Victoria paid her last visit to Ireland in 1900, Edward VII came in 1903 and George V in July 1911, on the eve of the revolution. Here were highly charged events which (as James Murphy and Senia Paseta have recently argued) have been largely written out of the political historiography of modern Ireland.[5] Victoria and Edward VII's visits attracted huge crowds onto the streets of Dublin, many of whom (though by no means all) were welcoming. The Irish Parliamentary Party, by and large, urged a low-key and polite acceptance of the royal visitors – the Lord Mayor of Dublin, Sir Thomas Pile, who had been elected as a Nationalist, presented a loyal address to Victoria on behalf of Dublin Corporation. In so far as these visits have attracted attention, then it is in the context of the important advanced nationalist reaction which they helped to create – they gave a spur to separatists, and inspired separatist organisations that claimed their place in the struggle which culminated in the revolution. But these royal visits also exposed a highly complex relationship between nationalist Ireland and the British monarchy; Edward VII, in particular, was held to symbolise a new and more generous relationship between Britain and Ireland, and he toured extensively in areas which only seventeen years later, during the 'Troubles', would have been out of bounds for an RIC constable, let along the King of England. The visits were structured to show-case the monarchy in a favourable light: Edward VII presented some gold antiquities to the Royal Irish Academy, and used the occasion of the death of the Pope, Leo XIII, to publicly underline his great affection for the departed pontiff.

It is difficult to fully decode these visits; but on the whole it might be suggested that they reinforced some passive sympathy for the monarchy, while also profoundly dividing Irish nationalism. Leading separatists like Arthur Griffith felt with some justification that these visits revealed the extent to which mainstream constitutional nationalism had been accommodated by the crown and within the British connection.

The army was a muscular arm of the British state in nineteenth-century Ireland. At one level, it had an obvious importance in support-ing British rule and the Union; the garrison veered between a strength of 15,000 and 30,000 in the course of the century, and generally stood at around 25,000. In the early part of the nineteenth century, this force was spread across the country in smallish detachments, but in later decades a massive garrison at the Curragh was constructed, perhaps (as the mili-tary historian Elizabeth Muenger has suggested) with the subconscious intention of overawing the population.[6] Either way, though the army was deployed comparatively rarely, its presence may be seen as a crude and important bolster to the Union.

However, the relationship between the Irish people and the British army was more complicated than this. The army recruited tens of thou-sands of Irishmen, particularly during the Napoleonic wars and (at the end of the nineteenth century) during the war against the Boers in South Africa. Edward Spiers has pointed out that in 1830, when the Irish repre-sented less than a third of the total population of the United Kingdom, the proportion of Irishmen in the British army stood at over 42 per cent; at this time there were in fact more Irish than English in the army. With the Famine, and the associated decline in the Irish population, this pro-portion also fell dramatically; but as late as 1900, when separatists were energetically campaigning against recruitment, the Irish proportion of the army (13 per cent) was still ahead of the Irish proportion of the United Kingdom population (11 per cent).[7]

The full social and political importance of the army to Victorian Ire-land is again difficult to decipher, but it should certainly not be oversim-plified. Recruitment to the army largely hinged on a variety of social and economic circumstances rather than on any overt political consideration; it blossomed in the context of the large and relatively poor population which characterised pre-Famine Ireland. Taking the Queen's shilling certainly did not automatically induce loyalism – there has been an intriguing overlap between service in the British army and revolutionary activism from the time of James Connolly and Dan Breen through to the recent 'Troubles'. Revolutionary separatists indeed actively sought to recruit in the ranks of the army from the 1790s through to the time of the Fenian movement, and beyond. But these recruitment figures suggest that the army was an intimately familiar feature of the lives of many Irish families; and this, in turn, is reflected in the surprising popularity which the army retained in Ireland throughout the nineteenth century. Moreover, the importance of the army in terms of acclimatising Irish people to the symbolism and strategies of the British state should also be considered.

The expansion of Victorian government meant both that there were ever more Irish people in public employment, and that the physical expression of the state was of increasing importance in everyday life; there is a spatial dimension to the Union which has (for the most part) completely eluded historians. Some attention has been paid by scholars to the architectural manifestations of nineteenth-century Irish Catholicism (in terms, for example, of the great ecclesiastical building programme which was undertaken through the Victorian era), attention has also been paid to the architectural and iconic significance of the Stormont parliament building, opened in 1932. But there is also a case for emphasising that the state was intruding ever more into the physical environment of Irish people in the nineteenth century. Some work has been done by Jane Leonard and Keith Jeffery on war memorials in British Ireland; more work needs to be undertaken on the rich variety of other, Victorian, monuments and their wider significance (republicans, for example, have doubtless seen a bleak appropriateness in the survival of a statue of Queen Victoria in front of Dáil Éireann until 1948).[8] The consolidation of the RIC brought with it the erection of police barracks; the battery of land legislation passed at the end of the nineteenth century brought both administrators and government offices. A major complex of official buildings was completed in Merrion Street, Dublin, shortly before the end of the British regime, and inherited by the new Irish authorities: the Irish Taoiseach (head of government) still works under the royal monogram of George V. The expansion of the Victorian post office necessitated buildings and post boxes bearing the royal insignia, and brought Irish people into contact with the state in ever more complex ways (sending letters, savings, pensions and national insurance). The richly symbolic significance of the revolutionaries' assault on the General Post Office, Dublin, during the 1916 Rising should not be missed.

The physical expansion of the British state in Ireland was of course directly linked to increasing bureaucratic control and intrusion into the lives of Irish people. More policemen and more civil servants in Victorian Ireland meant that more information was being gathered on the population, and on its social, economic, cultural and political characteristics. As Joseph Chamberlain complained in 1885, 'an Irishman at this moment cannot move a step; he cannot lift a finger in any parochial, municipal or educational work without being confronted with, interfered with, controlled by an English official'. Margaret O'Callaghan has illustrated the directly political uses to which this intelligence-gathering might be applied (as, for example, in the use of RIC and other official data during the interrogation of the nationalist leadership at *The Times* Special Commission of the late 1880s). She has also suggested comparisons between the categories and amount of information gathered in Ireland and that accumulated in India and other imperial domains.[9] In other words, there is a case for arguing not just that the state bureaucracy directly helped to bolster the Union, but that it also underpinned the semi-colonial nature of the British regime in Ireland.

On the other hand, it was Irish Catholic policemen who were gathering intelligence and who had been incorporated by this colonial-style administration; and scholars are increasingly interested by the complex and reciprocal nature of the Irish Catholic relationship with empire. Notions of Protestantism were certainly central to the construction of British imperial identity in the eighteenth century, and to its consolidation in later years. It is paradoxical, then, that the Irish Catholic middle classes should have contributed as extensively as was the case to the British and imperial project. Liberalism provided able Catholic lawyers like Lord O'Hagan or Lord Russell of Killowen with an avenue to British ministerial politics; the structures of élite enterprises like the Indian Civil Service provided ambitious middle-class Catholics with professional opportunities which (for a few, like Sir Antony MacDonnell, Lord MacDonnell of Swinford) would bring incorporation into the British political élite. Recent research by scholars like Donal Lowry or Senia Paseta has tended to emphasise the extent to which some sections of the Irish Catholic middle classes were prepared to work within the social and political structures of the Union and empire.[10]

By the end of the nineteenth century a section of the Catholic establishment had been partly accommodated within the union. Paseta's study of the Catholic élite in the Home Rule era suggests a highly conservative community which had only slowly accepted the inevitability of Home Rule, and which participated in the administration of the empire. The Union worked for Irish Protestants; but it also worked, however tardily and imperfectly, for some Catholics some of the time.

The emphasis of my argument has been on the malleability of the Union, as well as on some of the cultural means by which Britishness was insinuated into nineteenth-century Ireland. But, of course, the longevity of the Union is also to be explained in terms of military and police action. As I have argued, Ireland was permanently garrisoned by British soldiers, and by the armed policemen of the Irish or (after 1867) the Royal Irish Constabulary. The RIC were an essential arm of the state during the suppression of the Fenian Rising of 1867, and during the Land War and Plan of Campaign in the 1880s. As has been said, the RIC (certainly in terms of its lower ranks) was a predominantly Catholic enterprise, and much official reliance was placed upon its capacity to tackle political crime. But the RIC was also, effectively, a further means of accommodating a section of Catholic society to the British state. Its importance, in terms of both direct and indirect political control was immense, as indeed was recognised by the IRA in 1919–21, for whom the men of the RIC were a principal target.

It is also true that while the Union contained the potential to accommodate Catholics, this potential was often realised only with great difficulty. There were vested British and Protestant interests in Irish official and professional life which were often difficult to move. There were thus critical sections of Irish Catholic society which were not assimilated by the British state, and which sought an outlet for their abilities and ambition within an alternative environment. John Hutchinson has famously argued that the late nineteenth-century Irish cultural and political revival owed much of its force to the thwarted ambitions of educated lower-middle-class Catholics, men and women who aspired to a place in the sun, but who found that it was already occupied by Protestants (or by Englishmen).[11]

The slowness of reform often helped to stimulate anger and support for the national cause; but the very fact that reform, however tardy, was within the realms of the possible, meant that many Irish Catholics were disposed to work within the structures of the Union for gradual, incremental gains. Ultimately the fundamental problem with the Union was not simply that it failed to deliver for Irish Catholics; but rather that it continually held out the promise of change, and continually either reneged on that promise, or delivered short measure. The history of the Union is thus a history of crises of expectation – from Catholic emancipation in 1800, through the Famine in 1846 and after, land reform in the late nineteenth century, structural reform and ultimately Home Rule. In the end, expectations of legislative independence were created through the Home Rule Act of 1914, which, when crushed, marked the beginning of the end of the British regime.

The Union worked for a time because it was able to accommodate some key sections of Irish Catholic society at least in a provisional or contractual manner; it also (more obviously) attracted the support of Irish, particularly Ulster, Protestants, who saw it as a guarantee against Catholic political and economic supremacy in Ireland. Landlords came to fear the Catholic democracy; and they were often prepared to accept the creeping reforms imposed by Westminster as an alternative to the possibly more radical behaviour of a future Dublin assembly. The astonishing economic growth of eastern Ulster, the heartland of Irish Protestantism, was credited to the Union settlement; the prosperity of this region permitted, from the mid-1880s, the growth of an organised movement dedicated to the preservation of the Union. It is of course a matter for conjecture, but it might be suggested that this movement helped to prolong the life of the Union for a time at the cost of making the final break with Britain more complete. In the end Protestantism and Unionism became synonymous, and though this might seem a predictable outcome (given the failure of Catholic emancipation in 1800–1), the union had for a time possessed wider possibilities.

IV

The Agreement of 1998 may (or may not) be seen as evidence of the continued malleability of the Union. There are indeed parallels between Ireland in the late nineteenth and early twentieth centuries, and Northern Ireland at the turn of the millennium. It is often said, for example, that the politics of British Prime Minister Tony Blair have a Gladstonian resonance; and it might be argued that the reinvention of a devolved administration in Belfast is, like Home Rule in 1886, an effort to 're-negotiate' the Union. Gladstone's Home Rule Bill did not get past the Unionists – the stalling of Home Rule helped to generate a crisis of expectations which fed, in turn, into the revolutionary struggle and the end of the British regime. The Belfast Agreement just about got past the Unionists in 1998. But it remains to be seen whether the deal will administer a constitutional restorative – or a mercy killing – to the Union.

Ireland has had a difficult relationship with the Union. There is a popular image of the Union as a kind of detachable superstructure covering Irish society in the nineteenth century, but in reality the Union was pervasive, and impacted upon the physical environment, the market place, and the professional and recreational life of Irish people. We need a social, cultural and spatial definition of the Union which will allow a fuller understanding of the complex relationship between the Irish people and their government in the nineteenth century. We may even need a fresh definition of Irish political history in order to address this challenge.

Notes

1. Patrick Geoghegan, *The Irish Act of Union* (Dublin: Palgrave Macmillan, 2000), p. 119.
2. K. Theodore Hoppen, *Elections, Politics and Society in Ireland, 1832–1885* (Oxford: Clarendon Press, 1984), pp. vii–viii.
3. See, for example, R. V. Comerford, *The Fenians in Context: Irish Politics and Society, 1848–82* (Dublin: Wolfhound Press, 1985).
4. W. E. Vaughan, *Landlords and Tenants in Mid-Victorian Ireland* (Oxford: Clarendon Press, 1994), pp. 219, 224.
5. See James H. Murphy, *Abject Loyalty: Nationalism and Monarchy in Ireland during the Reign of Queen Victoria* (Cork: Cork University Press, 2001) and Senia Paseta, 'Nationalist responses to two royal visits to Ireland, 1900 and 1903', *Irish Historical Studies* 31, 124 (November 1999), 488–504.
6. Elizabeth Muenger, *The British Military Dilemma in Ireland: Occupation Politics, 1886–1914* (Dublin: Gill and Macmillan, 1991), pp. 2–4.
7. Edward Spiers, 'Army organisation and society' in Thomas Bartlett and Keith Jeffery (eds.), *A Military History of Ireland* (Cambridge: Cambridge University Press, 1996), p. 337.
8. Keith Jeffery, *Ireland and the Great War* (Cambridge: Cambridge University Press, 2000), pp. 107–43, 154–5.
9. Margaret O'Callaghan, *British High Politics and a Nationalist Ireland: Criminality and the Law under Forster and Balfour* (Cork: Cork University Press, 1994), p. 122.
10. Senia Paseta, *Before the Revolution: Nationalism, Social Change and Ireland's Catholic Elite, 1879–1922* (Cork: Cork University Press, 1999).
11. See John Hutchinson, *The Dynamics of Cultural Nationalism: The Gaelic Revival and the Creation of the Irish Nation State* (London: Routledge, 1987).

Further reading

Thomas Bartlett and Keith Jeffery (eds.), *A Military History of Ireland* (Cambridge: Cambridge University Press, 1996)

R. V. Comerford, *Ireland: Inventing the Nation* (London: Hodder, 2003)

Patrick Geoghegan, *The Irish Act of Union* (Dublin: Gill and Macmillan, 1999)

E. H. H. Green, *The Crisis of Conservatism: The Politics, Economics and Ideology of the British Conservative Party, 1880–1914* (London: Routledge, 1995)

K. Theodore Hoppen, *Elections, Politics and Society in Ireland, 1832–85* (Oxford: Clarendon Press, 1984)

John Hutchinson, *The Dynamics of Cultural Nationalism: The Gaelic Revival and the Creation of the Irish Nation State* (London: Routledge, 1987)

Alvin Jackson, *Ireland, 1798–1998: Politics and War* (Oxford: Blackwell, 1999)
    Home Rule: An Irish History, 1800–2000 (London, 2003)

Keith Jeffery, *An Irish Empire? Aspects of Ireland and the British Empire* (Manchester: Manchester University Press, 1996)
    Ireland and the Great War (Cambridge: Cambridge University Press, 2000)

Daire Keogh and Kevin Whelan (eds.), *Acts of Union: The Causes, Contexts and Consequences of the Act of Union* (Dublin, 2001)

Christine Kinealy, *This Great Calamity: The Irish Famine, 1845–52* (Dublin: Gill and Macmillan, 1994)

Lawrence J. McBride, *The Greening of Dublin Castle: The Transformation of Bureaucratic and Judicial Personnel in Dublin Castle in Ireland, 1892–1922* (Washington, DC: Catholic University of America Press, 1991)

Elizabeth Muenger, *The British Military Dilemma in Ireland: Occupation Politics, 1886–1914* (Dublin: Gill and Macmillan, 1991)

James H. Murphy, *Abject Loyalty: Nationalism and Monarchy in Ireland during the Reign of Queen Victoria* (Cork: Cork University Press, 2001)

Margaret O'Callaghan, *British High Politics and Nationalist Ireland: Criminality, Land and the Law under Forster and Balfour* (Cork: Cork University Press, 1994)

David Officer, 'In search of order, permanence and stability: building Stormont, 1921–32' in Richard English and Graham Walker (eds.), *Unionism in Modern Ireland: New Perspectives on Politics and Culture* (Dublin: Gill and Macmillan, 1996)

Senia Paseta, *Before the Revolution: Nationalism, Social Change and Ireland's Catholic Elite, 1879–1922* (Cork: Cork University Press, 1999)

3

Language, ideology and national identity

Language has operated as a vehicle for debates concerned with cultural identity and political legitimacy in Ireland for much of its modern history. While the incorporation of Ireland into the United Kingdom by the Act of Union of 1800 marks a milestone in the cultural no less than the constitutional history of Ireland, the direction and dynamic of the 'language shift', from Irish to English as the general vernacular, were already well established and, as it seemed, irreversible, by the end of the eighteenth century.

Language and, even more crucially, religion, were the key elements of cultural discrimination in the great convulsion of the sixteenth and seventeenth centuries, the outcome of which was the establishment of a Protestant, overwhelmingly planter, new ruling class in Ireland, together with the triumph of the English language, law and politico-administrative institutions throughout Ireland, and the defeat of the whole institutional edifice of the Gaelic political and social order which had sustained and been mediated through the Irish language.

In the centuries that followed, language, together with religion, remained at the centre of the debate on Irish culture, community and identity. But the language shift to English, the language of power and of all the avenues to advancement, soon gathered momentum among those who aspired to improve their condition or to progress and participate fully in the life of the country under the new order. By the late eighteenth century, Irish was already considered the language of the past and of the poor; not only by the planter society, but by the emerging Catholic middle class in town and countryside, who, while continuing to use Irish in transactions or social intercourse with the lower orders, had themselves made the transition to English as the language of their domestic as well as their public lives. For the literate, Irish was still largely a scribal language of manuscripts, with only a limited presence in the world of print.

Within this central process of language shift, however, there were complex sub-themes. From the outset some Protestants of planter stock had shown an interest in Gaelic culture, and the Irish language, either from an antiquarian or a practical evangelising impulse. In the later eighteenth century, a renewed interest among a minority of the ruling élite (mainly 'patriotic' Protestants of planter descent) in the nature of Irish cultural particularity, allied to an encounter with early European Romanticism, resulted in the first of a series of 'Celtic Revivals' in Ireland, the scholarly and antiquarian fruits of which included the founding of the Royal Irish Academy in 1785.

From the late eighteenth century, a further elaboration of concepts of identity and peoplehood congealed into the political ideology of nationalism. Among the disciples of the new political nationalism in Ireland from the later eighteenth century there were a few thinkers, notably Thomas Davis, who were especially alert to the cultural implications of the constitutional-legal claims being made for an autonomous Irish 'state' on behalf of an 'Irish nation'.

But while these currents – of antiquarianism and early cultural nationalism – carried forward into the nineteenth century, the actual position of the two main vernacular languages in the first decades of the nineteenth century reveals a complex bilingual society. It is estimated that Ireland in 1800 had a population of 2 million Irish-speakers, 1.5 million Irish–English bilinguals and 1.5 million English speakers. Notwithstanding the continuing language shift, the numbers of Irish speakers probably increased up to 1845. This was because Irish was very much the language of the poor, and it was among the poor that population increase was greatest in the pre-Famine decades. The Great Famine of 1845–50 decimated Irish-speaking Ireland through death and emigration. The 1851 census (which included a 'language question' for the first time) revealed that the total number of Irish-speakers had fallen to 1.52 million or just 25 per cent of the population, and would continue to fall. As Helen and Máirtín Ó Murchú have written: 'a precipitant shift to English was underway . . . So it continued. By 1891, for the whole of Ireland, the percentage of Irish-speakers in the under ten group had declined to 3.5 per cent and the language appeared to be on the point of extinction.'[1]

The massive abandonment of Irish as a vernacular language during the nineteenth century is a remarkable event in Irish cultural history.

Given that a key axis of ideological and political contestation through-out the Union era (1800–1921) was the very legitimacy of the Union frame-work itself (as outlined in chapter 1), it might be expected that in the nationalist critique of the legitimacy and benefit of the Union connec-tion, the language shift in Ireland would feature prominently in nation-alist political movements. Yet, with a few notable exceptions, this was not the case until the closing decade of the nineteenth century.

In fact, English was the dominant language of all Irish nationalist popular political movements from the United Irishmen of the late eight-eenth century through to the nineteenth century. In print and on plat-form, the political propaganda of nineteenth-century Irish nationalism was conducted through English. Political leadership was crucial. The great popular tribune, the Catholic lawyer, Daniel O'Connell, leader of mass movements for Catholic Emancipation and Repeal of the Union in the second quarter of the nineteenth century, was himself a native speaker of Irish who held a fatalistic view of the inevitable decline of Irish. Moreover, he viewed this prospect with relative equanimity. In this he was typical of the advancing Catholic bourgeoisie, who were gener-ally content to salute the glories of the Gaelic past, while mobilising to construct a strong national identity based upon their already historically founded religious identity as the 'Catholic Irish nation' coming into its own after enduring the long night of persecution and discrimination.

The intellectuals of the Young Ireland movement of the 1840s were more alert to the message of cultural nationalism and the centrality of language in its tenets. Thomas Davis, in particular, strongly advocated an essentialist position for the Irish language in the construction of a credible Irish national identity. However, the medium of preaching and propaganda for the Young Irelanders was English, particularly in their influential newspaper, the *Nation*. Among the separatist Fenians of the post-Famine decades, there were individuals who were alarmed at the decline of the Irish language, but they conducted their public politics, whether at home or among the Irish diaspora, overwhelmingly through English. The same is true of the Home Rule movement. The achieve-ment of political self-rule, and the form of that political sovereignty – a republic or a native parliament – were the chief concerns of these political movements; the role of language in identity-formation was not a central issue.

The leaders of the Catholic church were, in the main, reconciled to, if not actively encouraging of, the language shift. Individual bishops and priests had concerns for the pastoral care of Irish-speaking congregations, which prompted them to require competence in Irish of those charged with such care. A minority channelled their affection for the language into the collection or commissioning of manuscripts and the support of scribes. But there was no satisfactory provision for the teaching of Irish at the national seminary at Maynooth, Co. Kildare, throughout most of the nineteenth century, nor was there satisfactory provision of catechetical or devotional literature in Irish. Furthermore, as the Irish Catholic church began to take on the role of a missionary church, among the Irish of the diaspora and in the English-speaking lands in general, English was the language of their mission. The Irish spiritual empire of the modern period was English speaking.

Perhaps the most energetic attention to the actual community of Irish-speakers on pragmatic grounds came from Protestant evangelical societies from the 1790s to the third quarter of the nineteenth century. Élite Protestant patronage of scholarship and antiquities continued throughout the nineteenth century. But the increasing association of all aspects of Irish patriotic or national sentiment with political nationalism, from the Young Ireland movement forward, resulted in a recoil from involvement in 'Irish' cultural projects by Protestants whose politics were Unionist. This became most pronounced in Ulster where, in the intense political polarisation of the Home Rule crisis of 1886–1914, the habit of seeing 'British' and 'Irish' as mutually exclusive versions of cultural identity (a habit also indulged in by advanced Irish-Irelanders of the same era) was to have a major influence on the disposition of the Northern Ireland state after 1920 towards cultural identity and the role of language.

The post-Union state – the British state – was central to the language shift and the politics of language in Ireland. The role of the state expanded significantly during the nineteenth century; that is to say, it increasingly reached into different aspects of the lives of ordinary people. So far as the bilingual character of Irish society was concerned, the state only recognised one of those languages. This reflected the ideological assumptions of the imperial British state regarding assimilation, improvement and progress. In effect, becoming literate in English was seen as an essential enabling stage on the path to progress and civility for the Irish people. Thus, in the expanding reach of state activity in policing, public works schemes, ordnance survey mapping, poor relief systems, and, most crucially, in the state-directed system of elementary 'national' education introduced in 1831, English achieved ever-deepening penetration, both geographically and socially. Only in the closing decades of the nineteenth century did the state demonstrate a more permissive attitude towards the presence of Irish in the education system, partly in response to lobbying from educationalists and language activists, partly because the overwhelming dominance of English suggested that indulging the Celtic strain as an exotic ornament on the broader British culture posed no threat.

With such powerful forces driving the advance of English, and the fatalism towards the language which was the historical legacy of the defeat and inexorable abandonment of Irish since the sixteenth century, the story of any actions to counter this language shift is very much a chronicle of unavailing efforts made by numerous individuals, in Ireland and among the emigrant Irish in Britain and America, to make a stand for the preservation of Irish as a living language. But there is no sustained organisational effort until late in the nineteenth century.

It is from the last two decades of the nineteenth century that we come upon those ideas and programmes regarding cultural renewal, and language 'revival', that are commonly referred to as 'the philosophy of Irish-Ireland' or 'the Gaelic League idea'. The timing of this stirring of ideas was not accidental, and neither was its focus. By the closing decade of the nineteenth century, some form of devolved self-government or Home Rule for Ireland seemed imminent. At the same time, the census returns were clearly indicating that the death of the Irish language seemed now inevitable and hardly less imminent. It was at this juncture that a deliberate project of 'decolonisation' was formulated and adopted by a group of intellectuals and artists with, in time, significant support from a larger constituency of political activists who were to form the nucleus of the political leadership of the new Irish state eventually established in 1922.

Language was a central preoccupation of this project. Indeed, coming to terms with the language/identity predicament in late nineteenth-century Ireland would, in different ways, inspire and torment W. B. Yeats and his collaborators in the Irish Literary Revival, as it did the young James Joyce even as he went into exile.

While there were precursor 'revivalist' initiatives from the 1870s, the appropriate starting point for discussion of the cultural project of language 'restoration' is probably Douglas Hyde's seminal 1892 lecture, 'The Necessity for De-Anglicising Ireland'. While Hyde became committed to the 'extension of our [Irish] language among the people', he was especially exercised to preserve Irish as a living language among the base community of Irish-speakers whose vernacular it still was. By the late nineteenth century, these were largely concentrated in areas in the western counties of the Atlantic coast. When Hyde, with others, founded the Gaelic League in 1893, the primary objective of the new movement was declared to be 'The preservation of Irish as the National language of Ireland and the extension of its use as a spoken tongue.'

The League's objective of preservation and extension reflected Hyde's basic propositions regarding language and identity and the need for socio-cultural regeneration in late nineteenth-century Ireland. Hyde claimed that the purpose of the language revival mission was 'to render the present a rational continuation of the past'. For Hyde and his fellow Gaelic League enthusiasts, it would be a catastrophe if the continuity of cultural tradition, articulated and given form principally through language, were to be ruptured. Such a cultural tradition encompassed thoughts, feelings, perceptions and wisdom, a distinctive world-view based on a unique set of values. The case made for cultural continuity, through the medium of Irish, and, therefore, for language revival, rested on a set of assumptions and propositions that combined elements of general humanism with specific tenets of cultural nationalism.

Hyde's understanding of the relationship between language, thought and identity was unremarkable for his time. He quoted approvingly Henri d'Arbois de Jubainville's definition of language as 'the form of our thoughts during every instant of our existence'.[2] The abandonment of a language, therefore, to say nothing of its enforced abandonment, inevitably involved a disorientating rupture in cultural continuity at several levels; not only an alienation from landscape (placenames) and inherited historical narratives and communal myths, but also a deep psychological trauma, at an individual and communal level, caused by the loss of a rich inherited matrix of wisdom and knowledge. This elemental trauma, it was believed, had been exacerbated by a number of features particular to the language change in Ireland – in particular, a sense that the loss of Irish was the outcome of military and political conquest. The abandonment of the native communal language in the face of the dominant new language of the conqueror became internalised as part of the shame of defeat, dispossession, humiliation and impoverishment – the classic condition of the colonised.

The specifically cultural nationalist aspects of Hyde's propositions were shared by many of his contemporaries. The Irish continued to insist that they were a distinct nation, and demanded a national state.

Yet they were abandoning the most distinctive mark of nationhood, the Irish language. This debilitating contradiction could only be resolved by reversing the language shift of recent centuries. For Hyde and the Gaelic League activists the restoration of the Irish language as the national vernacular was the cornerstone of this project of national reconstruction, a healthy identity being a prerequisite for a reconstruction of the social and economic fabric and the collective energy and self-belief of the national community.

Of course, the alternative badge of communal identity in Ireland was religion. Religious identity was, for historical reasons, deeply and pervasively communal in Ireland, but also a divisive and exclusive instrument of cultural differentiation. This strong communal sense of religious identity would inevitably present a challenge to nationalist theorists seeking an inclusive definition of Irish identity, and specifically to a project of cultural revival based upon language as the key marker of identity. Indeed, the search for an alternative to the divisive religious affiliation as a defining mark of Irish identity goes some way towards explaining the disproportionate prominence of Protestants among the theorists of Irish linguistic nationalism.

One further feature of Hyde's claim for the revival of Irish was that it was not simply a general plea for the cultural particularity encoded in language to be allowed to live and develop, but a specific set of claims for the kind of cultural differentiation, which marked off the Irish from the English. This, it must be said, was fairly representative of the stereotyping common to cultural commentary in the later nineteenth century, benignly voiced by Ernst Renan, Matthew Arnold and others, but with its more morbid versions formulated in racist discourse. In effect, the artistic and imaginative and spiritual Celts were contrasted with the solid, practical and materialist Anglo-Saxons. A version of this particular stereotyping also informed Yeats and his collaborators in the enterprise of establishing an authentic Irish national literature in Hiberno-English, and certain Gaelic Leaguers gave the formula a more deeply religious hue.

Hyde's main collaborator in founding the Gaelic League, the historian, Eoin MacNéill, also emphasised the need for spiritual as well as social renewal in Ireland. Where MacNéill diverged from Hyde, perhaps, was in his emphasis on the way in which the glories of the Gaelic tradition and inheritance, still resonating in the living Irish vernacular, emerged from the uniquely rich cultural fusion of the Celtic genius with the light of Christianity. Again, the journalist and propagandist, D. P. Moran, describing Ireland's cultural predicament as 'a battle of civilisations', produced a more schematic model than Hyde of cultural absorption (with the Gael as the matrix absorbing all later arrivals), and a more astringently sectarian tone.

With partition and the establishment of the two states in Ireland in 1920–22, the language situation changed fundamentally. Two confessional states came into being, with mutually exclusive totalising official versions of cultural identity. Northern Ireland existed because it had rejected Home Rule in order to remain British. Its official identity would remain resolutely British, giving no recognition or place in its public life to such unambiguous symbols of distinctive 'Irishness' as the Irish language. The nationalist minority's general stance of cultural dissent within Northern Ireland included, for many, support for the Irish language. Seamus Heaney has described the language situation in Northern Ireland as inculcating a 'binary thinking about language. I tended to conceive of Irish and English as adversarial tongues, as either/or conditions rather than both/and'.[3] This binary thinking affected more than language in the life of the Northern state.

So far as the independent Irish state is concerned, its official culture was determinedly un-British. It is generally accepted that the first generation of political leaders of the Irish Free State included a significant cohort who had been influenced, some profoundly, by the cultural movements at the turn of the century, and by the Gaelic League in particular. Indeed, it could be argued that the Gaelic League created, in effect, the political élite of independent Ireland. This may be overstating the case. But the leaders of the main political groupings in the new state accepted that the government of an independent Irish state had an obligation to give official recognition and strong support to the Irish language, the principal marker of that Irish nationality on whose behalf a national state had been demanded. Accordingly, the Irish language was given privileged status in the constitution of the Irish Free State and this was repeated in the Constitution of 1937, which declared it the first official language of the state.

Moreover, in terms of government policies, in the 1920s and 1930s Irish was declared an obligatory subject in the school curriculum, for public examinations, and for entry to various branches of the public service. A range of incentives were introduced to encourage its use more widely within the apparatus of the state and in the wider society. With subsidised publications, a presence in the arts and broadcasting, and significant symbolic recognition for Irish (in the nomenclature of state offices and services, public companies, ritual use on solemn state occasions, frequent, if inconsistent use by many prominent leaders in all walks of life) it would be wrong to say that no progress was made. By the 1950s, a substantial cohort of secondary bilinguals, of varying levels of competence, had emerged from the schools, and Irish had achieved a degree of penetration and a presence in public domains in Ireland from which it had been excluded for many centuries.

Yet this achievement fell very short of the radical cultural project of decolonisation proclaimed by the more advanced Gaelic Leaguers. The constitutional status of Irish was not translated into statutory legal rights for Irish-speakers; the ritual symbolic use was often minimalist and increasingly seen as tokenism; the degree of real penetration by Irish even within the state services and the apparatus of government was very limited; and, above all, the actual base-communities or enclaves of Irish-speakers – the *Gaeltacht* communities – continued to contract at an alarming rate, due to the ravages of emigration and the continuing shift to English within the diminished communities. There seemed to be no coherent state strategy for arresting this accelerating decline.

In seeking explanations for this, however qualified, 'failure' of the cultural project of the Gaelic League and its political offspring, the nature of the new Irish state demands attention. In terms of economic and social power structures, the Irish Free State was from its inception conservative of existing interests. The state was also deeply confessional, predictably, perhaps, given the overwhelmingly large (over 90 per cent) majority of observing Roman Catholics among its citizens. Its civic culture was deeply imbued with a Catholic ethos. Indeed, the sheer size of the Catholic majority (as a result of the partition of the island), and the historic experience of Irish Catholics since the sixteenth century, meant that a strong communal identity based on religious loyalty was, so to speak, ready-made and available to the Irish Free State at its foundation. This Catholic communal identity was easily shared and culturally comfortable even for elements of the nationalist political leadership who, at a cerebral level, had a more inclusive, religiously pluralistic and republican version of 'Irishness' than that suggested by simple 'Catholic nationalist' sentiment. In fact, a language dimension to Irish identity which demanded nothing too burdensome, nothing beyond a symbolic recognition of the ancestral language and a care to ensure its presence in the ceremony and ritual of occasions of state, was probably the ideal 'finishing' of identity for many Irish Catholics, utterly secure in the historical identity and the civic culture defined and shaped by their religion.

The growing assurance of the Irish Free State in the decades after 1922 as a stable democratic entity in a very turbulent world meant that the Irish state came to be taken for granted by its citizens, and Irishness (or 'identity') became, as it were, a function of citizenship of the independent Irish state – a comfort not available to the Irish nationalists living in Northern Ireland, for whom issues of identity (and with them language) remained inevitably more fraught.

It would be wrong to suggest that some at least of the cadre of political leaders in the new state did not wish and work for a more substantial cultural change, and specifically for more substantial progress in respect of the 'preservation and extension' of the Irish language. Their own understanding of the enormity and complexity of the task being undertaken may, in retrospect, be seen as seriously deficient. Irish had been in a perilous state by the late nineteenth century. Moreover, the geocultural location of Ireland in the twentieth century, right in the middle of the Anglo-American highway of communications and entertainment, increasingly the main artery of a global technology whose dominant language was English, made the challenge of achieving any viable form of bilingualism – to say nothing of a reverse language 'shift' – especially daunting.

The large majority of monoglot English-speakers in Ireland at the turn of the century, and the reassuringly high status achieved by the 'English of Ireland' in the forum of world literature (W. B. Yeats's Nobel Prize came in 1923, George Bernard Shaw's two years later, while James Joyce's *Ulysses* was first published in 1922), as well as its robustly creative energies in all aspects of popular culture, further weighted the advantages in favour of English being overwhelmingly the dominant vernacular and of its continuing to erode the fragile base of the Irish-speaking community. English was also the language of the vast majority of the Irish of the diaspora and of the countries in which most of them had settled. And, for the leaders of the Irish Catholic Church, English was a vital instrument in their dynamic global missionary effort from the middle of the nineteenth century forward.

Signs of impatience and frustration with the progress of the language 'revival' were unmistakable from the later 1930s. The sincerity and commitment of political leaders was vigorously questioned, as was the effectiveness of the particular strategies and methods employed in the implementation of state language policy. A crop of new voluntary language organisations was established from around 1940 forward – concerned with publishing, communications and evangelising in key sectors. Many saw these developments as signs of new life and energy among the Irish-language community.

But for committed revivalists there were ample grounds for anxiety. The core-communities of Irish-speakers in the *Gaeltacht* continued to decline. No new 'communities' of secondary bilinguals were being established; no medium-sized town or urban area became substantially Irish speaking in its everyday life. Teachers and educationalists, upon whom the main responsibility for 'achieving' the language restoration breakthrough in the schools depended, became weary of being relentlessly exhorted on the language issue, while being ignored on the broad agenda of education needs and career issues with which they were chiefly preoccupied. There was loss of support for the revival from sections of the intelligentsia, mainly writers, whose critique of the oppressive conservatism and confessional claustrophobia of the culture of the Irish state increasingly identified the state Irish language policy, especially the formulaic exhortations and heavy bureaucratic aspects of its implementation, as one more aspect of the sterility of the 'official' culture of the new state.

The most radical response to the evidence of failure in maintaining or sustaining the *Gaeltacht* community came from groups of political and social activists within the *Gaeltacht* community itself, supported by a cadre of urban intellectuals. The Irish writer and political activist, Máirtín Ó Cadhain, was prominent and influential in this movement. Ó Cadhain came to adopt a recognisably Marxist position (with strong Gramscian elements) on the language question and the depopulation, through emigration, of the *Gaeltacht*. The cultural hegemony of English was the outcome of socio-economic interests inherent in the power structure; the breaking of this cultural hegemony, therefore, would require a revolutionary socialist assault on these power structures and the interests they served. Or, as he put it: *Sí athréimniú na Gaeilge athghabháil na hÉireann* ('The restoration of Irish means the repossession of the country').

Less radical language revivalists sought, at different times and in different ways, to advise, cajole, persuade, bully and shame the government of the day into showing more urgency and giving a higher political priority (and resources) to the language task than successive governments seemed prepared to do. Revivalists with some more sophisticated and scholarly understanding of the socio-linguistic complexities of language change, and of the need for sustained and intelligent language planning at state level, suffered their own frustrations when regularly finding government ministers and bureaucrats indifferent to their advice.

Yet, it is remarkable how little fundamental rethinking of the basic assumptions of the language revival project took place within the revival movement in the early decades of the state. The basic ideology of the Gaelic League continued to be articulated in much the same terms as those of the founders. Indeed, as late as 1964, a group of eminent scholars and leaders of the language revival movement, in the Report of a special government commission established to review the 'progress' of the Irish revival project to date, stated the *raison d'être* of the revival in terms almost identical to the terms used by Douglas Hyde and Eoin MacNéill. But the government response to this Report struck a new note, with positive references to the contribution of both vernaculars to Ireland's cultural stock, and with a viable bilingual society as the declared objective of policy.

In fact, the late 1950s and early 1960s mark a significant shift in government policy and in the public debate on the language issue in independent Ireland. Voices critical of the language revival policy of the state began to grow in volume and to address even the basic assumptions (as distinct from the effectiveness and implementation of policy) of the language revival project. This public interrogation of the role of language in state ideology and policy was taking place, however, in the context of a profound crisis of confidence in the entire project of national independence and state-formation in Ireland.

The 1950s was a crisis decade in independent Ireland. Poor economic growth and massive unemployment and emigration, together with the unmistakable evidence that the political energies and agendas of the post-revolutionary generation seemed utterly exhausted, resulted in a rejection of the protectionist (cultural no less than economic) policies which had marked the de Valera era since the 1930s, and the posing of fundamental questions about the whole project of Irish independence. The old political guard was moving on and with it much of the old rhetoric. Economic protectionism, the nationalist route to self-sufficiency, was abandoned, and free trade for a competitive small open economy was announced as the road to salvation. That road was to lead to membership of the European 'Common Market' (later the European

Union). The language of cultural protectionism became an embarrassment; the future prospects for the Irish language would lie in a bilingual pluralist Ireland, in which the rich cultural and linguistic diversity of Europe would provide just the setting and the stimulus needed to enable the Irish to become confident of their identity in the larger European family, in contrast to the difficulties experienced within the more claustrophobic Anglo-American grid. Optimists saw this final renunciation of the deeply 'protectionist' nationalism of Eamon de Valera as a welcome opening of the shutters and a breath of fresh air. Others were not so sure; there were some critics who analysed the failures of the Free State in standard neocolonialist terms.

The fact that the state did not insist on Irish – the first language of the Constitution – being granted status as an official language of the European Union at the time of Ireland's accession to the 'Common Market' in 1972 was a significant sign of the changing complexion of Irish 'identity politics'.[4] Furthermore, the widening access of educational opportunity in Ireland from the 1970s was accompanied by new kinds of schools and structures, by the relaxation of the Irish language requirement for state examinations, and by a new rhetoric on the objectives of education policy which valorised economic development and moved the language question down the agenda.

Paradoxically, as the state's declared objective in language policy shifted from an essentialist, restoration position on Irish, towards a more viable bilingual society, the Irish language community began to undertake new initiatives and to exert political pressure on successive governments to provide better support and services and to vindicate the language rights of Irish speakers. A new crop of educated *Gaeltacht* activists, using the language and methods of civil rights agitation then sweeping the world in the late 1960s, began to demand full civil rights (social and economic as well as cultural) for the *Gaeltacht* communities. New networks of activists began to establish Irish-language schools (*gaelscoileanna*), chiefly in growing urban areas. This renewed agitation and organisation paid dividends: a *Gaeltacht*-based all-Irish radio station (1972) and later television channel (1995), and an elected *Gaeltacht* Regional Development Authority (*Údarás na Gaeltachta*) were established, and an expanding network of Irish-language schools developed in the 1980s and 1990s.

In Northern Ireland, the explosion of long-festering conflict in the late 1960s brought back to the centre of political debate in Ireland and Britain issues of ethnicity, dignity and rights, both individual and communal, which by then had seemed largely exhausted or 'resolved' in the Irish state. Language rights featured in the contestation of identity and political legitimacy at the heart of the Northern conflict. But the increasing recognition that Ulster's historic cultural corridors were east–west (particularly to Scotland) as well as north–south within the island of Ireland enriched the debate on identity, language and cultural traditions which matured, often in a climate of lethal contestation, as an aspect of the general discourse of 'accommodation' in Northern Ireland. 'Binary thinking' on language and identity was giving way to a more open exploration of hybridity. A version of cultural pluralism had begun to emerge by the mid-1980s, as the search for political accommodation centred on parity of esteem for different cultural traditions as a prerequisite for any lasting peace.

Translation represents a complex portal between languages and cultures. The historical circumstances of modern Ireland's language shift posed, and continue to pose, particular challenges in the area of translation, for creative writers, scholars and language ideologues. Issues of authenticity and 'appropriation' punctuated the discussion of the purpose and consequence of translations from Irish to English throughout the nineteenth century. Translation was a central, and contested, aspect of the W. B. Yeats and Lady Gregory-sponsored project of creating an authentic Irish literature in Hiberno-English. The Irish state from the 1930s supported translations into Irish, from English and, to a lesser extent, from other languages. The result, though of interest to later scholars, had little impact on the language situation among the population at large.

On the other hand, there was real demand for translations from Irish to English. In addition to translations of old mythological, epic and folkloric material (where there was an established 'tradition' and a proven market), translations of selections of Gaelic poetry were published, together with a number of the classic autobiographies of *Gaeltacht* writers. The reception of translations of such *Gaeltacht* works was frequently conditioned by historico-anthropological considerations, their elegiac tone announcing that they were the testament to a way of life and antique world-view that was on the eve of disappearing. This, it may be assumed, probably reinforced among English-speakers in Ireland (and elsewhere) a certain fatalism about the inevitability of the decline of the *Gaeltacht* and of Irish as the language of living communities. Translation from Irish to English may have drawn some readers to learn the original language, but it may also have provided many Irish readers with an accessible vantage point from which to witness the vanished or vanishing world of their own forebears.

From the 1970s, translation has engrossed an increasing number of younger writers in both vernaculars. A modest body of works from languages other than English has been translated into Irish. Translation from Irish to English (and indeed to other languages) is buoyant in contemporary Ireland, with a relaxed and healthy dialogue between writers in the two languages; creative writers who write primarily in English but who have some command of Irish regularly translate or collaborate with Irish-language writers in providing English versions of works originally composed in Irish. Irish-language writers, poets in particular, are increasingly recognised internationally, as sensitive audiences throughout the world attend more closely to the works of writers in lesser-used languages. But the multiple implications of translation from minority to world languages have particular point in the context of Ireland's historical language situation.

Conclusion

By the early twenty-first century the terms of the debate in Ireland on models of language, by definition models of community, are markedly different to those that detonated in the cultural revival a century earlier. Certainly, language remains an important vehicle for debates concerned with cultural identity in Ireland, but it can scarcely be said to be the basis upon which central acts of political contestation are conducted within the main vernacular languages and their communities of users. As a site of ideological debate, the language issue – its historical predicament and contemporary position – resonates strongly primarily with cultural commentators and activists engrossed in the discourse of colonialism and post-colonialism.

At the level of popular political mobilisation, within Northern Ireland the status and significance of the Irish language (and, in a more complex manner, of Ulster Scots) remains an issue of real political consequence. Indeed, the determination of the Northern cultural nationalists to insist on a revisiting of the issue of language and identity, as part of any political accommodation based on parity of esteem for different cultural traditions, has, perhaps, been critical to the debate on language and identity in late twentieth-century Ireland. In the intensity of the political struggle in Northern Ireland from the later 1960s, a revitalised Irish-language movement emerged, strongly urban-based and frequently embedded in the most assertive communities of republican political dissent. Schools, publications, leisure facilities, all working through the medium of Irish, demonstrated the creative energy of the activists. Given the intensity of the debate on identity in Northern Ireland in these decades, it is not altogether surprising, perhaps, that in the 1998 Belfast Agreement, the attempt to construct a lasting political accommodation between the parties to the conflict, all the parties committed themselves to 'understanding and toleration in relation to linguistic diversity, including in Northern Ireland, the Irish language, Ulster Scots and the languages of various ethnic communities'.

So far as the independent Irish state of the late twentieth century is concerned, powerful waves of global liberal capitalism under American auspices have eroded much of the cultural landscape. The cultural logic of this immersion has been increased cultural homogenisation dominated by American consumerist imperatives. Ireland's membership of a European Union, whose integration seems ever deepening, has also diminished the intensity of debate and contestation on the nature and constituents of Irish identity. For the political class in general, language as an issue in Irish cultural identity seems no longer a pressing concern (though the existence of a lively Irish-language media, albeit with a minority audience, is a factor which politicians cannot afford to ignore). The language issue has largely been accommodated within the broad political discourse of minority rights in an increasingly pluralist society.

But the purpose of state support for Irish, and the terms in which even its strongest advocates now make their case, generally identifies the challenge for Irish as that of ensuring its 'survival' as a living language among the core *Gaeltacht* and the wider dispersed communities of Irish-speakers, rather than attempting its restoration as the main vernacular of a 'national community'. The cultural representation of such a national community – 'the Irish' – is increasingly concerned with public symbols and symbolic events. The Irish language is likely to remain a valued symbol of the official culture of that national community. The linguistic rights of the Irish-speaking community in its public business with the state may in time be strengthened, and state support for various initiatives and programmes of language maintenance and transmission is likely to be responsive to demand and political pressure from the Irish-speakers themselves. Indeed, a new Official Languages Act of 2003 aims at strengthening the rights and entitlements of Irish-speakers in conducting business and in communicating with public bodies and state agencies.

Whether or not this kind of state support and these community-based resources will be sufficient to ensure the transmission of the Irish language into the future is a question which will be only be answered with time. The fragility of the language as a community language in the *Gaeltacht* and the relatively thin dispersal of Irish-speakers in the wider community will have to be borne in mind. What can be stated with some certainty, however, is the proposition that an understanding of the language issue remains essential to any serious consideration of the cultural and political history of modern Ireland.

Notes

1. Helen Ó Murchú and Máirtín Ó Murchú, *Irish: Facing the Future* (Dublin: Irish Committee of the European Bureau for Lesser Used Languages, 1999), p. 2.
2. The texts of Hyde's main exhortatory lectures have been collected in Douglas Hyde, *Language, Lore and Lyrics*, ed. Breandán Ó Conaire (Dublin: Irish Academic Press, 1986), especially pp. 145–99.
3. Seamus Heaney, *Beowulf: A New Translation* (London: Faber and Faber, 1999), p. xxiv.
4. In mid-2004 the Irish government announced that it intended re-opening the issue of securing 'official language' status for Irish within the EU, in the light of the expanded membership of the EU and the corresponding increase in new 'official languages'.

Further reading

Patrick J. Corish, *The Irish Catholic Experience: A Historical Survey* (Dublin: Gill and Macmillan, 1985)

Tony Crowley, *The Politics of Language in Ireland, 1366–1922: A Source Book* (London and New York: Routledge, 2000)

Seán de Fréine, *The Great Silence: The Study of a Relationship between Language and Nationality* (Dublin and Cork: Mercier Press, 1978)

Reg Hindley, *The Death of the Irish Language: A Qualified Obituary* (London and New York: Routledge, 1990)

Adrian Kelly, *Compulsory Irish: Language and Education in Ireland, 1870s–1970s* (Dublin: Irish Academic Press, 2002)

Joep Leerssen, *Mere Irish and Fíor-Ghael* (Cork: Cork University Press, 1996)
   Remembrance and Imagination (Cork: Cork University Press, 1996)

Eoghan Ó hAnluain (ed.), *Léachtaí Uí Chadhain* (Dublin: An Clóchomhar, 1989)

Brian Ó Cuív (ed.), *A View of the Irish Language* (Dublin: Stationery Office, 1969)

Risteárd Ó Glaisne, *De Bhunadh Protastúnach* (Dublin: Carbad, 2000)

Helen Ó Murchú and Máirtín Ó Murchú, *Irish: Facing the Future* (Dublin: Irish Committee of the European Bureau for Lesser Used Languages, 1999)

Seán Ó Tuama (ed.), *The Gaelic League Idea* (Dublin and Cork: Mercier Press, 1972)

4

Religion, identity, state and society

Religion and everyday life

Being Catholic or Protestant has been fundamental to what Irish people have done and said over the past two hundred years. It has been central to family life, education, health care and social welfare and has influenced the schools people attended, the friends they had and who they married. Religion has reached into areas such as the businesses, shops and pubs used by people; as well as the sports played and the newspapers and magazines read. In many ways, Catholics and Protestants in Ireland occupied two different, divided, social worlds. These worlds necessarily overlapped in business and everyday life, of course, but the doctrinal division between Catholicism and Protestantism remained central to commonly held conceptions of national and individual identity.

Religious identity in modern Ireland has been as socially significant as gender, class, ethnicity or sexual orientation. There is nothing uncommon about this. Throughout history and in the contemporary world, religious affiliation has been a major social divider. What made Ireland exceptional throughout the twentieth century was that while the rest of Western Europe became increasing secularised, religious affiliation remained a strong social marker for the Irish. In the terms adopted in this chapter, what mattered was not so much that Irish people were labelled as Catholic or Protestant, but that they were good Catholics and Protestants and could be identified within their communities as having accumulated spiritual capital.

To understand why religious affiliation has remained so important in Ireland, it is necessary to raise issues beyond the particular historical circumstances and current politics of Ireland. This chapter suggests that we must conceptualise churches, denominations, sects and cults and their adherents as operating in a field of power in which there is a struggle for position, survival and dominance. It describes how and why the Catholic and Protestant churches came to dominate the Irish religious field, and the strategies and tactics they used to attain such dominance. To understand how individual Catholics and Protestants struggled to attain and maintain their position within the field, it is important to notice the gendered nature of the religious field and the different tactics employed by women and men to attain religious power. Furthermore, we also have to be aware of how smaller religious organisations and groups – and their followers – provided opposition and resistance and survived and operated within the field. To understand the religious field and the strategies and tactics deployed to attain power, we have to understand the social origins of religion. Why are people religious? How does religion define social and personal identity? Religious identity and practice frames everyday life; in Ireland, it became central to the struggle for a range of different kinds of authority and power. Understanding how religion is tied in with this everyday struggle for power is crucial to any attempt to understand why it became such a strong social force in Irish society.

Religion is a universal human interest, in so far as people posit the existence of a supernatural world and strive to attain transcendence and salvation. It unites people into a community based on shared beliefs and values. Through engagement in collective rituals and practices, the community develops a shared way of reading, understanding and interpreting the world. People develop a similar sense of what is right and wrong, good and bad. Everything that unites and protects the community – the beliefs, practices and symbols – is sacred. Everything that threatens or undermines the sense of community is profane. When what is sacred to the community is threatened, it threatens and undermines the sense of self.

Symbols and rituals generate and maintain the collective consciousness of the community – the intuitive, taken-for-granted way in which members of the community live and interpret their lives.[1] For both Catholics and Protestants in Ireland, going to church on Sunday is not just about individual efforts to attain salvation but rather acts as a public display of community solidarity.

Public displays, however, can alienate as well as unite and, as with churches and schools, can be seen as a form of symbolic domination. In the twentieth century in the Republic, the signs of Catholic Ireland were seen to be everywhere – clerical dress, statues, grottos, public prayers, the Angelus, religious processions, and so forth. These reminded Protestants of their minority status. Orange marches, Union Jacks, bonfires, bunting, painting of street kerbs, and the symbols and language of everyday life have had a similar effect on Catholics in the North.[2]

Such an approach helps us to describe and analyse religion, but fails to yield a fuller sense of how being religious – that is, fulfilling spiritual and moral interests – buttresses and supports the fulfilment of economic, political, social and cultural interests. The way in which religious interests are fulfilled depends in the first instance on the ideas that exist about religion within a culture. Within the religious sphere or field there are generally a number of different, often competing, ideas about how to be spiritual and moral. These ideas are put forward by religious virtuosi such as prophets, preachers and priests, and are formed into religious teachings and practices within churches, sects and cults. In Ireland, the Catholic church came to dominate in the Republic, while in the North, Protestant churches held sway.

However, the way religious interests are fulfilled is not dependent on religious ideas alone. Issues of power are central. Religious behaviour must be analysed side by side with economic and political factors, in line with the approach adopted by Max Weber, whose analyses of Protestantism and the religions of Ancient Judea, China and India showed the connections between being religious and creating and maintaining economic and political power.[3] Following Weber, the religious life of a society can be understood analytically as taking place within a particular social sphere. In other words, when it comes to understanding why, for example, the Reformation did not develop in Ireland, why the Catholic church developed a monopoly position in the Republic, or why people in the North became and remained so resolutely Protestant, we have to understand how the fulfilment of religious interest was linked into social, cultural and symbolic interests. In Ireland, religious identity has been tied in with the fulfilment of a wide spectrum of other interests. The corollary of this argument is that when religion cannot contribute significantly to the realisation of other interests, then its importance, along with the dominant position of churches, declines. In effect, then, the current decline in the Catholic church's monopoly over the ways to be spiritual and moral is linked to the waning importance of proper religious behaviour in the achievement of social, political and economic power. This is what is at the heart of secularisation.

In his study of religion, Pierre Bourdieu[4] analysed social life in terms of various social fields in which institutions and individuals struggle to attain power, which he saw as different forms of capital.[5] In the religious field, churches, sects and cults are the main institutions. They, along with members of the laity, struggle to attain religious capital which can be exchanged for other forms of capital. In other words, being religious can influence success in business and work (economic capital), access to resources and power of command (political capital), the development and maintenance of alliances and social networks (social capital), and the attainment of awards, honour and respect, particularly in education (cultural capital and symbolic capital).

Bourdieu emphasised the importance of collective consciousness – what he referred to as *habitus* – in influencing practices within any particular field. Attaining capital in any field necessitates embodying the particular *habitus* of that field. The religious *habitus* is based upon an inherited disposition to being spiritual and moral which is embodied through socialisation. It is helpful to think of *habitus* as an intuitive way of being religious or (what feels like) a deeply natural way of reading and interpreting one's life and the world. And yet each individual enacts this *habitus* differently; in a flexible and transposable manner depending on the context, but also strategically, as means of attaining religious capital. In the religious field, churches develop a monopoly over the means of being spiritual and moral. In this way, while there is a religious *habitus* in general which applies to all players in the field including Christians, Jews and Muslims, there is, for example, a specific Catholic and Presbyterian *habitus* – that is, a Catholic and Presbyterian way of being religious.

The history of nineteenth- and twentieth-century Ireland can be seen as a struggle for economic, political and religious interests. People mobilised throughout the island to attain ownership of the means of production (mostly land), political power (mostly access to political office and control over the apparatus of government) and religious domination (mostly churches). These interests were tightly interconnected and witnessed the emergence and dominance of a Catholic bourgeois class in the Republic and a Protestant bourgeois class in the North, each enshrined within largely confessional states.

Mapping the religious field in the Republic

The majority population in the Republic of Ireland – over 90 per cent – is Roman Catholic. During the second half of the nineteenth century, the majority of Protestants belonged to the Church of Ireland. Between 1861 and 1911 they represented about 8 per cent of the yet-to-be-constituted Republic. A dramatic decline followed. By 1981, less than 3 per cent of the population was Church of Ireland. There have always been a number of other Protestant denominations in Ireland, mostly Presbyterians and Methodists, but the number of adherents has been less than 1 per cent. On the island as a whole, Presbyterians are mainly confined to southern Ulster. Members of the Church of Ireland came mostly from the middle and upper classes and, in Kurt Bowen's terms, fitted the picture of a small and privileged colonial minority.[6] The decline of the Protestant population was due in the first instance to migration, but subsequently to intermarriage with Catholics. Here, the Catholic church ruling that children in mixed marriages had to be brought up as Catholics was an important factor not just in terms of leaking of numbers, but in terms of symbolic domination. Although religious interests are closely allied with economic and political interests, there is little evidence of people changing their religious affiliation for material gain.

To understand how religion operates in social life, we need to examine how it serves as a means towards other ends within, rather than across, denominations. For most people, religion is not a matter of choice. They are, for example, born and remain Catholics or Protestants. Churches, in Weber's terms, are 'compulsory organisations', they have rationally established rules.[7] Membership and the embodiment of these rules during socialisation produce identity, and a sense of self. This is important, for although the fulfilment of religious interests is closely allied to the fulfilment of economic and political interests, people do not easily change their religious affiliation. Indeed much of Irish history revolves around the refusal of Catholics to become Protestant, or *vice versa*.

To understand being Protestant and Catholic in Ireland, it is necessary to go back to the Reformation. Why did the Irish not become Protestant like the majority of people did in Britain? We know that the refusal to join the Church of England – recusancy – began among the Anglo-Irish mercantile and gentry classes in the major cities. However, it is not clear what social, political and economic interests were at work. Moreover, we do not know why recusancy spread so rapidly among all classes throughout the country. R. F. Foster suggests, however, that remaining loyal to the Catholic Church had less to do with religious commitment and more to do with issues such as taxation, land and political allegiance. This may be so, but over the next 150 years, identity and loyalty became so well established that when the Penal Laws – which effectively sought to eliminate Catholics from civil society – were introduced, they seem to have had little effect, particularly among the Irish landowning classes who were devastated by the Laws.[8]

If not religious identity, then, what were the social, economic and political interests at work that made Catholics so loyal to their church? What were the forces at play later in the nineteenth century that enabled Catholics to resist the missionary efforts of Protestant evangelists – the offer of soup in time of famine and the promise of a decent education? As J. H. Murphy has shown, most of the efforts of the evangelists to convert Catholics failed miserably, despite some successes in Dingle, Kerry and Oughterard, Co. Galway.[9] Despite all the evangelical efforts, Protestantism remained the religion of the gentry who, as a small minority, dominated Catholics economically (through ownership and control of most of the land), politically (through their allegiance to the British state), socially (through their dominance of civil society) and culturally (through their higher levels of education). It was this domination – symbolically reinforced through better churches, houses, schools, hospitals and so forth – which reinforced a determination among Catholics to become more moral and spiritual. And it was the resentment against this material and symbolic domination, built up throughout the nineteenth century, which accounted for much of the violence directed against Protestants during the Anglo-Irish War of 1919–21 and the Civil War of 1922–23.[10]

The loyalty of the Irish people throughout the nineteenth century meant that the Roman Catholic church developed and maintained a dominant position in the Irish religious field. The attempts by the British state, the Anglican church and various Protestant institutions to limit and control the influence of the Catholic church in Ireland during the eighteenth and early nineteenth century had failed. Slowly but surely throughout the nineteenth century, the British state ceded dominance of education, health and social welfare to the Catholic church.[11] The Church of Ireland was formally disestablished in 1869. However, the Catholic church had become the 'established' church in Ireland long before then. This came about partly because of the interest the British state had in peaceful conditions and the creation of a mature, democratic, civil society in Ireland. The centralisation of the global power of the Catholic church in Rome, the extension of orthodox Roman rule throughout the church and the eagerness of Rome to establish its power in Ireland by acting as a broker between London and Dublin also contributed. The Irish hierarchy played a significant part in Irish politics in the late nineteenth century, and Catholic priests were major players in turning political activity away from violent rebellion towards participation in parliamentary democracy. The establishment of the Catholic church as a dominant institution in Ireland was in the interests of Rome as much as it was of Irish priests, nuns and brothers. The church operated in unison with the British state in the pacification and ordering of Irish society. Together they emerged as the two pillars that symbolically dominated Irish society and dictated how the political game should be played. The church cooperated with the state in the distribution and allocation of resources, goods and services. This gave it enormous political capital, which enabled it to continue to hold a dominant position in the political field in both the North and South of the island when the new states were established in 1922.

The dominant position of the Catholic church in the religious field was also powered from below. The close ties which Irish Catholics had with the church since the time of the Counter-Reformation became, during the nineteenth century, a loyal adherence. A distinctly Catholic identity spread, in particular, among the new middle class of 'strong' tenant farmers. Their ability to develop their farms (economic capital) was linked to the development of cultural, social and symbolic capital, all of which could be obtained within the religious field. The standard of living that could be derived from a small farm depended on it being inherited intact. This meant not giving out parcels of land to children when they married. Maintaining and developing economic capital became dependent on controlling marriage. This, in turn, relied on controlling sexual relations. The bodily discipline, emotional control and ethos of self-denial that came from adherence to Catholic church teaching became central to acheiving religious capital, which became the dominant form of embodied cultural capital.

There were resistances, particularly from within the artistic and literary fields, to the monopoly position that the Catholic church developed in social and cultural life. However, the reality was that the church was successful in confining such resistances to these fields and to the urban élite who operated within them.

An important feature of the religious field in Ireland is its gender structure. All of the world religions are patriarchal institutions. Yet in Catholic Ireland, as elsewhere, women have tended to have higher levels of religious belief and practice.[12] Attaining religious capital through being spiritual and moral became an important source of power for women, particularly mothers, who did not have access to other forms of capital. Religious capital enabled them to attain honour and respect – symbolic capital – which legitimated their position within the family and community. It was this dependency by women on religious capital which was central to the Catholic church dominating social fields such as education, health and social welfare. The Catholic church's dominance of these fields declined from the 1960s as more women gained access to other forms of capital and were less dependent on religious capital.[13]

The creation of a state which catered for the interests of Protestants in the North and a state which catered for the interests of the Catholics in the Republic had different impacts on the minorities involved. Protestants in the Republic were, in general, a privileged minority. They did not lose out economically or politically, but rather culturally. Their identity as a cultural minority was eroded primarily through migration and intermarriage. At the same time, there was a policy – pursued by Catholic zealots such as Archbishop McQuaid of Dublin – of ensuring that Protestants had no influence over the minds, bodies or souls of Irish Catholics.[14] Being Protestant in the Republic was tolerated on these conditions only.

But Protestants also withdrew into an enclave. Again, this had to do with fulfilling other interests, such as honour and respect in the community – symbolic capital – and maintaining existing networks of family, friends, colleagues and neighbours – social capital.

Church and state in the Irish Republic

The Free State was established in 1922, and the Catholic church was a major institutional player in the political field and in influencing state polices and action. As Patrick Murray has argued, clerical political power was an essential means to the end of ensuring that Irish society functioned in conformity with Catholic moral and social principles.[15] At the same time, the church played a crucial role in the creation and maintenance of an open polity and a voter-driven electoral democracy.[16] The 1937 Constitution did not officially establish the Catholic church, but it did extensively reflect Catholic moral and social principles and officially recognised the special position of the Catholic church in Irish society.

Thus, while the Republic of Ireland did not become a theocracy, the special position of the Catholic church ensured that it became the leading interest group in Irish civil society. Furthermore, because its power stemmed from the monopoly it held over moral and social principles and the consciences of politicians, it was unlike any other interest group. With the formation of the new state in the south of the island, the influence of the Catholic church began to extend into the more general field of power. In particular, the church was able to maintain the importance of cultural capital – especially religious capital – over economic capital. In other words, it was not only that the church held a dominant position in the fields of health, education, social welfare, the media, politics and so forth, but also that it had the power to influence and emphasise the importance of religious capital within these fields. Position and advancement were often dependent on embodying a rhetoric and *habitus* of self-denial. People operating in these fields had to eschew any overt material interest in political and economic capital and claim vocational commitment instead. In this way, the church was able to increase not just the transfer value of religious capital in relation to other forms of capital, but the forms that this transfer took. A spirit of humility, piety and self-denial became important for political and economic success, and key to the development and maintenance of social networks, including access to education.

An understanding of how important the embodiment of a Catholic *habitus*, particularly an orientation towards self-denial, was in Irish social and organisational life, is crucial to understanding the relation between religion and society in general, and church and state in particular. This requires careful explanation. It is not simply that bishops held the threat of eternal damnation over those who did not acquiesce in their commands. There is no simple answer as to how the church influenced the state in modern Irish society or way of estimating the level of its influence.[17] Because the church held a monopoly over morality, it had authority over the moral conscience not just of politicians but of many of those who worked in various areas of institutional life. Throughout what we may think of as the long nineteenth century of Irish Catholicism (the period up to at least the 1960s during which the church dominated social and cultural life in the Republic) many Catholics adhered legalistically to the rules and regulations of the church.[18] Priests, politicians, civil servants, and those who dominated the various fields of Irish social life, grew up in a small, homogeneous society, were moulded by the same culture, educated at the same schools, and were often related to each other. These are the factors that made the Catholic church unlike any other interest group in Irish society.[19] In other words, even if we accept Liam Ryan's claim that the Catholic church in Ireland saw itself – formally since the 1970s but in reality since the foundation of the state – as the moral conscience of Irish society, what remains to be answered is how this conscience was declared, implemented and enforced in institutions, civil society and everyday life.[20]

To understand the influence of the Catholic church over the Southern state in twentieth-century Ireland, it is necessary to go beyond formal interactions on issues of social legislation and commence analysis at the level of everyday life and the struggle for power and position. The influence of the church in Irish society was based on Irish people seeing themselves first and foremost as Catholics. Loyalty and adherence to the Catholic church ranked with, and often surpassed, loyalty to the state, political party, interest group, family or friends. In a national survey in 1973–74, over 60 per cent of Irish Catholics said their religious principles influenced how they behaved with their family and in work and what they did in their leisure time. Over seven in ten respondents said that, in the event of a clash, they would choose their religion over their occupation and spare-time activities, and over half said they would choose it over their family.[21] Secondly, identification with and loyalty to the Catholic church helped create an orthodox Catholic disposition, an automatic, unquestioned way of thinking and being which was ingrained in the body as much as in the mind. Catholicism amounted to a set of values, attitudes, beliefs and practices, ways of communicating and relating, into which each new generation was socialised in homes and schools, and which became the accepted, unquestioned orthodoxy of everyday life. Thirdly, the embodiment of this Catholic *habitus* became central to the operation of civil society, institutions (particularly in those institutions in which the church had formal power), interest groups, and debate and discussion in the public sphere. Fourthly, at a personal level, the embodiment of this Catholic *habitus* became a central element of cultural capital, central to survival and achievement within the educational system, to obtaining employment, to gaining and attaining customers, to developing and maintaining contacts and alliances, to attaining the honour and respect of people, to being promoted, chosen or elected as a leader.

In this way, religious identity fused not just with the fulfilment of religious interests, but with economic, political, social and cultural interests. This is what made Ireland an example not so much of a theocratic state, but rather of a theocratic society. What makes a society religious rather than secular, and what made Irish society Catholic, was not only the extent to which the church was able to exercise control over the state in particular social fields, and the way the church shaped the vision, goals and policies of the state, but the way a Catholic *habitus* pervaded all aspects of social life. A society does not become secular until being religious becomes a thoroughly private matter, has little or no impact in everyday life in the ordinary process of greeting, speaking, relating to others, no longer symbolically dominates public life, begins to disappear from the arts, literature and media, and no longer constitutes a central element of how people see and understand themselves. The longer being religious remains central to identity, to communication and everyday life, and to attaining power, the more churches and religious organisations will dominate civil society and exert control over the state. This, in effect, is what makes Northern Ireland at present a more religious society that the Republic.

Northern Ireland

Following the success of the Plantation of Ulster at the beginning of the seventeenth century and, later, the Cromwellian plantation, the attempts to anglicise the Northern population had been much more successful than in the Republic. But, again, religious and class interests are connected. Marianne Elliot notes that in the seventeenth century, 'the social pressures to conform to the religion of one's class eventually eroded the few remaining Catholic gentry in Ulster. But lower down the scale, traffic was often in the opposite direction.'[22] Indeed, she argues that during the seventeenth century religious identity was quite fluid. But by the end of the century, religious identity hardened, largely because most of the Irish tenant farmers ended up paying rent not to landlords, but to substantial Protestant tenant farmers.[23] Religious loyalty and identity had been sharpened and intensified by class divisions.

Presbyterian settlers, like their Catholic counterparts, were dominated religiously and politically by Anglicans for most of the eighteenth and nineteenth centuries. Such was the level of domination in Ulster that an estimated quarter of a million Presbyterians emigrated to North America during the seventeenth century. During the eighteenth century the Presbyterians espoused radical views on equality and religious freedom, and were a major force of resistance and opposition to the Anglican ascendancy and British state. The strength of resistance meant that many Presbyterians were able to suspend their antipathy to Rome and (through the United Irishmen) join forces with Catholics to rebel against the ascendancy and state in 1798. However, the tide was already turning, and by the middle of the nineteenth century there was a growing political alliance across classes between Ulster Protestants against Catholics which led eventually to a strengthened Orange Order and organised Unionism.[24]

Given that Protestants were generally better off, the level of conversion among Catholics was remarkably low. Again, this gives an indication of the importance of religious identity. But religious identity was maintained and developed not just by different practices and beliefs, but by constituting the other as morally inferior. Stories were told and myths and images generated which demeaned and denigrated the other group, making it out to be socially inferior. This reinforced solidarity and identity. Elliot notes that 'Catholicism was believed to induce sloth and slavishness of mind in its adherents, making them incapable of liberty, virtue and entry to polite society.' Catholics, on the other hand, 'believed in the antiquity, superiority and greater spirituality of their religion and traditions'. Religious identity in Northern Ireland came to be based not so much on people belonging to different 'imagined' communities, but to cast-iron communities that had very real consequences for the social relations of everyday life. Elliot argues that there is plenty of evidence that Catholics who became Protestants back in the seventeenth century are still remembered today and despised as 'turncoats'.[25]

Although there was a growing political unity and alliance among Protestants during the nineteenth and twentieth centuries, there was much greater competition in the religious field. The Catholic church was the largest church, but the combined strength of the Presbyterians, Church of Ireland (and all Anglicans), Methodists and other Protestant sects and denominations ensured that the Protestant churches collectively outnumbered the Catholic church. The primacy of individual faith meant that Protestants were much more open to evangelical preaching, to the significance of personal religious experience and to conversion.

In this environment, Protestant evangelicalism became a substitute for nationalism.[26] Fervent anti-Catholic theology fulfilled religious interests but, at the same time, helped fulfil the more material interests of opposing the political threat of Catholic nationalism. Despite splits and the emergence of new religious sects, particularly within Presbyterianism, the affinity between religious and political solidarity continued to reach across class boundaries. Protestants in Northern Ireland may have been religiously divided, but they have tended to be politically united. Protestant and loyalist symbols, particularly marches, were used to define an anti-Catholic position and to unite Protestants into a single moral community. As John Brewer and Gareth Higgins note, 'anti-Catholicism survives in Northern Ireland when it has declined elsewhere, notably in Britain and the Irish Republic . . . because it helps to define group boundaries and plays a major sociological role in producing and rationalising political and economic inequality'.[27]

The connection between the religious and political fields is quite different in the North. There is no monolithic institution such as the Catholic church that dominates the religious field. Pressure on the state does not come so much from the Presbyterian church or Church of Ireland, but from fundamentalist religious groups such as Ian Paisley's Free Presbyterians, religious political societies such as the Orange Order and Apprentice Boys, and Protestant paramilitary groups. The Orange Order operates as an umbrella group; the Orange Hall is a symbol of Protestant unity and serves as the place where denominational differences are put aside for the cause of Ulster Protestant loyalism. However, as in the Republic, the influence of religion in the political sphere is not so much from direct pressure which loyalists and Orangemen exerted over the state – for example in the Ulster Workers' strike of 1974 which brought down the power-sharing executive – as from the creation and maintenance of a Protestant society. This society was founded on a Protestant *habitus*, a Protestant disposition and way of reading the world which united Protestants into a single community. As in the Republic, this *habitus* became a central part of religious capital which, in turn, became essential to attaining other forms of capital. In other words, being a good Protestant in the North remained central within Protestant society to economic, political and social success as well as to identity, communication and interpersonal relations in everyday life.

Catholics were excluded from the dominant culture and suffered economic and political discrimination. Evidence of continued inequality is still clear in the fields of income, housing, wealth and employment, most notably in the Protestant-loyalist alliance's embargo on the minority ever holding political office.[28] In Northern Ireland, the Catholic church and community became what Eamonn Phoenix describes as a state within a state, with its own social infrastructure of schools, hospitals, sporting activities, newspapers and businesses. This is structurally similar to what happened to Protestants in the Republic, who had their own schools, hospitals, welfare organisations, community and sporting activities, firms and businesses.[29]

What remains remarkable, however, is that while there is such a divergence in religious identity in the North, both groups have a similar lifestyle and share similar values. As John Fulton points out, results of research suggest that there are certain common features 'in ethical attitudes: puritanical attitudes in sexual matters, conservatism, friendliness, "down-to earthness", sense of duty to neighbours, critical attitudes toward officialdom, and similar judgements to what constitutes good and bad conduct'.[30] More importantly, survey results indicate that when it comes to the nature of their world-view and religious faith, particularly the extent to which people are pessimistic, oriented towards the supernatural, and have a Calvinistic approach to faith, there is little difference between Northern Catholics and Protestants.[31]

This indicates the extent to which religious identity in the North remains the cognitive map that serves to partition two groups who are quite similar in basic values and lifestyle. No matter how similar people are in their values and lifestyles, they see and treat each other as different. The *habitus* of Catholics and Protestants in Northern Ireland, particularly the way of the reading, understanding and interpreting people as being Catholic or Protestant, will not change until religious capital is no longer linked to the achievement of other forms of capital. In Northern Ireland, it is not so much a question of whether structural or cultural factors are the main cause of the conflict, or whether religion really matters; what is important is the way religious identity, culture and heritage are interwoven into the fulfilment of other interests.

Challenges to religious identity

The decline in the importance of religious capital in the Republic can be linked to the demise of Ireland's status as a chiefly rural society dominated by farming and agriculture. With the shift towards an economy based on manufacturing and services, the practice of each generation of married couples having large families declined. This considerably reduced the need for permanent celibacy, late marriage and emigration. As the mode of production changed, so society became more urbanised. The state embraced a new vision of Irish society and the media (particularly television) began to penetrate into Irish homes, hearts and minds. The uniform dominance of the almost universal Catholic *habitus* began to fragment. Throughout the last half of the twentieth century the Catholic sense of self, and the Catholic presentation of self in everyday life – based on a *habitus*, practice and rhetoric of self-denial – began to dissipate, and to be replaced by a new sense of self based on self-realisation and fulfilment. The rigorous system of policing bodies and the very expression of self, particularly in relation to sex, which was once central to large families living off small farms, began to be replaced by a system in which consumption and indulgence were central. In this new system, sex, sexual feelings and emotions were no longer hidden and denied; they were revealed, analysed and explored. These changes are reflected most in the demise of the image of the shy, pious, humble, pure, chaste and modest Irish colleen and her replacement in cultural representation by an urbane, confident, assertive and sexually adventurous young woman.[32]

From the 1970s there was a steady decline in the legal-orthodox adherence to the Catholic church. By the end of the twentieth century there were less than 100 vocations to all forms of the religious life (priests, nuns and brothers) – compared to almost 1,400 in 1966. The proportion of Catholics attending Sunday Mass declined from 91 per cent in 1974 to just over 60 per cent in the late 1990s. There was, at the same time, a sharp decline in adherence to the church's teachings on sexual morality. However, the decline of the institutional church has not lead to an automatic decline in Catholic culture. The Catholic *habitus* is still embodied in the understanding and presentation of self. This reflex way of reading the world lingers long after supporting institutional structures and discourses have fallen away. The legacy of the Catholic *habitus* is such that it still informs and guides people as to what is right and wrong, good and bad, even though they may not adhere to many of the teachings of the church, particularly in relation to sexual morality. Being Catholic, identifying oneself as Catholic, thinking and acting in a Catholic moral manner and engaging in Catholic rituals is still a central part of people's cultural heritage and sense of self. This will remain the case until people devise alternative ways of celebrating transitional events such as birth, marriage and death. In the interim, there will be ongoing struggles over ownership and control of these ceremonies, with the church struggling to maintain traditional formats and liturgies.

In the North, the forces of the market, consumerism and sexualisation are as dominant as in the Republic. Religious *habitus* also operates in and through class. Yet whereas being loyalist remains closely tied to being Protestant; being nationalist is no longer as closely tied to being Catholic, especially a rigorous unquestioned adherence to the rules and regulations of the church.[33] Moreover, as Desmond Bell argues, although the Protestant people of Ulster may see themselves as being loyal to Protestantism and the British crown, they are not loyal adherents to the teachings and practices of their churches, and they often find themselves isolated and at odds with the British state and British public opinion.[34] In effect, the identity of Ulster Protestants is based on a negative sense of what it means to be Catholic and Irish. As the peace process develops, the question is to what extent religious identity will diminish, and how far as a result the social and emotional gap between Protestants and Catholics will diminish, in the same way as have the gaps between the classes and genders elsewhere in Western society.

Conclusion

Being religious – that is, identifying with and belonging to a church, accepting its beliefs and engaging in its practices – has been, and still remains, a major feature of modern Irish social life. Nonetheless, the penetration of capitalist social relations into every aspect of everyday life, the growth of the state and the influence of the mass media have meant that the accumulation of religious capital has, in the last fifty years, become far less significant in fulfilling other interests and attaining other forms of capital. Religious identity and heritage remain strong, but in a secularised society religion becomes more private in expression and restricted in its influence. In Northern Ireland, on the other hand, religious identity remains significant in social relations and in the attainment of capital in other fields.

The significance of religious identity and being religious can be analysed by the extent to which it limits and controls what people do and say. In contemporary Irish society to what extent is being Catholic or Protestant more or less significant than class, locality (parish, county, city), political party, nationality, gender, sexual orientation, group and club membership or lifestyle? And to what extent does it influence what happens in social relations in these areas? Religious identity and church affiliation are badges; the question is to what extent they are worn openly and displayed publicly in everyday social life, and to what extent they are being replaced by other markers of identity. Answers to these questions are difficult, yet it is clearly the case that fewer people interpret their lives through the institutional discourse of churches and understand themselves – or others – as Catholic or Protestant.

Notes

1. Émile Durkheim, *The Elementary Forms of the Religious Life* (London: George Allen and Unwin, 1976).
2. John Hickey, *Religion and the Northern Ireland Problem* (Dublin: Gill and Macmillan, 1984), pp. 57–84; Desmond Bell, *Acts of Union: Youth Culture and Sectarianism in Northern Ireland* (London: Macmillan, 1990), pp. 13–21; Joseph Ruane and Jennifer Todd, *The Dynamics of Conflict in Northern Ireland* (Cambridge: Cambridge University Press, 1996), pp. 179–86; John Brewer with Gareth Higgins, *Anti-Catholicism in Northern Ireland, 1600-1998: The Mote and the Beam* (London: Macmillan, 1998), pp. 181–207.
3. Max Weber, *Economy and Society*, ed. Gunther Roth and Claus Wittich (Berkeley: University of California Press, 1978), pp. 399–634.
4. Pierre Bourdieu, 'Legitimation and structured interests in Weber's Sociology of Religion', in *Max Weber, Rationality and Modernity*, ed. Sam Whimster and Scott Lash (London: Allen and Unwin, 1987), pp. 119–36; Pierre Bourdieu, 'Genesis and structure of the religious field', *Comparative Social Research* 13 (1991), 1–43.
5. Pierre Bourdieu, 'Forms of capital' in *Handbook of Theory and Research for the Sociology of Education*, ed. John Richardson (Westport, CT: Greenwood Press, 1986), pp. 241–58.
6. Kurt Bowen, *Protestants in a Catholic State: Ireland's Privileged Minority* (Dublin: Gill and Macmillan, 1983), p. 10. It is important to recognise that although the number of Jews in the Republic never rose beyond 4,000 and has declined rapidly since the 1950s, they were very prominent in civil society. For example, between 1991 and 1997, three Jews were elected to the Dáil. See Dermot Keogh, *Jews in Twentieth Century Ireland* (Cork: Cork University Press, 1998), pp. 224, 238. Similarly, among Protestants, although the numbers of Quakers in the Republic have been small, they also were prominent in civil society. See Maurice Wigham, *The Irish Quakers* (Dublin: Historical Committee of the Religious Society of Friends in Ireland, 1992).
7. Weber, *Economy and Society*, p. 52.
8. Roy Foster, *Modern Ireland 1600–1972* (Harmondsworth: Penguin, 1988), pp. 41, 205.
9. J. H. Murphy, 'The role of the Vincentian Parish Missions in the "Irish Counter-Reformation" of the mid-nineteenth century', *Irish Historical Studies* 24, 94 (1984), 152–71.
10. See Bowen, *Protestants in a Catholic State*, pp. 22-3.
11. Tom Inglis, *Moral Monopoly: The Rise and Fall of the Catholic Church in Modern Ireland* (Dublin: University College Dublin Press, 1998).

12. See Máire Nic Ghiolla Phadraig 'Religion in Ireland: preliminary analysis', *Social Studies* 5, 2 (1976), 113–80 (135).

13. See Inglis, *Moral Monopoly*, pp. 178–200.

14. John Cooney, *John Charles McQuaid: Ruler of Catholic Ireland* (Dublin: The O'Brien Press, 1999), p. 324.

15. Patrick Murray, *Oracles of God: The Roman Catholic Church and Irish Politics 1922–37* (Dublin: University College Dublin Press, 2000), p. 419.

16. Tom Garvin, *1922: The Birth of Irish Democracy* (Dublin: Gill and Macmillan, 1996), p. 23.

17. John Whyte, *Church and State in Modern Ireland 1923–79* (Dublin: Gill and Macmillan, 1980), pp. 249, 376.

18. Inglis, *Moral Monopoly*, pp. 30–6.

19. Whyte, *Church and State*, pp. 366–70

20. Liam Ryan, 'Church and politics: the last twenty-five years', *The Furrow* 30, 1 (1979), 3–18.

21. See Nic Ghiolla Phadraig 'Religion in Ireland', pp. 126–7.

22. Marianne Elliot, *The Catholics of Ulster: A History* (Harmondsworth: Penguin, 2000), p. 126.

23. W. H. Crawford, 'The Ulster Irish in the eighteenth century', *Ulster Folklife* 18 (1982), 24–32 (28).

24. See David Miller, *Queen's Rebels: Ulster Loyalism in Historical Perspective* (Dublin: Gill and Macmillan, 1978), p. 72; Peter Gibbon, *The Origins of Ulster Unionism* (Manchester: Manchester University Press, 1975), pp. 34–5; John Fulton, *The Tragedy of Belief: Division, Politics and Religion in Ireland* (Oxford: Clarendon Press 1991), pp. 56–7; Brewer and Higgins, *Anti-Catholicism in Northern Ireland*, p. 48.

25. Elliot, *The Catholics of Ulster*, pp. 171, 183, 159.

26. Fulton, *The Tragedy of Belief*, pp. 14, 61.

27. See Brewer and Higgins, *Anti-Catholicism in Northern Ireland*, p. 211. Barkley argues that the sectarian conflict in Ireland has always been political more than religious. He argues that there is evidence of a conflict between the English and Irish even among religious friars as far back as the twelfth and thirteenth centuries and claims that religion was not the origin of this political sectarianism, 'but from 1534 it added fuel to the flames'. See John Barkley, 'Being Protestant', in *Being Protestant in Ireland*, ed. James McLoone (Dublin: Co-operation North, 1985), pp. 3–19 (9). However, there are many who would argue that there was no island-wide sense of Irishness prior to the Reformation. See J. C. Beckett, *The Making of Modern Ireland 1603–1923* (London: Faber and Faber, 1969); D. G. Boyce, *Nationalism in Ireland* (Dublin: Gill and Macmillan, 1982) pp. 15–93; Margaret McCurtain, *Tudor and Stuart Ireland* (Dublin: Gill and Macmillan, 1972).

28. Joseph Ruane and Jennifer Todd, '"Why can't you get along with each other?": Culture, structure and the Northern Ireland conflict', in *Culture and Politics in Northern Ireland*, ed. Eamonn Hughes (Milton Keynes: Open University Press, 1996), pp. 27–43; Fulton, *The Tragedy of Belief*, p. 96.

29. See Eamonn Phoenix, 'Northern Ireland: from the birth-pangs to disintegration', in *Ulster: An Illustrated History*, ed. Ciaran Brady, Mary O'Dowd and Brian Walker (Belfast: B. T. Batsford, 1989), pp. 192–202 (196). See also Bowen, *Protestants in a Catholic State*, pp. 166–94.

30. Fulton, *Tragedy of Belief*, p. 99.

31. Andrew Greeley, 'Religions of Ireland', in *Ireland North and South: Perspectives from Social Science*, ed. Anthony Heath, Richard Breen and C. T. Whelan (Oxford: Oxford University Press, 1999), pp. 141–60 (147–9).

32. Tom Inglis, *Lessons in Irish Sexuality* (Dublin: University College Dublin Press, 1998); Tom Inglis, 'From sexual repression to liberation?', in *Encounters with Modern Ireland*, ed. Michel Peillon and Eamonn Slater (Dublin: Institute of Public Administration, 1998), pp. 99–104.

33. Steve Bruce, *God Save Ulster: The Religion and Politics of Paisleyism* (Oxford: Clarendon Press, 1986), p. 258.

34. Desmond Bell, *Acts of Union: Youth Culture and Sectarianism in Northern Ireland* (London: Macmillan, 1990), pp. 13–23.

Further reading

Desmond Bell, *Acts of Union: Youth Culture and Sectarianism in Northern Ireland* (London: Macmillan, 1990)

Kurt Bowen, *Protestants in a Catholic State: Ireland's Privileged Minority* (Dublin: Gill and Macmillan, 1983)

John Brewer, with Gareth Higgins, *Anti-Catholicism in Northern Ireland, 1600–1998: The Mote and the Beam* (London: Macmillan, 1998)

Steve Bruce, *God Save Ulster: The Religion and Politics of Paisleyism* (Oxford: Clarendon Press, 1986)

John Cooney, *John Charles McQuaid: Ruler of Catholic Ireland* (Dublin: The O'Brien Press, 1999)

Colin Coulter, *Contemporary Northern Irish Society* (London: Pluto Press, 1999)

Marianne Elliot, *The Catholics of Ulster: A History* (Harmondsworth: Penguin, 2000)

John Fulton, *The Tragedy of Belief: Division, Politics and Religion in Ireland* (Oxford: Clarendon Press, 1991)

John Hickey, *Religion and the Northern Ireland Problem* (Dublin: Gill and Macmillan, 1984)

Tom Inglis, *Moral Monopoly: The Rise and Fall of the Catholic Church in Modern Ireland* (Dublin: University College Dublin Press, 1998)

Desmond Keenan, *The Catholic Church in Nineteenth Century Ireland: A Sociological Study* (Dublin: Gill and Macmillan, 1983).

Dermot Keogh, *The Vatican, the Bishops and Irish Politics, 1919–39* (Cambridge: Cambridge University Press, 1986)
    Ireland and the Vatican: The Politics and Diplomacy of Church–State Relations, 1922–1960 (Cork: Cork University Press, 1995)

Emmet Larkin, *The Roman Catholic Church and the Emergence of the Modern Irish Political System, 1874–1878* (Dublin: Four Courts Press, 1996)

Patrick Murray, *Oracles of God: The Roman Catholic Church and Irish Politics 1922–37* (Dublin: University College Dublin Press, 2000)

John Whyte, *Church and State in Modern Ireland, 1923–79* (Dublin: Gill and Macmillan, 1971, 1980)

5

Republicanism, nationalism and unionism: changing contexts, cultures and ideologies

Introduction: change and continuity

For over two centuries, republicanism and unionism/loyalism have marked polarities in Irish politics – the former committed to a 'sovereign' all-Ireland republic, the latter to the maintenance and consolidation of Ireland (and Northern Ireland since 1920) as part of the United Kingdom. Much has changed, however, in the period between the United Irish Rebellion of 1798 and the Belfast Agreement of 1998. In the first instance, the social composition of the constituencies supporting both ideologies have altered substantially over time, influenced by Ireland's complex integration into the global capitalist economy, by famine and war, and the outcome of political struggle. In the interim, too, the substantive issues at the heart of unionist–republican conflict such as the 'Union', the 'Republic', self-determination, government, democracy, the state, Irishness, Britishness and 'Ulster' have changed their scope and meaning. Irish unionism and republicanism also register the successive imprints of their changing international contexts – the republican revolutions in the US and France; the subsequent 'age of imperialism'; and imperial fragmentation and the growing significance of the national state in its aftermath.

Against this vast panorama of change, the first part of this chapter examines some of the reasons for the endurance of unionism and republicanism. It suggests that the roots of their survival are to be found in a resilient, if highly asymmetric power structure, the legacy of colonial and imperial Ireland and the working out of the Partition settlement. Within this power structure, nationalists and republicans have developed characteristic, if asymmetric, views of the relationship between state and nation, modes of remembrance and styles of political mobilisation. The second part of the chapter sketches how Partition reconstituted unionism and republicanism and discusses how the 'politics of culture' has come to be central in the Northern Ireland conflict and in the search for a solution.

Power triangles

Since the seventeenth century, the British state has been at the apex of an enduring power triangle in Irish politics and the major source of power on the Irish political landscape. Through the agency of a succession of British governments, it has variously sought to annex, colonise, incorporate, control and eventually partially withdraw from the island of Ireland. The other two elements of the power triangle are the complex of organisations and movements emerging from 'Protestant' and 'Catholic' Ireland respectively – constituencies partly created by the various policies of the British state. Indeed, the latter has played a central role in constructing the modern idea of Ireland as a single political, administrative and cultural unit, while simultaneously reproducing within it profound antagonisms. At their most intense and intractable these antagonisms have fused irreconcilable religious divisions with those between settler and native, coloniser and colonised, and dominant and subordinate classes.

Unionism in its most abstract form has been the ideology of the British state and empire-building in Ireland. In its various organisational manifestations it has worked to identify and maintain a coincidence of interests between Ireland's Protestant minority and those of the British state generally. Its *raison d'être* has been the support of the British state, if not always of particular British governments. Republicanism in the Irish context has been a largely oppositional ideology committed, in principle, to a secular all-Ireland state capable of overcoming the divisions institutionalised by British rule. Commitments to the 'Union/Empire' or to the 'Republic' are not in themselves stand-alone political philosophies. Their adherents have simultaneously seen themselves, for example, as liberals, socialists, trade unionists and feminists. More pervasively, however, they have been influenced by sectarian division. The unionist–republican divide overlaps, but has never fully equated with, the religious and cultural divide between Protestant and Catholic Ireland.

While the constituents comprising the triangular power structure have changed over time, its basic form has proved resilient. Under the Union, it involved the British executive in Dublin Castle, the Conservative-Unionist Party and the Irish constitutional nationalists in an uneasy relationship with republicans and sometimes allied with the Whigs. Partition created a new triangular structure whereby the British state and successive governments dealt with Northern Ireland via the Ulster Unionist Party (UUP) and the Irish state via nationalists or constitutional republicans. After 1970, yet another new triangular relationship became central – linking the British state and executive to the 'two communities' in Northern Ireland. The fate of the Belfast Agreement which has sought to move tentatively beyond this format, by involving the Irish government in the search for a solution, still hangs in the balance.

State and nation

In the struggle over state and nation formation, both republicans and unionists have focused primary attention on the state: its boundaries, constitution and institutional forms. In this they both differ from mainstream Irish nationalists who prioritise an Irish 'nation' which has long predated an Irish state. The central historical myth of Irish nationalists has been that of a pre-existing and long-oppressed nation in search of a state in which its cultural identity would be institutionalised. For loyalists and unionists, the state precedes the 'nation' – indeed, they perceive the English/British state as having historically constituted and supported their 'community' and 'birthright' – if not their 'nation'. The priority for republicans has been to establish a state which would then shape a unified Irish 'nation' on the basis of equality of citizenship that would transcend the inherited colonial and religious divisions. The initial republican attempt to build a sovereign Irish state which would forge an inclusive, unified nation was to fail but was to survive as an unrealised ideal and a focus for political dissent for the following two centuries.

Republicans and unionists also differ from constitutional nationalists in that the latter have been historically more flexible about the institutional forms that might be taken by the state. The nature and extent of Irish political autonomy has been seen as negotiable by mainstream nationalists from the Repeal movement, through to Home Rule and Sinn Féin in the early twentieth century, and on to the recent negotiations over the Belfast Agreement. Demands for national autonomy did not necessarily exclude formalised links with the UK or the British empire – this was consistent with a view of a diasporic nation not confined to the island territory. Even today, constitutional nationalists in Northern Ireland see a reformed 'Union' as a vehicle for advancing their political goals.

Republicans, on the other hand, reject monarchy and empire, prioritising the ideal of the citizen-people within the territorial boundaries of the island. In practice, of course, they use the 'transnational nation' of the Irish diaspora as a political and ideological resource. In the course of the nineteenth and twentieth centuries, republicans have taken on much of the baggage of romantic nationalism and have become more closely identified, by default if not always by conscious design, with the cultural and political organisations of Catholic Ireland.

Unionists' articulation of the link between state and nation has a dimension not shared by republicans or nationalists. The central historical myth of mainstream unionism is not that of a 'sovereign people' – but that of the continuity and unique intrinsic merits of the unwritten British constitution – the Protestant crown in Parliament.[1] For unionists, this 'constitution' has been defended historically in the state's successive wars against the Catholic powers of Europe and Catholic interests in Ireland.

To the extent that they identify themselves as carriers of an 'improving' or 'civilising' mission in Ireland, unionists are able to posit a durable link between antique merits of the 'British constitution' on the one hand, and modernity and universalism on the other. Unionists, therefore, identify themselves with Britain as the site of the first industrial revolution, the heartland of a huge world-wide empire, its global 'civilising mission' via military and territorial expansionism, colonisation, and its diffusion of advanced forms of religion (Protestantism), science and technology, language and culture, and administrative and political institutions to much of the world.[2] This identification was to persist not only through the high noon of the imperialised monarchy (1850–1950),[3] but also through the long twilight of imperial decline during which Britain lost its status as the dominant world power. It survives today in the manner in which some Ulster unionists celebrate the British state as a multicultural, modernising, progressive entity, typically contrasting it with parochial, violent and ethnic nationalisms, including that represented by what they see as the monocultural, backward-looking Irish state.[4]

Modes of remembrance

Both republicans and unionists have developed compelling and popular story-lines that reflect not just Irish conflicts but many of those which have shaped the modern world. The story of Irish republicanism is part of the historical republican revolt against monarchy and empire informed by the secular Enlightenment values that inspired the US and French revolutions. Its specific story, however, is less about its philosophical content than its enduring struggle for Irish political independence against overwhelming odds. It remains an unrealised ideal – a project yet to be completed. As the 'story' of idealistic, determined élites who have constructed a 'revolutionary' tradition, it is suffused with themes of personal heroism and betrayal, violence and repression, 'republican families', conspiracy, enforced exile, hunger strikes, sacrifice, internment without trial and long imprisonment. It is this which has captured the imagination of writers, poets, balladeers, film-makers and other artists who have helped the story to endure. Over the last three decades, it is a story that has been spread as much by bitter critics of the republican movement as by its supporters as the current outpouring of work on the IRA demonstrates.[5] Seán O'Fáoláin has remarked that, as a revolutionary idea or political philosophy, republicanism in Ireland aborted – Irish republicans were rebels rather than revolutionaries. He is in no doubt, however, about the emotional appeal and influence of the republican 'story'.[6]

The unionist grand narrative stands in stark opposition to its republican counterpart on a number of dimensions. It celebrates Irish unionists' role in British imperialism and colonialism, and as agents, beneficiaries, advocates and privileged clients of the British monarchy and state in Ireland. If the story of republicanism is about rebellion, that of unionism and loyalism is about the defence of the state, its Protestant constitution and its civilising role. As such, its personalities and their deeds, although part of a much broader historical canvas, appear less dramatic and magnetic. Its story is of a completed project, enshrined in the 'institutions of power and antiquity' – a legacy to be defended. While not short of an intelligentsia, unionism has lacked the type of 'political intellectuals' prominent in the nationalist and republican movements, who invent the 'nation' and map and justify the historic struggle for Irish independence.[7]

While the critics of republicanism might assert that it sacrifices the present to the past and the future, critics of unionism might suggest that it sacrifices the future to past and present. Oliver McDonagh has argued that nationalists (including republicans) and unionists share a historical cyclicalism. For nationalists, it is a cycle of insurgency and degeneration. (This cyclicalism needs to be qualified by republicans' unilinear understanding of their uncompleted project of national independence.) For unionists, cyclicalism is expressed by their sense of being besieged or beleaguered – a historical vision of an 'endless repetition of repelled assaults without hope of absolute finality or of a fundamental change in their relationship with their surrounding and surrounded neighbours'.[8]

Referring specifically to Ulster unionists, Brian Graham has noted a lack of a developmental narrative in favour of a view of the 'past as a series of tableaux' or reaffirmations of loyalty to monarch, country or the unionist Protestant community.[9] This fits with the metaphor of siege. Reaffirmations of loyalty are often ceremonial and highly ritualised – as in Orange marches, royal visits or war commemorations. There is a strong strand of fatalism in unionist ideology that proclaims the permanence of their historical predicament – caught between potentially unreliable and untrustworthy British governments and the machinations of their enemies. Their persistent demand for finality and permanence, associated with an implicit belief that it will be never truly possible, is deeply rooted in the triangular system of relationships between the unionists, the British state and republicans.

Of course, versions of the republican and unionist narrative vary across time, class and party organisation. To the extent that they impose a simplified coherence on history, they obscure far more than they reveal about the complexity and contradictory nature of historical reality. For the empirically minded historian, these 'stories' evoke spurious continuities, what Joe Lee has termed the 'triumphant tyranny of the living Irish over their dead generations'.[10] Their importance lies not in their empirical accuracy or otherwise, however, but in how they are embedded and used in contemporary relationships of power. In other words, for whom do they remain 'politically usable' as ideological weapons? This has become a particularly contentious question for protagonists of the Northern Ireland conflict.

Contemporary Ulster unionist parties trace their lineage directly to the political coalition mobilised against Home Rule in the late nineteenth century.[11] However, their grand narrative (and that of historic Irish unionism) goes back much further over a period of four centuries. The Tudor conquest, the Ulster Plantation, the Cromwellian and Williamite wars of the seventeenth century, the Anglo-Irish ascendancy of the eighteenth century and the Act of Union (1801) are claimed as landmarks in the history of a substantial pro-British Protestant minority on the island who saw their position as dependent on the support of the British state and who, variously, acted as its advocates, agents and privileged clients in Ireland and throughout the empire. Ulster unionists have developed a regional variant of this history around their sacred calendar of 1641, 1688–90 and 1912–14, all of which marked historical turning points for those who traced their ancestry specifically to Protestant settlement and plantation in Ulster.

Republicans generally trace the origins of the modern movement to the influence of the American and French revolutions, the United Irishmen and subsequent episodes such as Emmet's rebellion of 1803, Young Ireland's of 1848, the Fenians and the Land League of the 1860s and 1880s, and the Irish Republican Brotherhood (IRB) inspired insurrection of 1916. The 1790s mark an important turning point in the politically 'usable pasts' of unionists and republicans alike. For the former, the foundation of the Orange Order, the defeat of the United Irishmen and the subsequent Act of Union (1801) are major milestones. For the latter, the United Irishmen mark the beginning of a long and as yet unfinished struggle to establish an independent Irish Republic aimed at transcending the sectarian differences between Protestant, Catholic and Dissenter. However, republicans have also borrowed from the nationalist canon a much older story-line of resistance by a Gaelic, Catholic nation to British involvement in Ireland. The insurrectionary history of republicanism has been woven into a much wider nationalist narrative. While militant episodes – often lacking popular support – have always divided nationalists as they occur, they nonetheless have been retrospectively adopted and legitimised as part of the struggle for national independence. For example, they have served to unite the two strands of the national movement – as in the centenary commemorations of the 1798 and 1803 risings, or as in the retrospective legitimation of the 1916 rising.

Styles of mobilisation

In the case of unionism and republicanism, their respective styles of mobilisation have been perhaps more important historically than the substantive content of the ideologies themselves. Ways of mobilising resources over two centuries have decisively shaped the cultures and identities of unionists and republicans. In broad terms, unionists' actual and potential capacity to draw on the superior economic, political and coercive power of the British state has forced republicans (and nationalists) to rely more heavily on cultural and ideological resources, on extraterritorial support, as well as on their majority status on the island of Ireland.

In so far as unionists and republicans have been committed to 'state-making', they have been committed to the use of violence and organised coercion. As Charles Tilly puts it: 'war makes states, as much as states make war'.[12] In general, larger states and empires are able to mobilise much more violence and coercion than those smaller states that seek to supplant them.[13] Historically, the reliance of the British state and its unionist supporters on violence, coercion and war (much of it extraterritorial) has dwarfed that of Irish republicanism and nationalism. Official militarism as practised in imperial wars abroad or in attempts to pacify Ireland involved large numbers of Irish Catholics typically serving under an officer class in which Irish unionists were prominent. Irish unionists, in so far as they drew on their historical legacy as 'citizen- colonists' prioritised two tasks: surveillance of the 'native' or 'disloyal' population, and the obstruction of 'native' efforts at self-organisation.[14] This combined with an independent resort to violence by plebeian elements in the unionist community such as the Orange Order and its predecessors.[15] Unionist mobilisations against Home Rule, the subsequent policing, paramilitary and 'security' culture in Northern Ireland, current debates over arms and decommissioning are comprehensible in the light of this history.

The mobilisation of Irish Protestants and unionists into the British armed forces and in successive wars and military campaigns is a critical part of their identification with the state. Annual remembrances of past war sacrifice, most notably in the First World War, are a central part of unionist self-identity. By contrast, the republican and nationalist commitment to militarism and myths of sacrifice is more circumscribed, even if it has received more attention from historians. One of the features that differentiates the Irish and British states is the minimal role accorded to a military culture in the official ideology of the former and its continued prominence in the latter.

Radical republicans' historic commitment to the 'armed struggle' should not be abstracted, therefore, from the wider picture of military mobilisation and policing in Ireland. Their resort to violence and coercion has been far more episodic and militarily ineffectual than that of unionists backed by the state. Yet it has taken on a huge symbolic and cultural significance, often *post hoc*, as a statement of Irish people's right to self-organisation and independence. In revolutionary contexts, tight-knit conspiratorial groups were prone to claim for themselves the right to act on behalf of the Irish 'nation' or 'Republic'. Thus Theobald Wolfe Tone's idea of a 'nation-in-arms' translated into the Irish Revolutionary Brotherhood's calling themselves the 'government of Ireland' in 1873,[16] and to the IRA's claim from 1919 to be the guardians of the Republic. One of the persistent themes of republican activism is its view of electoral politics within empire and Union as corrupting and corruptible. This approach became harder to sustain with the spread of democratisation in the twentieth century and led to a successive splintering of the movement as Fianna Fáil, Clann na Poblachta, Offical Sinn Féin, and eventually Provisional Sinn Féin became involved in parliamentary politics. Smaller coteries always remained, however, committed to physical force as a means of guarding the 'purity' of the Republican ideal.

In some respects, republican styles of mobilisation have never matched the varied and complex forms practised by the early republicans of the United Irish movement in the 1790s. That movement combined constitutional methods at the outset with revolutionary conspiracy, mass organisation and rebellion. The Catholic–Dissenter alliance, and its middle-class leadership in Belfast and Dublin,[17] spread propaganda in newspapers such as *The Northern Star* and *The Press*, circulated pamphlets, including those by Thomas Paine and Wolfe Tone, and serialised various treatises, handbills and broadsheets, popular songs and ballads.[18] Meetings, marches and celebration dinners were supplemented by wakes, race meetings and potato diggings as a cover for recruiting support. As the government began to use armed force and terror to suppress the movement, the republicans increasingly turned to revolutionary organisation and conspiratorial oath-bound activity. They began to enlist Defenders' organisations with a record of resisting government repression and the violence of local loyalist groups. The Defenders had a widespread network of lodges with a federated, cellular structure while their ideology was a hybrid of pro-French sentiments combined with religious sectarianism, embryonic nationalism and millenarianism.[19]

The political thought of the United Irish leadership is best characterised as Enlightenment republicanism. It is not to be understood as romantic separatism or a claim for self-determination based on ethnic and cultural difference but as 'an assault on ancien regime pillars of monarchy, aristocracy and church in the name of a non-sectarian republic'.[20] The movement represented a brief opportunity for republican mass mobilisation across sectarian boundaries. This was created by a new fluidity in political allegiances within Protestant, Catholic and Dissenter populations, and by support from revolutionary France. The hybrid organisational form of the United Irish movement left it exposed to internal divisions and to government infiltration and manipulation. As in all complex political movements, members had diverse backgrounds and objectives. Its defeat was salutary and had far-reaching consequences for Irish republican organisation, reducing popular and cross-sectarian involvement and driving it underground into the hands of smaller conspiratorial and frequently militaristic élites.

The Irish Republican Brotherhood was founded in 1858 as an amalgamation of French and American varieties of revolutionary republicanism. Committed to ending British rule, its influence was crucial in the 1916 Easter rebellion. Its relatively narrow separatist focus meant that the great issues of Irish society, the economy, land, religion and education were largely the preserve of representative Catholic politicians. Although the IRB was to forge an alliance with Parnell's party in the 1880s, and Sinn Féin after 1916, it remained highly suspicious of electoral politics. The Fenians offered a revolutionary methodology rather than an ideology – their conspiratorial methods often implying a 'utopian contempt for actually existing people'.[21]

Caught between state power and the growth of popular democracy in the nineteenth century, republican revolutionaries developed strategies of mobilisation, protest and commemoration which proved extraordinarily durable. Graveside orations, speeches from the dock, mass funerals of republican activists, accounts of prison experiences, popular histories and ballads of republican heroes and events, created a cross-generational consciousness which linked Emmet's rebellion to the 1916 rebellion over 100 years later and Terence Bellew McManus's funeral in 1861 to Bobby Sands's in 1980. By the last quarter of the nineteenth century, however, the IRB were developing entryist methods vis-à-vis the emerging new cultural organisations such as the Gaelic League and the GAA. Patrick Pearse was to widen the appeal of revolutionary republicanism further by linking it to Gaelic revivalism and eventually to a form of devotional Catholicism in the 1916 rebellion.[22] It was a potent mix that was to revitalise popular republicanism after 1916 while rendering it even more alien to Northern unionists, including the descendants of the Presbyterian United Irishmen. Moreover, a version of this republicanism was to re-emerge in response to the conditions faced by Northern Catholic communities from the 1970s onwards.

Partition and its consequences

Partition was to fragment both republican/nationalist and unionist Ireland while creating the conditions for the cementing of an Ulster unionist political coalition in Northern Ireland. As the border gradually metamorphosed into a fully fledged inter-state boundary, each entity developed homogenised and antagonistic official cultures – one, Protestant, British and pro-imperial, the other Catholic, Gaelic and anti-imperialist. Different regional forms of economic integration into the wider capitalist economy, the decline of the Anglo-Irish ascendancy, and the distinct state-consolidating programmes of the dominant parties widened the gulf between North and South even further.

In the absence of a constructive rationale for the Northern Ireland state, other than the prevention of an all-Ireland unit, the UUP sought to engage popular Protestant support through a system of patronage, electoral gerrymandering and paramilitary policing designed to offset the potential threat from the 'disloyal' minority. Culturally, the state embarked on a series of elaborate royal and civic ceremonies. These included the unveiling of Carson's statue at Stormont, the Festival of Britain in Northern Ireland, and royal visits, especially that of Elizabeth II after her coronation. Here, the state was represented as a united Protestant entity, endorsed by the monarchy and by the state élites.[23] The themes of loyalty, empire, monarchy, Britishness, and unionist unity were counterposed to the subversive, backward-looking pipedreams of nationalists and republicans. The ornamentalism, public ceremony and ritual of the British state and its empire were adapted to the political needs of the Northern Ireland unionists. The regional parliament in Northern Ireland had taken on all the elaborate constitutional and ceremonial paraphernalia of Westminster. The virtues of the founders of Northern Ireland were celebrated through biography and popular history as were the characteristics of the 'Ulsterman'. The effect was to render the 'disloyal minority' invisible in the public sphere, other than as a nominal parliamentary opposition and as the source of periodic threat to the state.

Partition marked a severe reversal for the republican project but allowed for its re-emergence as the constitutional republicanism of De Valera and Fianna Fáil from 1927 onwards. Embracing a majoritarian strategy, and a socioeconomic programme based on self-reliance and protectionism, Fianna Fáil (the republican party) became the dominant political party of the Irish state. Dissident republicans coalesced around an IRA army council claiming a mandate from the Second Dáil (1919) and committed to a physical force strategy to end Partition and a policy of abstaining from the two parliaments on the island. Periodic military activities proved completely ineffectual – such as the bombing campaign in England in 1939–40 and the abortive 'Border campaign' between 1956 and 1962. However, they maintained in existence a marginalised culture of resistance, subject to successive splintering, based on shared prison experiences, commemorations and low-intensity conflict with the security forces of both states. Attempts to broaden republican strategy in a socialistic direction failed to engage wider democratic support in the 1930s,[24] although republicans played an active role in the Civil Rights Movement in Northern Ireland in the 1960s.

The conditions leading to the outbreak of the Northern Ireland conflict in the early 1970s were to create new opportunities for republican mobilisation, and for a level of popular, if localised, support that it had not achieved since 1919–21. After the movement split in the early 1970s between the Official and Provisional IRA, the latter went on to prosecute a prolonged three-cornered conflict with the British government and loyalists lasting nearly thirty years. In the wake of the hunger strikes, Sinn Féin began to develop a broader political strategy in Northern nationalist communities alongside the military campaign. With the Belfast Agreement of 1998, they have entered parliamentary politics in both Irish jurisdictions and have asserted their commitment to 'take the gun out of Irish politics'. As in the past, dissident republicans have remained. Republican Sinn Féin, the Continuity IRA and the Real IRA retain little support but continue to prioritise the armed struggle as a means of achieving Irish unification.

One of the effects of Partition has been to distance and insulate Northern Ireland from the mainstream politics of Britain and the Irish Republic. However, after 1945 the spread of the post-war British welfare state had begun undermine the capacity of the Unionist Party to dictate the terms of the Union in key areas. This provided political opportunity and a ready international audience for the Northern Ireland Civil Rights

Movement in the 1960s. This movement highlighted the contradiction between the discriminatory policies of the Stormont administration and the universalistic provisions of the welfare state, thus beginning a long process of reforms which were generally imposed by successive British governments over the opposition of unionists.

The initial destabilising factor, however, proved to be the nature of unionist response to civil rights demands, interpreting them in traditional terms as an 'attack on the state' from republicans and nationalists. This proved to be a self-fulfilling prophecy, as sectarian conflict and British army intervention provided the opportunity for the re-emergence of militant republicanism and recurring cycles of violence involving the Provisional IRA, loyalist paramilitaries and the official security forces.

Over the last thirty years, the balance of political, economic and demographic power has slowly shifted in Northern Ireland as British governments (with growing Irish government involvement) have sought to reconfigure its administration via institutionalised power-sharing between the 'two communities'. This overall policy of both governments was one of 'containing' the conflict within Northern Ireland while developing agreed measures to deal with it. Of course, among the protagonists, definitions of the conflict varied wildly. At one end of the spectrum, unionists portrayed it as a problem of law and order, crime and terror; at the other, militant republicans saw it as an anti-colonial liberation struggle. A politics of reform targeted on the British government emphasised class and sectarian inequality, the lack of human rights and the persistence of discrimination.

A politics of cultural identity

With few prospects of agreement on the nature of the conflict, both governments and influential political intellectuals began to redefine it as a cultural conflict – involving a clash of national and religious identities. To the 'permanent' Northern Ireland politics of 'power', security and control of territory was now added new layers: an intensified politics of culture, propaganda and the mass media. Among the products of this shift was a whole new political vocabulary including such terms as the 'two traditions', 'education for mutual understanding', 'peace and reconciliation', 'cultural traditions', 'parity of esteem' and a new emphasis on human rights, consent, dialogue, negotiation and ultimately the 'peace process'. The Belfast Agreement is the working out of this new politics of cultural recognition and agreement. The traditional politics of the 'Union' and the 'Republic' are now prosecuted with a new vocabulary but in the process are being reconfigured themselves.

One of the paradoxes of the new 'politics' of cultural identity is that it has appeared, initially at least, to bring about a remarkable level of élite accommodation as witnessed in the Belfast Agreement while, on the other hand, there are clear signs of intensified levels of popular sectarianism and division. Above all, it has been embraced enthusiastically by a Provisional Republican movement that is phasing out 'armed struggle' and has agreed to the principle that majority consent in Northern Ireland is necessary prior to establishing a sovereign all-Ireland state. Unionists have been less enthusiastic but it has encouraged a group of new unionist intellectuals to debate the changing nature of the Union and the basis for a settlement.[25]

Nevertheless, the new 'politics of cultural identity' has also encouraged political fragmentation, making accommodation problematical within Northern Ireland. Long-standing fissures within unionism have become more apparent – between secularists and evangelicals, working-class loyalism and middle-class and suburban unionism, self-confessed bigots and ecumenists, and between what are variously described as cultural and liberal unionists,[26] Ulster loyalists and Ulster British,[27] and the 'constitutional people' and the 'sovereign people'.[28]

The influence of extreme forms of evangelical Protestantism contributes to a universe of moral certainty in unionism which transcends many of its internal divisions and tends to make notions such as 'parity of esteem' and 'mutual understanding' redundant. An enduring strand of cultural unionism, most visibly associated with Ian Paisley, draws on an abiding tradition of anti-Catholicism[29] which stretches back to the seventeenth century. The opposition to 'popery' in all its manifestations has been most durably institutionalised in the Orange Order. From this perspective, unionist identity is dependent not just on allegiance to the British state but on a permanently or exclusivistic relationship with Irish Catholics and nationalists. It follows that to engage in dialogue or negotiation with non-unionists has the potential to undermine unionist identity. Norman Porter has noted the extension into unionist politics of the model of the evangelical sermon most obviously practised by Ian Paisley but practised by secular unionists also.[30] Unionists arrogate to themselves the role of 'prophetic witnesses' against the evils and wrongdoing of republicans. Confrontation, judgement and denunciation pervade the language. Republican hostility and indifference are taken as confirmation of their status as unrepentant sinners who have hardened their hearts against truth. Unionists therefore are sceptical of the notion of dialogue 'since it is to allow the unthinkable, namely that republicans' views may be as valid as unionists, that error may be as valid as truth, that bad may have something to teach the good'.[31]

This stance is influential even among secular unionists. It has deep historical roots which go back to the Home Rule campaign and beyond.[32] It holds that there is no moral equivalence between those who uphold and defend the law of the state and those who seek to overthrow it. This is why unionists bitterly reject any suggestion that law-breaking by police, army, intelligence services (and even at times loyalist paramilitaries) belongs to the same moral universe as that carried out by republicans.

Duncan Morrow suggests, however, that fundamentalist Protestantism only provides a central focus for unionist politics in the face of republican violence.[33] While it would be a major obstacle to the integration of unionists into a United Ireland, he suggest that it only unifies unionists in the face of an enemy. For Morrow, the ultimate choice for unionists is more likely to be between fundamentalism and Britishness. Nevertheless, such a cultural analysis of unionism raises serious questions about long-term unionist willingness or capacity for genuine dialogue and negotiation with their political opponents, whether it be in the Belfast Agreement or in related disagreements over arms decommissioning or the routes of Orange marches. Signs that a majority of unionists now oppose the Agreement are in part rooted in a growing unionist belief that it infringes the moral superiority of their case by implicating them in an administration shared by untrustworthy evildoers. Just as good and evil are morally irreconcilable, so also unionism and republicanism are politically irreconcilable.

Dialogue on cultural divisions – plausible within middle-class settings and in private discussion among politicians – takes on a different aspect in the context of 'street politics'. In the aftermath of the 'ceasefires' the ideological struggle has transmuted into an intensified 'grassroots' struggle to 'claim' territory symbolically (and physically) via marches, street signs, flags, murals and graffiti.[34] The result has been even more communal segregation. The latter's logical outcome is a *de facto* re-partition of a type that would replicate and even exacerbate the divisions associated with the initial Partition of 1920.

Both unionism and republicanism as political ideologies are embedded to varying degrees in a culture of popular sectarianism which they periodically seek to challenge, utilise and manage. The strengthening of sectarianism is one of the enduring legacies of the thirty-year conflict. It is characterised by a vocabulary of communal 'hate-speech'– scumbags, animals, rats, bastards, Huns, Prods, Taigs, Fenians. It is the language of insult, provocation and contempt of the 'other', not just on the streets, but in politics, and in the more polite terminology of the middle classes. Drawing on a long history with its roots in the plantation, economic competition, agrarian violence and its translation into an urban industrial environment, popular sectarianism combines a sense of communal superiority with a 'disdain' for the 'other community' – yet a conviction of victimhood at the hands of the 'other'. As a form of popular culture, sectarianism is imbued with the sense of two communities fated to be permanently locked in a deeply antagonistic relationship, yet one which intimately shapes each community's identity. This sectarianism is totalitarian, even racist, committed to a zero-sum view of the 'struggle' that is most visibly represented in the struggle to control territory.

Popular sectarianism translates into more 'respectable' politics in a number of ways – most notably into the ideologies of those who assert the impossibility of accommodation or compromise, who see politics as a zero-sum process between two irreconcilable sets of political and religious beliefs. To the extent that the consociationalism of the Belfast Agreement institutionalises this sectarianism, the Accord will be self-defeating. The Agreement poses huge challenges for unionists and republicans alike. The key issue is the extent to which they can represent their communities while effectively challenging the appeal of popular sectarianism. This will require a more fundamental accommodation than has yet been achieved. It is dependent on a greater equality of power within and between both 'communities' promoted consistently by the British state. But sustainable agreement will also depend on major changes in the distinctive modes of remembrance and styles of political mobilisation associated with unionism and republicanism in the past.

Notes

1. Thomas Hennessey, 'Ulster unionist territorial and national identities 1886–1893: island, kingdom and empire', *Irish Political Studies* 8 (1993), 21–36 (28).
2. Linda L. Colley, *Britons: Forging the Nation, 1707–1837* (London: Pimlico, 1992).

3. David Cannadine, *Ornamentalism: How the British Saw their Empire* (London: Penguin, 2002).

4. John Wilson Foster (ed.), *The Idea of the Union: Statements and Critiques in Support of the Union of Great Britain and Northern Ireland* (Vancouver: Belcouver Press, 1995); Arthur Green, 'Unionist horizons', *Irish Review* 4 (1988), 27–32; Robert McCartney, *Liberty and Authority in Ireland* (Derry: Field Day Theatre Co., 1985); Field Day Pamphlet No. 9.

5. Richard English, *Armed Struggle: A History of the IRA* (London: Macmillan, 2003); Ed Moloney, *A Secret History of the IRA* (London: Allen Lane, 2002).

6. Seán O'Faoláin, *The Irish: A Character Study* (Old Greenwich, CT: The Devin-Adair Company, 1949), pp. 112–28.

7. Liam O'Dowd, 'Intellectuals and political culture: a unionist–nationalist comparison', in *Culture and Politics in Northern Ireland, 1960–1990*, ed. Eamonn Hughes (Milton Keynes: Open University Press, 1991), pp. 151–73.

8. Oliver MacDonagh, *States of Mind: A Study of Anglo-Irish Conflict, 1780–1980* (London: George Allen and Unwin, 1983), p. 14.

9. Brian Graham, 'Contested images of place among Protestants in Northern Ireland', *Political Geography* 17, 2 (1998), 129–44.

10. Joe Lee, 'The Ribbonmen', in *Secret Societies in Ireland*, ed. T. Desmond Williams (Dublin: Gill and Macmillan, 1973), p. 35.

11. Stephen Howe, *Ireland and Empire: Colonial Legacies in Irish History and Culture* (Oxford: Oxford University Press, 2000); Alvin Jackson, 'Unionist history', in *Interpreting Irish History: The Debate on Historical Revisionism*, ed. Ciaran Brady (Dublin: Irish Academic Press, 1994), pp. 253–68.

12. Charles Tilly, *Coercion, Capital and European States, AD 990–1990* (Oxford: Basil Blackwell, 1992).

13. Benedict Anderson, 'The new world disorder', *New Left Review* 193 (1992), 3–13.

14. Frank Wright, *Northern Ireland: A Comparative Analysis* (Dublin: Gill and Macmillan, 1987), p. 1.

15. Frank Wright, *Two Lands on One Soil: Ulster Politics before Home Rule* (Dublin: Gill and Macmillan, 1996).

16. John O'Beirne Ranelagh, 'The Irish Republican Brotherhood and the revolutionary period 1879–1923', in *The Revolution in Ireland 1879–1923*, ed. George Boyce (Dublin: Gill and Macmillan, 1988), pp. 137–56 (141).

17. Nancy Curtin, *The United Irishmen: Popular Politics in Ulster and Dublin, 1791–1798* (Oxford: Clarendon Press, 1994).

18. H. T. Dickinson, 'Irish radicalism in the eighteenth century, Review Article', *History* 82 (1997), 266–84 (271).

19. Jim Smyth, *The Men of No Property: Irish Radicals and Popular Politics in the Late Eighteenth Century* (London: Macmillan, 1992).

20. Ian McBride, 'Ulster Presbyterians and the passing of the Act of Union', in *The Irish Act of Union, 1800: Bicentennial Essays*, ed. Michael Brown, Patrick M. Geoghegan and James Kelly (Dublin: Irish Academic Press, 2003), pp. 68–83 (82).

21. MacDonagh, *States of Mind*, pp. 81–2.

22. Ibid., p. 86.

23. Gillian McIntosh, *The Force of Culture: Unionist Identities in Twentieth Century Ireland* (Cork: Cork University Press, 1999), p. 22.

24. Richard English, *Radicals and the Republic: Socialist Republicanism in the Irish Free State, 1925–1937* (Oxford: Clarendon Press, 1994).

25. Liam O'Dowd, 'New unionism, British nationalism and the prospects for a negotiated settlement in Northern Ireland', in *Rethinking Northern Ireland: Culture, Ideology and Colonialism*, ed. David Miller (London: Longman, 1998), pp. 70–93.

26. Norman Porter, *Rethinking Unionism: An Alternative Vision for Northern Ireland* (Belfast: Blackstaff Press, 1996).

27. Jennifer Todd, 'Two traditions in unionist political culture', *Irish Political Studies* 2 (1987), 1–26.

28. Arthur Aughey, 'The character of Ulster unionism', in *Who Are "the People": Unionism, Protestantism and Loyalism in Northern Ireland*, ed. Peter Shirlow and Mark McGovern (London: Pluto Press, 1997), pp. 16–33.

29. John Brewer and Gareth I. Higgins, *Anti-Catholicism in Northern Ireland, 1660–1998: The Mote and the Beam* (London: Macmillan, 1998).

30. Norman Porter, *The Elusive Quest: Reconciliation in Northern Ireland* (Belfast: Blackstaff Press, 2003), p. 126.

31. Porter, *The Elusive Quest*, p. 127.

32. Margaret O'Callaghan, 'Franchise reform, "first past the post" and the strange case of unionist Ireland', *Parliamentary History* 16, 1 (1997), 85–106.

33. Duncan Morrow, '"Suffering for righteousness sake": fundamentalist Protestantism and Ulster politics', in *Who Are "the People"*, ed. Peter Shirlow and Mark McGovern, pp. 55–71.

34. Neil Jarman, *Material Conflicts: Parades in Northern Ireland* (Oxford: Berg, 1997); Dominic Bryan, *Orange Parades: The Politics of Tradition and Control* (London: Pluto Press, 2000).

Further Reading

J. Bowyer Bell, *The Secret Army: The IRA* (Dublin: Poolbeg Press, 1998)

Richard Bourke, *Peace in Ireland: The War of Ideas* (London: Pimlico, 2003)

Richard English and Graham Walker (eds.), *Unionism in Modern Ireland: New Perspectives on Politics and Culture* (London: Macmillan, 1996)

Tom Garvin, *Nationalist Revolutionaries in Ireland 1858–1928* (Oxford: Oxford University Press, 1987)

James Loughlin, *Ulster Unionism and British Identity since 1885* (London: Pinter, 1995)

Oliver MacDonagh, *States of Mind: A Study of Anglo-Irish Conflict 1780–1980* (London: George Allen and Unwin, 1983)

Gillian McIntosh, *The Force of Culture: Unionist Identities in Twentieth-Century Ireland* (Cork: Cork University Press, 1999)

David Miller, *Rethinking Northern Ireland: Culture, Ideology and Colonialism* (London: Longman, 1998)

Robert W. White, *Provisional Irish Republicans: An Oral and Interpretive History* (Westport: Greenwood Press, 1993)

6

Irish feminism

The wrongs of woman

In the period of the European Enlightenment, a modern feminist discourse emerged out of complimentary concerns with what the English writer, Mary Wollstonecraft, named 'the wrongs of woman' and 'the rights of women'. There were earlier speculations on the possibility that women might constitute a class of people who suffer, and may demand rights, but there was no systematic attempt to theorise the position of women in Irish society – with a view to bringing about a change in that position – before the mid-eighteenth century. In the eighteenth century the wrongs of which women were conscious included unequal access to education, vulnerability to domestic violence and to sexual violence from family and strangers, limited rights of property and inheritance and exclusion from all levels of government and the judiciary. The groundswell of complaint about the wrongs suffered by women in Ireland tended to be particular and dispersed in this early period. Women and men who complained about specific aspects of women's lives did not couch those complaints within a thorough analysis of an Irish class system or social contract.

The absence of an overarching narrative immediately draws attention to perhaps the single greatest problem facing an historian of feminism in Ireland, which is the question as to whether the evolution of feminist discourses in Irish and in English constitute separate discourses and separate development. The large majority of Irish women were Irish-speaking. Literary sources from eighteenth-century Ireland suggest that there was some consciousness of a potential war between the sexes: men and women wanted different things from their lives and complained about one another as groups. *Cúirt an Mheán-Oíche* (*c*. 1780) by Brian Merriman uses an imaginary court of women to conduct a comic complaint by women and defence by men. One would have to be circumspect in reading this poem for evidence that women voiced particular grievances, but it does point to an awareness that women could be thought of as an oppressed class. The sources of unhappiness in women's lives were likely to be differentiated, however, depending on class position, occupation and area of habitation. Women in Dublin, Cork and Belfast had some different concerns from rural women, and women on the west coast and the islands were experiencing rural life differently, for example, from those involved in farming in Leinster. Aristocratic Gaelic women, like their old English and new English counterparts, had access to political influence if not directly to the exercise of political power. Women sometimes managed large estates in the absence of husbands, or in the minority of sons and brothers. At most levels in society marriages were arranged and in some cases they became business partnerships in which the woman, through superior intellect, willpower or family backing, or because she had brought more capital into the business, was the dominant partner.

In several other European countries, the evolution of a bourgeois feminist discourse was entwined with the development of the realist novel and particularly with the interest in female self-consciousness developed in the novel. The fact that the Irish language did not adopt print culture for realist fiction in any significant way in the eighteenth century contributed to – or was a product of – the dominance of other literary genres, and as far as we know there are no novels by women in Irish from this period. The attention to women's issues in other genres has to be carefully filtered through literary conventions. Love poetry often has more to say about the ideal than the particular woman, although poetry from the Dublin literary circle centred on the family of Seán and Tadgh Ó Neachtain, Úna Ní Bhroin and Máire Ní Reachtagáin suggests that it was possible to express an appreciation of intellectual companionate affection.

A better sense of women's anxieties may be derived from the *caoineadh*, the oral lament poetry composed collaboratively by women to memorialise a dead individual. Although this ritual poetry follows generic conventions, it can also incorporate local and particular issues, and it is a form which allows women to express anger in specific contexts: in *Caoineadh Shéamuis Mhic Choitir* (*c*. 1720) by a nurse, *An tAthair Nioclás Mac Síthigh: Caoineadh do Chum a Dheirfiúr* (*c*. 1766) by a sister Cáit de Búrca, and

Tórramh-Chaoineadh Airt Uí Laoghaire by Art Uí Laoghaire's widow Eibhlín Dubh Ní Chonaill, the particular losses of the women who knew these men are coloured by a profound sense of injustice against an alien and oppressive government. Máirín Nic Eoin has argued that any analysis of patriarchal forms in Gaelic Ireland in this period should recognise that notions of political and cultural dominance are scarcely applicable to any class. Instead, she suggests that the gendered ideologies of the indigenous Irish culture might have to be read as a reaction to colonial control:

> Notions of political or cultural dominance can scarcely be applied to any class in Irish-speaking Ireland since the seventeenth century. Nevertheless, the Irish-speaking communities did have cultural leaders who continued to disseminate aspects of pre-colonial ideology. It can be argued that the Gaelic poets and learned classes who disseminated gendered thought systems right through the seventeenth, eighteenth and nineteenth centuries may have done so unconsciously as a form of defence against the erosion of native cultural practices.[1]

The wrongs of women are inseparable from the other wrongs suffered by the Irish people, and this entwining of feminist and nationalist discourses is the most distinctive feature in the evolution of Irish feminism. Its clearest expression in eighteenth-century anglophone Ireland appears in the anonymous novel, *The Triumph of Prudence over Passion* (1781):

> I see no reason why women should not be patriots; for surely, if tyranny and oppression are established in a country, they are more likely to suffer for it, both in their persons and properties than men, because less able to defend themselves; it, therefore, concerns them much, to use all their influence in opposing it; and doubtless that influence is more powerful than people are aware of.[2]

The rights of women

There is some evidence that women who supported the ideals of the United Irishmen, the republican movement that led a French-assisted rebellion in the summer of 1798, may have been meeting in groups. However there is no real sign that a demand for female franchise was part of their agenda. The democratic and republican aspirations that emerged in the late eighteenth century had obvious implications for the political representation of women, but the defeat of the 1798 rebellion stymied the development of such arguments. Furthermore, the ideological interpretations of violence against women in the course of the rebellion and its suppression seemed to involve a calcification of women's roles as domestic and family-centred in the period immediately after the Act of Union. There were, however, other outlets for female political activism. Philanthropic projects to aid the poor, the sick, the elderly, children and sinners allowed religious and lay women to gather together in meetings and committees, to write letters, raise subscriptions and petitions, while Irish support for the campaign to abolish the slave trade encouraged women to lobby and to use their economic power as consumers to influence public policy. Nano Nagle, Theodosia Blachford, Arabella Denny and Mary Leadbeater are notable philanthropists and campaigners in pre-Famine Ireland, while writers such as Maria Edgeworth, Sydney Owenson, Anna Maria Hall and Charlotte Elizabeth Tonna all examined various ways in which Irish women's lives were expressed or occluded in public and private spheres.

Public lobbying for the rights of women begins to emerge as a separate argument in the 1820s, at a point when the dominant political force in Ireland was the campaign for Catholic emancipation. Anna Doyle Wheeler is generally acknowledged as the first Irish woman to campaign publicly for the emancipation of women. Wheeler left Ireland after an unhappy marriage and her argument in favour of women's rights was developed in dialogue with British utilitarian philosophers and members of the cooperative movement. With William Thompson she co-wrote *Appeal of One Half of the Human Race, Women Against the Pretensions of the Other Half, Men* (1825), published in England and with no explicit Irish argument.

During the 1840s almost all discussion of the condition of women in Ireland was routed through commentary on the causes and effects of the Famine, when the vulnerability of women and children to the consequence of events in which they had no decision-making roles was made particularly obvious. Women philanthropists from Ireland and abroad were active in famine relief. In that trauma, and in the subsequent period of high emigration, it is not clear to what extent women thought of themselves as a separate class of sufferer. The famine may have contributed directly and indirectly to proportionately greater emigration by women, to the movement of greater numbers of women into prostitution, to new political and popular campaigns for land reform, to the development of cultural nationalism, and to the perception abroad that Ireland was a site of British colonial abuses. In the second half of the nineteenth century all these factors had a bearing on the evolution of feminism.

Women who contested the authority of the churches and the pervasiveness of restrictive family values in regulating sexuality, reproduction, dress, demeanour, education, employment and freedom of expression may have chosen to evade conflict through emigration rather than to stay and battle for change. Eleanor Butler and Sarah Ponsonby (known in the late eighteenth century and since as the Ladies of Llangollen) were the first famous Irish lesbians to run away, but it seems probable that anyone who preferred openly to express a sexual identity beyond that of marriage within her own class and clan would leave if she could. It would be unwise, however, to extrapolate from this presumption the thesis that women who left Ireland were necessarily more independent and radical than those who stayed. It could be argued, for example, that emigrants were more like to display a privatised, free market attitude to the commodification of sexuality, while those who stayed often negotiated a subtle and complex place for sexual expression within their families and communities.

The large number of women from the lowest economic classes who were moving in and out of prostitution were increasingly perceived as a problem by the middling and upper classes. For privileged feminists, sex workers became an important cause. The Contagious Diseases Acts, the first of which was passed in 1866, initiated the compulsory inspection for venereal diseases of women in specified garrison towns in Britain and Ireland. For feminists, these acts, which instiued the inspection of women rather than men, enshrined a sexual double standard. Furthermore, by seeking to regulate (rather than root out) prostitution, they could be seen to foster rather than contain 'vice'. In Ireland, Isabella M. S. Tod and Anna Haslam were involved in founding branches of the Ladies National Association for the Repeal of the Contagious Diseases Acts. Tod was a Belfast woman who established Ireland's first suffrage society in 1871. She also campaigned for the repeal of the married women's property acts, was active in the temperance movement, in philanthropic societies and was in favour of women's education. From the introduction of the first Home Rule Act in 1886 she was associated with unionist politics. At that point a marked schism in Irish feminism emerged, with unionist and nationalist feminists working essentially in separate spheres. Anna and Thomas Haslam (husband and wife) established the Dublin Women's Suffrage Association in 1876, eventually to become the Irish

Women's Suffrage and Local Government Association. The Haslams were both feminists and Quakers, and it is worth pointing out here that Quakers played a disproportionately significant role in nineteenth-century feminist activism.

It had not wanted the Great Hunger to expose the ways in which the systems of land ownership and management in nineteenth-century Ireland were dysfunctional, but the crisis caused by famine gave new impetus to calls for reform. The Land War of the late 1870s and the early 1880s began with tenant demands for rent abatements and escalated into a campaign against the corruptions of landlordism itself. The Irish Land League, founded by Michael Davitt in 1879, was headed by Charles Stewart Parnell. In 1881 Davitt proposed a women's Land League to conduct the Land War in the event of its leaders being jailed. Parnell's sister, Anna Parnell, was leader. Although the Ladies' Land League was actively involved in recruitment, public meetings, resisting evictions and other forms of tenant support, it was never able to become a completely self-determining body, and its apparently subservient relation to the men's Land League seemed to reinforce the stereotype developed during the evolution of the United Irishmen, the Young Irelanders and the Fenians, that women were helpmeets rather than potential theorists and leaders in nationalist campaigns.

It was during the Land War that British feminists such as Josephine Butler and Annie Besant began to identify Ireland as a site of particular feminist concern, and Irish women as in a continuum with women in other British colonies who were suffering abuse from the state. Irish contributions to literature on the New Woman, and in particular the contributions of Sarah Grand, George Egerton and Rosa Mulholland, fostered this analogy. The phrase 'New Woman' is said to have been coined by the Ulster-born Sarah Grand, and describes a new generation of women who believed in women's suffrage, abolition of the double standard in sexual matters, rational dress and educational opportunities for women.

From the 1840s writers had been attempting to take a leading role in the formation of an emergent romantic nationalist identity. Literary women first participated in the project as poets writing for *The Nation*. The interest taken by writers and readers of *The Nation* in ballads and popular culture, and – at least theoretically – in the Irish language revival might be seen as progressing quite naturally towards the end of the century into the folklore and Celticism popularised by Jane Wilde and Augusta Gregory.

In nineteenth-century Ireland feminism can be seen to have become gradually constituted as a set of specific arguments articulated by the English-speaking middle classes. As Angela Bourke has demonstrated in *The Burning of Bridget Cleary* (1999), however, it is possible to identify gender as a faultline in many places, rural and urban, Irish-speaking, English-speaking and bilingual, across the classes. Newspapers and railways represented the technological sides of a modernity that was spreading through the country; areas of the countryside most remote from Belfast and Dublin might be in regular contact with Glasgow and Boston; members of religious orders were part of a world-wide network of missionary workers; and there was a regular internal migration of women into apprenticeships, factories and domestic service. At the cultural level, while university-educated and middle-class women members of the Gaelic League were travelling to the *Gaeltachts* to learn Irish, they also saw the setting up of women's branches in the *Gaeltacht* to teach reading and writing to native Irish speakers. This is how Úna Ní Fhaircheallaigh describes women's participation in the Gaelic League:

> Each Sunday night the girls used to come to the branch of the Gaelic League which had been set up for the men. It was not long before they too were taken by a strong desire to learn Irish and they soon became jealous that they did not have their own branch of the League. They were, however, given cause for hope as regards this matter. One of them said – 'We will have a branch for ourselves now without being beholden to the men.'[3]

National independence

The Irish Women's Franchise League, established in 1908, made a point of its nationalist sympathies and from the beginning of the twentieth century Irish feminist organisations, like Irish socialists (allowing always for some overlap between the two constituencies), conceded some priority to the struggles for and against national independence. Although some suffrage organisations, such as that in Munster, brought together nationalist and unionist members, many women felt compelled to choose between feminism and their other political commitments, with some Southern unionist women, for example, retreating from suffrage organisations. There were other women who avoided such conflict by focusing their political activities in more apparently neutral spheres such as social purity or philanthropy; but even here there were appreciable sectarian divides, with separate Catholic and Protestant organisations addressing issues such as temperance or vice reform.

The various relations between the suffrage question and other national questions were debated in newspapers, periodicals and in literature. The suffrage newspaper, *The Irish Citizen* (1912–20), insisted that gender was central to an understanding of citizenship. *Bean na hÉireann* (1908–11), the newspaper of *Inghinidhe na hÉireann*, the nationalist women's organisation founded by Maud Gonne in 1900, examined feminism in relation to its broadly socialist and nationalist agenda. From 1914, *Cumann na mBan*, the women's auxiliary corps to the Irish Volunteers, replaced *Inghinidhe na hÉireann* as the locus for female nationalist activism. There was criticism from the start that *Cumann na mBan* accepted a subservient status for women in the struggle for independence, and that they were willing to postpone the achievement of equality for women until after the settlement of the national question. This priority is clear in their Manifesto:

> We would point out to our members that it is their duty in all controversial matters to abide by the principles of nationality, which are the bedrock on which alone any vital national movement can safely be built.[4]

In contrast, the Irish Citizen Army, founded in 1913 and led by James Connolly from 1914, accepted women and men on an equal footing as members. Connolly is largely credited with the commitment to equality for the sexes that was included in the document proclaiming an Irish Republic at the time of the 1916 rising. Women from the Citizen Army fought in the rising and Constance Markievicz, Connolly's lieutenant, was sentenced to death after the rising, with the sentence commuted to life imprisonment. She was in fact released from prison in 1917 and in 1918 became the first woman ever elected to the British House of Commons; by then a Sinn Féin member, she refused to take up her seat and joined the Provisional Government of Ireland and the first *Dáil Éireann* (Irish parliament).

There are many autobiographical accounts by women of the 1916 rising, the War of Independence and the subsequent civil war. There are interesting contrasts between these narrative memoirs and the various ways the period has been represented in fiction and cinema, where a number of stereotypes regarding women as passive sufferers and mourners were quickly established and have remained surprisingly resilient. The work done by *Cumann na mBan* in the period immediately after the rising may have itself contributed to the establishment of these tropes – for several years they were active in forging a cult around the executed leaders of 1916 through commemorative events. Moreover, it became commonplace after 1916 for women to stand for election to parliament based on their familial relationships – sister, widow, daughter – to nationalist martyrs. This did deliver several women members into the first and second *Dáil* and, along with the involvement of women in the Citizen Army and in *Cumann na mBan*, helped to secure equal franchise rights for women in the constitution of the Irish Free State in 1922. Women in Northern Ireland received full adult franchise along with British women in 1928.

Feminism after Partition: Northern Ireland

Ruth Taillon and Diane Urquhart have characterised both the Ulster Women's Unionist Council (UWUC) and the Ladies' Auxiliary of the Ancient Order of Hibernians (a female nationalist association) as conservative bodies, which discouraged women from parliamentary politics and relegated them to providing support systems for male politicians.[5] There is little evidence of a thriving feminism in Northern Ireland before the 1960s, although it is important to note that women were almost accidentally entrusted with the dissemination of religious and ethical values and with the education of children into the ideologies of unionism and nationalism. It is also possible to identify key times and places where the tensions inherent in a divided, sectarian and deeply violent society were narrativised in terms of home and family. This produced some strange, unhappy and interesting fiction and drama centred on frustrated and arrested erotic and family relationships, but also inclined to allegorise the fallout from Partition as a family drama. Reaching out for romantic allegory was already imminent before Partition. In 1908 James Douglas described Belfast in the following terms, in his novel *The Unpardonable Sin*:

> Bigotsborough is a city which suffers from unsatisfied aspirations and baffled aims. Its imagination is starved, and it is oppressed by an intolerably grey monotony. It is the loneliest city in the world. It would be happy if it were on the Clyde, for its blood is Scottish. But it lives in exile among an alien race. It has ceased to be Scottish and it is too proud to be Irish. It has the hunger of romance in its heart for it has lost its own past, and is groping blindly after its own future. It cannot identify itself with Ireland or with Scotland or with England,

and it vehemently endeavours to give itself to each country in turn. It is like a woman who dallies with three lovers, and cannot make up her mind to marry any of them.[6]

One way of accounting for the critical neglect of women writers before 1960 is to look at how many of them chose to work within a particular genre of romance fiction that addressed the internecine divisions in Irish society more directly that the work of their more 'literary' peers. This was not exclusively the work of women, of course, as reference to Douglas indicates, but it is a genre dominated by women. A genealogy of fiction about inter-religious romantic relations would include the work of Kathleen Coyle, Nan C. Rogers, Patricia O'Connor and Anne Crone, while Sam Hanna Bell, Joseph Tomelty, Michael MacLaverty and Brian Moore explore ways in which the overarching violence of Northern society is mimicked in the domestic sphere. This work is interested in issues of repetition and reproduction. It also throws light on the emergence in Irish writing of lesbian fiction (in the work of Janet McNeill, Molly Keane, Kate O'Brien and Elizabeth Bowen) as high art, whilst heterosexual romance remains apparently base and unproductive.

In terms of feminist political activism, life in the North was not completely bleak. Women who eschewed the sectarianism and conservatism of parliamentary politics could be active in local government, and particularly in trades unions, although many of the major industries were dominated by Orangeism. The Catholic church's obsession with anti-communism deterred many Catholics from joining socialist organisations, while the power of the Orange Order acted as a similar deterrent on Protestants. Women such as the trade unionist Saidie Patterson were very effective in leading labour disputes, in campaigning for the redress of poverty and for children's rights, and in smaller numbers many were active in peace movements in the First World War and in much greater numbers during the Cold War, although other feminists such as Betty Sinclair gave priority to the role of women in fighting fascism.

Feminism after Partition: Free State and Republic

If the Catholic church did much to stifle potential feminism in the North, in the new Irish Free State its influence has been represented as devastating. The cult of the Virgin Mary was reinvigorated in the late nineteenth and early twentieth centuries by way of the Marian apparitions at

Lourdes, Fatima and Knock, Co. Mayo, and recruited to the church's anti-communist crusade. The cult of Mary had a deep influence on the lives and imaginations of Catholic Irish women. Although the Catholic church apparently promoted versions of the Gaelic revival and celebrated – indeed insisted on – Irish difference, mariology was often imported to loosen local ties to older and potentially more subversive modes of religious observance such as those associated with wakes, patterns and holy wells. Margaret O'Callaghan argues that, 'after independence the Catholic church sought an extended moral control in compensation for the loss of its historical role as the "public voice of a wronged nation"'.[7] The church might reasonably have feared that a revolutionary discourse could quickly adopt pro-secular, anti-clerical attitudes, even in nations previously considered devoutly Christian. The French and Russian revolutions raised these fears. The response of the Catholic church in Ireland to this possibility was to identify itself closely with a vision of an essential Irish character, and to demonise the attractions of liberalism or socialism as quintessentially 'foreign', where the 'foreign' was always a form of English power. It is deeply significant for the history of Irish feminism that the Catholic church chose to battle secularism (which it all too often named as Protestantism) in terms of regulating sexuality. Whether they were influencing the Censorship board to censor the work of Marie Stopes, the advocate of family planning, or even writings by Catholic obstetricians on the 'rhythm method' of contraception, influencing the League of Mary's attack on female prostitution and managing Magdalen asylums, forcing single mothers to give up their children for adoption, attacking dance halls and films as the site of foreign vices, or attempting to destroy the political careers of politicians believed to be sympathetic to socialism or divorce, the leaders of the Catholic church in Ireland repeatedly entwined discourses of racial purity, national pride and patriarchal authority. In 1925 the archbishops and bishops of Ireland meeting at Maynooth issued a statement which gives a flavour of their argument and tone:

> Purity is strength, and purity and faith go together. Both virtues are in danger in these times, but purity is more directly assailed than faith. The danger comes from pictures and papers and drink. It comes more from the keeping of improper company than from any other cause; and there is no worse fomenter of this great evil than the dancing hall.[8]

The influence of Free State Catholicism is strongly imprinted on the 1937 Constitution of the Irish Republic, drawn up by Eamonn de Valera. Article forty-one proclaims that:

> The State recognises the Family as the natural primary and fundamental unit group of Society, and as a moral institution possessing inalienable and imprescriptible rights, antecedent and superior to all positive law.
>
> In particular the State recognises that by her life within the home, woman gives to the State a support without which the common good cannot be achieved.
>
> The State shall, therefore, endeavour to ensure that Mothers shall not be obliged by economic necessity to engage in labour to the neglect of their duties in the home.
>
> The State pledges itself to guard with special care the institution of Marriage, on which the Family is founded.[9]

This emphasis on marriage is a response to the recurring debate over divorce in the Irish senate during the 1920s and 1930s. W. B. Yeats was one of the senators who argued that Ireland's prohibition on divorce fundamentally discriminated against the Protestant minority and revealed the Free State to be under Catholic control. One of the effects of such arguments was to enable Northern unionists to position themselves as defenders of liberal values, despite the many ways in which Northern Ireland was extraordinarily misogynist and homophobic in legal and social terms.

Women senators seem to have found it easier to speak out in favour of women's rights to education and employment rather than on issues of sexuality. Senator Jennie Wyse Power and Louie Bennett, head of the Irish Women's Worker Union (established 1911), opposed government plans in 1935 to restrict female employment, but Articles forty and forty-five of the constitution – ostensibly designed to protect mothers – in fact enabled public service employers to restrict many jobs to unmarried women and led to the creation of what Margaret O'Callaghan has described as a 'public sphere that was virtually exclusively male'.[10]

Women's liberation

At the start of the 1960s there was some sense that Ireland was about to embrace certain kinds of modernisation, that might involve social as well as economic change. Sean Lemass (*taoiseach* from 1959 to 1966) and Terence O'Neill (prime minister of Northern Ireland from 1963 to 1969) both fostered the belief in a new era, and raised expectations, especially amongst disenfranchised groups, that economic growth would be accompanied by forms of liberalism and tolerance. Both parts of Ireland, however, proved to be resistant to change. Partition fuelled a sectarian party politics and blocked the development of socialist and feminist critique. The early 1960s might be viewed as a period in which women began to develop a renewed consciousness of the wrongs by which they were oppressed, but they were only slowly beginning to organise forms of resistance. Edna O'Brien struck out against Irish censorship with *The Country Girls* trilogy (*The Country Girls*, 1960; *The Lonely Girl*, 1962; *Girls in Their Married Bliss*, 1964), which also sent out a signal that Irish women were fretting under the repressive codes governing female sexuality, language and decorum. An attentive reader of women journalists such as Monica Carr, Angela MacNamara, Mary Maher, Maeve Binchy, Mary Kenny, Nell McCafferty and Elgy Gillespie would have seen other signals of the accumulating sense of grievances felt by women, and these grievances became central to a growing public debate from about 1968.

In 1967 the United Nations Commission on the Status of Women had initiated a process whereby women's groups around the world would examine the status of women in their own countries. An Ad Hoc group of representatives of Irish women's organisations in the Republic gathered information on discrimination against women in education and employment, and on the habitual demeaning of women in public arenas such as advertising and broadcasting. In October 1968 they requested the government to set up a National Commission on the Status of Women. The *Report of the Commission on the Status of Women* was published in 1972; it made recommendations on employment, education, jury service, taxation, law, social welfare, rural life, political and cultural life. A Council for the Status of Women was established to press for implementation of the report, and, by 1976, 75 per cent of recommendations had been fully implemented, with a further 17 per cent partially implemented.[11]

The Irish Women's Liberation Movement (IWLM) grew out of meetings of women radicals and activists; in 1971 they published *Irish Women – Chains or Change?* outlining the group's key demands. In March that year those demands were given wide publicity when the RTE television presenter Gay Byrne offered the IWLM an entire edition of his magazine format *Late Late Show* to present their cause. A subsequent public meeting in the Mansion House, Dublin, attracted over 1,000 people. The movement was able to harness broad support as long as it stuck to what were perceived as women's issues and eschewed the left-wing politics of some of the founder members. The ban on contraception in the Republic emerged as a key issue and in May 1971 a group of women went to Belfast to purchase contraceptives, and returned with them to Dublin, flouting Customs officials.

The IWLM was very successful in identifying and publicising important issues for feminism, but it broke apart partly because of an over-reaching ambition to organise affiliate groups into too rigid a structure, and partly because there had never been a consensus amongst nationalists, socialists and liberal feminists either on the causes of women's oppression or on strategies for resistance. Subsequent women's liberation groups were founded but one can also trace the legacy of the IWLM in the foundation of special interest groups such as AIM (founded 1972 to help women suffering marital breakdown), ADAPT (founded 1973 for Deserted and Alone Parents), Cherish (founded 1972 for unmarried mothers), Women's Aid (for battered wives, first refuge opened in 1974), and in the later 1970s campaigns for Lesbian and Gay Liberation, and against violence against women. These groups concentrated on campaigns to redress the wrongs of women, while the Women's Representative Association (WRA, founded 1970, known as Women's Political Association or WPA from 1973) fostered women's entry into parliamentary and local government politics, sponsored political discussions, and encouraged support for women candidates regardless of their party affiliation.

In Northern Ireland in the 1960s the work of women as activists in trade unions and community politics fed into the evolution of the Northern Ireland Civil Rights Association (NICRA, founded 1967). From 1969 one could detect three broad strands in feminist politics in the North: there were women who identified as feminists but insisted on the priority of nationalist, unionist or anti-imperialist affiliations; there were women who pursued a women's liberation agenda and tried to achieve non-sectarian consensus around special issues such as support for Rape Crisis Centres, Lesbian and Gay Liberation, victims of domestic violence and single parents; and there were people who argued that true feminism must be non-sectarian and opposed to all forms of violence. All these strands had their successes and failures. Within republican and loyalist communities there were remarkable examples of women's activism in support of prisoners, for example, and in building resources within the community. On the other hand, there were also a number of utopian projects to ground peace movements in Northern Ireland in alliances between women. Whatever their political affiliations women in the north became resourceful at organising themselves, and at communicating in different media from local freesheets and newsletters to television and newspapers world-wide. The vocalisation of women's concerns reinvigorated established genres such as poetry, fiction, drama and memoirs. Community theatre, for example, became an arena for collaborative creativity.

Sexuality and public scandal

From the early 1970s, women's groups in Northern Ireland and in the Republic began to use international law and international human rights discourse to pressure home governments into changing the status of women. Membership of the European Economic Community from 1973 brought support by way of funding and also put pressure on the British and Irish governments to redress injustices that were anomalous in Europe, particularly in matters relating to privacy. Other European countries moved towards permitting divorce, contraception, abortion and the decriminalisation of homosexuality. The story of feminism in Ireland since the 1970s has not, however, been one of smooth progress towards liberalisation. In 1979, Pope John Paul II visited Ireland and advised the Irish to preserve their country's distinctive Catholic values. In the 1980s and 1990s conservative forces mobilised to contest any moves towards reforming Ireland into a more secular and liberal state. These conservative forces had successes: in 1983 a referendum led to the adoption of a constitutional amendment guaranteeing the right to life of the unborn foetus; in 1986 another referendum confirmed a constitutional ban on divorce. Mags O'Brien describes the bitterness of the activists in the Divorce Action Group who realised that the vote was not an indication of strongly held moral views but rather of an unwillingness to face change. Their perception was that while many had supported divorce in theory, they wished to preserve their separatist vision of an Ireland somehow more moral and more upright than other nations.[12]

Although Irish feminists seemed to take up the causes of privacy and reproductive rights after these positions had been argued and thought through in other places such as the United States and Western Europe, and thus Irish feminism could be viewed as belatedly espousing derivative causes, its struggle with the conservative backlash in defence of family values and foetal rights was an advanced warning to feminist movements in other countries where such a backlash was only beginning.

In the 1980s and 1990s public debates over issues to do with privacy, reproductive rights and alternative sexualities were centred on a series of scandals in which print and broadcast media personalised the issues through sensationalised exemplary cases: the death in childbirth of 15-year-old Ann Lovett and her baby in 1984; the trial of Joanne Hayes for the murder of the Kerry babies in 1984; the decision of rape survivor Lavinia Kerwick to renounce anonymity and speak on a radio programme in 1990; the rape in 1992 of a 14-year-old known as 'X' and the attempt of the state to prevent her from travelling to England for an abortion; the exposure in 1993 of Eamonn Casey, bishop of Galway, who was revealed to have fathered a child twenty years previously; the conviction in 1994 of Brendan Smyth, a Catholic priest, whose career as a child abuser had been shielded by the church and whom the Fianna Fáil government had failed to extradite on request to Northern Ireland. In these cases campaigning journalists confronted their readers, viewers and listeners with the human costs of Ireland's Catholic ethos, but popular journalism also played a role in policing normative heterosexual values and demonising figures in public life – especially politicians – who might challenge the supremacy of family life.

These scandals may have moved public opinion in Ireland, but it is doubtful that they raised many difficult problems for feminist theory. Many Irish feminists, particularly people with religious convictions, underwent personal struggles over marriage and reproduction, but there was never any serious doubt that feminism must be pro-choice. For all the attention given to these cases, they demanded activism rather than debate. Perhaps the most interesting aspect of these scandals was the difference between public opinion as expressed in elections and referendums and as expressed in radio phone-ins and opinion polls. These differences seemed to suggest that citizens were searching for a gap between the edicts of church and state, where they hoped to preserve the vision of a morally pure Ireland, separate from the practice of private morality.

The signal that public opinion was moving in favour of reform came with the election in 1990 of Mary Robinson as Ireland's first female president. In Robinson's previous career as a barrister and in her twenty-year period in the Irish senate (1969–89) she had been strongly associated with feminist causes and with the campaign to decriminalise homosexuality.

Her election produced some euphoria amongst feminists, particularly in the light of her successful mobilisation of women voters. As a non-executive head of state Robinson worked largely with symbols and gestures, but she was effective in changing the tone of Irish public life and in suggesting that a distinctive Irish identity could be imagined in terms of diversity rather than homogeneity. Her presidency coincided with a period of economic prosperity and for a while she was regarded as herself a symbol of a new Ireland, more confident and generally more liberal than before. She decided not to run for a second term of office and in 1997 became United Nations Commissioner for Human Rights.

Travelling: feminist futures

The election of a feminist lawyer as Ireland's first woman president indicated both a disillusion with the domination of an apparently stale version of nationalism in mainstream politics and a belief that women were finally moving towards some kind of parity of esteem in Irish life. Some of the utopian impulses that were liberated at the time of Robinson's election helped to foster a more self-assured feminism. This confidence can be seen in development of a feminist cultural critique that is in dialogue with, rather than merely in debt to, international feminist debates. Groups such as Women Against Imperialism anticipated the evolution of post-colonial theory in Ireland. Literary and cultural critics have subjected Irish culture to a variety of feminist readings that have been particularly attentive to the 'double colonisation' of Irish women. This trope has made numerous appearances in contemporary creative writing by women, of which there has been something of an explosion in the last fifteen years. There have also been productive comparisons between Irish writing and writing from former British colonies in Africa and India; whilst membership of the European Union has drawn attention to parallels in the experience of Irish women and women in regions such as the Basque country, southern Italy, Wales, Greece, and, more recently, in eastern Europe. These European analogies have been highlighted by the numbers of migrants and asylum seekers coming to Ireland from Romania, Albania and the former Yugoslavia.

These various frameworks have contributed to the development of current interests and concerns in Irish feminism. In the last ten years there has been a growth of interest in traditional forms of knowledge. This has involved a renewed commitment to the Irish language and to folklore and the oral tradition, but has also stimulated an interest in collecting and representing women's narratives, in facilitating groups that have had difficulty in gaining access to the public sphere – travellers, the economic underclasses, sex workers, survivors of violence, lone parents, recent immigrants – to develop and present their own interpretations of their needs and objectives. Contemporary feminism offers a fairly robust critique of the urban, professional, post-feminist women who are most visible in the media, and tends to celebrate the knowledge and skills of an older generation of 'oppressed' women, observing the resourcefulness with which they negotiated their oppression. Servants, sex-workers, single parents and travellers are now the typical protagonists of literature and cinema. Sentimental attitudes to the representation of poverty and marginality are not necessarily producing a more generous society, however, according to the testimonies of minority communities both old and new.

In the North, where feminism could never even temporarily evade or bracket the national question, there is a women's political party (although in 2004 it currently holds no seats), paralleling the earlier unsuccessful women's peace movement of the 1970s and 1980s. There has been much greater exploration in the North of the umbrella or coalition models, in which women retain special issue identities within federations that share resources and search for affiliations.

Women writers, artists, film-makers and critics have been more obviously prominent and successful in the last ten years than for many decades previously, but they continue to have very limited institutional power. There are very few feminist critics prominent in Irish universities and women artists continue to have difficulty in attracting support for large-budget projects. This institutional weakness may yet have long-term consequences for the development of an indigenous feminist theory: the recent growth in diaspora studies, particularly in the United States, could produce a useful dialogue between Irish feminism and its Irish-American counterpart, but that dialogue will be less useful if the ground is yielded for American interests to dominate the agenda.

It is not easy to identify the most crucial issues for feminism at the start of the twenty-first century, especially as they may emerge from grassroots movements. Much has been accomplished in terms of equality legislation in the last twenty years, but attitudes and practices have not been so clearly reformed. Ireland's relative economic prosperity in this period has encouraged feminists to argue more about international responsibilities and globalisation. Arguments about pornography and prostitution, for example, need to be rethought in terms of new migrations and new technologies. Feminism could take the lead in thinking through the opportunities offered to Ireland as it becomes a more multicultural society through new immigration, but in other European countries this issue has been a source of deep division amongst feminists. Some people argue that the proper role of feminism in immigration debates is to demand that women newly arrived, from Muslim countries for example (almost always the example), should be empowered to take up the more equal distribution of rights between the genders in Western Europe, and that this is best accomplished through a model of assimilation. The exemplary immigrant should adopt European customs, practices and languages and thereby experience a form of liberation. The feminist investment in this argument is made acute through concern for the oppression of non-Western women. A counter-argument proposes that the foundation of feminism is resistance to oppression and discrimination, and that the immediate crisis caused by immigration into Ireland is the rise of racism. Feminism should first oppose racism, and since the assimilation model both panders to racism and xenophobia, and also dictates to women what freedoms they should want, rather than responding to their demands, it should be treated with caution.

Language might well be a key issue here. While all European countries are multilingual, Ireland has bilingualism more deeply inscribed into theories of national identity than some other nations. Feminists working in the Irish language have long argued that the Irish language is an important feminist issue, as is the fate of all minority languages. Minority languages are often mother-tongues, primarily used in the home rather than in the public sphere, and their position in society may be understood as analogous to the position of women. In recent years there has been a significant popular revival of the Irish language, particularly as a medium for educating children. A new constituency of young activists identifies the Irish language as one site of resistance to the homogenising aspects of the European Union and of wider globalisation. Irish feminism is turning to the promotion of a multilingualism that includes Irish, English and the new immigrant languages, rather than to assimilation, as a way of enabling new forms of citizenship. In the 1960s Irish travellers were forced into settlement by the state, but far from promoting assimilation, this assault on their indigenous culture exposed them to new forms of racism, impoverishment and exclusion. Then, Irish feminism failed adequately to defend minority rights: now is the time to engage in that defence.

Notes

1. Máirín Nic Eoin, *B'ait Leo Bean: Gnéithe den Idé-eolaíocht Inscne i d'Traidisiún Liteartha na Gaeilge* (Dublin: An Clóchomhar, 1998). Translation by Máirín Nic Eoin. Reprinted in *The Field Day Anthology*, vol. V, pp. 1576–7. Máirín Nic Eoin's original text reads as follows: 'Ní fhéadfaí a mhaíomh go raibh ceannas polaitiúil ná cultúrtha ag aicme ar bith de phobal na Gaelige ón seachtú haois déag ar aghaidh, mar shampla. Mar sin féin, is cinnte go raibh ceannairí cultúrtha ag an bpobal sin agus go raibh gnéithe den idé-eolaíocht réamhchoilíneach fós á gcraobhscaoileadh acu. Tá an chosúlacht ar an scéal gur mar chosaint ar a n-ionad féin mar bhaill speisialta d'aicme a bhí faoi chois a chuir filí agus aos liteartha na Gaeilge tuiscintí áirithe maidir le hidirdhealuithe inscne chun cinn le fórsa is le fuinneamh sa seachtú, san ochtú is sa naoú haois déag, nuair ba mhó a bhí gnéithe den chultúr dúchasach faoi bhrú is faoi léigear' (*Field Day Anthology*, vol. V, p. 1570).

2. *The Triumph of Prudence Over Passion; or, The History of Miss Mortimer and Miss Fitzgerald*. By the Authoress of Emeline. 2 vols. (Dublin: Stephen Colbert, 1781), vol. I, p. 125.

3. Úna Ní Fhaircheallaigh, *Smuainte Ar Árainn* (1902). Translated by Bríona Nic Dhiarmada. Reprinted in *The Field Day Anthology of Irish Writing*, vol. V, pp. 1047–8. Bríona Nic Dhiarmada's original text reads as follows: 'Bhíodh na cailíní ag teacht isteach gach Domhnach go dtí an chraobh do Chonnradh na Gaedhilge do cuireadh ar bun le haghaidh na bhfear. Níor bh'fhada gur ghabh fonn foghlumtha na Ghaedhilge go mór iad, agus go dtáinig éad orra fa gan chraobh do'n Chonnradh do bheith aca dhóibh féin. Tugadh misneach dhóibh 'n-a thaoibh sin agus do b'é adubhairt ceann aca' 'Béidh craobh ághainn anois dúinn féin gan bhuidheachas do na fearaibh' (*Field Day Anthology*, vol. V, p. 1047).

4. Cumann na mBan, *Manifesto* (1914). Reprinted in *The Field Day Anthology*, vol. V, pp. 103–4.

5. Ruth Taillon and Diane Urquhart, 'Introduction to women, politics and the state in Northern Ireland, 1918–66', in *The Field Day Anthology*, vol. V, pp. 353–4.

6. James Douglas, *The Unpardonable Sin* (London, 1907).

7. Margaret O'Callaghan, 'Introduction to women and politics in independent Ireland, 1921–68', in *The Field Day Anthology*, vol. V, pp. 120–34 (125).

8. Archbishops and Bishops of Ireland, Maynooth Statement, 6 October (1925). Reprinted in *The Field Day Anthology*, vol. V, p. 154.

9. Article forty-one of the Constitution of Ireland, 1937. Reprinted in *The Field Day Anthology*, vol. V, p. 330.

10. Margaret O'Callaghan, 'Introduction to women and politics in independent Ireland, 1921–68', in *The Field Day Anthology*, vol. V, pp. 120–34.

11. See June Levine, 'The Women's Movement in the Republic of Ireland, 1968–80'. Reprinted in *The Field Day Anthology*, vol. V, pp. 177–87.

12. Mags O'Brien, *Divorce? Facing the Issues of Marital Breakdown* (Dublin: Attic Press, 1995). Reprinted in *The Field Day Anthology*, vol. V, p. 273.

Further reading

Angela Bourke, *The Burning of Bridget Cleary: A True Story* (London: Pimlico Press, 1999)

Angela Bourke, Siobhán Kilfeather, Maria Luddy, Margaret MacCurtain, Gerardine Meaney, Máirín Ní Dhonnchadha, Mary O'Dowd and Clair Wills (eds.), *The Field Day Anthology of Irish Writing, Volumes 4 and 5: Irish Women's Writings and Traditions* (Cork: Cork University Press in association with Field Day, 2002)

Linda Connolly, *The Irish Women's Movement: From Revolution to Devolution* (Basingstoke: Palgrave, 2001)

Margaret Kelleher and James H. Murphy (eds.), *Gender Perspectives in Nineteenth-Century Ireland: Public and Private Spheres* (Dublin: Irish Academic Press, 1997)

Susan Knight, *Where the Grass is Greener: Voices of Immigrant Women in Ireland* (Dublin: Oak Tree Press, 2001)

Maria Luddy and Cliona Murphy (eds.), *Women Surviving: Studies in Irish Women's History in the 19th and 20th Centuries* (Dublin: Poolbeg Press, 1990)

Margaret MacCurtain and Mary O'Dowd (eds.), *Women in Early Modern Ireland* (Edinburgh: Edinburgh University Press, 1991)

Máirín Nic Eoin, *B'ait Leo Bean: Gnéithe den Idé-eolaíocht Inscne i d'Traidisiún Liteartha na Gaeilge* (Dublin: An Clóchomhar, 1998)

Ailbhe Smyth (ed.), *The Abortion Papers* (Dublin: Attic Press, 1992)

Margaret Ward, *Unmanageable Revolutionaries: Women in Irish Nationalism* (London: Pluto, 1995)

MARY J. HICKMAN

7

Migration and diaspora

Introduction

Irish migration in the nineteenth century is one of the most significant movements of population in modern European history, in terms of the total number of people involved and the proportion migrating. Between 1801 and 1921 (the period of Union with Britain), approximately 8 million people left Ireland. Ireland's contribution to the outflow of approximately 44 million people from Europe between 1821 and 1914 was the largest of any other country, relative to the size of the island's population. In the twentieth century, outward migration continued; but it was marked by two periods of very heavy out-migration, the 1950s and the second half of the 1980s, and by two periods of net inward migration, the 1970s and the second half of the 1990s. These patterns reached a point in Ireland such that, for all but the eldest son and sometimes daughter, emigration was a life event as 'normal' as leaving school or getting married. Altogether in the period 1949–89 800,000 people left Ireland. There are two consequences following this sustained emigration over the past two centuries. One is that at any one time a significant proportion of people alive who were born in Ireland were living abroad. The second is that there are many millions of people across the globe who are of Irish descent and who can claim an Irish heritage and identity should they so wish.

In terms of numbers received the two most important destinations for Irish migrants have been Britain and the United States of America. In the nineteenth century, almost 80 per cent of the huge outflow crossed the Atlantic. After 1920, however, there was an almost complete reorientation of these patterns, so that, overall, 80 per cent settled in Britain during the rest of the twentieth century. Australia is also an important destination, because while at most 5 per cent of Irish migrants in the nineteenth century went to Australia, they formed 25 per cent of the settler population in that country; since the 1950s there has continued to be a small but notable on-going movement to Australia. These settlements, and other significant destinations such as Canada, South Africa and New Zealand and increasingly the rest of the European Union, form the basis of any discussion about an Irish diaspora. My aim here is to indicate the complexity of the issues in understanding these movements and settlements and their contemporary relevance.

Migration and diaspora are closely interlinked. The contemporary currency of the term diaspora begs the question: do all migrations produce diasporas? For some diaspora theorists, the answer would be in the negative, because only a forced migration creates the requisite conditions. Many historians of ethnic groups would argue that unless an immigrant group's position was correlated with social disadvantage, then an assimilatory trajectory ensures that 'the homeland' remains of only residual interest. There are reasons to question both these conclusions. On the one hand, all exit streams are heterogeneous in social composition, resulting in diverse motives and decisions to migrate within the same time span. This entails heterogeneous diasporas from the moment of inception. On the other hand, the assimilation paradigm ignores the extent to which being ethnic and being diasporan can be mutually constitutive on settlement elsewhere. In this chapter, I consider Irish migration and diaspora from 1800 onwards. I commence by summarising the main theoretical approaches to analysis of diasporas prior to discussing how certain themes as applied to the study of the Irish diaspora might illuminate the internal dynamic and tensions between migration and immigration, 'being diasporan' and 'being ethnic'. A final section deals with Irish diaspora identities and contemporary multiculturalisms.

Defining diaspora

There are broadly two approaches to defining diaspora: a traditional paradigm which sees diaspora as produced by some form of coercion that leads to the uprooting and resettlement outside the boundaries of the homeland of large numbers of people; and a post-modern reading of diaspora by anthropologists and cultural critics, which sees it as expressing modes of 'hybrid' consciousness and identity. In the traditional account, derived from the Jewish diaspora, six features are significant: dispersal, collective memory, alienation, respect and longing for the homeland, a belief in its restoration, and self-definition in terms of this homeland.[1] Since the late 1960s, broader definitions of diaspora have emerged in this tradition; and diaspora has come to be used for a wide range of dispersions of populations: expatriates, expellees, political refugees, alien residents, immigrants and ethnic and racial minorities.

In its post-modern version, the hallmark of diasporic experience is a process of unsettling, recombination and hybridisation.[2] One consequence is that a diasporic space is created that transgresses the boundaries of ethnicity and nationalism. In his study of *The Black Atlantic*, Paul Gilroy observes that diaspora provides a 'third space', or alternate public sphere, which allows for both identification outside, and permanent living inside, the national time-space. This 'post-modern' version of diaspora emphasises that what distinguishes a diasporic community is its sense of being a 'people' with historical roots and destinies outside the time-space of the 'host' nation. Avtar Brah argues that diaspora-space marks the intersectionality of the transmigration of people, capital and culture, and therefore diasporic identities are at once local and global. All those who inhabit diaspora space – whether 'indigenous' or 'immigrants' – are subject to transformation. The concept of diaspora space thus takes account of the entanglements of genealogies of 'dispersal' with those of 'staying put', so that the 'nativised subject' is rendered as much a diasporian as the diasporic subject is nativised. All parties to an encounter are deeply marked by it, albeit differently depending upon the specific configurations of power mobilised by the encounter, and the differential impact of asymmetries of power on different social groups.[3]

In recent years, perhaps as a result of the exponential increase in the use of the term diaspora, attempts have been made to produce typologies of diaspora. For example, Robin Cohen distinguishes five different categories of diaspora: victim, labour, imperial, cultural and trade. Cohen's categorisation of the Irish diaspora is as one of the classic 'victim' diasporas, based on the trauma of the Great Famine of the 1840s, the size of migration between 1845 and 1852, and the extent to which recent post-revisionist scholarship has demonstrated that the British government had a hidden agenda of population control, designed to facilitate the modernisation of agriculture and land reform. In Cohen's view, all of these aspects closely connect Irish patterns to those that propelled the

Jewish, African and Armenian diasporas.[4] This is a convincing account of the development of the Irish diaspora in the middle of the nineteenth century, a period in which the primary destination of Irish peasant migration was the United States of America. However, given the volume and longevity of Irish migration, the typology of diasporas Cohen advances could just as well provide the means of differentiating discrete phases of the Irish migrant stream during the past 200 years, or of differentiating the displacement and placement of distinctive social groups among those emigrating from Ireland at any one time.

In a recent overview of the diaspora literature, Pnina Werbner critiques typologies of diaspora that list approaches according to whether their stress is on the empirical realities of ethno-transnational connections or on questions of diasporic consciousness and subjectivity. She argues that these divisions serve to separate analytically what needs to be read as mutually constitutive: in her view, diasporic culture is always both materially inscribed and organisationally embodied. Werbner instead points to a growing consensus that diasporas are characterised by social heterogeneity, that they are historical formations in process and that they encompass a dual orientation: to fight for citizenship and equal rights in the place of settlement, alongside continuing efforts to foster transnational relations. She critiques the post-modern versions of diaspora for marginalising the continued imbrication of diasporas in nationalist rhetoric and for underplaying the continued significance of attachments to a place of origin and/or collective historical truama for the late modern organisation of diasporas. In Werbner's view, diasporas are both ethnic-parochial and cosmopolitan. The challenge is 'to disclose how the tension between these two tendencies is played out in actual situations'.[5]

How can these different ways of defining diaspora enhance discussion of the Irish diaspora? And how can analysis of the Irish diaspora contribute to this general discussion? On the one hand, it might be shown how the Irish, upon migration, have a set of features deemed to distinguish diasporic formations in one typology or another. On the other hand, it is possible to establish whether the post-modern concept of diaspora offers fruitful possibilities for analysing the experiences of a global dispersion of people who identify as Irish. Both these approaches would yield valuable material on the Irish diaspora, especially if they encouraged comparative research rather than the more usual single-country focus.[6] Alternatively, we could explore the possibility of constructing an explanatory framework which allows us to expand on

Werbner's observation about diasporas as historical formations in process, changing over time and responding to the different political and social contexts in which their members find themselves. This seems the most fluid approach as it allows for multivariation across space and time, and is the method I adopt in what follows.

This chapter suggests further analysis of the Irish diaspora as a historical formation in process might usefully revolve around two organising themes: first, the importance of 'the Irish' in constructing ethnic, racial, religious, gender and class hierarchies in societies of settlement and, second, the multitrajectories of Irish immigrants in different nation-state contexts and their positionings within the diaspora. The first theme subjects assimilation arguments to interrogation while the second involves unpacking the enagagement of a heterogeneous diaspora with various nineteenth-century industrialising and nation-building contexts and with globalisation and various multiculturalisms in the twentieth century. Engaging with both these themes entails examining the impact of the presence of particular diasporic groups on formative moments or processes in the development or re-formulation of nation states and in the transition from one economic mode to another. It also focuses on the framing that those processes give to the subsequent trajectories of immigrant groups and their descendants. I am separating these themes for analytical purposes, but it should be clear that they are closely connected. In studying the Irish diaspora these processes can be perceived through the lens of the 'invention' of one important element in the populations that contributed to the history and formation of the United States of America, Britain and Australia. The story is different in each case.

Diaspora, race, ethnicity and the nation-state

How can we conceptualise the constitution, trajectories and survival of ethnic identities of Irish migrants within specific nation-state contexts and place these analyses in a diasporic context? What has been the role of contestations over Irish identities in the historical formation of the 'nation' in each of these major places of settlement for Irish emigrants? What have been the roles of different groups of Irish migrants in constructing or contesting the dominant lines of social cleavage in each of these societies? This entails analysing the intersectionality of Irish immigration with: class and the particular ethno-racial regime which developed in Britain; race and ethnic hierarchies in the United States; and with constructions of ethno-national identity and the marginalisation of indigenous peoples in Australia. Is it possible that diasporic identities were constituted in ways that challenged rather than reinscribed hegemonic power relations?

Contemporary research about the Irish diaspora uses the concept of assimilation as the standard framework within which to understand the trajectory of Irish experiences since the mid-nineteenth century. The focus is rather more often on how the Irish were assimilated than on whether the evidence about the Irish informs us about the adequacy or inadequacy of the assimilation paradigm. The accepted orthodoxy is that the disadvantages and discrimination Irish people experienced in Britain hindered the process of assimilation there to some degree, but that this can be contrasted with Irish 'success' in all the other major destinations, especially the United States of America. Underpinning this assumption is the idea that (except for the peculiarities of the British context) the Irish benefited from being a white, English-speaking people as part of the outflows from Europe in the nineteenth century. This perspective fails to recognise the differently constituted elements within the Irish diaspora and homogenises the largest constituent element of that body: Irish working-class Catholics, who on settlement in nineteenth-century Britain and America were identified as 'the Irish'.

To illustrate the complexity of these questions, I will examine an aspect of the first of my two themes: the importance of the category of 'the Irish' in constructing ethnic, racial, religious and class hierarchies in societies of settlement (the historical research on the gendered aspects of these processes is still too scanty to afford much confidence in including it in this analysis). In particular I want to focus on the significance of populations constructed as 'Irish' for the (re)establishment of the central social cleavage and mode of nation building in both the United States of America and Britain. The processes of ethnic and racial formation involved are linked to the evolution of hegemony, unpacking the way in which societies are organised and ruled.

United States of America

Nineteenth-century migration from Ireland to the United States of America is seen as fulfilling the criteria of a classic 'diaspora'. Irish immigrants arrived during a century in which the United States of America became a post-slavery society, at a time when the racial differentiations cleaving America were reconfigured after the civil war and a bifurcated hierarchy emerged: 'race shifted from being slavery's justification to being its replacement'.[7] It was also the century in which an ethnic hierarchy was established which classified categories of white immigrant labour in terms of their qualifications to belong to the republic. Ideas of race and processes of racialisation were central to the vicissitudinous patterns that resulted. Although the Irish in nineteenth-century America have been subject to considerable analysis, both in respect of the positioning of Irish immigrants in terms of the racial divide and of the ethnic hierarchy, these accounts have mostly been driven by the concerns of ethnic historiography or new labour history, rather than providing an overview of the relationship between these different processes.

Richard Williams examines how the Irish immigrants in antebellum America were moved from being a lower race (Irish and Catholic as opposed to English and Protestant) into the lower slot of the upper race (Irish and white as opposed to African and black). As unskilled workers, Irish immigrants in the nineteenth century occupied the lowest slot within the free labour system, a position understood in terms of their ethnicity. Williams suggests that through a parallel process to the creation of race 'a segment of Irish society became identified as the Irish in the United States'.[8] The creation of an Irish ethnic identity (a group of individuals with a specific social value, as reflected in stereotypes) in the United States, he argues, was similar to the process by which a sector of the African population became black.

Dale Knobel describes how an Irish stereotype gestated in America in the late antebellum period. Not solely derived from anti-Catholicism or borrowed from notions of the 'wild Irish' held in England, the Irish stereotype of this period was shaped strongly by prevailing popularised understandings of character, ethnicity and nationality. The late antebellum stereotype drew boundaries, as Knobel writes,

> not just between native-born and foreign, Protestant and Catholic, well-educated and ill, but between Celt and Saxon (or, more to the point, Anglo-American), setting the Irish outside the pale of 'true' Americanism much more thoroughly and finally than the other principal white ethnic minorities in the United States.[9]

Thus, the antebellum Irish stereotype represented the character and condition of one rapidly accumulating element of the immigrant population as borne in the blood and resistant to improvement. In contrast,

Anglo-American blood, it was vouchsafed, guaranteed the United States a fundamental unity that could never be fully fractured. Knobel charts the transition from this antebellum stereotype which treated the Irish 'almost as an alien "race"'[10] to their re-racialisation, patchily commenced during the civil war and continuing through the 1860s, as part of a white Anglo-Celtic racial majority. Knobel connects this process of re-racialisation with the concomitant efforts of civil war science to assert the adaptability of all white blood to 'true' Americanism, the corollary being the inadaptability of all black blood. In effect, whatever their legal status, blacks still lacked the nature that qualified them to be 'true' Americans. The Irish stereotype did not disappear and, according to Knobel, was still capable of generating inter-ethnic hostility but this was now ethno-cultural in character rather than racial. It should be added, however, that the drawing of boundaries along lines of ethnicity forms a terrain in which processes of racialisation can still be generated.

A number of authors in the United States have studied the ways in which race was central to the formation of an American working class. This has included the analysis of the Irish in the United States of America as the first immigrant group to provide unskilled free white manual labour. David Roediger's proposition in the early 1990s, that 'Working class formation and the systematic development of a sense of whiteness went hand in hand for the US white working class', was a catalyst for this debate.[11] Roediger also emphasises the role of the Democratic Party, that 'alliance of slaveholders, financiers, and white labourers',[12] and its bid to build a northern power base as a critical factor in the 'whitening' of the Irish. Kevin Kenny challenges historians who argue that the Irish 'opted for' or 'chose' whiteness in order to deliberately distance themselves from African-Americans and advance themselves socially. He thinks this argument overestimates the degree of conscious agency involved rather than seeking the explanation in part in the structure that determined individual actions. Kenny argues that the American Irish did not create the social and racial hierarchy of the society into which they immigrated and they cannot be expected to have overturned this hierarchy in the course of earning their livelihoods. Furthermore, he cites many Irish immigrants who acted to promote racial justice and social reform.[13] Although Kenny's caution as to the specific relationship of agency and structure in this context is worth heeding, there is a danger of seeming to posit a static view of the relationship that does not appear to embrace the notion of an historical formation in process.

Kenny considers that one source of Irish-American racism was that Irish immigrants were themselves 'racialised' as inferior in social practice and popular stereotype and faced abundant discrimination. This may have made their claims to 'whiteness' all the more assertive. Irish immigrants were, however, eligible for citizenship after a five-year waiting period, and when they became citizens male Irishmen could vote. The point is, argues Kenny, that there are degrees of racial discrimination, and that racism cannot be understood at the level of cultural stereotype alone; the perspectives of labour, politics and citizenship laws must also be added to the picture. Kenny's proposition is not entirely convincing, however. Are we examining degrees of racial discrimination or different processes of racialisation that had their own specificity? In particular, what has to be accounted for is the consolidation of two hierarchies, with one fundamentally underpinning the existence of the other. The category of race helped to manage the phenomenon of ex-slaves, as definitions of blackness (one drop of blood) created a seemingly unassailable positioning for whites in the race hierarchy. However, differentiations within whiteness were manifold and were generated from the varied ethnicities of immigrant populations.

The change in the positioning of the Irish after the civil war is usually related to the coming of later immigrant groups not to the changes wrought by emancipation and processes of re-racialisation. The ethnicised hierarchy of the white population installed by the post-bellum period had its own determinations. What it afforded was a mode of classifying and regulating an expanding immigrant labour force. At the same time it opened a route to Americanisation, although this was a far from straightforward process. The arrival of new immigrant groupings in the second half of the nineteenth century was therefore the terrain upon which the re-racialisation of the Irish as ethnic (now with a positive connotation) was confirmed. After all, Roediger's argument is that ethnicity was not an option in the antebellum period (because of nativist campaigns), so the Irish had to position themselves within the dominant racial group. This was hotly contested until the postbellum period, as traced above. Subsequently, the Irish played a critical role in the process of 'becoming American' for other immigrant groups, to the point that incorporation amounted almost to an Irish version of being American (especially true in northern cities).[14]

Kenny's work usefully sets the discussion in a diasporan context. He cites the dynamics of Irish society in the eighteenth and nineteenth centuries, with its religious sectarianism and segregation, as providing an important background and argues that the Irish immigrants arriving in nineteenth-century America came equipped with a notion of group solidarity and a familiarity with militant force that translated easily into racism and violence. The battles they fought over identity in the United States were similar to the ones they and their ancestors had fought in Ireland and thus many of them 'turned to racial politics and even violence in America as though it was the natural state of affairs'.[15] In fact, as Kenny himself points out, significant numbers did not turn to racial politics and violence. In addition, most of the research about the Irish and whiteness is based on histories of Irish male immigrants; given the distinctiveness of the Irish immigrant stream in the post-Famine period as made up more evenly of single men and women than any other European immigration to the United States we need more thorough investigation about the gendered patterns of these interactions. What all of this suggests is that a more complex mapping of origins, differentiations and contexts is required in order for us to be able to ascertain the heterogeneous positionings of Irish America in general and within the group constructed as 'the Irish', that is Irish working-class Catholic immigrants.

A general argument about incoming European immigrants in the United States is that they were subject to the parallel processes of assimilation and nationalisation, going through various stages *en route* to becoming American. The literature on whiteness has been a necessary corrective to most of the previous theories about the Irish in the United States, which assessed assimilation mostly in terms of such a staged movement from a position of militant Irish nationalism, through ethnic nationalism and dual nationality towards becoming American. It is perhaps more fruitful to consider these as the dual processes of becoming American and participation in a diaspora (both of which inevitably change over time). Without a diaspora, for example, it is arguable that outrage at the imprisonment of Young Irelanders or the Fenians would not have had political effect. The stagist approach (with its notion of an assimilatory trajectory) may however obscure the extent to which, simultaneously, from the moment of arrival, an individual or group experiences both processes – that is, they are becoming something else in a diasporic and a specific nation-state context. These processes are not necessarily experienced as either contradictory or antagonistic although they can be. My point on simultaneity is that being diasporan informs being ethnic, just as being positioned as ethnic informs being diasporan.

Many might argue that it is the longevity of Irish nationalism amongst Irish Americans that has to be explained rather than its disappearance. I will return to this point in the final section.

Britain

American scholarship on migration and whiteness has been conducted with reference to the intersection of racialisation processes and the construction of particular ethnicities. In Britain, however, with rare exceptions,[16] discussions of whiteness operate as an extension of class analysis rather than as the deconstruction of a racialised category. For example, Alistair Bonnett cites the presence of Irish immigrants in the metropolitan centre in nineteenth-century Britain as indicative that whiteness may not be solely about the racial ordering of the working class, but simultaneously restores and privileges the class axis by arguing that middle-class alienation was founded on fears of the 'urban poor' far more than 'immigrants' at that time.[17] This failure to deal with submerged ethnicities within 'whiteness' is a feature of histories of Britain.

By the beginning of the nineteenth century, accelerating industrialisation, rapid urbanisation, colonial expansion, increasing immigration and the development of a more complex state apparatus were the context for nationalisation and civilisation strategies within Britain. A code of breeding was cemented that enabled the alliance of the new hybrid élite (aristocracy and industrial capital) and different national élites (English, Welsh, Scots and the Anglo-Irish Protestant ascendancy). Positioned as members of a superior island race, this code enabled the English/British to classify and hierarchise all human beings.

At different times in the nineteenth century, therefore, the English working class were designated by the ruling class as 'a different breed' or an uncivilised 'race', but in other circumstances, as a constituent part of the English (British) 'race'. As Robert Miles comments:

> The result was a racialized nationalism or a nationalist racism, a mercurial ideological bloc that was manipulated by the ruling class (or rather by different fractions of it) to legitimate the exploitation of inferior 'races' in the colonies, to explain economic and political struggles with other European nation states, and to signify (for example) Irish and Jewish migrants as an undesirable 'racial' presence within Britain.[18]

Ideas of race and hierarchy were, therefore, a constant feature of much of the public discourse in the domestic arena as well as in various parts of the empire.[19] Immigrants with political demands came to be identified with an invasive and highly contagious virus, which must be isolated if the body politic was to survive. It is important to note that this distinction between immigrants and the indigenous population powerfully combined elements of class and 'racial' signification, because as an ideology it had to be the basis of a nation-state underpinned both by class and ethno-national differentiations. The two arenas of differentiation intermesh; calls to the national interest mask class relations and debates about the primacy of socio-economic divisions mask important ethno-racial or ethno-national hierarchies.

In Britain, Irish immigrants filled certain niches in the labour market. The Irish Catholics amongst them were, however, stygmatised, both because of the historical relationship between Britain and Ireland and because they represented a threatening 'other' in class-divided British cities. The boundaries of the nation which were socially constructed to bind together different classes of Protestants in Britain did not accommodate Catholics easily, even after Catholic Emancipation in 1829. Thus, although they were formally citizens of the state in the nineteenth century, Irish Catholics were not imagined as part of the nation in the same way. Dichotomies of race and nationality were constantly conflated in commentaries about the Irish. The national characteristics which separated and raised the British above the people they colonised – their economic pre-eminence, Protestantism and 'way of life' – always depended on the proof of difference. In the scientific register of the code of breeding which developed in Victorian England, the Irish were made unconsciously to represent a missing evolutionary link between the 'bestiality' of black slaves and that of the English worker. Further, the Irish living in British cities were cited as evidence of the 'missing link' between the gorilla and the Negro.

In the nineteenth century anti-Catholicism was ingrained amongst all social groupings in Britain and was significantly intertwined with anti-Irish hostility. In cultural terms anti-Catholicism remained the sentiment which most clearly defined the nation and the decades that followed emancipation were a period of resurgent anti-Catholicism.[20] Further, the popular discourse of the Protestant nation intersected with anti-Irish sentiment and helped define where the danger to the nation lay.[21] These fears were made manifest in the shape of Irish immigrants, who were perceived as threatening the union of church and state, which was the embodiment of 'the English people'.[22] In Britain, an ethno-religious hierarchy paralleled and intersected with a class hierarchy, and both were underpinned by processes of racialisation in the course of producing national subjects. The resuscitation of anti-Catholicism after emancipation is not dissimilar, in some respects, to the expanding significance of modes of racial thinking in Britain after slavery was abolished.

The discourses generated about the Irish both at national and local levels in the 1830s and 1840s differentiated them as immigrants from the rest of the working class, and resulting discriminatory practices effectively segregated them. This can be seen by examining how Catholic schools came to be state funded. The context of the establishment of state-funded Catholic education in 1847 was the Famine immigration from Ireland. The government pushed the funding of Catholic schools through parliament against considerable opposition. Their articulated motivation was the harm that would accrue to the Protestant nation if the children of Irish Roman Catholics were to be 'as at present, ignorant, sensual and revolutionary infidels'.[23] They were also responding to objections that were voiced about the presence of the children of Irish Catholic immigrants in the same schools as other working-class children.[24] The objections centred on a fear of 'contamination' from the children of Irish Catholic immigrants who were problematised as a social and political threat.[25]

A peculiar process of segregation and involution therefore took place. The children of Irish Catholic immigrants were set aside in their own church schools. Catholicism was equated with culture and became the main way of 'being Irish' in the public domain. Catholicism became increasingly respectable and remained an anglicised institution, so that beginning as an agent of segregation, the church eventually became one of incorporation. The school was therefore a site where the identities of people with Irish-born parents were contested. The aim of the government and the intention of the Catholic church was that Catholicism would be the cement to bind Irish Catholic migrants to their subordinated place in the nation. One consequence was the masking of Irishness both within official discourse and for the children of working-class Irish Catholic immigrants. Catholic schools held up a mirror to their pupils in which their Catholicity was reflected rather than their Irishness.

The most important effect of these strategies was that many Irish people maintained a low profile (outside Irish areas) about being Irish and about Irish national issues. The partial success of the incorporatist strategy of the church, therefore, lay in its being the agency of a low public profile for the Irish in Britain, frequently misrecognised as a process of assimilation. The private sphere of the family and sometimes local communities provided other sources of identifications and were also the sites where the Irish elements of children's identities were more likely to be expressed. It is in these locations that processes of denationalisation and incorporation have been variously resisted, transgressed, sidelined, accommodated or embraced. The process of incorporation is never total, however, and is typically characterised by instability and incompleteness.

Issues about the integration and segregation of an ethnic minority were, therefore, of crucial significance in shaping the development of the British education system in the nineteenth century. Within the Enlightenment, education was the means by which 'man' was perfectible and thus schooling was to confer access to civilisation. Education was, therefore, central to the construction of modernity. The racialised discourse which ensured that Irish Catholic children were not educated with other working-class children established an ethnically segregated, religiously distinctive, state education system with far-reaching consequences for both the Irish Catholic children educated within Catholic schools and those educated in the rest of the sector.[26]

Perhaps one of the important differences between the United States and Britain in the nineteenth century was that the social construction of whiteness as a unifying concept across class and ethnic demarcations for European immigrant groups was critical for the formation not only of the working class in America, but for the basis of the whole society. The nation was produced in tandem with this process of assimilation. In Britain, on the other hand, it was the social construction of a national ideology of Britishness/Englishness and the colonial enterprise which was crucial for underpinning class alliances and for shaping the particular ethno-racial regime that developed. Studying the Irish in the United States and Britain illuminates both nation-building contexts, facilitates comparison across the diaspora, elucidates differences in ethno-racial regimes in each country and is suggestive of the ways in which a diasporic context remained significant for Irish migrants and their descendants.

Diasporan identities and contemporary multiculturalisms

It is important to examine the relationship between the 'invention' of 'the Irish' in the nineteenth century and the persistence of Irish identities in the contemporary period. One response to the persistence of ethnic identifications has been the suggestion that people of Irish descent are just availing themselves of an ethnic option in an era in which such identifications have acquired some leverage. Further, it might be suggested that the Irish are 'tailing' on the struggles of other ethnic communities to gain recognition in the public sphere. I think these arguments can be simplistic. Groupings constituted as Irish have responded to the transition to official discourses of multiculturalism by a resurgence of Irish identifications, activities and organisations, but in complex and varied ways (for example, in the United States in the 1960s/1970s after Civil Rights, in the 1980s in Australia and in the 1990s in Britain).

There is now a general assumption that the term 'symbolic' best describes the relationship to ethnicity of white ethnic groups in the United States. Mary Waters argues that with the achievement of middle-class surburban status, ethnicity becomes a lifestyle option, a costless form of community. But when ethnicity is correlated with class disadvantages, a more complex phenomenon emerges. Waters argues that this is primarily a function of the racial/colour divide in today's United States and, therefore, applies to African-Americans and racialised groups (e.g. Asian and Latino groups) amongst the post-1965 migrants to the United States.[27] In fact, ethnicity does not necessarily remain solely symbolic for Irish Americans. Waters may miss this because she did not include any analysis of diasporic consciousness in her study and because she treats Irish Americans as a homogenous formation, in the process eliding internal differentiations based, for example, on social class and generation.

As Khachig Tölölyan comments, lines separating ethnic groups and diasporas are not clear cut. They shift in response to a complex dynamic.[28] Sometimes it is possible to describe individuals and communities as behaving as ethnics in one sphere of life, as diasporan in others and frequently as shifting from one to another. The distinguishing diasporan feature, he argues, tends to be the existence of a multitiered community, consisting of degrees of activism. Some evidence for this can be found in the Irish diaspora. The same community, therefore can contain, for example, ethnicised Irish Americans and committed disasporans; or, to borrow a distinction made by Paul Arthur, could include those with an awareness of diaspora and those with a consciousness of diaspora.[29] The continuing salience of social class for Irish Americans has been brought out in research in the past thirty years and this has been followed in the 1990s by biographies of working-class Irish Americans. These biographies portray working-class Irish Americans sympathetically but depict polarised relations with and towards local working-class African-American communities.[30] Surburban ethnic whiteness is not, therefore, the full story of the Irish in contemporary America. However, Irish America has largely conformed to the reinforcement of the race divide and new immigrants, particularly if in working-class jobs, very quickly learn where they stand in relation to the central race cleavage: 'A hostile posture toward resident blacks must be struck at the Americanizing door before it will open . . . Only when the lesson of racial estrangement is learned is assimilation complete.'[31]

Irish identities in England have had a very low profile. There has been a widespread assumption by academia, politicians and the public at large that twentieth-century Irish immigrants unproblematically assimilate into the 'white' population within a fairly short space of time and that their children are simply 'English'. The complexity of the experiences and positionings of Irish people in Britain are, therefore, not fully acknowledged in debates about a multicultural or multiethnic Britain. These complexities are charted by Breda Gray in research which reveals the positioning of Irish women in England as cultural 'outsiders' and racial 'insiders'. The women's accounts demonstrated the impossibility of meeting the criteria for cultural belonging in England and the unrealisability of a racial belonging based on looking 'white' when the Irish are culturally racialised.[32] There was a sharp debate in the 1980s and 1990s within Irish communities in Britain over whether to seek 'ethnic minority' status in governmental and public terms. Despite the subordinated positioning it involved, about 60 per cent of Irish when surveyed agreed with the designation.[33] Those who opposed it were either anxious about any raised profile for the Irish or were middle-class professional Irish immigrants who regarded notions of Irish stereotyping and discrimination as part of an outdated victim mentality. They took an ostensibly politically correct position that 'race'/racialisation did not apply to the Irish and in the process they firmly staked their claim to a racialised, de-ethnicised upper-middle-class élite positioning.

Conclusion

Economic rationalism may have taken the Irish to Britain, the United States of America and to various British dominions where they could maximise any advantages that accrued to them by knowing the English language and familiarity with British-derived institutions and procedures. However, in all these contexts Irish migrants encountered a political and cultural establishment that was British or British in origin and a common feature of all these diasporic contexts was that Irish ethnic identities were forged against anti-Irish stereotypes and as part of ongoing interaction with the 'homeland'. In the United States of America and in Australia, Irish Catholic migrants had opportunities (to varying degrees) to climb beyond subordinate positionings and were often keen to prove their loyalty to their new state of residence in the face of systematic questioners. In nineteenth-century Britain, Irish migrants neither necessarily had opportunities for advancement (though some did) nor necessarily wanted to prove their loyalty (although for some this was a concern). Proving loyalty to the state was, however, an overt objective of the Catholic church, the hierarchy of which was not taken over by the Irish. These arguments have largely been made about the groups who left Ireland and became part of Irish Catholic working-class communities in the expanding cities of the United States of America and Britain. This was the major, but by no means the only, migration from Ireland between 1800 and 1970.

My intention here has been to explore some of the ways in which we can understand the Irish diaspora as a historical formation in process. Even when restricting consideration to the groups who left Ireland and became part of Irish Catholic working-class communities elsewhere, it is a demonstrably heterogeneous formation. Much more research is required about the role of this part of the diaspora and others (for example, the role of Irish Protestants in eighteenth-century America in the creation of the republic) in order to fully assess the importance of 'the Irish' in constructing ethnic, racial, religious, gender and class hierarchies in societies of settlement and the multitrajectories of Irish immigrants in different nation-state contexts and their consequent positionings and identities. In addition, the complexities of the diasporic networks over these two centuries are only beginning to be traced. If this research agenda can be harnessed to the urgent task for interdisciplinary study of how Irish migration and diaspora shaped social, cultural, economic and political formation in Ireland itself, we might be well on the way to mapping the full significance of Irish migration and diaspora.

Notes

1. William Safran, 'Diasporas in modern societies: myths of homeland and return', *Diaspora* 1, 1 (1991), 83–99.

2. See James Clifford, 'Diasporas', *Cultural Anthropology* 9 (1994), 302–38; Paul Gilroy, *The Black Atlantic* (London: Verso, 1993); Stuart Hall, 'Cultural identity and diaspora', in *Identity: Continuity, Culture, Difference*, ed. Jonathan Rutherford (London: Lawrence and Wishart, 1990).

3. Avtar Brah, *Cartographies of Diaspora: Contesting Identities* (London and New York: Routledge, 1996).

4. See Robin Cohen, *Global Diasporas* (London: UCL Press, 1997) for a highly nuanced typology. See also Khachig Tölölyan, 'Rethinking diaspora(s): stateless power in the transnational moment', *Diaspora* 5, 1 (1996), 3–36.

5. Pnina Werbner, 'The materiality of diaspora: between aesthetic and "real" politics', *Diaspora* 9, 1 (2000), 5–20.

6. A significant exception is Donald Harman Akenson, *The Irish Diaspora* (Belfast: Institute of Irish Studies, The Queen's University, 1993).

7. Patrick Wolfe, 'Race and racialisation: some thoughts', *Postcolonial Studies* 5, 1 (2002), 51–62 (58).

8. Richard Williams, *Hierarchical Structures and Social Value: The Creation of Black and Irish Identities in the United States* (Cambridge: Cambridge University Press, 1990), p. 100.

9. Dale T. Knobel, *Paddy and the Republic: Ethnicity and Nationality in Antebellum America* (Middleton, CT: Wesleyan University Press, 1986), pp. 166–7.

10. Ibid., p. 169.

11. David R. Roediger, *The Wages of Whiteness: Race and the Making of the American Working Class* (London: Verso, 1991), p. 8.

12. Noel Ignatiev, *How the Irish Became White* (London and New York: Routledge, 1995), p. 181.

13. Kevin Kenny, *The American Irish* (Harlow, Essex: Longman, 2000).

14. See Timothy J. Meagher, *Inventing Irish America* (South Bend, IN: University of Notre Dame Press, 2001); James R. Barrett and David Roediger, '"Irish Everywhere": Irish Americans and the "Americanization" of the "New Immigrants" in the United States, 1900–1930', unpublished paper given at Re-Writing Irish Histories Conference (University College London, 4–6 April 2002).

15. Kenny, *The American Irish*, pp. 67–71.

16. Philip Cohen, 'The perversions of inheritance: studies in the making of multi-racist Britain', in *Multi-Racist Britain*, ed. Philip Cohen and Harwant S. Bains (London: Macmillan, 1988), pp. 9–118; Mary J. Hickman and Bronwen Walter, 'Deconstructing whiteness: Irish women in Britain', *Feminist Review* 50 (Summer 1995), 5–19; Gail Lewis, *Forming Nation, Forming Welfare* (London: Routledge with the Open University Press, 1998).

17. Alistair Bonnett, *White Identities: Historical and International Perspectives* (Harlow, Essex: Prentice Hall, 2000).

18. Robert Miles, *Racism after 'Race Relations'* (London: Routledge, 1993), p. 96.

19. Catherine Hall, 'The rule of difference: gender, class and empire in the making of the 1832 Reform Act', in *Gendered Nations: Nationalisms and Gender Order in the Long Nineteenth Century*, ed. Ida Blom, Karen Hagerman and Catherine Hall (London: Berg, 2000).

20. Linda Colley, *Britons: Forging the Nation 1707–1837* (London: Yale University Press, 1992); John Wolffe, 'Evangelicalism in mid-nineteenth-century England', in *Patriotism: The Making and Unmaking of British National Identity*, vol. I, ed. Raphael Samuel (London: Routledge, 1989).

21. Geoffrey F. A. Best, 'The Protestant constitution and its supporters, 1800–1829', *Transactions of the Royal Historical Society* 8 (1958), 105–27.

22. K. Robbins, 'Religion and identity in modern British history', in *Religion and National Identity*, Studies in Church History, 18, ed. S. Mews (Oxford: Basil Blackwell, 1982), pp. 465–87 (469).

23. Mary J. Hickman, *Religion, Class and Identity* (Aldershot: Ashgate, 1995), p. 154.

24. James Murphy, *The Religious Problem in English Education: The Crucial Experiment* (Liverpool: Liverpool University Press, 1959).

25. Hickman, *Religion, Class and Identity*.

26. Ibid.

27. Mary Waters, *Ethnic Options. Choosing Identities in America* (Berkeley: University of California Press, 1990).

28. Tölölyan, 'Rethinking diaspora(s)'.

29. Paul Arthur, 'Diaspora intervention in international affairs: Irish America as a case study', *Diaspora* 1, 2 (1991), 143–62.

30. Marjorie Fellowes, *Irish Americans: Identity and Assimilation* (Englewood Cliffs, NJ: 1979); Pete Hamill, *A Drinking Life: A Memoir* (Boston: Little, Brown and Company, 1994); Michael Patrick MacDonald, *All Souls: A Family Story from Southie* (Boston: Beacon Press, 1999).

31. Toni Morrison, 'On the backs of blacks', *Time Special Issue: America's Immigrant Challenge*, 142, 21 (Fall 1993), 57.

32. Breda Gray, '"Whitely scripts" and Irish women's racialised belonging(s) in England', *European Journal of Cultural Studies* 5, 3 (2002), 257–74.

33. Hickman and Walter, *Discrimination and the Irish Community*.

Further reading

Donald H. Akenson, *The Irish Diaspora* (Belfast: Institute of Irish Studies, The Queen's University, 1993)

Andy Bielenberg (ed.), *The Irish Diaspora* (Harlow: Longman, 2000)

Gray, Breda, *Women and the Irish Diaspora* (London: Routledge, 2003)

Mary J. Hickman, *Religion, Class and Identity* (Aldershot: Ashgate, 1995)

Kevin Kenny, *The American Irish* (Harlow: Longman, 2000)

Jim Mac Laughlin, *Location and Dislocation in Contemporary Irish Society: Emigration and Irish Identities* (Cork: Cork University Press, 1997)

Timothy J. Meagher, *Inventing Irish America* (South Bend, IN: University of Notre Dame Press, 2001)

Kerby A. Miller, *Emigrants and Exiles: Ireland and the Irish Exodus to North America* (New York and Oxford: Oxford University Press, 1985)

Patrick O'Farrell, *The Irish in Australia* (Sydney: New South Wales University Press, 1986)

Roger Swift and Sheridan Gilley (eds.), *The Irish in Victorian Britain: The Local Dimension* (Dublin: Four Courts Press, 1999)

Bronwen Walter, *Outsiders Inside: Whiteness, Place and Irish Women* (London and New York: Routledge, 2001)

8

The cultural effects of the Famine

Introduction

This chapter shows how the Great Famine of 1845 to 1852 was the single most important event in Ireland in the modern period. In European terms, famine had become an increasingly remote event, and that Ireland should suffer a devastating episode was made all the more unusual in that it then formed part of the richest, most powerful and centralised state in the world – the United Kingdom created by the Act of Union in 1800. The Famine disproportionately impacted on the 3 million potato-dependent people who comprised the notoriously poverty-stricken base of Irish society. These effects were compounded by doctrinaire government policies, designed as much to appease British opinion and to promote social engineering as to alleviate poverty or save lives. Over 1 million people died and 2 million more emigrated within a decade: the population of the island halved by 1900, the result of endemic emigration by young people, delayed marriages and abnormally high rates of celibacy.

The Famine therefore marked a watershed in many areas of Irish life – demographics, economics, society, culture. Yet the immediate response appears sluggish. Indubitably, Ireland remained culturally comatose in the immediate post-Famine period. The period from the 1880s, when the post-Famine generation took over, witnessed the creation of a series of radical responses to the Famine legacy, of which the Irish literary revival is one. Many other initiatives were also undertaken, inspired by people themselves born during the Famine. The best-known examples include Michael Davitt, founder of the Land League in 1879, and Michael Cusack, founder of the Gaelic Athletic Association in 1884. They belonged to a generation that sought to reshape Ireland in fundamental ways following the Famine and the hollowing-out of indigenous Irish culture.

In this chapter, I explore a sequence of these responses – the devotional revolution, the decline of the *caoineadh* (keen), dance and hurling – and discuss these in the context of the memory of the Famine. I conclude with an exploration of the concept of radical memory. The devotional revolution is a term used by historians to describe the startling transformation within Irish Catholicism that occurred within a generation of the Famine. An entirely revamped religious practice hardened into a powerful and rigid cultural formation that essentially remained intact for over a century, only slowly dissolving from the 1960s onwards. While most commentators describe this cultural formation as 'traditional' Irish Catholicism, it was in fact a new form, which belongs to modernising rather than archaic forces within Irish society, and which was dependent on the cultural carnage of the Famine for its emergence. Commentaries that neglect this deeper history in favour of a foreshortened version run serious risks of distortion and shallowness.

A more specific account of the cultural changes induced by the Famine can be provided by looking at the fortunes of the *caoineadh* (keen), the demise of which demonstrates the drastically altered status of Irish women and of oral culture in post-Famine Ireland. Both dance and sport also witnessed dramatic changes in the last quarter of the nineteenth century, changes which could readily be slotted into an 'invention of tradition' model. However, in Ireland these inventions offer radical rather than conservative possibilities, sharply distinguishing Irish cultural practice at this time from elsewhere in Europe. The concept of radical memory provides a useful conceptual framework for understanding these processes. The larger point is that it is dangerous to simply import models generated from the historical experience of other cultures and to apply them unmodified to the Irish scene. This is especially the case when these models originate from metropolitan and imperial cultures.

The Devotional Revolution

The Famine accelerated the transformation of the Catholic church in Ireland. In the pre-Famine period, a vernacular Catholicism had established deep roots among those social formations that the Famine would decimate. This vernacular inheritance evolved organically within an agrarian society, its ritual rhythm dominated by calendar custom and inhabiting a numinous landscape of holy wells and pilgrimage sites like Croagh Patrick and Lough Derg. In this cultural matrix, behaviour was regulated by custom and tradition: central religious events were the rites of passage and communal occasions that included the pattern, wake and station. The trauma of the Famine, the associated decline of vernacular religion and popular culture and the erosion of the Irish language created a cultural vacuum that was filled by the more ritualistic practices associated with the devotional revolution – the institutionalisation of mass-going, new devotional practices such as novenas, forty-hour devotions and the exposition of the host.

This devotional revolution was made possible by a formidable increase in plant and personnel and a tightening of internal discipline, which in turn acted as the basis of a transformation in popular religious practice. A surge in mass attendance, an increasingly exhibitionist architectural display and a stricter social discipline were all part of the revolution. Irish Catholicism became more public, more assertive, more Roman in character, as the institutional church eclipsed its vernacular predecessor. The devotional revolution therefore represented the triumph of a canonical belief-system over older informalities. Its success was seen in the spread of churches, convents, schools, orphanages and hospitals. Irish Catholicism became a crucial bearer of order and identity in a nineteenth-century world of unprecedented flux, accelerated by the devastating impact of the Famine and selective emigration. These simultaneously obliterated the demographic base of vernacular Catholicism in the Irish poor and fatally weakened the older particularistic cultural formations rooted in the Irish language.

The devastation wreaked by the Famine strengthened the church's hand in imposing its modernising crusade. Catholicism invaded the vacated cultural space and solved an identity crisis by offering a powerful surrogate language of symbolic identity in which Irishness and 'Catholicism' were seen as reciprocal and congruent. The symbiosis of 'Irish' and 'Catholic' was strengthened, and religion articulated an artificial, symbolic language of identity to replace the living one being swept away by famine, emigration and jolting socio-cultural transformations. The institutional Catholic church could also take advantage of the more homogenised post-Famine social structure, as the pre-Famine potato people – the *bruscair an bhaile* (or trash of the town, as one Catholic shopkeeper in pre-Famine Ireland put it) – with their vigorous popular culture, were decimated and demoralised. The church injected a new social discipline of respectability.

A growing political rapprochement with nationalist politicians cemented an unusually cohesive marriage of church and nation. These developments were stiffened by the post-Famine institutionalisation of the church and by the surge of self-confidence it got from involvement in the creation of an Irish Catholic spiritual empire overseas. The new Irish identity was exported to the Irish diaspora, making Irish Catholicism an epiphyte on empire in the English-speaking world. At the First Vatican Council of 1867–70, 30 per cent of the 730 bishops were either Irish or of Irish descent. The novelist, Canon Sheehan, noted in 1881: 'Wherever the mightier race has gone, the weaker race has followed and established a spiritual empire coterminous with that political empire.'[1] The College of All Hallows, established to educate missionaries in 1842, had 1,500 alumni by 1900. By the 1880s, the Christian Brothers operated in China and in Calcutta and the Loreto Sisters in Madras. The Society of African Missions was founded in 1877. These global pretensions within Irish Catholicism intensified markedly after the founding of the Free State. The Maynooth Mission to China (established in 1911, with its College built in 1918) extended to the Philippines in 1929, to Korea in 1933, and to Burma in 1936. The Missionary Sisters of Our Lady of the Rosary (ministering in Nigeria) were founded in 1924, followed by the Medical Missionaries of Mary (also based in Nigeria) in 1937. By 1964, there were over 6,000 Irish missionaries. A heroic historiography also allowed Irish Catholicism to envisage itself as the historical, psychic and functional core of the Irish experience, thereby seamlessly linking itself with the national identity.

In Ireland, as population fell, the number of clergy rose. By the early twentieth century, the Irish priest–people ratio, at 1:1,100, was the lowest in the world. Between 1800 and 1900, the number of nuns increased from 120 to 8,000. This vocational surge also ensured the marginalisation of the laity within the power structures of the church itself, even at a time when that laity was becoming more pious. By 1861, only 146 people (including deists and atheists) claimed to have no religious affiliation. In post-Famine Ireland, religious affiliation increasingly became a surrogate for national identity as the effective agent of communal solidarity. Linked to a shared experience of marginalisation, this clerical-nationalist alliance could also transcend and neutralise class division as a basis of political action.

The keen

A further result of the Famine was to alter the Gaelic tradition of grieving the dead. The high mortality rate made people callous towards death. In these appalling circumstances, death itself – or at least its social significance – died. Talking about the demise of the *caoineadh*, an observer in Clare noted that 'especially since the Famine of 1848, the practice has not been much in use. The innumerable deaths which at that time had daily taken place, together with the hunger and destitution which prevailed throughout the country deprived the people in fact of that natural feeling and regard which they were wont to have for the dead.'[2]

While Gaelic culture was still vibrant and intact, two styles of *caoineadh* coexisted. One was formal and literary, composed retrospectively, utilising a long line containing a regular number of natural speech stresses.[3] These intricate and sophisticated compositions (like the celebrated eighteenth-century lament poem *Caoineadh Airt Uí Laoghaire*) were a valued component of the Gaelic repertoire, with a venerable literary genealogy. The second style of *caoineadh* was more informal, improvised and extempore, using a restricted metre with one stress per line.[4] By the mid nineteenth century, the literary tradition had almost entirely collapsed, and the oral *caoineadh* was all that survived.

The *caoineadh* furnished formal and public acknowledgements of women's responsibility for the ceremonies of death as well as for birth. It functioned as a transition ceremony, a cathartic, therapeutic theatre of death, which explored both the emotional experience of loss and the necessary continuity of the surviving community. The carnival quality of the wake was a precise response to this liminal ambiguity. Far from being the 'wild and inarticulate uproar' heard by outsiders, the *caoineadh* was structured, rhythmic and orchestrated, utilising iterative procedures drawn from a rich formulaic repertoire, composed in performance and adhering to strict metre. While the pre-existing compositional vocabulary structured it, there was flexibility of improvisation within it.

Because the *caoineadh* was pre-eminently a woman's genre, it could code gendered rhetorics of resistance within the mourning formalities. It could also give a direct voice to marital strife and conflicts between kin groups, precisely because the wake brought the two families together physically, and because the shock of death exposed or released raw emotional states. Exchanges between priests and women-keeners are frequently recorded. While robust exchanges between poets and priests were frequent in the eighteenth century, there was a deal of intimacy and respect between the two in the Gaelic tradition. However, once the church began to distance itself from the tradition and once the devotional revolution took hold, a new sense of distance between priests and people emerged. Because it was women's work and rooted in a vernacular culture of expression and structure of feeling, the *caoineadh* was opposed by the institutional church.

If the keen was anathema to a modernising, institutional church determined on obliterating its vernacular competitor, it also occupied a prominent position in British attacks on Gaelic culture, as a consistent signifier of Ireland's cultural and political incivility. In one account, the keen is compared to 'the counterfeit and barbarous clamour of howling savages that would disgrace the funeral of a Hottentot or the obsequies of a native of Otaheite [Tahiti]'.[5] The keen was thus assessed as a barbaric mark of primitivism, an animal howl inhabiting the ambiguous borderlands between nature and culture; a sinister sound which embodied the strange danger of Irish emotion in all its raw and violent excess. Its affront to the canon of polite taste was all the more unsettling in that it had a formulaic, ritualistic and even professional dimension (in the case of keening women). This effect was heightened by the keen's theatrical performance of emotion, which signified Gothic Catholic excess as opposed to Protestant privacy and inwardness in response to grief. The shocking coexistence within the wake of laughter and lament, of a wildly oscillating emotional register, came to signal Celtic inconsistency, the lack of the fully formed, regulated, rational personality of civil Anglo-Saxon society.

This ethical critique focused obsessively on the mouth, the vector of oral culture, insistently envisaged as lax and unstable – the site of drunkenness, sedition and the excessive emotion of the keen. Hence arose the concern to impose the Kantian hierarchy of the sense – to promote the distantiated and objectifying eye and ear in place of the profligate immediacy, the inferior taste of the mouth. The anglicisation of Ireland in the nineteenth century required a reordering of the Irish senses, the acquisition of the stiff upper lip in place of raucous loose talk. This newly disciplined Irish body could then participate in the formation of a new ethical subject – rational, self-interested and above all consistent. The overlap of the political and emotional economy is nowhere so transparent as in this discourse. In her convent boarding school at Bruff in County Limerick, Sissy O'Brien was struck by the nuns' emphasis on strict silence, believing that she and her classmates would have been 'lively and joyous, but for incessant repression and the haunting fear of breaking rules, especially of breaking silence'.[6]

Dance and its transformations

In a culture of poverty, body language could offer joyous liberation, an exuberant display of flamboyant theatricality lifting out of the material world. Dancing became a cultural statement, the somatic and kinetic intelligence of which blended into a richly expressive vernacular art. The accomplished traditional dancer rode the rhythm, consummately mastering the movement. But s/he also oscillated along the porous boundary between respect for tradition and an assertive individuality. For the spectators, the attraction was the expressive tension between tradition and the individual talent; the dancer, bound to the strictly prescribed music, could also innovate within and against it. Where male and female danced together, there was also sexual theatre – expressed through the heavier 'hit' of the male dancer (culminating in the 'batter', heavy rhythmic drumming with the full foot), counterpoised against the quicker, buoyant step of the female performer. In the crowded social settings of pre-Famine Ireland, the challenge and the spectacle was heightened by the rigid limitations of space. The rich pre-Famine repertoire of Irish dances involved the creative interplay between indigenous and exogenous forms, resulting in popular hybrids like the 'sets' and 'reels' (an Irish adaptation of the continental 'quadrille'). The itinerant dancing masters customised these new forms, translating them into a popular idiom and then propagated them in their newly standardised forms through their itinerant teaching circuit. Dance was a malleable, inherently portable art form that could easily transfer from one place to another.

The Catholic church turned against the robust tradition of dance, because it could be free, intoxicating, spontaneous and sexual. It involved close encounters between male and female and could occur in unregulated spaces, like public houses and at cross-roads. Dance belonged to the participants without mediators or masters. The church moved to domesticate its wilder energies and to control the time and places of performance. This occurred simultaneously with the increasing dominance of industrial time (regulated by the clock) over agrarian time (regulated by the daily and seasonal cycle). In the post-Famine period, the dance tradition was leached of its vitality, exuberance and hybridity; like the hedge schoolmasters, the dancing masters were inexorably squeezed out as the churches increasingly frowned on their activities.

By the end of the nineteenth century, a remarkable transformation occurred in Irish dance, spearheaded by Fionán MacColuim.[7] MacColuim, a clerk in the India Office in London, fitted the classic profile of a nationalist intellectual. Active in the Gaelic League in London, he was struck by the lack of a social dimension to the language movement, especially as compared with the vigorous Scots *céilithe* nights he saw in the city. Imitating the Scots model, he organised the first Irish *céilí* at Bloomsbury Hall in London in 1897. MacColuim was perturbed, however, by the lack of variety in the Irish dances, and by the absence of large-scale, rapidly moving dances, covering the entire floor space of a hall that could involve everybody as participants rather than as spectators. He then met an old Sliabh Luachra dancing master, Patrick Reidy, who introduced him to a more extensive repertoire of Irish dances. Thus encouraged, MacColuim accompanied Reidy on a collecting trip to Ireland – drawn inevitably to Reidy's native ground in Kerry, but also attracted to the county as a bastion of 'pure' or literary Irish (as opposed to the *patois* of Connemara, or the deplorably Scots-tainted Donegal dialect). Thus, the 'Highlanders', 'Lancers' and 'Flings' of Donegal and the *sean-nós* (old style) dance style of Connemara were rejected in favour of a Munster-based canon of Irish dance, just as 'Munster' Irish was promoted as the canonical dialect by the (Munster-dominated) Gaelic League.

This new canon of Irish dance involved a number of principles. Invented group dances like 'The Walls of Limerick' and 'The Siege of Ennis' were adapted as ideal for large social occasions, because they involved large numbers and traversed the whole floor (unlike the traditional style, which valued the ability to 'dance on a sixpence' in tightly restricted domestic space). The stepping style was simplified and rigidified to eliminate the vulgar batter (seen as English clog dancing in disguise) and to curtail flamboyance (as in the theatrical arm-flailing of the Connemara style). The tempo of the music was also slowed, to create a more stately, refined style. The distaste for the batter was also because of its raw male sexual libido, an insistent theatrical performance of masculinity, displayed in covert competition with other males.

These developments were linked to the movement away from 'house' and 'cross-roads' dances to hall-based *céilis*, a move approved and promoted by the Catholic clergy, and culminating in the Dance Hall Act of 1935. This effectively outlawed house dances (allegedly on hygiene grounds, more accurately on moral hygiene grounds). Hall settings could be much more tightly supervised, as opposed to house dances – especially once the car introduced a new form of mobility for what Cardinal MacRory in 1931 saw as urban sexual predators – 'unsuitables from a distance'. The Carrigan Commission of 1931 attributed great moral perils to 'the opportunities afforded by the misuse of motor cars for luring girls'. The impact of the 1935 Act was draconian, making it practically impossible to hold dances without the sanction of the trinity of clergy, police and judiciary. Both the setting as well as the style of the new Irish dances acted to dampen down sexuality. The invented dance style was purposely asexual, involving minimal physical contact, as opposed to the full-blooded, full-frontal engagement of, for example, the traditional sets. This evolution from passion to pallor, from erotic to neurotic, almost buried the existing forms. Increasingly, and predictably, the new form appealed most to pre-pubescent children, a development aided by the Gaelic League-sponsored dancing schools in the 1920s. This had three repercussions: insistence on Irish language competence as a prerequisite for teaching excluded the last of the old-style dancing masters; a competitive element was introduced, which increasingly confined dancing to the stage rather than the dance floor; a new costume-culture was invented, elaborately 'Celtic' in style, making the children look as if they had been 'bespattered by the Book of Kells'[8] (while an added refinement of pinning on medals won in competition gave them the incongruous look of retired field marshals).

Hurling

The writing of Irish cultural history has tended to focus excessively on high culture, usually from a political perspective. Historians mesmerised by high politics and literary scholars preoccupied by the high deeds of Yeats and Joyce have spared little time to researching the broader cultural dynamics of sport within Irish culture. In this section, I take the example of hurling in an effort to write sport back into cultural history and try to broaden and deepen the appropriate contexts in which to consider the role of sport in post-Famine Ireland.

By the eighteenth century, there were two principal and regionally distinct versions of hurling. 'Commons' was akin to the modern Scottish game of shinty: it did not allow handling of the ball which was wooden and hard; it used a narrow-bladed crooked stick. A winter game, it was played by both Presbyterians and Catholics and it was confined to the northern third of the island, especially Antrim, Derry and Donegal. *Báire* or *iomán*, the second version, was by contrast a summer game of southern provenance. The soft animal hair ball (the *sliotar*) could be handled or carried on the hurl, which was flat and round headed. Unlike 'commons', this version was extensively patronised by the landed gentry as a spectator and gambling sport. The gentry formed and captained the teams, issued the challenges, supplied the hurling greens and supervised the matches. These gentry hurlers were especially active in Cork, Tipperary, Kilkenny, Wexford and Galway. This game required level, well-drained pitches of the type especially found in limestone areas, which also produced abundant ash, the best material for making hurls.

Landlord patronage was essential to the southern game. But the impact of the French Revolution, which sharpened class and political divides, and the spread of metropolitan behavioural norms, eroded the landlords' local loyalties. The Famine also accelerated the decline of hurling from its mid-eighteenth-century heyday, when the game had been sponsored by the landed gentry. Post-1798, the gentry withdrew their patronage and the game degenerated into crudity. A modernising Catholic middle class abandoned the game as an embarrassing vestige of a past from which they wished to distance themselves. This modernising thrust was also aided by the impact of Fr Matthew's temperance campaign, whose 'moral revolution' (as described by the German traveller Johan Georg Kohl in 1842) seconded O'Connell's political one. Both stressed the utilitarian, progressive strand of the Enlightenment, and both were hostile to popular culture and to non-respectable forms of behaviour.

After the Famine, faced with both gentry and Catholic disapproval, the game survived precariously in three isolated pockets: in east Galway (the Gort–Ardrahan–Kinvara area), around Cork city (the Aglish–Carrigaline area) and north of Wexford harbour (the Blackwater–Skreen–Castlebridge area). This precipitous collapse had other causes besides the Famine. In the late 1830s, commentators in Killarney and Kilkenny recorded the explicit hostility of Catholic priests to the game. Attacks on the game by anglicising Catholic clergy, by sabbatudinarians and by magistrates who feared its crowd-gathering and therefore subversive potential contributed to the sharp decline. This formed part of the rapid anglicisation of Irish culture in the second quarter of the nineteenth century, which saw the Catholic middle classes engaging in a precipitate retreat from vernacular cultural forms, a retreat conducted at a break-neck speed unprecedented in nineteenth-century Europe. Lacking support and controlling influence, the games disintegrated, allowing priests to demonise them as immoral and disreputable displays of atavism, occasions of violence, drunkenness and the promiscuous mingling of the sexes. The opprobrious term *cailín báire* (hurling girl) evolved to mean a girl of loose morals. Thus, in hurling, as with faction fights, patterns, wakes, the keen, the priests intervened to quell robust expressions of vernacular culture.

Police and magistrates also intervened. The veteran Fenian Jeremiah O'Donovan Rossa claimed that magistrates forbade hurling and that he had personally witnessed police setting out to halt a match.[9] To this trinity of landlord, parish priest and policeman could be added the figure of the strong farmer, as the key agent who sounded the death knell of hurling. The game did not die; it was killed. The Young Irelander Michael Doheny noted how the game was 'fast dying away' and identified clerical distrust as a first cause. But he then identified a second, and more important factor: 'the disinclination of the farmers to allow the hurling on their grazing lands'.[10] As the socially respectable withdrew themselves from participation, the game was kept alive by boys and the very poor. Because meadows were increasingly unavailable, the game was literally squeezed out into the roadside (where it assumed the dangerous form of road hurling) or into the coarse countryside (where it declined into *scuaibín*, a rough and tumble cross-country scramble, devoid of the grace, skill and discipline of its elegant predecessor).

It is against this vacuum that the work of Michael Cusack and the Gaelic Athletic Association should be set. It fits the scenario envisaged by Miroslav Hroch for the development of *risorgimento* nationalism. This involved a tripartite sequence: initially recuperation of national identity (history, language, folklore); then, the progressive reworking of this by ideologists of nationalism; and finally, the transition from cultural revival to political demands.[11] A national community must be nurtured, its identity carefully recuperated out of the shards of history, language and folklore. This new cultural vocabulary had then to be inserted into a grammar of political action. In its redefined form, national culture could be harnessed to political demands. This sequence required a number of social processes to underpin it: an increase in the number of educated people (facilitated in Ireland by the National School system); a dislocation in the settled sedentary culture (in Ireland, the Famine and a traumatic language shift); a rise in mass communications (the penetration of print culture is a logistical imperative); and cheap transport which made popular mobilisation possible (in Ireland, the railway system contributed significantly). Where these social processes combined with a political tendency towards the eclipse of empire, then cultural nationalism was empowered. Janus-headed, it simultaneously homogenised (stressing the unity of the Irish people) and differentiated (stressing their distinctiveness from the British people). Nationalism became a classifying protocol, which reordered relationships between peoples.

While cultural nationalism underpinned the GAA at a macro-level, a more pragmatic concern with codification did so at a micro-level. The Victorian period was the great era of sports codification, both in the regulation of existing sports (Australian rules football in 1858, the English Football Association in 1863, the Queensberry rules in boxing in 1865) and in the creation of new ones (Lawn Tennis in 1873, basketball in 1891). Initially, an English phenomenon based around the public schools, codification was rapidly exported to the empire and to the anglophone world. Codification eased the transition in sporting forms from rural to urban, participating to spectating, and recreational to competitive. The rise of mass spectator sports for urban consumption was facilitated by enhanced spending power, the associated commercialisation of leisure, improved communication networks and the invention of the weekend. Codification also linked to a new rhetoric of high moral purpose of character building, the cult of masculinity and of racial stereotyping. This led to a sustained effort to organise and then control working-class sport and to develop 'national' games. Baseball in the USA, rugby in New Zealand, soccer in England and Australian Rules football emerged almost simultaneously as national games.

Cusack explicitly visualised Gaelic games as a disciplined performance of Irish masculinity, a calculated corrective to the Victorian caricature of the Irishman as a slouched simian brute, comic caperer or childlike innocent. The robust physicality of the games symbolised and performed a fully developed masculine character, a recovery of the male body from its emasculated and emaciated Famine forms. Cusack believed that the post-Famine Irish male had internalised 'degeneracy'. The body itself was now reinscribed politically and made explicit as a site of renewal and rectification. The Gaelic male specifically rejected corporeal colonialism, reshaping an Irish body politic as an antidote to dehumanisation, degeneracy and depoliticisation. The concepts of discipline, organisation, tactics and self-control associated with the games strengthened military potential as powerful enactments of tactical solidarities, patriotism and political muscle.

Cusack's organisation of Gaelic games fits neatly into the wider evolution of European cultural nationalism and of the sports codification movement. The genius of Cusack was the welding of these two strands together in an Irish context. He realised that the initial momentum behind sports codification in Ireland was emanating from Trinity College and the Dublin public schools, and infiltrating the boat clubs, rugby, hurling, athletics and cricket. In an era of the six-day working week, the refusal to sanction games on Sunday was inevitably construed as an anti-Catholic and anti-working-class manoeuvre, as was the insistence on the 'gentleman amateur' ethos (patently modelled on English precedents) which refused participation to 'mechanics' and 'labourers'. Cusack realised the need for a game for the Irish rural poor and especially the labourer class; hurling and football could emancipate the small man from the tyranny of the existing athletic clubs and thereby help in eroding paternalism.

The shrewd application of the principle of territoriality was a crucial element in the GAA's success. The GAA met national and social needs while retaining the territorial allegiances which imparted cohesion and emotional solidarity to Irish rural life. Similar forces of territoriality have been identified behind the success of rugby in the Welsh villages, cricket in the West Indies,[12] and rugby league in Yorkshire and Lancashire. In Ireland, the games spread with astonishing rapidity. There were over 1,000 clubs by 1890 and the GAA is acknowledged by sports historians as the most speedily and extensively established sporting organisation in the world. In the absence of Cusack's intervention, hurling might now be an antiquarian footnote or a furtive survivor, like road bowls or cock fighting.

From its inception in 1884, the GAA found itself in an intensely competitive relationship with other sports, notably rugby and athletics. Codification was deployed on an inter-sport, competitive principle. The 1880s was the pre-eminent decade of codification – of cricket, golf and tennis, for example, when permanent sporting organisations and grounds were established. The notorious GAA 'Ban' on participating in other sports evolved in this context.[13] Initially non-political, its aim was to force players to declare their sole allegiance to the GAA for affiliation fees, strengthening the fragile financial base of the game. It was only later and secondarily that the 'Ban' acquired its political purposes, before it was finally rescinded in 1971.

Cusack and his GAA backers also used the game as a nationalising idiom, a symbolic language of identity filling the void created by anglicisation. It had therefore to be sharply fenced off in organisational terms from competing 'anglicised' sports like cricket, soccer and rugby. Thus, from the beginning, the revived game had a nationalist veneer, its rules bristling like a porcupine with protective nationalist quills on which its perceived opponents would have to impale themselves. Its principal backers were those already active in the nationalist political culture of the time. Its spread depended on the active support of an increasingly nationalist Catholic middle class. Gaelic games received their greatest support from those active in nationalist politics, especially the Irish Republican Brotherhood (the Fenians). Gaelic games were a crucial conduit to that mass backing which increasingly gave cultural nationalism its democratic mandate.

The spread of the new game also depended on the active support of a nationalist Catholic middle class. The GAA's social base came especially from journalists, schoolteachers, clerks, priests and publicans, the social constituency behind cultural nationalism across nineteenth-century Europe. Thus hurling's early success was in south Leinster and east Munster, the same region which powered popular nationalist movements like Daniel O'Connell's campaign, the Devotional Revolution in Irish Catholicism, Fr Matthew's temperance campaign, the Fenians, and the take-over of local government. The GAA was a classic example of the radical conservatism of this region – conservative in its ethos and ideology, radical in its techniques of organisation and mobilisation. The spread of hurling can be closely matched to the spread of other radical conservative movements of this period, notably the diffusion of the indigenous Catholic teaching orders and the spread of cooperative dairying.

Framed in a longer time perspective which embraces the eighteenth century, the game of hurling represents a textbook example of the relationship between European élites and vernacular cultures. The model of élite participation in popular culture is a threefold process:

first immersion, then withdrawal and finally rediscovery, invariably by an educated élite, and often with a nationalist agenda. 'Rediscovery' involved an invention of tradition, creating a packaged, homogenised and idealised popular culture. The relationship of hurling and the newly established GAA in the 1880s shows this third phase with textbook clarity. Looked at in this way, hurling can be envisaged as a classic example of 'the invention of tradition', but with the crucial distinction that its invention was deployed for radical rather than conservative purposes, in constructing the nation as an imagined community. That national consciousness itself had to be imagined, or constructed, and then disseminated. In Ireland, it has been fashionable to denigrate the fabricating impulse in that construction; it is equally valid to celebrate its creativity and emancipatory potential, a creativity evident in Cusack's magnificent obsession. Joyce's focus in *Ulysses* on Cusack's Cyclopean fixity relates to the later and embittered man when the initial creativity had hardened into the sclerotic institutional structures of the GAA, overseen by its first generation of professional administrators.

In this achievement, hurling became a resonant symbolic language, speaking from the space voided by the brutal dissolution inflicted on vernacular forms by the Famine. If the games became a classic example of the invention of tradition, the really significant question becomes not how, but against what was it invented? In the Irish case, the invention of tradition was also an inversion, seeking to redress the bruising encounter with colonialism, with its persistent hollowing effect on indigenous culture. In contrast to the conservative orientation of arguments centred on the invention of tradition in Victorian Britain, memory in Ireland was deployed for radical political purposes: a spur to agency, rather than a prop to passivity.

Conclusion: radical memory

As we can see in all of these case studies, the recourse to the past in Ireland was deployed for radical political purposes. This stands in contrast to the conservative orientation of arguments centred on the invention of tradition in Victorian Britain. Cultural memory in the hands of activists like Cusack and Davitt deployed the past in a radical way to challenge the present and reshape the future, to restore into possibility historical moments that had been blocked or unfulfilled earlier.[14] There is more in the past than simply what happened; at any given point in time, multiple trajectories towards the future are open. Radical memory in the post-Famine period deployed a prospective rather than an elegiac nostalgia, a nostalgia for the future, not the past. This dialogue of cultural memory and expectation keeps alive the memory of suffering and defeat against the obliterative force of the victors' narrative. Radical memory opens a space for a counterpoint history. These post-Famine projects in their diverse ways treat history as rememorative, seeking to write back in that which had been erased or submerged. 'Rememoration', a term invented by Toni Morrison, displays an acute awareness that 'the act of imagination is bound up with memory' and that individual memory and social memory are inextricably linked.

The most alert and engaged cultural thinkers of the post-Famine generation differentiated between two modes of memory: an individualist, self-obsessed, disabling one, which internalises damage as melancholia, and a culturally induced enabling form, which seeks wider explanations and political strategies. The second approach allows for legitimate translation from the personal to the public sphere, while avoiding the internalisation of damaging notions of fate, destiny and providence, all of which had wreaked enormous damage during the Famine, by encouraging political passivity. The second form of public memory accepts responsibility for the past and historicises memory; by doing so, it restores agency and prevents the slide of memory into nationalist nostalgia. In that way, it radicalises historicism.

This redemptive model of radical memory must also continue to acknowledge the irredeemable losses that lie at the core of historical injustice, loss so absolute as to be beyond redemption, as has been powerfully argued in the case of the slave trade, the Shoah or the Irish Famine. A historical negative space of absolute loss exists, a limit that theory cannot transgress, that ethics cannot redeem, a disconsolate future that has lost its past. This is also the realm of contingency and necessity, of Marx's piercing aphorism that people make their own history but not in conditions of their own choosing.

Notes

1. Patrick Sheehan, 'The effect of emigration on the Irish church', *Irish Ecclesiastical Record* 3, 3 (1882), 611.
2. Royal Irish Academy, MS 12, Q 13, p. 10.

3. Breandán Ó Buachalla, *An Caoine agus an Chaointeoireacht* (Dublin: Cois Life, 1995); Breandán Ó Madagáin (ed.), *Gnéithe den Chaointeoireacht* (Dublin: An Clóchomhar, 1978); Sean Ó Coiléan, 'The Irish lament. An oral genre', *Studia Hibernica* 24 (1984–88), 97–117.

4. Angela Bourke, 'The Irish traditional lament and the grieving process', *Women Studies International Forum* 11 (1988), 287–91; Angela Bourke, 'Performing, not writing', *Graph* 11 (1991), 28–31; Angela Bourke, 'Caoineadh na marbh', *Oghma* 4 (1992), 3–11.

5. *Wexford Herald*, 29 November 1792.

6. Mary Carbery, *The Farm by Lough Gur: The Story of Mary Fogarty [Sissy O'Brien]* (London: Longmans, 1937), p. 100.

7. See Diarmuid Breathnach and Máire Ní Mhurchú, *Beathaisneis: 1882–1982* (Dublin: An Clóchomhar, 1986), pp. 37–9.

8. I owe this phrase to Eileen Battersby.

9. Jeremiah O'Donovan Rossa, *Rossa's Recollections: 1838 to 1898* (New York: Mariner's Harbour, 1898), p. 203.

10. Michael Doheny, 'The autobiography of an agitator', *Irish American*, 19 February 1859.

11. Miroslav Hroch, *Social Preconditions of National Revival in Europe: A Comparative Analysis of the Social Composition of Patriotic Groups among the Smaller European Nations*, trans. Ben Fowkes (Cambridge : Cambridge University Press, 1985), pp. 61–83.

12. C. L. R. James, *Beyond a Boundary* (Durham, NC: Duke University Press, 1993).

13. 'The Ban', as it became known, prevented GAA members on pain of expulsion from participating as players or spectators in 'foreign games', notably soccer, rugby and hockey.

14. Kevin Whelan, 'The memories of "The Dead"', *Yale Journal of Criticism* 15, 1 (2002), 59–97.

Further reading

Angela Bourke, 'More in anger than in sorrow: Irish women's lament poetry', in *Feminist Messages: Codings in Women's Folk Culture*, ed. Joan Radner (Urbana: University of Illinois Press, 1993), pp. 160–82

Helen Brennan, *The Story of Irish Dance* (Dingle: Brandon, 1999)

Peter Burke, *Popular Culture in Early Modern Europe* (London: Temple Smith, 1978)

James Donnelly, *The Great Irish Potato Famine* (Sutton: Stroud, 2001)

Tom Hayden (ed.), *Irish Hunger: Personal Reflections on the Legacy of the Famine* (Dublin: Wolfhound, 1997)

Kerwin Lee Klein, 'On the emergence of memory in historical discourse', in *Representations* 69 (2000), 127–50

Emmet Larkin, *The Historical Dimensions of Irish Catholicism* (Washington, DC and Dublin: Catholic University of America Press and Four Courts Press, 1997)

David Lloyd, 'Colonial trauma/postcolonial recovery?', *Interventions* 2, 2 (2000), 21–8

David Miller, 'Mass attendance in Ireland in 1834', in *Piety and Power in Ireland, 1760–1960*, ed. Stephen Brown and David Miller (Notre Dame, IN: University of Notre Dame Press, 2000), pp. 158–79

Liam O'Caithnia, *Scéal na h-Iomána Ó Thosach Ama go 1884* (Dublin: An Chlóchomhar, 1980)

Cormac Ó Gráda, *Black '47 and Beyond: The Great Irish Famine in History, Economy and Memory* (Princeton, NJ: Princeton University Press, 1999)

Robert Scally, *The End of Hidden Ireland: Rebellion, Famine and Emigration* (New York: Oxford University Press, 1995)

Kevin Whelan, 'The geography of hurling', *History Ireland* 1 (1993), 27-31

'The memories of "The Dead"', *Yale Journal of Criticism* 15, 1 (2002), 59–97

II

Cultural practices and cultural forms

9

Modernism and the Irish revival

While the attempt to recover or revive a traditional native culture was a key element of Irish cultural nationalism since the late eighteenth century, the moment of the so-called Celtic Revival, at around the turn of the twentieth century, remains distinctive and significant for a number of reasons.

In no other period has Ireland produced so many writers of such extraordinary quality. Moreover, the reputations and achievements of W. B. Yeats and J. M. Synge are inextricably bound up with the revivalist features of their Irish subject matter, and those of James Joyce and Samuel Beckett are at least in part moulded by their rejection of the aesthetics and politics of the revival. The contemporary 'branding' of the Irish cultural heritage continues to exploit the fame of these literary stars. The works of Yeats, Joyce and Beckett, of course, are all also central to the history of European modernism. Indeed, it could be argued that this unique instance of a modernist movement in a colonial setting presents an important challenge to theorists of modernism; certainly, this literature demands from its critics a nuanced understanding of modernity in relation to Irish history.

A variety of popular cultural and political movements flourished during the years of the revival, including Sinn Féin, Irish Ireland, the Irish Literary Theatre (later the Abbey Theatre), the Gaelic League, the Gaelic Athletics Association, and the Cooperative movement. These were crucial to the historical development of twentieth-century Ireland. Yeats's involvement with the Abbey Theatre and with certain key controversies when a number of plays, most significantly Synge's *Playboy of the Western World* (1907), were dismissed by enraged nationalist audiences, provides an opportunity to consider some of the ironies and even contradictions inherent in the revival, and in the conjunction between aesthetic innovation and the project of cultural decolonisation.

Yeats wrote in 1900:

> I think that our Irish movements have always interested me in part, because I see in them the quarrel of two traditions of life, one old and noble, one new and ignoble. One undying because it satisfies our conscience though it seemed dying and one about to die because it is hateful to our conscience, although it seems triumphant throughout the world. In Ireland wherever the Gaelic tongue is still spoken, and to some little extent where it is not, the people live according to a tradition of life that existed before the world surrendered to the competition of merchants and to the vulgarity that has been founded on it; and we who would keep the Gaelic tongue and Gaelic memories and Gaelic habits of our mind would keep them, as I think, that we may some day spread a tradition of life that would build up neither great wealth nor great poverty, that makes the arts a natural expression of life that permits even common men to understand good art and high thinking and to have the fine manners these things can give.[1]

Yeats's conception of *fin-de-siècle* Ireland as the site of a collision between ancient tradition and commercial civilisation is central to his work. It need hardly be stated, though, that his analysis falls short of the complexity of his historical situation, and that modern Ireland did not effectively resist, much less overturn, industrialism or capitalism. Athough Yeats does not specifically mention the horror of the Great Famine (and here his sketch is characteristic of revivalist discourse which frequently veiled such historical trauma), the changes it had brought about were clearly evident by the end of the nineteenth century. For example, who exactly are the 'we' on whose behalf Yeats speaks? Irish peasant culture had been decimated (surviving only in a few western enclaves, memorialised by the revival in Yeats's Sligo and Synge's Mayo and Aran Islands); the old ruling class, the Anglo-Irish or ascendancy, had largely lost possession of its estates in the wake of the Land War of the 1880s and the legislation of the subsequent quarter century; and the emerging Catholic bourgeoisie, rural and urban, stood to inherit the Irish earth.

Yeats represents a mainly anglophone movement for cultural 'revival', spearheaded by the Anglo-Irish at the very moment of their historical eclipse. Ireland had already, by virtue of its colonial history, been incorporated into the imperialist system, and possessed a highly modernised state. Many Irish nationalists demanded unfettered economic development and greater democracy in a style which was anathema to Yeats. For him, a cultured élite would naturally take the lead in the tasks of recording, translating, editing or adapting Irish stories and songs, and of seeing them into print or onto the stage for the first time. Yeats had been deeply impressed by such works as Standish O'Grady's *History of Ireland, Vol. One* (1878) and Augusta Gregory's *Cuchulain of Muirthemne* (1902), which depicted an aristocratic and heroic Irish antiquity. All such writing, for Yeats, involved the regeneration of the contemporary artistic imagination, rather than its subordination to any particular political end. The protesters in the Abbey, speaking up for a self-consciously 'respectable' Catholic Ireland, evidently did not agree; they could not tolerate images of an Irish woman eloping with a beggar, as in Synge's *In the Shadow of the Glen* (1904), or of Mayo peasants lionising a man they believe to be a murderer in *The Playboy*, as authentic expressions of the spirit of the nation.

Obviously, this was more than a quarrel between tradition and modernity. The various forces at work in the revival have been understood in several ways, then and since. For Yeats, the riots which greeted *The Playboy* were an instance of 'Culture' being howled down by 'Barbarians'. D. P. Moran, self-styled spokesman for 'Irish Ireland', dubbed this a 'Battle of two Civilisations', in which only one, the native, had both force of numbers and moral right on its side. His phrase has been adopted by historians such as F. S. L. Lyons, considerably more sympathetic to Yeats's view than to Moran's.[2] However, during most of the last century, many Irish writers and intellectuals have called down a plague on both houses, in what Terence Brown has described as the movement of 'counter-revival', encompassing such figures as Sean O'Faolain and Patrick Kavanagh.[3] From a certain viewpoint (which we might call, in the Irish context, 'revisionist'), both the misty, idealistic romanticism of Yeats and the puritanical, narrow-mindedness of his opponents, might equally be seen as symptoms of the failure of the Irish to embrace the liberation of secular modernity. Some more recent commentators have attempted to transcend any simple view of class or sectarian antagonism in the revival period, or of any straightforward opposition between pro- and anti-modernisers, in order to acknowlege progressive tendencies on all sides which may have been compromised or suppressed during the consolidation of the newly independent Irish nation state.[4]

These early remarks of Yeats's may also help to illuminate the question of modernity and colonialism. The modern, in colonial conditions, is associated with 'foreignness', domination and violence; it is in no sense naturalised in the course of a long process of economic and social development. It is precisely in such a situation that the culturally 'old' appears most intensely valuable, and becomes the object of political contestation. For while it may virtually obliterate traditional culture, such an experience of modernisation also confers an auratic significance on the remnants of the archaic. Yeats and his friends who would keep 'Gaelic habits of mind' (even if not themselves 'Gaels') are engaged in a salvage mission which ideally would transform an entire society – but the political implications of this transformation are ambiguous.

The wider cultural dimensions of Yeats's project remind us of his connections with William Morris and the Arts and Crafts movement in late Victorian Britain. His consciousness of the arts more generally should not surprise us, given that his brother, Jack B. Yeats, was Ireland's greatest modern painter, and his sisters, Lily and Lolly, ran the innovative Cuala Press, which produced remarkable books illustrated in neo-Celtic styles. Indeed, the revival was never a purely literary affair: some of its earlier writers, including George Russell (Æ) and George Moore, started out as painters, and this was also something of a Golden Age in Irish craft and design.[5] Both Yeats (impressed by Morris as a publisher as well as a writer) and later James Joyce (despite his indifference to modernist visual art) shared in the modernist preoccupation with the printed book as aesthetic artefact.[6] However, it is clear that Yeats envisions his ideal society as a clearly stratified and hierarchical one. Although intense critical debate has continued over the question of whether Yeats's politics, especially in his later years, can strictly speaking be described as 'fascist', this is probably less important to the reader of the poetry and plays (as no individual literary text could usefully or coherently be so described) than the necessity of acknowledging the deeply anti-democratic tenor of his thought throughout his long career.[7] And if Yeats looks to Ireland as the place where a harmonious neo-feudal society might re-emerge, it is surely problematic that, despite his best efforts to 'retrieve' an anti-modernist intellectual Anglo-Irish tradition, no even mildly compelling historical images of such a condition from the recent past could survive scrutiny.[8] The Anglo-Irish ascendancy (whom despite his own middle-class origins Yeats always regarded as his 'people') had presided over the destruction, in the sixteenth century, of what was regarded in the popular view as Ireland's only true aristocracy – the old order of chieftains and kings.

It is by now well recognised that while the discourse of nationalism may gather its material from the enclaves of tradition, it generally does so in order to create a version of the colonial state in new cultural dress. It is, therefore, usually entirely committed to the desideratum of 'modernity'.[9] Yeats's project is sufficiently like that of the nation-builders of early twentieth-century Ireland for him to be acknowledged as their poet (who, as Edward Said puts it, 'articulates the experiences, the aspirations, and the restorative vision' of a colonised people),[10] although he never shares their view of the modern state. His constant laments about the philistinism of the Catholic middle class can be comfortably absorbed by that class itself (and indeed recited by its sons and daughters in the classrooms of independent Ireland) while all the time he in fact delivers a radically conservative critique of the society which it has created.

But this is just one of the many ironies that attend W. B. Yeats's great fame and the enduring popular reverence for his work in Ireland. The image of the lovelorn poet of the 'Celtic Twilight' period, celebrating the beauty of the Irish landscape and expressing his melancholy and loneliness in words and images borrowed from simple country folk (see 'The Stolen Child', 'Down by the Salley Gardens', 'He Hears the Cry of the Sedge') has remained vivid. During the 1890s, he sought to reconcile his devotion to Ireland (and to its nineteenth-century traditions of patriotic verse), with his typically *fin-de-siècle* preoccupations with the occult and the séance:

> Nor may I less be counted one
> With Davis, Mangan, Ferguson,
> Because, to him who ponders well,
> My rhymes more than their rhyming tell
> Of things discovered in the deep,
> Where only body's laid asleep.
>
> ('To Ireland in the Coming Times')[11]

Yeats's favouring of simple diction and of the ballad form distinguish his poetry from that of modernist contemporaries such as Ezra Pound or T. S. Eliot. But as the decades pass, he grows increasingly alienated from popular political feeling, and from the Irish separatist movement. Yet even as his mysticism and nostalgia for pagan Ireland become elaborated into highly arcane theories concerning universal history (which are comparable to those of his international poetic counterparts), deeply hostile to Christianity, mass society and to any notion of historical amelioration, his best poems remain remarkable for their rhetorical bravado and their extraordinary 'quotability' (see 'The Second Coming', 'Leda and the Swan', 'Long-legged Fly'). Yeats at times seemed to regard the new Irish state as the unruly child of the alliance between the Catholic bourgeoisie and a number of radical Anglo-Irish women, including the revolutionary leader Constance Markievicz. This dreadful union was symbolised for him by the disastrous marriage of John MacBride (one of the nationalist martyrs of 1916), and Maud Gonne (whom Yeats loved in vain for most of his life, as every Irish schoolchild knows). This is how Yeats commemorates MacBride's ambiguous achievement:

> Yet I number him in the song;
> He, too, has resigned his part
> In the casual comedy;
> He, too, has been changed in his turn,
> Transformed utterly:
> A terrible beauty is born.
>
> ('Easter 1916')[12]

Ultimately, Yeats offers an ideal of femininity totally opposed to his earlier portrayals of his first love (see 'Prayer for my Daughter'), and produces his most suggestive and disturbing writing on feminine sexuality, violence and politics in the wake of his repudiation of Gonne (see 'Meditations in Time of Civil War').[13] But again, the spectacle of Yeats as a disillusioned and embittered man, isolated in his tower in Co. Galway or railing in the Senate against the repressiveness of the Free State, sits easily enough with the image of the Romantic artist who was bound, in any case, to be frustrated by politicians and businessmen. And his strategic deployment of 'Irishness' continued to be powerfully resonant, no matter how narrow his own ideology. This is from as late as 1938, when Ireland's heroic adventure in decolonisation was apparently well and truly over:

> When Pearse summoned Cuchulain to his side,
> What stalked through the Post Office? What intellect,
> What calculation, number, measurement, replied?
> We Irish, born into that ancient sect
> But thrown upon this filthy modern tide
> And by its formless spawning fury wrecked,
> Climb to our proper dark, that we may trace
> The lineaments of a plummet-measured face.
>
> ('The Statues')[14]

The poem's analogy between the triumph of ancient Greece over Asia and Ireland's defeat of modern degeneration demonstrates that Yeats's blending of the esoteric and the nationalist had survived, although it was no longer in harmony with any wider cultural movement in his own society.

The analysis of Yeats in relation to Romanticism and modernism illustrates the difficulties presented by any discussion of Irish literature in this period in terms of the established histories of English and indeed European writing. To begin with, we must consider the relationship between the revival and modernism. Are these entirely antithetical categories, the latter (especially in the Joycean mode) born out of a reaction against the former? This judgement would evidently be supported by the fact that Yeats, largely because of his imbrication in nationalist rhetoric, was never regarded as a valued precursor by that minority of later writers who were committed to pursuing modernist experiment; from the point of view of the generation of the 1930s and later, modernism in Ireland certainly began with Joyce, not Yeats.[15] Against this, it must be conceded that very little of the writing associated with the revisionist 'counter-revival' was at all radical in formal terms, owing far more to the naturalism of Joyce's *Dubliners* and *A Portrait of the Artist as a Young Man* than to his *Ulysses* or *Finnegans Wake*. Certainly, Yeats's attitude towards nineteenth-century English poetry and Romanticism was very different to Ezra Pound's or T. S. Eliot's, and he was particularly influenced by William Blake and the Victorian critique of industrialism; his views on Celtic spirituality owed a great deal to Matthew Arnold. It is a commonplace to suggest that with *Ulysses*, a work which imitated, parodied and transcended the nineteenth-century novel, a country which had never produced a major realist novel suddenly leapt to the forefront of twentieth-century fiction. But, equally, if we set Yeats's poetry beside the sentimental patriotism of Tom Moore or Thomas Davis, or consider Synge and Sean O'Casey, with their dramatisations of Irish vernacular eloquence within the constrictions of their respective versions of rural and urban Irish society, beside the 'stage-Irishism' of Boucicault or even Shaw and Wilde, it is hard to avoid the conclusion that literary development in this period cannot be explained by any nationally based, evolutionary model of inheritance and innovation. Irish literature abruptly ceased to be a self-consciously colonial branch of English literature, always painfully aware of its minor status and its London-based audience. We are surely obliged to reach for the idea of modernism and its 'revolution of the word' to account for this creative explosion. And here, the parallels between English and Irish literary history break down, for the 'advanced' metropolitan tradition undergoes no comparable re-making. Perry Anderson and other critics in the Marxist tradition have mapped the phenomenon of aesthetic modernism in relation to 'uneven' or 'incomplete' development: in part a consequence of grappling with the modern where the memory of what it supplants is fresh.[16] The applicability of this vision of the historical conjuncture between the *avant-garde* and the archaic to the colonial situation is obvious; but it is also significant, as Terry Eagleton puts it, that the idea of time associated with *nationalism* is more 'modernist' than 'modern', 'at once traumatized and enraptured by the new, mournfully arrested and dynamically open to the future'.[17] In this light, the family resemblances between O'Grady, Gregory, Yeats *and* Joyce become clearer. Terence Brown points out that even the literary forms sponsored by the revivalists, dependent on 'the ancient Celtic sagas, on folktale and on the self-conscious interlacing narratives of the storyteller's oral art, as well as on the revelatory capacities of myth' influenced the understanding of textuality itself in Yeats, Joyce and even Beckett.[18]

Such reminders of the connections between Joyce and the revival are instructive, not least because Joyce himself is such a savage satirist of the revival's idealism and social pretension. In his broadside 'The Holy Office' (1904), Joyce begs not to be accounted one of the 'mumming company' of Yeats, Synge, Russell and the rest, and declares his own artistic mission to be one of 'Katharsis'.[19] He has as much scorn for the earnest Gaelic Leaguers of the Catholic middle class, whom he regards as obsessed with ethnic and sexual purity, as he has for the mystic feminists and vegetarians of the largely Anglo-Irish circles of Yeats and Russell. Russell's absurd sermonising, overheard by Bloom in *Ulysses*,[20] is matched by the parodies of Yeats, Synge and Douglas Hyde scattered throughout Joyce's works. Some of this hostility can be explained as the resentment of the young, ambitious writer who needs to outdo his contemporaries, just as an anxious Stephen Dedalus tries to dominate the literary debate unfolding in the National Library in chapter 9 of *Ulysses*. But the image of Joyce as the deflator of revivalist dreams also appears to support a long-established view of this author as a thoroughgoing demythologiser of all forms of nationalist imagining, implacably opposed to 'essentialist' identities and the violence they must inevitably bring in their wake.[21]

Joyce's relationship with early twentieth-century Ireland is surely more complex than this, although it is certainly tempting to regard him as the antithesis of Yeats in every conceivable way – and, therefore, like his most celebrated creation, Leopold Bloom, an enthusiastic cosmopolitan, offering an exuberant and optimistic vision of the urban environment, everyday modern life, technology and consumerism. In the first place, we need to understand the difficulty Joyce, as an English-speaking Dubliner, experiences with the concept of authentic 'Irishness' which rarely troubles others in this period. Near the end of *A Portrait*, when Stephen confronts the image of an Irish-speaking peasant (who himself speaks in fear and wonder of 'the terrible queer creatures at the latter end of the world'[22]), we can appreciate Joyce's recognition of alterity, which cannot simply be overcome by any voluntaristic identification with the 'people'. Gabriel Conroy has a comparable experience at the end of *Dubliners*, as he contemplates all that divides him from his wife Gretta, who is from the west of Ireland; the story 'The Dead', as a whole, represents an exploration of the process by which 'the fragments of the nation' (in Partha Chatterjee's words) are gathered up by the nationalist project. But this does not mean that Joyce is insensitive to the trauma of modernisation, or that he is only interested in depicting Ireland as a 'normal' place.[23] Moreover, acting as the 'purgative' to the revivalist mystifications of the Irish past, Joyce's up-to-date frankness about biology, sexuality and what Mikhail Bahktin calls the 'lower bodily stratum', finds an echo in the very crudeness, chaos and extravagance of the very Gaelic sources which the revivalists so often sanitised. Joyce's grotesque parodies of Gregory's translations of the stories of Cuchulain (in chapter 12 of *Ulysses*) demonstrate another mode in which the archaic and *avant-garde* may enter into explosively creative conjunction with one another. Joyce, although his texts have never been as widely known as Yeats's, is perhaps more 'popular' in this sense: although Joyce makes no programmatic declarations about seeking to recover the traditional, his experiments with the carnivalesque (especially in *Finnegans Wake*) do appear to suggest that he, too, may be inspired by the idea of an Irishness older and more profound than the repressive Romanised Catholicism of the late nineteenth century.[24]

In the light of this, it might be more accurate to say that *Ulysses* is a book in which the notion of the emancipatory power of modernity is interrogated, and indeed put under considerable pressure, rather than one in which the modern is uncritically ratified. Bloom is certainly in some respects a Hibernian version of Baudelaire's *flâneur*, the urban pedestrian whose liberated creative vision transforms the art of the modern metropolis.[25] But he is also a melancholic figure who yearns for a lost idyll of domestic happiness that is always mediated through the commodity. His fond memories of his baby daughter's 'tubbing night', for example, are inextricably associated with red wallpaper from Dockrell's at 'one and ninepence a dozen' and special American soap.[26] Bloom dreams of escaping the city altogether for a secluded, suburban residence, picturing to himself its olive green hall door and ivy-covered porch.[27]

This serves to remind us, as Walter Benjamin comments, that the bourgeosie created not only the phantasmagoric world of the commodity and the modern city environment which corresponds to it, but also the private home as the refuge from emotional overstimulation and alienation.[28] And just as pornography and advertising promise consolation to lonely individuals whose stories unfold in the streets, shops, pubs and brothels of Dublin, so too capitalism and nationalism offer an escape from the 'Famine, plague and slaughter'[29] of the past. But the city street, as Benjamin puts it, always leads downward, conducting the *flâneur* 'into a vanished time . . . into a past that can be all the more spellbinding because it is not his own, not private'; and for Joyce, too, the 'dreamworld' of modern commerce inevitably 'reflects back upon the primal past' as it imagines a utopian collective future.[30] In this sense, Joyce's forward-looking modernism, so concerned with consumption and excess, can never entirely be divorced from the supposedly regressive, nostalgic impulses that gave rise to other forms of revivalist writing.

This interweaving of some of the many strands of Joyce's modernist practice may perhaps be illustrated here by reference to just one of the interpolations from 'Cyclops' (chapter 12) – that portion of the text most directly concerned with specifically nationalist imaginings of the future. At this point in the episode, Paddy Dignam, who was consigned to his grave in Glasnevin earlier on the day of 16 June 1904, speaks to his friends in Barney Kiernan's bar:

> Interrogated as to whether life there resembled our experience in the flesh he stated that he had heard from more favoured beings now in the spirit that their abodes were equipped with every modern home comfort such as tālāfānā, ālāvātār, hātākāldā, wātāklāsāt and that the highest adepts were steeped in waves of volupcy of the very purest nature . . . It was then queried whether there were any special desires on the part of the defunct and the reply was: *We greet you, friends of earth, who are still in the body. Mind C. K. doesn't pile it on*. It was ascertained that the reference was to Mr Cornelius Kelleher, manager of Messrs H. J. O'Neill's popular funeral establishment, who was responsible for

carrying out the funeral arrangements. Before departing he requested that it should be told to his dear son Patsy that the other boot which he had been looking for was at present under the commode in the return room and that the pair should be sent to Cullen's to be soled as the heels were still good. He stated that this had greatly disturbed his peace of mind in the other region and earnestly requested that his desire be made known. Assurances were given that the matter would be attended to and it was intimated that this had given satisfaction.[31]

Joyce's immediate target is a then fashionable Theosophy (of which Yeats was a devotee), comically deflated here with talk of undertakers, boots and commodes. But here, even dreams of Nirvana have been overtaken by images of a domestic paradise (one closed to souls as yet as unrefined as Dignam's), with all those mock-Sanskrit mod. cons. In passages such as this one, *Ulysses* constantly traces the relationship between all sorts of material and spiritual deprivation, and concomitant fantasies of plenitude and pleasure, in its mapping of the dreamworld of modernity. This is as much the case with the bored and neglected housewife Molly as it is with her husband Leopold and with the xenophobic citizens of Dublin who eventually assault Leopold in the pub. From sexual shame and longing to the ultraliberated enjoyment of all the 'sweets of sin'; from provincial paralysis to self-aggrandising myth-making; from colonial boredom to the making of one little town an everywhere, a cosmopolis: as one of the many popular songs quoted in *Ulysses* puts it, your head it simply swirls. Joyce never simply satirises or dismisses the inhabitants of Dublin because his entire text is in some regards a larger scale reproduction of their own imaginative and political fantasies. But as *Ulysses* finally achieves publication in 1922, the Anglo-Irish Treaty is about to partition the island, in order to create the Irish Free State and the 'statelet' of Northern Ireland. The modernist phase of Irish nationalism, so to speak, was drawing to a close, and Joyce's continuing linguistic experiments (culminating in *Finnegans Wake*) are increasingly remote from any sense of a particular national context or audience.

Ireland's modernism, although precocious by comparison with developments elsewhere, was almost entirely confined to literature. Its influence on later developments in the visual arts, music and architecture was mediated by an intense and protracted anti-modernism, sometimes indistinguishable from anti-revivalism, which was itself pre-eminently literary. There was certainly a return to conventional forms of representation that was at times almost aggressively eager to dispense with the experimentations and heroics of the earlier decades. This reversion is highly visible in the careers of artists such as Seán Keating and Paul Henry in the 1930s.[32] But in literature, naturalism, associated in fiction with O'Faolain, and in poetry with Kavanagh, became dominant. It prided itself on its attention to the actual, on its readiness to emphasise limitation and the absurdity of any pretence to transcend it; this set of attitudes was remarkably appropriate to the Free State's post-revolutionary pursuit of security and authority.[33] Thus modernism in Ireland is not followed by post-modernism (which does not appear until much later) but almost by the reverse – a disenchantment with and dismissal of much that the revival had inaugurated.

There are of course some exceptions to this general retreat. These would obviously include Samuel Beckett, whose late-modernist preoccupations link him to the era of the revival, although chronologically he lies outside it,[34] and Máirtín Ó Cadhain, whose extraordinary novel *Cré na Cille* was published in 1949. In an extended comparison between Beckett and Ó Cadhain, Declan Kiberd suggests that Ó Cadhain's decision to write in Irish is analogous to Beckett's use of French: both were thereby freer to disengage from literary stereotypes of Irishness, while Ó Cadhain also broke with the revivalist emphasis on the folkloric roots of 'authentic' Irish-language writing in his characteristically modernist stylistic practice.[35] In Beckett, however, scattered echoes of Synge, O'Casey or Yeats seem to commemorate a grander dream of Irishness, and of its challenge to and by the modern world. Those who inhabit the catastrophically reduced conditions of his fiction and drama – Molloy, Malone and the Unnamable of the famous trilogy and the tramps, Vladimir and Estragon, of *Waiting for Godot* – can no longer dream of any such heroic confrontation. They have lapsed back into 'blather', an endless verbality that they long to escape from, to reach the silence that lies beyond it. Their furious energy is an inverted version of the energy that once made Irish modernism so dazzling an enterprise. 'Beckett's *Ecce Homo* is what human beings have become', as Adorno writes, for the greater the aspiration, the greater the possibility of failure.[36]

Flann O'Brien's version of counter-revivalism involved a curious inversion of modernism's cosmopolitan ambitions, while retaining many of its experimental formal procedures. O'Brien evidently reacted against the ambitions and the reputation of Joyce, although in his case we can identify the effects of Irish political introversion, enhanced by neutrality during the Second World War. But it was Thomas Kinsella who turned the Joycean achievement to his own purposes in verse, rewriting Joyce in an idiom that owes a good deal to Pound. Kinsella's poetry, however, has been increasingly erased from public consciousness by the emergence of new work that has forsaken the epic ambitions of modernism, making a virtue of the modesty that disclaimed for art the capacity to repair the destitution of the cultural world. This is represented most importantly by Seamus Heaney, who has regularly acknowledged his indebtedness to Kavanagh, and more recently by the distinctively postmodern Northern Irish poets, Paul Muldoon and Medbh McGuckian.

One of the more familiar political charges levelled against literary revivalism in Ireland is that it helped to inspire the militaristic, masculinist heroics that led to 1916, and that it also contributed to the grimly patriarchal regime that succeeded in the Irish Free State. While more nuanced and detailed readings of Yeats, as well as of such figures as Patrick Pearse, should by now have served to contextualise and qualify this critique, it might further be argued that the institutionalisation of the great male modernists in itself, regardless of the politics of their literary practice, served to inhibit later writers, and, especially, women. Simply put, the presentation of Joyce, for example, as the exemplary Irish literary genius may have had oppressive implications for Irish women writers, despite or maybe even because of the fact that he has often been read as alert to women's experiences and concerned to find ways to express their voices. Certainly, most contemporary Irish women's writing, from the south of Ireland at least, has more in common with the naturalism and feminism of the early fiction of Edna O'Brien, for example, than to any revivalist precursors. Nevertheless, recent feminist recovery work, straying well beyond the more familiar names of Augusta Gregory, Elizabeth Bowen and Kate O'Brien, may call into question whether either nationalism or modernism as such were fundamentally disabling affiliations for Irish women writers.[37]

But while most later Irish writers may have forgone the egotistical hubris and uncompromising obscurity of the late Yeats and Joyce, they may also have missed out on their central insight: that Ireland's 'backwardness' can offer a privileged vantage point for the exploration of the modern itself, and one that might be shared by other non-metropolitan cultures. Elleke Boehmer, for example, has suggested that an 'expanded picture of a globalized and constellated modernism' might encompass the ways in which 'nationalist movements in the empire's outer regions were inflected through modernist prisms'.[38] Despite their renewed reverence for the local and the regional, counter-revivalists instead often couched their critiques of the constrictiveness of independent Ireland in the much less critical terms of what has come to be known as the ideology of modernisation; suggesting, in other words, that it was the business of the Irish merely to 'catch up' with their more enlightened and emancipated neighbours.[39] The simple ambition to become modern is far removed from the complex condition of modernity, most especially when it becomes so eager to abandon, as a hindrance and as a form of excess, those modernist positions that were so hard won and so memorably represented by the generation of Joyce and Yeats.

Notes

1. W. B. Yeats, 'A postscript to a forthcoming work of essays by various writers', *Uncollected Prose*, ed. J. Frayne and C. Johnson (London: Macmillan, 1975), vol. II, p. 245.
2. F. S. L. Lyons, *Culture and Anarchy in Ireland* (Oxford: Oxford University Press, 1982).
3. See Terence Brown, 'The counter-revival', in *The Field Day Anthology of Irish Writing*, ed. Seamus Deane (Derry: Field Day, 1991), vol. III.
4. See Luke Gibbons, 'Constructing the canon: versions of national identity', in *The Field Day Anthology of Irish Writing*, vol. II; and P. J. Mathews, *Revival: The Abbey Theatre, Sinn Féin, The Gaelic League and the Co-operative Movement* (Cork: Cork University Press, 2003).
5. Brian Fallon, *Irish Art, 1830–1990* (Belfast: Appletree Press, 1994), p. 14.
6. See Jerome McGann, *Black Riders: The Visible Language of Modernism* (Princeton: Princeton University Press, 1993).
7. See Conor Cruise O'Brien, 'Passion and the cunning: an essay on the politics of W. B. Yeats', in *In Excited Reverie: A Centenary Tribute to W. B. Yeats*, ed. A. N. Jeffares and K. G. W. Cross (New York: St. Martin's Press, 1965); and Elizabeth Cullingford, *Yeats, Ireland and Fascism* (London: New York University Press, 1981).
8. Marjorie Howes explores Yeats's conception of Anglo-Irish identity as a 'nationality in crisis', which Yeats repeatedly exposes as no more than a 'willful, imaginative response' to the absence of stability. See *Yeats's Nations: Gender, Class, and Irishness* (Cambridge: Cambridge University Press, 1996).
9. See Partha Chatterjee, *The Nation and its Fragments* (Princeton: Princeton University Press, 1993).
10. Edward Said, *Culture and Imperialism* (London: Chatto & Windus, 1993), pp. 265–6.
11. W. B. Yeats, *The Poems*, ed. R. J. Finneran (London: Gill & Macmillan, 1983), p. 50.
12. Ibid., p. 181.
13. For recent feminist reassessments of Yeats, see Elizabeth Cullingford, *Gender and History in Yeats's Love Poetry* (Cambridge: Cambridge University Press, 1993); Howes, *Yeats's Nations*.
14. Yeats, *Poems*, p. 337.

15. See Patricia Coughlan and Alex Davis, Introduction, *Modernism and Ireland: the Poetry of the 1930s*, ed. Patricia Coughlan and Alex Davis (Cork: Cork University Press, 1995), p. 1.

16. See Perry Anderson, 'Modernity and revolution', in *Marxism and the Interpretation of Culture*, ed. C. Nelson and L. Grossberg (London: Macmillan, 1988).

17. Terry Eagleton, *Heathcliff and the Great Hunger* (London: Verso, 1995), p. 280.

18. Terence Brown, 'Ireland, modernism and the 1930s', in *Modernism and Ireland: The Poetry of the 1930s*, p. 34.

19. Joyce, *Poems Penyeach* (London: Faber, 1966), pp. 36–7.

20. Joyce, *Ulysses*, ed. H. W. Gabler (London: The Bodley Head, 1986), p. 135.

21. See Richard Kearney, 'Myth and motherland', in *Ireland's Field Day* (London: Hutchinson, 1985).

22. Joyce, *A Portrait of the Artist as a Young Man* (London: Penguin, 1992), p. 274.

23. As argued by Joep Leerssen, *Remembrance and Imagination* (Cork: Cork University Press, 1996), p. 230. Against this see, for example, Luke Gibbons's analysis of Joyce's account of the 'pathology of post-Famine Ireland', especially in *Dubliners*, '"Have you no homes to go to?": Joyce and the politics of pathology', *Semicolonial Joyce*, ed. D. Attridge and M. Howes (Cambridge: Cambridge University Press, 2000), pp. 150–71.

24. For the classic account of popular European carnival, see Mikhail Bakhtin, *Rabelais and His World*, trans. H. Iswolsky (Cambridge, MA: MIT Press, 1968).

25. See Walter Benjamin's speculations on Baudelaire, 'Paris, the capital of the nine-teenth century', in *The Arcades Project*, trans. H. Eiland and K. McLaughlin (Cam-bridge, MA: Harvard University Press, 1999).

26. Joyce, *Ulysses*, p. 128.

27. Ibid., pp. 587, 585.

28. Benjamin, 'Paris, the capital of the nineteenth century', p. 20.

29. Joyce, *Ulysses*, p. 38.

30. Benjamin, 'Paris, the capital of the nineteenth century', p. 416.

31. Joyce, *Ulysses*, p. 248.

32. See Brown, 'Ireland, modernism and the 1930s'.

33. See Seamus Deane, *Strange Country: Modernity and Nationhood in Irish Writing since 1800* (Oxford: Clarendon Press, 1997), p. 162.

34. Fredric Jameson defines 'late modernism' or 'neo-modernism', post-1945, as a replay and repetition of a 'high modernist practice', which has now been codified and taken as a model. See *A Singular Modernity: Essay on the Ontology of the Present* (London: Verso, 2002), Part II.

35. Declan Kiberd, *Irish Classics* (London: Granta, 2000), pp. 574–89.

36. Theodor Adorno, 'Commitment', in *Aesthetics and Politics*, ed. Ernst Bloch *et al.* (London: Verso, 1977), p. 190.

37. See Antoinette Quinn, 'Ireland/Herland: women and literary nationalism, 1845–1916', and Gerardine Meaney, 'Identity and opposition: women's writing, 1890–1960', in *The Field Day Anthology of Irish Writing*, ed. A. Bourke *et al.* (Cork: Cork Uni-versity Press, 2002), vol. V.

38. Elleke Boehmer, *Empire, the National, and the Postcolonial, 1890–1920* (Oxford: Oxford University Press, 2002), p. 175. For the influence of Irish revivalist writing in other regions of the world, see Tracy Mishkin, *The Harlem and Irish Renaissances: Language,*

Identity and Representation (Gainesville: University of Florida, 1998); and (in relation to Joyce) Gerald Martin, *Journeys through the Labyrinth: Latin American Fiction in the Twentieth Century* (London: Verso, 1989).

39. See Conor MacCarthy on the ideology of modernisation in Ireland: *Modernisation, Crisis and Culture in Ireland, 1969–1992* (Dublin: Four Courts Press, 2000).

Further reading

David Cairns and Shaun Richards, *Writing Ireland: Colonialism, Nationalism and Culture* (Manchester: Manchester University Press, 1988)

Seamus Deane, *Celtic Revivals* (London: Faber, 1985)

R. F. Foster, *W. B. Yeats: A Life*, 2 vols. (Oxford: Oxford University Press, 1997 and 2003)

Declan Kiberd, *Inventing Ireland* (London: Jonathan Cape, 1995)

P. J. Mathews, *Revival: The Abbey Theatre, Sinn Féin, The Gaelic League and the Co-operative Movement* (Cork: Cork University Press, 2003)

Emer Nolan, *Joyce and Nationalism* (London: Routledge, 1995)

G. J. Watson, *Irish Identity and the Literary Revival* (London: Croom Helm, 1979)

10

Poetry in Ireland

To give an account of poetry in modern Ireland is not an entirely straightforward matter, for several reasons. To begin with the most obvious, using the title 'Poetry in Ireland' rather than 'Irish Poetry' sidesteps a vital issue. Since the Middle Ages, poetry has been written on the island in both Irish and English. Recently there has been some dispute over whether the poetry in the two languages can sensibly be seen as a single entity at all, as 'Irish Poetry'. The classic claim in favour of such a shared poetic tradition was made by Thomas Kinsella, both in his book *The Dual Tradition*, and in the introduction to his *New Oxford Book of Irish Verse* in 1986:

> It should be clear at least that the Irish tradition is a matter of two linguistic entities in dynamic interaction, of two major bodies of poetry asking to be understood together as functions of a shared and painful history . . . To limit a response to one aspect only, as is often done – to the literature in Irish, through specialized academic concerns or out of nationalist emotion, or to the literature in English as an annexe to British literature . . . is to miss a rare opportunity: that of responding to a notable and venerable literary tradition, the oldest vernacular literature in Western Europe, as it survives a change of vernacular.[1]

The aspiration towards such a dual, shared tradition was stated a long time ago by the Cork poet and Professor of Literature Denis Florence McCarthy. McCarthy was one of the artistic leaders of the nationalist journal, *The Nation*, in the 1840s. The terms in which he puts the aspiration seems to concede the chimerical nature of the project: 'that we can be thoroughly Irish in our writings without ceasing to be English;

that we can be faithful to the land of our birth without being unfaithful to that literature which has been "the nursing mother of our minds".[2] So Kinsella's view is far from unique, nor is it especially eccentric, even if he does express it with more vigour than his predecessors. The view that Irish literature shares common features across its two languages had for example been taken – equally famously – by Vivian Mercier in his great study of *The Irish Comic Tradition*.[3] The idea that the same literature can share two languages was most vigorously contested by Conor Cruise O'Brien, who argued at different times against both Mercier and Kinsella that it is absurd to say, in Kinsella's terms, that a poetic tradition has changed languages and remained the same literary whole.[4]

So a chapter such as this has to address the dilemma of what exactly 'poetry in Ireland' entails, taking into account both of the languages in which poetry has been written since the Middle Ages. Quite apart from modern scholarly disputes, there is a real issue here in historical terms. It is not simply an argument between literary historians of opposed persuasions: Kinsella's 'nationalist emotion' versus the inclination to see modern Irish literature as Anglo-Irish or 'an annexe to British literature'. Vivian Mercier, who argued for the integrity of the dual tradition, was a friend of O'Brien and wrote one of the most valuable studies of Anglo-Irish literature.[5] It has been a particularly vexed issue over the past two centuries because by 1800 there is a complex relationship between poetry in Irish, much of which was composed and preserved orally as it had been since the Elizabethan period, and developments in the wider European poetic world, dominated by individualistic Romanticism, of which English poetry formed an important part. It is clear, for example, that Johann Wolfgang von Goethe in German, Giacomo Leopardi in Italian, Victor Hugo in French, and Lord Byron and Percy Bysshe Shelley in English, all belonged to the same broad European development, but that Irish poetry did not. As a final complicating factor, we will see that by 2000 it was no longer just a matter of writing poetry in Irish or English; a series of symbiotic complexities involving the languages and their interrelations are also at issue, through cross-reference, translation and influence, conscious or unconscious.

A second introductory caveat when tracing a heritage for the Irish poets of the past two centuries is to remember that the poetic world inherited by the Irish poets of the nineteenth century was not an inferior or client one; it was fundamentally different, in aesthetic and ethical terms, founded in a tradition of great learnedness and virtuosity whose roots go back to the early Middle Ages. This point is illustrated abundantly in the most important anthology of poetry in Irish from the first of the two centuries under consideration here, *An Duanaire* by Seán Ó Tuama and Thomas Kinsella.[6] The editors of this book make high claims for the Gaelic poets of their whole period, especially between 1650 and 1800, but emphasise how much those poets stood outside their contemporary European traditions. In their introduction, Ó Tuama and Kinsella can claim, with some plausibility, that 'the dozen or so lyrics of high quality which [Aodhagán Ó Rathaille] shaped out of his own personal chaos make him perhaps the greatest of Irish poets, writing in Irish or English, between the seventeenth century and the twentieth'.[7] Even popular anonymous poetry in Irish is entirely distinct, both in subjects and forms (often having more in common with medieval European poetry than with contemporary writing), from the ballads that were shared across Europe.

This claim for autonomy and literary sophistication needs to be advanced not just in response to the colonising relegation suffered by the Irish language, ever since the Elizabethan period, and dramatically accelerated in the nineteenth century, but also because the criticism of poetry in Irish made such a bad beginning. At its worst, criticism like Douglas Hyde's in his 1902 pamphlet *Irish Poetry* (which it is only fair to remember was an entry in an Irish language competition)[8] set the tone for a kind of chauvinistic critical infantilism, mercilessly mocked by Flann O'Brien both in his 'Cruishkeen Lawn' columns in the *Irish Times* and in more extended fictions in both Irish and English such as *An Béal Bocht* (*The Poor Mouth*) and *At Swim-Two-Birds*. More damagingly, Hyde's slightly earlier and much more significant *Literary History of Ireland* was also dominated by a kind of legend-based critical atavism (in conjunction, in both books, with Hyde's own excellent English versions of the Irish poems).[9] Hyde's *Literary History* is a powerful piece of cultural campaigning, but its coverage hardly reaches the eighteenth century and it makes no mention of writing in English. Despite distinguished exceptions, such as Austin Clarke's brief but brilliant *Poetry in Modern Ireland*,[10] it proved difficult to get beyond the beleaguered defiance of such criticism, and it is only in recent years that a genuinely evaluative criticism has been applied to poetry in Irish, by writers like Alan Titley and Frank Sewell in his discussion of four major poets of the second half of the twentieth century.[11] What is most crucially needed is a modern criticism, in Irish and/or English, of the major poetic writings in Irish between the Middle

Ages and the twentieth century.[12] Without that it is difficult to see where modern Irish poetry stands, or on what it is founded. We cannot assess its effectiveness without a criticism that clarifies its aims in the light of its heritage.

There are two final introductory factors to be borne in mind before proceeding to the substance of this summary of poetry in Ireland over the past two centuries. First, it is characteristic of most anthologies of Irish poetry, in Irish, English or both, to give far greater representation of poetry in the oral tradition and popular songs (Ó Tuama's *amhráin na ndaoine* or songs of the people) than in most canonical assemblages. Even W. J. McCormack's lively millenial anthology from New York, whose distinctive approach is to include brief representations of many poets (including some in Irish) from the start of the Anglo-Irish period, ends with a brief section of such poems.[13] The second, and related, factor is that there is a much more marked tolerance of the political in poetry in Ireland and about Ireland than is normal in English: from Jonathan Swift, to W. B. Yeats, to Seamus Heaney, to Nuala Ní Dhomhnaill, to Tom Paulin (with a predictable reaction from traditionalist critics against poetry's right to be political, something which has always been resisted in the English tradition, from the seventeenth century but perhaps dating as far back as the age of Chaucer). In Ireland, there has always been a socio-political counter-tendency.

This tradition of the political and the popular was already an important part of what distinguished poetry in Ireland at the end of the eighteenth century, the beginning of the two centuries under discussion here. As an example, it is instructive to consider Eoghan Rua Ó Súilleabháin. Ó Súilleabháin has been repeatedly taken as the figure of the Gaelic poet: for instance by Yeats in 'Red Hanrahan' and elsewhere, and by Thomas Flanagan in *The Year of The French*. Ó Súilleabháin wrote in the generation before 1800 as a semi-folk poet of great technical accomplishment. Moreover, although his writing does not fit into European romanticism, he was not writing in an atavistic or outmoded tradition; he had little to do, for example, with the eighteenth-century world of European neoclassicism (with which, as it happens, poetry in Irish did sometimes have rather closer affinities than with the Romantics). And, though he wrote in well-established Irish forms and genres, Ó Súilleabháin was decidedly modern, writing of current events in terms which were political ('Rodney's Glory', celebrating a British naval victory in which he was involved), sociological (*An Spealadóir*) and personal (*A Chara Mo Chléibh*). His writing is not reactionary; it is at once modern and traditional. In many ways indeed, it could be claimed that he – like Raifteirí – was writing from a more modern, forward-looking mentality than the introversions of the great European Romantic poets. Most importantly, he was the inheritor of a fully formed tradition of poetry unique to Irish in its period, the eighteenth-century convention of the political aisling, a descendant of the medieval dream-vision. This tradition has links with European love poetry since the Middle Ages but took quite distinct forms in Irish from the late seventeenth century onwards, as described in Daniel Corkery's great study *The Hidden Ireland*.[14] Corkery shows how the vision-poetry of the European tradition developed political forms in Ireland in ways entirely unparalleled elsewhere in Europe.[15] Finally, we should note that the centrality of anonymous popular songs does not mean that there was no 'cult of authorship'. This was just as influential in the Irish popular oral tradition as in Romanticism. Indeed 'the poet' – '*an file*' in Irish – has a long pre-history as a figure of authority in Irish literature, something which Yeats represents as a political reality in his heroic play, *The King's Threshold*.

The main reason for dwelling on Ó Súilleabháin, who slightly predates our period, is to establish that in 1800 the poet writing in Irish was much better established as an authoritative precedent than the Irish poet writing in English, despite the relatively slight representation of Gaelic poetry in printed texts. There are quite different problems in placing Irish poetry in English at the start of the nineteenth century. Here there are writers who certainly were part of the world of European Romanticism: Thomas Moore belongs to the milieu, if not always to the subjective spirit, of the European Romantic poets in English. But, apart from Moore, the contribution of Ireland to nineteenth-century poetry in English is not greatly significant – or at least its place in the traditional canon is not.[16] Generally speaking, the heritage offered by early nineteenth-century Irish poets in English to their successors was not found inviting by the revivalists of the later nineteenth century in the way that a cult figure like Eoghan Rua Ó Súilleabháin was.

There is a further poetic field of particular importance in Ireland beyond what was written as original poetry in Irish or English: translation, especially translation into English by Irish writers. The most productive area here was translation from Irish, though Irish poets (led by the late Romantic James Clarence Mangan) also play a noticeable part in translating European poetry into English. However, Mangan's European poems have not generally been seen as a corpus of great influence in its own right. What did have greater impact as a component of the Irish poetic whole was translations from Irish – the traditions of Hyde and Augusta Gregory. Mainly through their versions, translation exerted important, though sporadic, formal influence on some Irish poets in English. What has come to be called the 'voice' of Irish poetry in English was partly developed by the translators.[17]

So the Irish situation in 1800 was anomalous in several ways; poetry in Irish was a major cultural phenomenon in its own terms but played little part in the mainstream of European developments; Irish poetry written in English had aspirations to be part of the cultural-political centre but did not, on the whole, make a major impression there. So far I have given most emphasis to the Gaelic tradition because that is the heritage least likely to be readily familiar to the modern reader. But it was a constant presence in the mind of Irish poets in Irish and English from the beginnings of the Celtic Revival in the eighteenth century, onward through Yeats and his fellow-revivalists, to twentieth-century poets like John Montague, Seamus Heaney and Paul Muldoon. To take one example, it is impossible to have a proper sense of the force of Muldoon's use of terms like *'aisling'* (vision) or *'immrami'* (voyaging) without seeing them in the context of Gaelic poetry.

The most authoritative treatment of developments in Irish poetry in all its senses through this period is the chapters in *The Field Day Anthology of Irish Writing*, especially the opening section of Volume II 'Poetry and Song 1800–1890' compiled by the project's general editor Seamus Deane.[18] The broad subdivision he makes – 'Poetry and Song' – recognises the centrality of the oral and popular element I have noted above. Broadly speaking, Deane accords with the principles outlined by Kinsella in the *New Oxford Book* by taking together the three categories I have distinguished: poems in English, poems in Irish and translations. His Introduction is an admirably brief outline of these three traditions (though poetry in Irish is not much represented in this part of the *Anthology*), and he performs a crucial service by placing the poetry in its original context of publication, showing, for example, how James Clarence Mangan published a different kind of poem in the Unionist *Dublin University Review* than in the nationalist *The Nation*. In a way this division of outlet is a microcosm of much larger differences of context: between the poems published in Irish and English, or in popular or literary forums. Even writing in English, Mangan distinguishes the established

existence of two kinds of audience and two kinds of poetry associated
with them: the Gaelic tradition with its tendency towards the oral and
popular song (Ó Tuama's *amhráin na ndaoine*), and canonical European
poetry. But Mangan is a European, and – like Ó Tuama and Deane
himself – he is aware of the links between Gaelic poetry and the medieval
traditions of European poetry in which it is founded.

In distinguishing in this very brief survey the three poetic worlds
that prevailed in Ireland across the past two centuries, there must be –
if we are to speak of distinctively Irish poetry at all – important mutual
influence between those categories, as there is. Maybe the most persuasive example of this interrelationship is formal analysis, something that
Deane does not have space for in his excellent and canon-shaping section in *The Field Day Anthology*. Deane notes that Jeremiah Callanan 'is
often said to have been one of the first translators from the Irish to have
achieved something like a natural fluency in English'.[19] This claim was
advanced most famously by Yeats in the introduction to his anthology of
Irish verse: 'An honest style did not come into English-speaking Ireland
until Callanan wrote three or four native translations from the Gaelic.'[20]
A lot of weight is being put on the words 'native' and 'natural' here, to
distinguish Callanan's versions from a perfectly fluent kind of Irish translation in English derived from eighteenth-century English models. The
history of Irish poetry in English from 1800 is a story of a consciously
revivalist venture, starting at the latest from Charlotte Brooke's *Reliques
of Irish Poetry* (1789).

In order to see what exactly it was that constituted the 'native' and
'natural' in Callanan's translations, we have to cite for contrast the kind of
poetry written in standard English diction in Ireland by the first revivalists and in the early nineteenth century, the period when Irish poetry first
seems to aspire to being thought of as a coherent and separate corpus.
Even if we follow Mercier, O'Brien, McCormack and others in dating
the beginnings of Anglo-Irish literature with the Restoration dramatists
and Jonathan Swift in the late seventeenth and early eighteenth centuries, it is only with Romanticism and the revivalists that something distinctively Irish or Celtic can be claimed. Yeats's much-quoted triad from
'To Ireland in the Coming Times' sets the scene well; for him, Mangan,
Davis and Ferguson illustrate the similarities and differences in the Irish
corpus. Mercier notes that there were two styles available to the Irish
poets in English in the early nineteenth century, and that it is perfectly
easy to distinguish them. There is the late eighteenth-century 'poetic

diction abhorred by Wordsworth' of which Mercier gives these lines from William Leahy's version of the wonderful Finn-cycle lyric 'The Blackbird of Derrycairn':

> Hail tuneful bird of sable wing,
> Thou warbler sweet of Carna's grove!
> Not lays more charming will I hear
> Tho' round th'expansive earth I rove.[21]

Here is a poetic language practised by an Irish poet, predating Callanan's naturalness. If anyone doubts the existence of *anything* that can be called 'the Celtic note', they have only to contrast this quatrain, derived from the English eighteenth-century tradition, with the long line that the gifted translators beginning with Callanan and Ferguson derived from Irish.

It could be argued that the distinction of Callanan is not that he achieved natural fluency in English, as claimed by Yeats and Deane, but that he and the other translators brought into English poetry formal qualities that are at once entirely foreign to it and totally successful within it, and which thereafter remained a permanent option within English. But it is a poetic form that is entirely unparalleled in standard English, often alternating the loose long lines with short lines of plain-style. The most commonly quoted examples are well chosen: Callanan's mysteriously effective 'The Outlaw of Loch Lene':

> My bed was the ground, my roof the greenwood above,
> And the wealth that I sought one far kind glance from my love.

Or Ferguson's masterpiece, his 'Lament for Thomas Davis' which is perhaps the finest achievement of this very un-English poetic:

> I walked through Ballinderry in the springtime,
>   When the bud was on the tree,
> And I said, in every fresh-ploughed field beholding
>   The sowers striding free,
> Scattering broadcast for the corn in golden plenty,
>   On the quick, seed-clasping soil,
> Even such this day among the fresh-stirred hearts of Erin
>   Thomas Davis is thy toil.

The extreme variation in line lengths here is matched by another much-quoted minor masterpiece by a revivalist colleague of Yeats's, T. W. Rolleston in his translation 'The Dead at Clonmacnoise' (1909):

In a quiet-water'd land, a land of roses
Stands Saint Kieran's city fair,
And the warriors of Erin in their famous generations
Slumber there.

A characteristic note has become recognisable through the century: a vernacular freedom, derived from popular songs and far removed from the artificialities of eighteenth-century English diction – lines like this much-quoted *cri de cœur* from a translation by Edward Walsh:

I've the cold earth's dark odour
And I'm worn from the weather.[22]

By the end of the century this vernacular anti-doggerel has gained unmistakeable confidence, for example in the freedom of this line amidst the elegant regularity of Thomas Caulfield Irwin's elegant 'Sonnets on the Poetry and Problems of Life':

The tide's sad voice ebbing towards loneliness.[23]

Without an awareness of this heritage, it is not possible to understand Yeats's place among the modernists in English or what lies behind Patrick Kavanagh's notes played on 'a slack string'. In his opening chapter Mercier shows how the vapid versions of eighteenth-century formal verse took on such new notes with the revivalists, with linguistic effects drawn at least in part from the Gaelic tradition, though by no means entirely so. When William Larminie made his famous proposal that so excited Yeats, that Irish poets could make 'their mark on English literature' by bringing into its prosody a body of metres drawn from the Irish, he was partly prescribing a course of action that had already been put into practice by the translators: a style of lineation and assonance which, in Larminie's phrase, was 'rich with unexhausted possibilities'.[24]

The different styles of representation can be illustrated by comparing the versions of Seán Ó Coileáin's '*Macnamh an Duine Doilíosaigh*' by Mangan and Ferguson, both accomplished prosodists. The titles of the two translations give an indication of the two approaches: Mangan's 'Lament Over the Ruins of *Teach Molaga*' keeps the placename in Irish; Ferguson's title, like his version, is more fully translated: 'Lament over the Ruins of the Abbey of Timoleague'. When Mangan translated the poem there were already two earlier translations: by Thomas Furlong in Hardiman's *Irish Minstrelsy*, and Ferguson's which was printed in the *Dublin*

University Magazine in the course of his review of Hardiman. Here is Ferguson's version of the first two stanzas:

> Lone and weary as I wander'd
>   By the bleak shore of the sea,
> Meditating and reflecting
>   On the world's hard destiny;
> Forth the moon and stars 'gan glimmer
>   In the quiet tide beneath, –
> For on slumbering spray and blossom
>   Breathed not out of heaven a breath.[25]

Mangan's version was first published in *The Nation* (on 8 August 1846).

> I wandered forth at night alone,
> Along the dreary, shingly, billow-beaten shore.
> Sadness that night was in my bosom's core,
> My soul and strength lay prone.
> Musing of Life, and Death, and Fate,
> I slowly paced along, heedless of aught around,
> Till on the hill, now, alas! ruin-crowned,
> Lo! The old Abbey-gate![26]

Clearly Mangan's version is much more foreign to the prosodic norms of English at the end of the eighteenth century (there is not much influence from the English Romantics in these translators). But what is particularly Gaelic here is not the diction ('heedless of aught around' is typical of the unexpressive slackness of English poetic diction at its least inspired) but the formal properties: the metrical patterns and the variations in line length. These effects, at least as an option, become typical of Irish poetry in English.

These nineteenth-century applications of the traditions of poetry in Irish, both through translation and through adaptation of formal effects, were a preparation for much more significant developments in the twentieth century. Obviously Yeats is central here; but he was only the leading figure in a widespread movement to create a new poetry in Ireland as part of the cultural revival. The body of work produced between Yeats and Heaney's successors is clearly very substantial. There is an irony in the view of Austin Clarke, followed by a number of commentators such as R. F. Garratt,[27] that Yeats's success meant that he used up the poetic moisture that might have nourished later growths. Yeats's generation was at the start of a new tradition, drawing on preceding formalities, but creating a larger heritage themselves. Yeats was an enabler, not a hoarder. Moreover, at the start of the twentieth century poetry in Irish begins to show a net gain again, no longer only offering forms and subjects to poetry in English, but starting a new tradition which borrowed lyric forms from English and other modern poetic worlds. In the space available here all I have been able to do is to suggest the broad circumstances in which that happened. I will conclude by describing twentieth-century developments in similarly broad terms.

One way of assessing how 'Irish Poetry' has been seen in the twentieth century is to consider anthologies. Here we find a strikingly circular development; earlier sectional anthologies, such as *The Spirit of the Nation* (1843), Douglas Hyde's *Love-Songs of Connacht* (1893), and George Sigerson's *Poets and Poetry of Munster* (1860) and *Bards of the Gael and Gall* (1897) are succeeded by attempted complete surveys, such as the various Oxford Books, before a return to more definitive anthologies devoted to different areas or periods – such as, say, Frank Ormsby's *A Rage for Order*.[28] The significant period here is the middle one, roughly the first two-thirds of the twentieth century, when it was felt that 'Irish Poetry' was both unitary and definable enough as a category to be encompassed within the covers of a single book. The first major compilation of this kind was Stopford Brooke and T. W. Rolleston's *Treasury*, timed for the start of the new century,[29] as was Yeats's rather more whimsical *Book of Irish Verse*. Donagh MacDonagh and Lennox Robinson's *Oxford Book of Irish Verse* (1958) begins at the recognised starting-point of Anglo-Irish literature in the Restoration period, and includes poems in English and some translations from the Irish. This became typical of anthology coverage: the two most popular anthologies in the later twentieth century, by the poets John Montague and Brendan Kennelly, feature the same mixture.[30]

Thomas Kinsella's controversial 1986 *Oxford Book*, mentioned at the start of this chapter, was the last attempt – at least to date – to cover Irish poetry as a whole.[31] Most recent anthologies have given up the attempt to be all inclusive. Important recent anthologies have all reverted to a partial coverage, particularly of the modern period, mostly defined as the twentieth century. Anthologies occur in cycles: the early 1970s saw the publication of several. Derek Mahon's *Sphere Book of Modern Irish Poetry* (1972) ran from middle Yeats (starting at *Responsibilities*, 1913) to very early Muldoon, presciently drawing on a pamphlet 'Knowing My Place' published when Muldoon was 20. David Marcus edited *Irish Poets 1924–1974* for Pan in 1975, and there were two significantly selective Ulster collections, both published by Blackstaff in Belfast in 1974: Padraig Fiacc's *The Wearing of the Black: An Anthology of Contemporary Ulster Poetry* with a firm commitment to the traditional Irish inclination towards political poetry, observable since the eighteenth century; and John Hewitt's *Rhyming Weavers and other Country Poets of Antrim and Down*. And at the same time as Kinsella's *New Oxford Book* there appeared two modern anthologies. The first of these, Paul Muldoon's *Faber Book of Contemporary Irish Verse* (1988) was accused of having a bias towards Northern writers: not too surprising a bias, one might feel, given the dominance of poetry in English by the generation of Ulster poets who emerged in the 1960s: John Montague, Derek Mahon, Seamus Heaney, Michael Longley and James Simmons. The second of the modern anthologies from that point was *The Penguin Book of Contemporary Irish Poetry* (1990), edited jointly by Derek Mahon and Ireland's foremost publisher of poetry, Peter Fallon of Gallery Press, which was seen as partly offering a southern corrective to Muldoon's *Faber Book*. A more determinedly southern emphasis was given by Gabriel Fitzmaurice in 1993.[32] The most successful overall anthology of the period since Yeats is Patrick Crotty's *Modern Irish Poetry*, which represents all the kinds of poetry in Ireland in all its languages and mixtures from the 1930s up to the 1990s.[33]

Of course anthologies, although they may be influential, are reactive, not proactive, so the question that arises is: what is the implication of the way anthologies have evolved for the conception and coverage of Irish poetry? There are some obvious historical developments that anthologists had to take account of. One is already evident in the previous paragraph: the leading role in English poetry taken by the Ulster poets of the 1960s, which indeed may be extendable back by a generation to the writing of Louis MacNeice, W. R. Rodgers and Patrick Kavanagh. An equally obvious new development is the strengthening of poetry in Irish, throughout the twentieth century, but accelerating in its second half, inspired perhaps by the lead of Máirtín Ó Direáin, Seán Ó Riordáin and Máire Mhac an tSaoi. New *duanairí* (anthologies) had to emerge to represent this development, and they have: initially the two elegant and scholarly volumes edited by Séamas Ó Céileachair.[34] A confident millenial culmination of such anthologies was Gréagóir Ó Dúill's *Fearann Pinn* in 2000 which is a substantial representation of twentieth-century poets in Irish.[35]

Ó Céileachair's volumes in fact immediately preceded the most significant development for poetry in Irish of the modern, printed era, which was the emergence of the *Innti* group of poets from University College

Cork in the late 1960s. Their emergence there was largely inspired by the scholarly leadership of Seán Ó Tuama, professor of Modern Irish at UCC, and by the example of Seán Ó Riordáin, the first great modern lyric poet in Irish. The principal members of the *Innti* group were Gabriel Rosenstock, who has become recognised as the leading contemporary translator into Irish of poetry from several languages; Michael Davitt; Liam Ó Muirthile who is a journalist in Irish as well as one of the country's leading lyric poets; and Nuala Ní Dhomhnaill.

It is not a slight to the other three of this gifted foursome to say that Ní Dhomhnaill's eminence is the most striking; indeed it is one of the most remarkable phenomena in contemporary Irish poetry. Ó Riordáin, the poetic guru of this group, had grown up speaking English but wrote only in Irish, discouraging the translation of his works into English. Ní Dhomhnaill (who also knew English before Irish) followed this lead with variations; she too writes only in Irish and doesn't translate her work into English herself.[36] Unlike Ó Riordáin though, she does encourage the translation of her work by other poets. As a result, one of the most important poetic volumes to appear over the past generation is *Pharaoh's Daughter* (1991), a collection of Ní Dhomhnaill's poems with parallel translations by many of the leading contemporary Irish poets in English: Heaney, Longley, Montague, Carson, Muldoon and others.[37] Her earlier poems had been translated by a writer who is of comparable interest for this debate, the Limerick poet Michael Hartnett. Hartnett too grew up speaking English, the language he first wrote in. In 1978 he wrote a long poem 'A Farewell to English' in which he declared his intent only to write in Irish thereafter. Hartnett was a skilled two-way translator of his own work and predictably grew impatient with the self-denying ordinance that prohibited his exercising his gift as a writer of spare and beautiful English lyrics. In the last decade of his short life, Hartnett returned to writing in the vernacular of his local Co. Limerick English. But the point of the choices open to the Irish poet, and the complex of loyalties they entailed, could not have been expressed more effectively.

It is very evident that I am weighing this outline heavily towards the writers in Irish. I am assuming that access to Irish poets in English, from Yeats onwards in particular, is readily available. What I have attempted to do here is to present the less familiar context for 'poetry in Ireland'. What at any rate is evident is that the condition of that poetry at the end of the twentieth century is immensely intricate. The majority of published poets, North, South and expatriate, write in English, fitting more or less directly into a tradition that extends backwards through Yeats to the revivalists and translators of the nineteenth century. There is a very powerful minority of writers of poetry in Irish, who are creating a major poetic corpus of their own which is totally separate from poetry in English, but who at the same time often write in modern lyric forms which are new to Irish (Liam Ó Muirthile is a particularly convincing example) and on subjects of contemporary urgency: the evocations of gay relationships by the exceptionally talented Donegal poet Cathal Ó Searcaigh, and the variations on Irish myths woven by Ní Dhomhnaill to express such dilemmas as feminism and her concern for world peace. There is no reason of course why a language which is founded in an uncosmopolitan culture should not express the political and the contemporary, as we found with Eoghan Rua Ó Súilleabháin in the eighteenth century.

Between these poles of English and Irish there are several other combinations. Some writing in English is more aware of an Irish linguistic prehistory or of such local linguistic variants as Ulster Scots (Heaney's 'Broagh' is a particularly luminous evocation of the sociopolitical implications of the mixed language of Ulster).[38] As throughout the preceding two centuries, many poets write in more standard forms of English; the choices remain fundamentally the same. I have noted writers like Hartnett who grew up speaking English and then wrote in Irish; a contrary case is Ciaran Carson who grew up speaking Irish and writes poetry in English. A more obvious negotiator between Irish and English is the use of parallel text, as with Hyde and Clarke, discussed above. Two representative anthologies might be noted: the first, *Taisce Duan* performs the admirable service of introducing the great twentieth-century translators into English in parallel with the poems they translated from the Middle Ages to the nineteenth century.[39] For the modern period – the second half of the twentieth century – there is a particularly attractive anthology, *An Crann Faoi Bláth*.[40] And, following on from the nineteenth-century revivalists, a series of distinguished English poems were produced by great translators such as Frank O'Connor in his *Kings, Lords and Commons* (1959).

Finally, it should be noted that, while criticism of the major canon of poetry in Irish over the centuries remains underdeveloped, a vigorous criticism of modern Irish poetry is developing. This has sometimes concentrated on the Gaelic tradition and its intersections with contemporary writers, as in Seán Mac Réamoinn's *The Pleasures of Gaelic Poetry*

(1982). Other writers, notably Edna Longley, see the modern traditions of Irish poetry as more importantly involved with the heritage of English poetry. Several attempt to construct a tradition starting after Yeats and the revivalists.[41]

The standing army of Irish poets, Patrick Kavanagh declared gloomily, has never fallen below 5,000. What this essay has attempted to do is to give a sense of poetry in Ireland as a cultural and linguistic phenomenon over the past two centuries, rather than to give a roll-call of the major practitioners. That can be found in many of the anthologies itemised in the later pages here; as can the texts from great tradition of Irish poetry – Moore, Mangan, Yeats, MacNeice, Kavanagh, Murphy, Heaney, Longley, Muldoon, Ní Dhomhnaill. The more urgent task is to place these writers within their complex heritage, and to give an indication of the kinds of choices that have been open to Irish poets since 1800. To return to the opening paragraph, the argument about whether Irish literature has remained a unified whole since the Middle Ages now looks outdated. It is clear that poets writing in and about Ireland at the start of the twenty-first century are broadly aware of a complex inheritance and the intricacies of how they might align themselves to it, historically and lin-guistically. These choices mirror the cultural complexity that the politics of modern Ireland – North, South and *émigré* – entail, which of course is what poetry must do if it is to be of general interest.

Notes

1. Thomas Kinsella, 'Introduction', in *New Oxford Book of Irish Verse* (Oxford: Oxford University Press, 1986), p. xxvii.
2. D. F. McCarthy, 'Introduction' in *The Book of Irish Ballads* (Dublin, 1846), pp. 22–3.
3. Vivian Mercier, *The Irish Comic Tradition* (Oxford: Clarendon Press, 1962).
4. Conor Cruise O'Brien, 'Our wits about us' (a review of Mercier's *The Irish Comic Tradition*), in *Writers and Politics: Essays and Criticism* (1965; Harmondsworth: Penguin, 1976), pp. 136–41.
5. Vivian Mercier, *Modern Irish Literature: Sources and Founders*, ed. and presented by Eilís Dillon (Oxford: Clarendon Press, 1994).
6. Seán Ó Tuama and Thomas Kinsella, *An Duanaire 1600–1900: Poems of the Dispossessed*, presented by Seán Ó Tuama with translations into English verse by Thomas Kinsella (Mountrath, Portlaoise: The Dolmen Press, 1981).
7. Ó Tuama and Kinsella, 'Introduction', *An Duanaire*, p. xxi.
8. Douglas Hyde, *Irish Poetry: An Essay in Irish with Translation in English and a Vocabulary*. MacTernan Prize Essay 2, published for the Society for the Preservation of the Irish Language (Dublin: Gill, 1902). Throughout this essay, where texts occur in both Irish and English, I will quote in English.

9. Douglas Hyde, *A Literary History of Ireland* (London: T. Fisher Unwin, 1899; reprinted by Ernest Benn Limited, London, 1967).

10. Austin Clarke, *Filíocht Éireannach na Linne Seo/Poetry in Modern Ireland* (Cork: Mercier Press, 1951). Published for the Cultural Relations Committee of Ireland. The unusual parallel-text form of Clarke's book, identical to that of Hyde's *Irish Poetry*, suggests that the latter may have been a conscious precedent.

11. Frank Sewell, *Modern Irish Poetry: A New Alhambra* (Oxford: Oxford University Press, 2000). See, too, the excellent chapter by Alan Titley, 'Innti and onward: the new poets in Irish', in *Irish Poetry Since Kavanagh*, ed. Theo Dorgan (Dublin: Four Courts Press, 1996), pp. 82–94, and the equally enlightening survey by Caoimhín MacGiolla Léith in the same collection, 'Modern poetry in Irish, 1940–1970', pp. 42–51. Titley's various monographs in Irish on several of the major modern Irish language poets are the most important recent contribution to the development of a sophisticated poetic criticism in Irish.

12. An exemplary beginning to such a project is the essays in Seán Ó Tuama, *Repossessions: Selected Essays on the Irish Literary Heritage* (Cork: Cork University Press, 1995).

13. W. J. McCormack, *Irish Poetry: An Interpretive Anthology from Before Swift to Yeats and After* (New York: New York University Press, 2000).

14. Daniel Corkery, *The Hidden Ireland: A Study of Gaelic Munster in the Eighteenth Century* (Dublin: Gill and Macmillan, 1924).

15. See Seán Ó Tuama, *An Grá in Amhráin na nDaoine* (Dublin: An Clóchomhar, 1960) for an excellent account of the whole of this tradition from the Middle Ages onwards.

16. This is not to say that the extensive canon of Irish poetry in English in the nineteenth century was negligible. For a stimulating discussion of some of its major figures, see Robert Welch, *Irish Poetry from Moore to Yeats* (Gerrards Cross: Colin Smythe, 1980).

17. See, for example, Robert Welch, *A History of Verse Translation from the Irish, 1789–1897* (Gerrards Cross: Colin Smythe, 1988) and Bernard O'Donoghue 'The translators' voice: Irish poetry before Yeats', *Princeton University Library Chronicle* 59, 3 (1998), 299–320.

18. Seamus Deane (ed.), *The Field Day Anthology of Irish Writing* (Derry: Field Day Publications, 1991), vol. II, pp. 1–114.

19. Deane, 'Poetry and song 1800–1890', in *The Field Day Anthology*, vol. II, p. 20.

20. W. B. Yeats, 'Introductory Essay', in *A Book of Irish Verse* (London, 1900), p. xix.

21. Mercier, *The Irish Comic Tradition*, p. 6.

22. 'From the Cold Sod That's O'er You' ('*Táim Sínte Ar Do Thuama*'): quoted in *The Field Day Anthology*, vol. II, p. 81.

23. *Field Day Anthology*, vol. II, p. 59.

24. William Larminie, 'The development of English metres', *Contemporary Review* 66 (November 1894).

25. Deane, 'Poetry and song 1800–1890', *The Field Day Anthology*, vol. II, p. 45.

26. Ibid., p. 30.

27. Robert F. Garratt, *Modern Irish Poetry. Tradition and Continuity from Yeats to Heaney* (Berkeley: UCLA Press, 1986).

28. Frank Ormsby, *A Rage for Order: Poetry of the Northern Ireland Troubles* (Belfast: Blackstaff Press, 1992).

29. Stopford A. Brooke and T. W. Rolleston, *A Treasury of Irish Poetry in the English Tongue* (1900).

30. John Montague, *The Faber Book of Irish Verse* (London: Faber, 1974) and Brendan Kennelly, *The Penguin Book of Irish Verse* (Harmondsworth: Penguin, 1970, revised and updated 1981).

31. Kinsella (ed.), *New Oxford Book of Irish Verse*.

32. Gabriel Fitzmaurice (ed.), *Irish Poetry Now: Other Voices* (Dublin: Wolfhound, 1993).

33. Patrick Crotty (ed.), *Modern Irish Poetry: An Anthology* (Belfast: Blackstaff Press, 1995).

34. Séamas Ó Céileachair, *Nuafhilí 1 1942–'52* (Dublin: Oifig an tSoláthair, 1957); *Nuafhilí 2 1953–63* (Dublin: Oifig an tSoláthair, 1968).

35. Gréagóir Ó Dúill (ed.), *Fearann Pinn: Filíocht 1900–1999* (Dublin: Coiscéim, 2000).

36. The emphasising here of Ní Dhomhnaill's importance serves as a reminder of how this kind of survey underrepresents women poets. In a dashing and astute essay (first a talk for RTÉ) in Dorgan's 1996 collection (see note 11 above), Ní Dhomhnaill makes an impassioned attack on the neglect of her contemporary women poets whom she sees as the new 'Hidden Ireland', mentioning Eiléan Ní Chuilleanáin, Eavan Boland, Medbh McGuckian and others.

37. Nuala Ní Dhomhnaill, *Pharaoh's Daughter* (Dublin: Gallery Press, 1991).

38. Seamus Heaney, *Wintering Out* (London: Faber, 1972), p. 27.

39. Sean McMahon and Jo O'Donoghue (eds.), *Taisce Duan: A Treasury of Irish Poems with Translations in English* (Swords: Poolbeg, 1992).

40. Declan Kiberd and Gabriel Fitzmaurice (eds.), *An Crann Faoi Bláth/The Flowering Tree. Contemporary Irish Poetry with Verse Translations* (Dublin: Wolfhound Press, 1991).

41. Interesting examples of this are Patricia Coughlan and Alex Davis (eds.), *Modernism and Ireland: The Poetry of the 1930s* (Cork: Cork University Press, 1995); John Goodby, *Irish Poetry Since 1950* (Manchester: Manchester University Press, 2000).

Further reading

Seamus Deane, 'Poetry and song 1800–1890', in Seamus Deane (eds.), *The Field Day Anthology of Irish Writing* (Derry: Field Day Publications, 1991), vol. II, pp. 1–114

Robert F. Garratt, *Modern Irish Poetry: Tradition and Continuity from Yeats to Heaney* (Berkeley: University of California Press, 1986)

John Goodby, *Irish Poetry Since 1950* (Manchester: Manchester University Press, 2000)

Declan Kiberd, *Irish Classics* (London: Granta, 2000)

Thomas Kinsella, *The Dual Tradition: An Essay on Poetry and Politics in Ireland* (Manchester: Carcanet, 1995)

W. J. McCormack, *Irish Poetry. An Interpretive Anthology from Before Swift to Yeats and After* (New York: New York University Press, 2000)

Gréagóir Ó Dúill (ed.), *Fearann Pinn: Filíocht 1900–1999* (Dublin: Coiscéim, 2000)

Sean Ó Tuama and Thomas Kinsella, *An Duanaire 1600–1900: Poems of the Dispossessed*, presented by Seán Ó Tuama with translations into English verse by Thomas Kinsella (Mountrath, Portlaoise: The Dolmen Press, 1981)

Frank Sewell, *Modern Irish Poetry: A New Alhambra* (Oxford: Oxford University Press, 2000)

Robert Welch, *A History of Verse Translation from the Irish, 1789–1897* (Gerrards Cross: Colin Smythe, 1988)

11

Irish sport

Introduction

The historical development of a sporting culture in Ireland reflects the island's political and cultural history as a whole. It is a story of accommodation and resistance, and of an uneasy relationship between these attitudes, dialectically intertwined in Irish history. As Mike Cronin observes, 'until there is only one idea of Irish nationalism, and a singular and commonly shared expression of identity, then sport will continue to reflect the multifaceted and ever changing nature of Irishness'.[1] Not only has sport in Ireland been greatly affected by economic and political change, it has also impacted both directly and indirectly on Irish society. It is worth noting, however, that the story of Irish sport as a cultural practice is to a large extent his/story. As in other areas of public life, women have had a relatively low profile in the sporting world. Much has changed since the 1960s, and yet Irish sport remains a preserve of gender inequality: men run the games, are the best rewarded participants, make up the bulk of sporting audiences and receive most publicity from the sporting media.

Sport matters to the Irish people, and in particular to Irish men. They play it, read about it, watch it and speak about it to a degree that, whilst by no means unique, certainly suggests that it is an aspect of Irish cultural life deserving of notice. The extent to which Irish soccer captain Roy Keane's departure from the World Cup Finals in 2002 and his criticisms of association football's ruling body in the Irish Republic, the Football Association of Ireland (FAI), held virtually the entire nation in thrall is clear evidence of sport's ability to supersede almost all other domestic and international matters. Arguably Keane has been one of the most iconic and certainly one of the most controversial sports stars that Ireland has produced in modern times. Having begun his playing career in the League of Ireland with Cobh Ramblers he then took the route followed by so many Irish people before him, and went to ply his trade in England. He played first with Nottingham Forest and then with England's most famous club, Manchester United. Indeed, it is possible to argue that the relationship between Ireland and England represented a significant part of the context within which Keane's decision to desert the Irish world cup squad can be partially understood. On the one hand, it was reputed that Keane had derided the English-born manager of the Irish team, Mick McCarthy, both for his lack of ability and for the fact that he was not really Irish. On the other hand, critics of Keane were quick to suggest that he had abandoned the national side in order to undergo medical treatment which would lengthen his career with Manchester United, the team to which he owed his greatest loyalty.

The full truth of the matter will probably never be known. What is significant, however, is how much creative tension centres on Ireland's close social and cultural links to Britain. The Irish have been profoundly influenced by the British, or to be more precise the English, approach to sport. And yet the Irish have consistently used sport to establish their distinctiveness from the British, either by beating them at their own games or by cherishing indigenous ludic traditions. As a cultural practice, therefore, sport can be regarded as a microcosm of Irish cultural life. Neither unequivocally a part of the British cultural imperialist project nor wholly postcolonial, Ireland has walked a fine line between accommodation to British cultural practice and resistance to the culture of a foreign power. Arguably it is this that has been largely responsible for the emergence of a dynamic, creative and highly successful cultural way of life not least in the world of sport.

The story of Irish sport can also be said to be the story of at least three different Irelands, as well as a variety of contemporary readings of Irishness. This is the story of sport in pre-Partition Ireland, of sport in the Irish Free State (subsequently the Irish Republic), and of sport in Northern Ireland. It is also a story that involves Catholic and Protestant Ireland, urban and rural Ireland, post-imperial and post-colonial Ireland, traditional Ireland, modern Ireland and perhaps even postmodern Ireland.

Before sport?

In many respects it would be defensible to begin an account of the historical development of sport in Ireland, as elsewhere, in the mid to late nineteenth century. The sporting revolution that began in England and specifically in its public schools transformed sporting activity from a series of random and relatively unorganised events into the codified and bureaucratised form that we now recognise as modern sport. Of course, an alternative case could be made for arguing that the Ancients got there even earlier with events like the original Olympic Games exhibiting a degree of rational organisation. Certainly this era saw athletic contests moved away to a limited extent from their purely functional roots – practising to hunt, equipping oneself to survive and preparing for combat. In the long period from the collapse of the Roman Empire to the nineteenth century, however, sport was largely anarchic in Ireland as elsewhere.

It is sometimes claimed that Ireland possesses a rich sporting heritage that can be traced back to ancient times and that organised Irish sport pre-dated the English revolution by centuries. It is undeniable in this regard that striking games as well as rough and tumble football matches were an established feature of Irish life. It should be noted, however, that similar activities were commonplace throughout Europe during the Middle Ages. Indeed, they have been a virtually universal indicator of humanity's urge to celebrate its physical dexterity and engage in competitive rituals. In this, as in most things, the Irish were in no way unique. Early forms of football, such as *caid*, that were played in Ireland are certainly amongst the progenitors of the various codes that are popular today, and rudimentary forms of hurling have undeniably been played for many centuries. The English sporting revolution served to provoke a response from Irish nationalists, however, that led to these native forms of folk games acquiring the status of national sports complete with their own partly imagined histories.

Prior to the mid-nineteenth century the concept of sport in Ireland had another meaning far removed from the rough and tumble activities of the agricultural labouring class. A good day's sport for the Irish gentleman, just as for his English counterpart, consisted of hunting. The Anglo-Irish gentry were as keen as their English equivalents to participate in a range of field sports, whilst their employees were allowed to disport themselves only on high days and holidays with bacchanalian excesses such as those associated with the annual Donnybrook fair, the very name of which in time was to become a generic expression for mayhem and disorder. By the middle of the nineteenth century the leisured classes had also taken up cricket, that most quintessentially English sporting pastime, and it was they who were also to feel the initial impact of the revolutionary approach to sport that was already afoot in English public schools such as Rugby, Eton and Harrow.

Sport arrives

The ties that bound the Anglo-Irish ascendancy to the metropolitan core were, of course, considerable, with education playing a crucial role. Generations of Irish gentlemen, and a few Irish ladies, attended the great English public schools and universities, and it was inevitable that they would embrace the games that were to be central to the sporting revolution and thereafter to British ludic imperialism. They returned to Ireland with radically different ideas from those of their fathers about what constituted good sport. The result was a dramatic increase in the number of people playing cricket in Ireland and the emergence of rugby in those Irish educational establishments that sought most strenuously to emulate the ideals of English public school education. Nor was it only the Protestant ascendancy that was attracted to sport organised on the English public school model. Catholic schools also began to find a place for rugby and cricket, and amongst those who played the latter were young men who would subsequently be leaders of the constitutional nationalist cause, including Charles Stewart Parnell and John Redmond.

Antipathy to English sporting imperialism did not emerge in a straightforward way. The colonial administration and also the military were active agents in the diffusion of English sport. As a consequence, it was easier for nationalists to see the English sporting revolution not so much as a means whereby the physical education of young people was being actively promoted but as a subtle way of further underpinning British rule in Ireland. Furthermore, the sporting revolution appealed only to particular sections of the Irish population. In essence it was a middle- and upper-class affair. The one important exception to this latter rule emerged in the shape of association football, which rapidly spread into working-class areas, especially Belfast, which was nineteenth-century Ireland's most industrialised city. This in no way served to diminish its British image in the eyes of watchful nationalists.

That said, however, as football, or soccer as it became known in many parts of Ireland, spread throughout the world, it would prove to be increasingly difficult for nationalists to dismiss it as simply 'the garrison game'.

There is no doubt that by the beginning of the 1880s organised sport had become an increasingly significant feature of Irish social life. For the most part, it had done so primarily as a consequence of certain groups of Irish people endorsing the principles and main characteristics of the English sporting revolution with Irish gentlemen playing a range of British sports as amateurs. As promoted by the pioneers of public school sport in England, the principal objective was to build the character of a middle-class élite. However, in this same period, sport had also acquired a very different goal, that of helping to advance the cause of Irish nationalism in the face of British sporting imperialism. Indeed, it was inevitable that some nationalists would feel the need to challenge British cultural dominance in this area as in so many others.

Ourselves alone

Michael Cusack took full advantage of the spread of modern sport to Ireland. He had been an active participant in a number of sports and was keen to support sports development in the widest sense. He was also concerned, however, that organised sport remained essentially exclusive and that working-class people in Dublin and elsewhere were being denied the opportunity to maximise their sporting potential. Furthermore, in politics, Cusack was a nationalist who had signed the Fenian oath some years earlier. In many respects, therefore, the logical outcome of his sporting and political ideals was the leading role that he was to play in the formation of the Gaelic Athletic Association (GAA) in 1884.

Established in Thurles, Co. Tipperary, with links to the Gaelic League and initial support from a relatively broad spectrum of public opinion, the GAA's main objective was to revive and promote a range of Irish cultural practices, amongst them hurling and Gaelic football. This in turn was intended to assist in the democratisation of access to sport in Ireland. The GAA's emergence meant that, from that moment on, sport in Ireland would not only be implicated in confirming the close cultural ties between Ireland and Britain but would also serve as an important vehicle for the transmission of a counter-hegemonic cultural and political ideology. Indeed, in the early years of the GAA's existence, despite attempts by

Cusack and others to ensure the involvement of all of the main strands of Irish nationalist opinion, the association quickly came under the control of the most revolutionary group within the nationalist camp at that time, namely the Irish Republican Brotherhood. Thereafter, the GAA's leaders were vigorous in their efforts to make sure that the association would not fall into the hands of any single political faction. Rather, the GAA was to become an umbrella in which all shades of nationalist opinion would find themselves united even in periods such as the civil war when the nation as a whole was bitterly divided and in the wake of partition when a constitutional line was quite literally drawn through the map of Ireland.

It would probably be fair to say that the games that were most actively promoted by the GAA represented an invention of tradition at least as much as a revival of indigenous pastimes. Hurling of some sort or another had certainly been in existence for centuries. Whether it was peculiarly Irish or not is, however, another matter altogether. One historian of the sport cites 'the evidence of Irish myth and legend' to show that 'the game had its devoted followers more than a thousand years before Christ'.[2] In reality, however, hurling's origins are uncertain, although in so far as it is now regarded as the Irish game *par excellence* its precise provenance is virtually irrelevant. Similarly, despite the evidence of rough and tumble versions of football, including most notably the game of *caid*, having been played in Ireland for centuries, the modern sport of Gaelic football was to all intents and purposes an invented tradition. Today, however, its Irishness is no less authentic for all that. What should certainly be noted though is that the approach to sport that the GAA adopted was ironically very much in line with the ideology that had inspired the British sporting revolution. Amateurism, Christian values and character formation were at least as cherished by the leadership of this Irish nationalist sporting organisation as they had been by the muscular Christians of the English public schools some years earlier. Indeed, in addition to rooting Gaelic sport in Ireland's Catholic parishes, competition between counties (administrative legacies of British colonial rule) was also initiated and remains vibrant to the present day. Competition culminates in the all-Ireland (county) finals held each year at Croke Park in Dublin. Against all of this, however, is the fact that the GAA provided Ireland and the Irish with a distinctive sporting identity. In reality, it matters little whether the games that it fostered were centuries old or relatively recent inventions. In sporting terms at least, they helped to set the Irish apart not only from the British but from most other people within the British Empire, where the British way of playing sport was being adopted with almost as much enthusiasm as the English language. This process was aided in no small measure by a series of bans enacted by the GAA aimed at preventing Gaels from playing and watching foreign games. Despite these bans, however, the 'foreign', that is to say British, games that the GAA despised so much were also flourishing in Ireland.

In the Belfast area in particular, association football was becoming increasingly popular, at first amongst the Protestant working class whose affinity to Britain is a partial explanation, but then within Catholic areas of the city as well. The interest in football expressed by urban nationalists is highly significant, not least in light of the fact that the GAA had banned its members from playing or even watching foreign games. It is apparent that the GAA's leaders believed that participation in a foreign game such as football indicated a willingness to accommodate oneself to the British influence in Ireland. However, with the establishment of Belfast Celtic Football Club, nationalists in the North could argue that they were involved in their own form of sporting cultural resistance which consisted of taking on the British or at least their Ulster unionist supporters at their own game and, in more cases than not, beating them. This debate has implications not only for football but also for other British sports in Ireland.

A nation at play

Any analysis of the national significance of sport in Ireland must take into account two particular dichotomous relationships – that which exists between the Irish Republic and Northern Ireland and that which distinguishes Gaelic games from other sports. The Irish Republic's sporting culture is essentially one that can be participated in by the entire population. Regional differences abound. For example, Gaelic games, and in particular hurling, are considerably more popular in predominantly rural counties such as Tipperary and Kilkenny than in the urban sprawl of Dublin city. Rugby union, whilst popular throughout the Republic, sheds its largely middle-class image successfully only in Limerick. Individual sports also vie with each other for funding as well as for adherents. The fact remains, however, that it is relatively easy for citizens of the Irish Republic, especially men, to move between different sports. The division between Gaelic games and foreign games persists and relations between the GAA and the ruling body of association football in the Irish

Republic, the FAI, have never been particularly cordial. But players and fans alike can make the transition from games of resistance to games of accommodation safe in the knowledge that all of their activities are ultimately bound up with the broad identity of Irish sport.

Since partition and the formation of the Irish Free State, later to become the Republic of Ireland, the GAA has served an almost unique function in giving the fledgling nation state a highly distinctive sporting culture. For that very reason, however, it finds it difficult to assist the nation to compete on the world stage. In the early years of the state, the Tailteann Games, yet another attempt to revive an ancient Irish tradition, were intended to give the newly established state an element of international sporting recognition. Their success was limited, however, and thereafter, the GAA, having played a significant role in the games, has been obliged to content itself with facilitating domestic competition, which on occasions reaches high levels of skill and intensity. Regular matches between Irish hurlers and Scottish shinty players take place and more high-profile contests involving Gaelic and Australian Rules footballers have been played according to evolving sets of compromise rules. Their impact has so far been relatively short lived.

Foreign games, on the other hand, have always had the capacity to allow Irish athletes to compete internationally. Although they do not pass the 'cultural purity' test, sports such as football, rugby, golf, distance running and boxing, whilst in no way peculiar to Ireland, have on numerous occasions provided the opportunity for national celebration as Irish sportspeople have competed with and beaten international opposition. It would be difficult to argue that in the contemporary era such successful sportsmen and women as Niall Quinn, Keith Wood, Padraig Harrington, Sonia O'Sullivan, Steve Collins and even Roy Keane are anything other than patriotically Irish. Furthermore, their names are recognised throughout the world whereas even the most successful Gaelic footballers and hurlers are known only in Ireland and in those parts of the world where the Irish diaspora has ensured that Gaelic games enjoy some sort of global presence.

None of this is intended to suggest that the GAA is a wholly insular organisation that simply turns its back on the rest of the sporting world. Its attitude towards foreign games has mellowed and there now exist no formal regulations preventing members from taking part in other sporting activities although, at the time of writing, the GAA's Rule 42 in theory continues to preclude foreign games from being played on

GAA-owned premises. An exception has been made in the past for American football, thereby fuelling the suspicion that in the mindset of the GAA 'foreign' really means British. It is evident from this that the guardians of the Gaelic games tradition still feel threatened by the attractions of other sports despite overwhelming evidence testifying to the continuing popularity of the Gaelic games movement. Indeed throughout most of Ireland, the GAA's strength resides in its ability to provide sport and leisure opportunities to huge numbers of people, particularly in rural areas where the organisation remains at the heart of everyday life.

Inasmuch as sport represents contested terrain in the context of the Irish Republic, it would seem as if the main area of contestation is centred on rival meanings of Irishness. On the one hand, there exists a traditional, almost pre-modern, reading of Irishness that is at ease with even the more conservative strategies of the GAA. At the opposite end of the spectrum is the view that Ireland is a modern, perhaps post-modern, pluralist and multicultural society and that the exclusiveness of organisations such as the GAA are little more than unpleasant reminders of the bad old days. Sport, for such critics, must be inclusive and outward-looking if it is truly to represent the new Ireland as well as to contribute to its quest for international recognition. Of course, these are extreme positions and arguably the overwhelming majority of people in the Irish Republic are able to live comfortably with both of these visions of Irishness as embodied in national sporting practices.

Overall, therefore, as a direct consequence of the efforts of the GAA and also of its sporting rivals, the Irish Republic today possesses a vibrant sporting culture. It is undeniable that women are less likely to be included in this culture than men. In addition, it is apparent that economic status as well as socialisation impact on a person's choice of and access to leisure opportunities. At the same time, the sporting culture of the Irish Republic reveals a degree of equity, which is likely to grow in the years ahead. Men and women from across the social spectrum celebrate the achievements of national sporting heroes and support the numerous sports events that take place in Ireland itself, as well as major international events in which there is some Irish involvement. Although people have their own sporting preferences and the question of whether to accommodate or resist remains a live issue, more often than not sport has a tendency to bring the Irish together to play and watch such diverse activities as Gaelic games, association football, basketball, golf, horse-racing, hockey, rugby and the rest. In Northern Ireland, however, the sporting culture is considerably more complex.

Sport divided

As in the Irish Republic, the GAA in Northern Ireland not only serves to confirm the existence of a distinctive Irish sporting culture, but also offers leisure and entertainment amenities to many people, particularly in the more nationalist and rural west and south but also in nationalist pockets in the more eastern counties including the Glens of Antrim and the Ards Peninsula. In addition, however, because the six counties of Northern Ireland are constitutionally part of the United Kingdom, the GAA continues to operate in the North in much the same way as it did throughout Ireland at the time of its formation. Whereas in the Republic it now plays an essentially hegemonic role, assisting the state both in terms of marketing and social control, in Northern Ireland at one level at least it remains a fundamentally counter-hegemonic organisation. Whilst it willingly accepts money from the British government in order to pursue its sports development objectives, it has also consistently allied itself to the nationalist agenda that demands at the very least social justice for Catholics in Northern Ireland and, less unequivocally, the formation of an independent thirty-two-county Irish republic.

This political aspiration, which has tended to be exaggerated by the GAA's enemies, has created problems within the association itself and has also led to the demonisation of the organisation in the eyes of some members of the British establishment, many Ulster unionists, rogue elements in the locally recruited security forces and the overwhelming majority of loyalist paramilitaries. One gruesome consequence has been the murder of a significant number of GAA members in Northern Ireland which, alongside harassment at the hands of the security forces, the occupation of property owned by the GAA and objections from unionist local councillors to planning applications from Gaelic clubs, has helped to strengthen nationalist attitudes within the GAA. All of this is recorded in considerable detail by Desmond Fahy.[3] It is worth bearing in mind, however, that, despite its harrowing experiences, the organisation rescinded its ban preventing members of the British security forces from joining the GAA in 2000, in a gesture of support for the unfolding peace process in Northern Ireland. Even though only one Northern county, Down, was in favour of this change, it is clear that even in the six counties of Northern Ireland, the association has for the most part come to recognise that things have changed for the better for Northern nationalists as a result of the Good Friday Agreement, and that it is reasonable for the GAA to move with the times. It is also worthy of note that media coverage of Gaelic games, particularly football, in the North is now at its highest level ever and there is a mood of confidence about Northern Gaels as they parade a sporting identity that had in the past to be hidden.

In Northern Ireland the division between Gaelic and British games is further complicated as a result of the existence of a different and largely ignored cultural divide based on social class. Studies of cultural practices in Northern Ireland have tended to think in terms of two competing monoliths.[4] It has been convenient to deal in broad generalisations that indicate that the two major traditions live entirely and relatively homogeneously within separate cultural spheres. In relation to sport, therefore, there has been a widespread assumption that Catholics play Gaelic games as a mode of resistance and Protestants play British games, thereby confirming not only their accommodation to but also their almost total immersion in a British way of life. There is of course much truth in these broad generalisations. The GAA has done little to reach out to Northern Protestants over the years, for example, and for its part, the Irish Football Association, soccer's governing body in Northern Ireland, has presided over events such as the departure of both Belfast Celtic and Derry City from local competition in circumstances that have led many nationalists to feel generally unwelcome. However, the reality, as is increasingly being recognised, is rather more complex, not least in light of the influence of gender and social class.[5]

As in the Irish Republic, moreover, regional variations also impact on sporting preferences and ensure that claims for the existence of rival monolithic and homogeneous sporting cultures are further undermined. With reference first to gender, it is simply not the case that for the majority of women in Northern Ireland sport plays a crucial role in the construction and reproduction of national identity. Once social class is added, the argument for the existence of two monolithic sporting cultures becomes all the more difficult to sustain, with working-class urban nationalists and unionists being equally drawn to association football albeit in ways that are as likely to divide as to integrate. Meanwhile, middle-class nationalists are far more likely to have an affinity with Gaelic games, whilst their middle-class Protestant counterparts are almost certain to have been exposed since schooldays to traditionally

British sports such as rugby, hockey and cricket. A doubly divisive school system that separates the overwhelming majority of children along religious as well as academic lines is the single major factor in ensuring that this high level of sporting 'apartheid' is maintained. Meanwhile, association football with its broad appeal across the community divide has tended to be seen as instrumental in maintaining and actually strengthening sectarian identities. In fact, the role of football in relation to community relations is worthy of closer scrutiny.

Despite the obvious popularity in Northern Ireland of a range of sporting activities, not least various forms of motor sports, association football clearly attracts most interest on a day-to-day basis. Whilst much of the early enthusiasm was reserved for Irish League clubs such as Belfast Celtic and their main rivals from the unionist community, including Glentoran and Linfield, there has also been a long-standing devotion on the part of nationalists and unionists respectively to Scotland's 'Old Firm' of Celtic and Rangers. While interest in the domestic game has decreased dramatically since the 1970s, support for the Glasgow clubs remains at a high level with thousands of fans making regular trips to see their favourites, usually as members of the many Celtic and Rangers supporters' clubs that are to be found throughout Northern Ireland. In addition, support for Scotland's Big Two has now been equalled if not actually surpassed by interest in English football. A number of Premiership teams receive widespread support in Northern Ireland with Manchester United and Liverpool being the main beneficiaries. This enthusiasm for English football, and in particular for Manchester United (with other fans becoming known colloquially as ABUs – Anybody But United), is matched in the Irish Republic, where support for Celtic is more muted. This may be simply because support for Rangers is virtually non-existent but it also reflects the ways in which sport in the Republic is far less implicated in making statements about a particular community in relation to its significant other. One interesting by-product of the enthusiasm in Northern Ireland for English football is a degree of cross-community contact that is largely unthinkable in the context of support for local football or Celtic and Rangers. Given that many fans follow at least two teams and sometimes three (one in Northern Ireland, one in Scotland and one in England), the fact that supporting an English team unites people across the sectarian divide is at least worthy of note. More contrived attempts to use sport as a basis for cross-community accord have tended to be far less successful.

It is a widely held view, not least within sporting hierarchies, that sport is uniquely placed to bring people together. This view, of course, largely ignores the extent to which sport is deeply implicated in the very processes that keep people apart and can cause them to be antagonistic towards each other. Various schemes aimed at exploiting the integrative potential of sport have been instituted in Northern Ireland since civil unrest gave way to sectarian violence in the late 1960s and early 1970s. Many of these have been directed towards young people. In addition, there has been substantial provision of publicly funded leisure facilities, particularly in the city of Belfast. The purpose of these strategies was twofold; first, in the best traditions of rational recreation, to keep young people occupied, off the streets and engaged in activities that would burn up excess energy and, second, to allow people from the rival traditions to meet in contexts that were deemed to be neutral, especially by those who are ignorant of the passions that sport arouses. There is little evidence that these techniques have met with any real success. Sport in Northern Ireland, as elsewhere, is intimately bound up with cultural differences and traditions, the very factors that have been largely instrumental in keeping the two communities apart. It is unlikely that artificially created sporting contexts can exercise much influence even on young people when more organic aspects of everyday life – education, churches, housing and, of course, sport in its natural condition – are consistently pushing them apart. The levels of contact that cross-community schemes can establish may have a temporary impact on how young people view the other. The fact remains, however, that much of the surrounding society is so polarised that, for the most part, only children living in areas where there is a relatively high degree of residential integration (mainly middle-class areas) are in a good position to build on the relationships forged through sport. There are of course some exceptions to what is otherwise a somewhat gloomy scenario.

Just as support for English football clubs can bring people together, so too can participation in certain individual sports, which do not attract a significant fan base. These include golf, tennis and lawn bowls. Other sports that have a good record in terms of transcending sectarian boundaries include boxing and ladies' hockey. It is also worth recording that high-level performers in a whole range of sports, even those most closely linked to one or other of the two traditions, are generally able to shed the worst signs of sectarian animus as they endeavour to improve their own sporting performance. Thus, Catholics have traditionally played for the

Northern Ireland national football team despite the fact that very few of their co-religionists in the North are prepared to support that team and prefer instead to follow the representatives of the Irish Republic. Meanwhile, rugby players from an Ulster unionist background represent an Irish national team surrounded by the trappings of the Irish nation. The important distinction to be made in this regard is between sports people who engage with the other organically in the furtherance of their sporting ambitions, and people who are brought together by way of sport in an almost wholly artificially constructed setting. The latter approach is unlikely ever to have major implications for society as a whole. As for the example of high-level performers revealing a greater ability to mix, the unfortunate truth is that this is largely facilitated by an obsessive preoccupation with sport which means that the performers in question tend to operate in their own relatively self-contained sphere of activity and exert little influence on society at large. Thus, neither example would suggest that sport has integrative potential in Northern Ireland in the absence of wider structural change.

One sporting example above all underlines this point. Regardless of who is selected to play for Northern Ireland at soccer, few Northern nationalists are willing to support the 'national' team. Furthermore, the problems encountered by Celtic's Neil Lennon in the later years of his career as a Northern Ireland player, first being subjected to abuse from his own fans and subsequently receiving a death threat purporting to come from loyalist paramilitaries, indicate that Catholic players are less than welcome by some sections of the Protestant community. Regardless of what has been achieved as a result of the peace process, the Northern Ireland soccer team, like Northern Ireland itself, is undoubtedly a matter for cultural and political contestation and no amount of cross-community work in sport can alter this fact.

Conclusion

The Irish, as popular wisdom would have it, love their sport. Indeed, they have loved their sport albeit in many different manifestations since earliest times. But not all Irish people have loved or even participated in sport. Furthermore, at no stage have the people of Ireland enjoyed equal access to sporting opportunities. Another cliché, regularly applied to sporting cultures across the world, also needs to be countered. It is widely presumed that sport is a bit of fun, that people play sport in a spirit of friendly competition and where there are genuine grounds for discord, that sport can help to heal the wounds. The example of Northern Ireland tends to prove otherwise. In addition, a cultural analysis of sport in what is now the Republic of Ireland would also indicate, although perhaps with less damaging implications, that sport is at least as bound up with what sets people apart as with what unites them. The nature of the division in Northern Ireland is more obvious although less simple than some analyses might have led us to believe. Throughout Ireland, however, there has existed a historic tension that runs through the sporting culture and in so doing reflects a major faultline that has divided Ireland in broader social, cultural and political terms.

Sport has given the Irish a sense of their own unique identity. Alongside other cultural practices, including the advancement of the Irish language, traditional music and dance, the Gaelic games movement has been of enormous significance in terms of the construction and reproduction of a particular reading of Irishness. At the same time, though, it is important to note the role of sport in allowing newly independent states to enter the world of nations. To almost as great a degree as joining the United Nations, being allowed to participate in international sporting competition represents a major step in the coming of age of any nationstate. For independent Ireland this rite of passage has been fraught with danger, perhaps more imagined than real. To play international sport as opposed to Gaelic games inevitably means engaging with that sporting universe for which the English were, if not the main protagonists, at the very least overwhelmingly influential figures. Yet without availing themselves of the opportunity to take on the world (the English included) at sport, the Irish would have been limited to a kind of introspection in relation to sport, which would have contributed to a narrowing of national identities. Modern Ireland, in the shape of the Irish Republic, appears to live reasonably comfortably with this sporting and cultural dilemma, although evidence of the rift can still be found. In Northern Ireland, however, the divide in sport, like the divisions that affect the wider society, will be much harder to reconcile.

Sport is one of the most popular and influential cultural practices in contemporary Ireland. Many of the island's sports stars are internationally known and respected. Representative teams from both parts of Ireland have enjoyed success on the international stage. Simultaneously, Ireland has played host to a number of sports events and competitions and sport, especially in the form of activities such as golf and fishing, plays its part in making the island a popular tourist destination. Gaelic games in particular are also important not only as a community resource but also as part of a marketing strategy, even though the 'Irish Ireland' that they depict does not conform to the total reality of modern Ireland. Sport thus reflects all of the country's main sources of division and provides a window through which Ireland and Irish culture as whole can be examined.

Notes

1. Mike Cronin, *Sport and Nationalism in Ireland. Gaelic Games, Soccer and Irish Identity since 1884* (Dublin: Four Courts Press, 1999), p. 190.
2. Seamus J. King, *A History of Hurling* (Dublin: Gill and Macmillan, 1998), p. 1.
3. Des Fahy, *How the G.A.A. Survived the Troubles* (Dublin: Wolfhound Press, 2001).
4. John Sugden and Alan Bairner, *Sport, Sectarianism and Society in a Divided Ireland* (Leicester: Leicester University Press: 1993); and John Sugden and Scott Harvie, *Sport and Community Relations in Northern Ireland* (Coleraine: Centre for the Study of Conflict, University of Ulster, 1995).
5. Alan Bairner, 'Sport, politics and society in Northern Ireland: changing times, new developments', *Studies* 90, 359 (Autumn 2001), 283–90; and Alan Bairner, '*Sport, Sectarianism and Society in a Divided Ireland* Revisited', in *Power Games: A Critical Sociology of Sport*, ed. John Sugden and Alan Tomlinson (London: Routledge, 2002), pp. 181–95.

Further reading

Alan Bairner, *Sport, Nationalism and Globalization. European and North American Perspectives* (Albany, NY: State University of New York Press, 2001)

J. J. Barrett, *In the Name of the Game* (Bray: The Dub Press, 1997)

Malcolm Brodie, *100 Years of Irish Football* (Belfast: Blackstaff Press, 1980)

Padraig Coyle, *Paradise Lost and Found. The Story of Belfast Celtic* (Edinburgh: Mainstream, 1999)

Marcus de Búrca, *The G.A.A.. A History*, 2nd edn (Dublin: Gill and Macmillan, 1999)

Neal Garnham (ed.), *The Origins and Development of Football in Ireland* (Belfast: Ulster Historical Foundation, 1999)

Paul Healy, *Gaelic Games and the Gaelic Athletic Association* (Cork: Mercier Press, 1998)

Grant Jarvie (ed.), *Sport in the Making of Celtic Cultures* (London: Leicester University Press, 1999)

W. F. Mandle, *The Gaelic Athletic Association and Irish Nationalist Politics, 1884–1924* (London: 1987)

Art Ó Maolfabhail, *Camán: 2,000 Years of Hurling in Ireland* (Dundalk: Dundalgan Press, 1973)

12
_____

Projecting the nation: cinema and culture

From the earliest period, cinema in Ireland has contended with two apparently conflicting forces: the 'esperanto of the eye' promulgated by the globalising drive of Hollywood, and the localising lens adopted by the Irish Literary Revival. Part of the cultural power of Hollywood in its formative decades lay in its appeal, as a cheap form of entertainment, to the working class and immigrant populations rapidly expanding in American cities at the turn of the century. To facilitate cross-cultural markets, story-lines, narrative forms and visual styles were devised that addressed spectators not as 'Irish', 'Italians' or 'Jews' but at the most general, human interest level – shorthand for the individualism and universal aspirations of the American way of life. Notwithstanding its crass commercialism, the movie industry also performed a powerful civic function: by divesting viewers of their ethnicity or inherited loyalties, or at least making them redundant on entering a film theatre, it promoted the assimilation of widely divergent cultural minorities into the white American mainstream. It was not entirely coincidental that D. W. Griffith called his landmark film *The Birth of a Nation* (1915) – though its white supremacist vision and replaying of the civil war also betrayed some of the underlying narratives of that nation.

But while cinema was establishing a commodified public sphere in the United States – what Robert Sklar refers to as 'movie-made America'[1] – theatre and literature were spearheading a national renaissance of a different kind in Ireland. As if emphasising the very cultural ties endangered by Hollywood, the Irish literary movement looked to the past, the vernacular and the local to stage its version of the nation. It would be a mistake, however, to see this solely in terms of the backward look of romanticism. A profound sense of the local, however discrepant and discomfiting, was no less prominent in James Joyce's Dublin than in W. B. Yeats's isle of Innisfree. It is this vernacular modernism,[2] at once rooted in a culture yet very much part of the new media technologies, that has informed the best of Irish cinema, even if critical acclaim has not always yielded similar market success. Romanticism posed no threat to the Hollywood dream factory (indeed was part of the dream), but the prospect of alternative routes to modernity from the cultural periphery offered a more serious challenge, one that went to the heart of the Hollywood system itself.

In this, it may be argued, lay one of the main *cultural* obstacles to the development of an Irish national cinema, a factor that has come into play with even more prominence since the resurgence of the Irish film industry since the 1970s. To be sure, many other forces have militated against a strong, indigenous cinema since the founding of the state, amongst which may be numbered the lack of an economy of scale and adequate industrial base; the hostility to mass culture, fuelled by cultural protectionism in the early decades of the state; the existence of an anglophone audience which made a fledgling Irish cinema unduly susceptible to Anglo-American influence; and – not least – the absence of a strong visual tradition. All of these found their specific cinematic articulation, however, in attempts to work out specifically 'Irish modes of address' that would counter the culturally homogenising thrust of classic Hollywood cinema. As Miriam Hansen argues, the assimilationist aesthetic of Hollywood called for a plot structure of an internal, formal integrity (often driven by 'genre', parallel action and clear narrative closure) which required no special or 'non-diegetic' knowledge on the part of the viewer.[3] Irish culture, by contrast, lent itself to forms of modernity that were more cognisant of time and place, a requirement for cultural specificity that has presided over films from the earliest silent period to *Michael Collins* (Neil Jordan, 1996) and on into the twenty-first century.

More often than not, the demand for specific Irish modes of address presents itself as a protest against stage-Irishry, against the kind of hollowed-out representations that show little knowledge of, and less sympathy with, the multilayered complexities of Irish culture and history. The unspoken assumption here is that such local knowledge is required if a film is to do justice to Irish themes and subjects – even films originating within the Hollywood system. Is an adequate response to Neil Jordan's *Michael Collins*, for example, enhanced by an understanding of Irish history and politics, or not? What is one to make of the response, heard after a screening in an American multiplex, that while the character of Collins was 'awesome', the 'gay Nazi dude' in the leather overcoat (that is, Eamon de Valera, founding father of the Irish Free State) 'sucked'?[4] Notwithstanding Jordan's efforts to package the film within Hollywood conventions drawing on the war epic and gangster genres, it was his resolute commitment to grounding the story in Irish historical memory (however controversial) that proved the film's undoing at the American box-office – while, of course, making it the most successful and bitterly contested Irish film at home.

Silent cinema: vernacular visions

It may have been this pressure to acknowledge the weight of history on the landscape that first induced an American production company, the Kalem Company of New York, to shoot on location outside the United States – as if their target Irish, or Irish-American, audiences would not settle for less. *Ben-Hur* was filmed on a Manhattan dirt-track by the same company, but upstate New York or Vermont could not pass for Ireland in the eyes of the early Irish cinemagoers, whether at home or abroad. In 1910, the Kalem production team, under the direction of Sidney Ollcott and Gene Gauntier, travelled to Killarney to pioneer a new topographical realism in cinema. As a review of their first feature, *The Lad from Old Ireland* (1910) declared: 'The picture is genuine Irish and needs no labelling to prove it. It carries its authenticity on its face.'[5] This authenticity was carried across the Atlantic in 1914 when clay was transported from the 'real Colleen Bawn rock' at Killarney, Co. Kerry, and placed in the foyer of a cinema so that patrons might step on Irish soil on their way in to see another Kalem production, *The Colleen Bawn* (1911).[6] Nothing could be further removed from the conditions of viewing described by Hansen, which required that audiences bring nothing – mentally, and still less physically – to the enjoyment of cinema. The paradox of this insistence on actual locations and (quite literally) pieces of 'the ould sod' was that instead of leading to coherent, realist narratives, it produced a radical disjunction between story and setting, narrative and history.

These discontinuities can be seen at work in the film of *The Colleen Bawn*, based on Dion Boucicault's enormously successful Victorian melodrama and shot in Killarney in 1911. The opening titles of *The Colleen*

Bawn assure us that 'Every scene, including interiors, in this Irish production was made in Ireland, and in the exact location described in the
original play.' As the story progresses – or digresses – the intertitles pro-
ceed to introduce topographical non-sequiturs, at least where the story
is concerned, such as 'The inn shown is over 100 years old', followed by
a landscape shot of 'a real bog near Killarney's lake'. That both narrative
and setting are at cross-purposes becomes even more apparent in the next
series of intertitles which convey the information that the exact reproduction of the original Danny Mann's cottage is on the screen, followed
by the scene of the attempted murder, 'the exact location including the
real Colleen Bawn rock and cave' (the source of the 'ould sods' transported
to the US). The problem with these claims to authenticity is that there
were no originals in the first place, as both the characters and the inci-
dents depicted were fictitious and passed into Killarney lore through the
invented traditions of tourism. This tension between story and spectacle
is stretched to breaking point when one intertitle finally announces, having described Danny Mann's remorse after his attempted drowning of the
Colleen Bawn: 'The bed used in this scene belonged to Daniel O'Connell
and was occupied by him.' Not surprisingly, the logic of these intertitles
is to split the screen – and by extension, audiences – in two: the top half
narrates the story in a manner presumably intelligible to mass audiences,
but the lower part increasingly relapses into topographical and historical
asides that could only be of interest to Irish viewers, drawing on popular
history or cultural memory.

Though ostensibly celebrating 'Romantic Ireland' in the search for
authenticity and picturesque locations, the resulting aesthetic effects are
jarring. Films like *The Colleen Bawn* share techniques with modernism: as
in the fiction of James Joyce, both narrative and history are skewed and
distorted by media technologies. In *Ireland a Nation* (Walter MacNamara,
1914–21), the most ambitious epic of the War of Independence, this incongruity is taken to further extremes when narrative closure is constantly
frustrated by the tacking-on of new actuality footage, as developments in
the war constantly outstrip the narratives of the nation. It was as if, in the
cultural ferment of a revolution, Irish modernism turned to the discordant effects of the new media technologies, whether in cinema or other
forms, for an unsettling aesthetic that energised insurgent impulses,
and assisted an often torpid nationalist movement to throw off colonial
rule.

Romantic Ireland

It was not simply the case that these fractured narratives in early Irish cinema cut across the universalising designs of Hollywood: they also called into question the conservative ideological leanings of the emergent nation-state, at least in so far as the latter were underpinned by a romantic fusion of faith and fatherland. In keeping with Joyce's example, the challenge posed by cinema and popular culture to the cultural retrenchment of the Free State was not just political in nature, but also extended to the private sphere: the domain of gender, sexuality and the family. As a signal that the revolutionary energies were now being run to earth, one of the first pieces of legislation passed by the new state was the Censorship of Films Act (1923), and in succeeding decades, the popular press, pulp fiction, radio, jazz and popular music all fell foul, in different ways, of the censor.

Hollywood's challenge to the centrality of the family in the national romance of Irish life derived primarily from its emotional individualism and privatisation of desire, particularly as idealised in the cult of romantic love. It is important to note that when film tapped into particular currents in Irish culture, it gained the approval of the new state – even when it was still speaking from what was essentially an American position. Hence the extraordinary official reception accorded to Robert Flaherty's *Man of Aran* in 1934, which transformed its Dublin premiere into a state occasion, attended by Eamon de Valera and his cabinet, members of the diplomatic service and dignitaries from all walks of life, including 'Dr and Mrs W. B. Yeats'. Flaherty's documentary can be seen as an expression of romantic primitivism, the fascination in American culture with the struggle between man and the wilderness, but with one crucial qualification: it was the *family* rather than the individual that was pitted against nature. Its title notwithstanding, it was, as one review put it, not just 'a story of man against the sea' but also of 'woman against the skyline' – several scenes depicting Maggie Dirrane engaged in the backbreaking work of gathering kelp from the seashore and, indeed, risking her life attempting to save fishing nets and equipment after the tumultuous storm.

In John Ford's *The Quiet Man* (1952), the other classic representation of romantic Ireland, the claims of family, inheritance and communal ritual are also counterposed to American individualism. Not surprisingly, Sean Thornton (John Wayne) returns to Ireland with all the Hollywood trappings of romantic love and immediate gratification of desire: 'I don't get this', he complains to the matchmaker Michaeleen Oge (Barry Fitzgerald) who chaperones his first date with Mary Kate Danagher (Maureen O'Hara): 'Why do we have to have you along? Back in the States, I'd drive up, honk the horn, a gal would come running out . . .' Sean discovers the way to Mary Kate's heart involves not just individual desire but an apprenticeship in the mores and protocols of Irish society – the kind of cultural repertoires which Irish audiences were expected to bring to early cinema. The need for change and adaptation works both ways, however, and if the storm that breaks when Mary Kate throws caution to the winds and embraces Sean in a country churchyard indicates a woman on the verge of revolt,[7] then it could be said that cinema itself provided an early warning of the storm clouds that were gathering over both church and state as modernisation took hold in the late 1950s.

Many of the anxieties about film expressed in censorship debates suggest that the true rival of Catholicism was not Protestantism, or even communism, but cinema itself, especially in view of its powerful seductive appeal to the senses and obsessive forms of identification. At one point in Thaddeus O'Sullivan's *The Woman Who Married Clark Gable* (1984), based on a story of Sean O'Faolain's set in the 1930s, the eponymous woman confides her troubled fantasies about her husband (whom she thinks has become Clark Gable) to a priest. The scene in the confessional is carefully shot as a dark, enclosed space facing a rectangular frame or grid. As the woman leaves, however, she is shown emerging from a film theatre, as if both forms of rapt devotion are competing for the same part of her inner life. It is not surprising that when Irish society underwent a series of profound transformations beginning in the 1960s, film should play a prominent role in charting and precipitating these changes, while at the same time, in the form of an indigenous film industry, giving a new lease of life to the vernacular modernism of earlier attempts to project Ireland on the screen.

The resurgence of Irish cinema

The resurgence of contemporary Irish cinema since the early 1970s was due to a number of factors: the emergence of a disparate group of highly gifted directors, actors and other related personnel; the capacity of visual expression to come out from the shadow of a powerful literary tradition; the success of Irish popular culture, particularly rock music, at a global level; and the impact of a successive range of measures taken by the government to support the film industry. From a handful of independent films in the 1970s, over fifty feature films have been produced since the reactivation of *Bord Scannán na hÉireann* (The Irish Film Board) in 1993. Two decades of achievement have seen Irish (or Irish-themed) films win several Oscars (*My Left Foot*, Jim Sheridan, 1989; *The Crying Game*, Neil Jordan, 1992), major awards at Cannes (*Cal*, Pat O'Connor, 1984; *The General*, John Boorman, 1998) and Venice (*Michael Collins*, Neil Jordan, 1996; *The Magdalene Sisters*, Peter Mullan, 2002), and have led to the emergence of major film directors such as Neil Jordan and Jim Sheridan, as well as leading players such as Gabriel Byrne, Liam Neeson, Stephen Rea, Aidan Quinn, Pierce Brosnan and Colin Farrell.

The initial phase of filmmaking was spearheaded by a number of independent directors in the 1970s. The first noteworthy indigenous production by Bob Quinn, *Caoineadh Airt Uí Laoire* (*Lament for Arthur Leary*, 1975) used a series of Brechtian devices to place a classic eighteenth-century Gaelic poem against a contemporary setting in the west of Ireland, thus drawing a vernacular tradition and modernist techniques into dialogue from the outset. Quinn followed this with *Poitín* (1978), a dark comedy about illicit distilling which parodied the romantic comedy of *The Quiet Man* (1952); and *Atlantean* (1983), an ironic three-part documentary exposing the myths of Celticism.

The contestation of the official myths of romantic Ireland was also carried forward in the 1970s in representations of working-class life in Dublin in Joe Comerford's short *Withdrawal* (1974) and the critical naturalism of his *Down the Corner* (1976). An *avant-garde* approach to landscape and perception was given a new complexity in the 'No Wave' experimental films of Vivienne Dick, *Visibility Moderate* (1981), *Like Dawn to Dust* (1983) and *Rotach* (1985), and was explored at feature length in three innovative films: Thaddeus O'Sullivan's *On a Paving Stone Mounted* (1978), an experimental meditation on landscape, exile and memory; Joe Comerford's *Traveller* (1981), dealing with the beleaguered travelling community in Ireland, and Pat Murphy's remarkable *Maeve* (1981), a milestone in modern Irish cinema. Using innovative forms of narrative, flashbacks, and voice-over, *Maeve* dealt with the return of a young feminist to her republican background in Belfast, and her subsequent critical engagement with the marginalisation of women in Irish nationalist history. Informed by feminism and the *avant-garde*, but also by a deep immersion in cultural memory, *Maeve* more than any other film negotiates the tension between narrative and location, depicting landscape itself as a series of submerged narratives often cutting across the main story-line, much like the clashing intertitles of early cinema. In 1981, the Irish government established *Bord Scannán na hÉireann* (The Irish Film Board) to provide institutional support for film production in Ireland. What was at stake, perhaps, at this developmental level was the capacity of Irish films to tell their own stories in a manner that addressed Irish audiences, but which also aimed at international distribution, whether on the art-house and festival circuit, or the more commercial mainstream controlled by Hollywood. Among the most important films produced under the aegis of the film board were *Angel* (Neil Jordan, 1982), *Anne Devlin* (Pat Murphy, 1984), *The Outcasts* (Robert Wynne-Simmons, 1982), *Pigs* (Cathal Black, 1984), *Eat the Peach* (Peter Ormrod, 1986), *Clash of the Ash* (Fergus Tighe, 1987) and *Reefer and the Model* (Joe Comerford, 1987). *Angel*, the film that first brought Neil Jordan to international attention, explored the murky moral underworld of political violence in Northern Ireland, even when it had justice on its side – a theme that was to recur in much of Jordan's later work. 'The Troubles' also provided the setting for Pat O'Connor's fatalistic *Cal*, as a young man is caught up in the maelstrom of violence only to fall in love with the widow of one of his victims.

Pat Murphy's visually stunning second feature *Anne Devlin*, set during Robert Emmet's fateful insurrection in 1803, involved a radical reworking of female stereotypes, particularly the pietà-like figure of the suffering heroine which has exercised such influence over nationalist popular memory. *The Outcasts* (Robert Wynn Simmons, 1984) was also set in pre-Famine Ireland and, like Tommy McArdle's *The Kinisha* (1977), explored the clash of pagan folklore and Catholicism, and its effects on gender and sexuality. Though the representation of modern Dublin on the screen is often attributed to the success of the Roddy Doyle trilogy in the 1990s – *The Commitments* (Alan Parker, 1991), *The Snapper* (Stephen Frears, 1993) and *The Van* (Stephen Frears, 1997) – other films had already dealt sympathetically with the working-class casualties of urban decay, as it manifested itself in homelessness, drug abuse and the terror inspired by drug barons (Joe Comerford's *Down the Corner*, 1976, Cathal Black's *Pigs*, 1984, and Joe Lee's *Sometime City*, 1986 and *The Courier*, 1988).

Eat the Peach (Peter Ormrod, 1986) was one of the first films to deal with what later became known as the 'Celtic Tiger' economy, highlighting with often comic effect the economic and cultural insecurities that constituted the underside of Japanese high-tech investment in Ireland. The closing down of the Japanese factory in the film might have been a fitting epitaph for the abolition of the first Irish Film Board in 1987, which came ironically at a time when Irish cinema was just making its presence felt on the international stage. The flagship film was John Huston's memorable version of James Joyce's *The Dead* (1987), filmed with an uncanny sensitivity for the seemingly throwaway details and the cadences of the voice in Joyce's story. In Huston's film, the tension between modernity and tradition, male and female voices, the east and west of Ireland, is brought to the screen visually with all the charged emotion and subtle political undercurrents of Joyce's original story. Though the action turns mainly on conversations and choreographed actions, it is the camera in the end that captures the tonality of Joyce's prose. In Pat Murphy's *Nora* (2000), this understated visual eloquence becomes part of the inner life of Joyce's life-long partner Nora Barnacle (Susan Lynch) as she strives to come out from under the shadow of his verbal mastery. The struggle between word and image is given a powerful reflexive turn in one scene where she seeks refuge in a movie theatre that is screening Irish films (including Kalem productions): here we see the woman from the 'traditional' west of Ireland looking to modernity and new cultural technologies to find her own muted voice.

Fracturing the family

The breakthrough films for the rapid expansion of Irish filmmaking in the 1990s were Jim Sheridan's *My Left Foot* (1989), which was nominated for five Oscars, winning in the Best Actor (Daniel Day-Lewis) and Best Supporting Actress (Brenda Fricker) categories, and Neil Jordan's *The Crying Game* (1992), which earned Jordan an Oscar for Best Original Screenplay and was for a while the most successful independent film of all time.

Sheridan's film was an evocative story of a struggle against adversity set in working-class Dublin, based on the autobiography of the writer Christy Brown, who suffered from cerebral palsy. His next film, *The Field* (1990), also received an Oscar nomination (Richard Harris for Best Actor), and gave epic expression to the time-honoured Irish hunger for land, as tradition falls victim to the forces of modernisation. Like Bob Quinn's *Poitín*, *The Field* is in many ways a dark, parodic engagement with *The Quiet Man*, except in this case, the visiting American meets his doom, and the dysfunctional family of the Bull McCabe self-destructs rather than triumphs over the traumas of the past. In the more recent *How Harry*

Became a Tree (Goran Paskaljevic, 2002), the tenacity with which the farmer clings to the land becomes a metaphor for the fanatical impulses within nationalism itself – whether in an impoverished rural Ireland, or the contemporary Balkans (a sub-text brought to the film by the director's Serbian background). As if the sinners are now more sinned against, the well-heeled business type and land-grabber, the town shopkeeper (Adrian Dunbar), is the unlikely victim in the story, and the powerless smallholder, Harry (Colm Meaney), the villain – a symptomatic contemporary reversal, perhaps, of the ethos of classic westerns such as *Shane* (George Stevens, 1953).

One key strand in contemporary Irish cinema has sought to lay the ghost of Ford's *The Quiet Man*, as if to rescue Ireland from the illusions of an Arcadian past, the myth that the periphery offers a therapeutic cure for the ills of the modern world. Beginning with the classic television drama *The Ballroom of Romance* (Pat O'Connor, 1982), Eamon de Valera's Ireland from the 1930s to the 1950s became the dark night of the soul from which people had to escape, whether through emigration, the flight to the city or, more generally, modernisation. *Angela's Ashes* (Alan Parker, 2000) is perhaps the culmination of this trend, reversing the logic of *The Quiet Man* by construing America as the cure for Ireland's ills, rather than the other way around.

One of the reasons Irish films have looked back more in anger than nostalgia is that for those sections of society whose story has not yet been told, the past is still not over. Cathal Black's *Our Boys* (1981) was an early uncompromising depiction of the Catholic church's stranglehold on education, a subject which also featured as the tragic backdrop to a Christian Brother's elopement with a young epileptic boy in *Lamb* (Colin Gregg, 1985), the film that brought Liam Neeson to prominence. Bob Quinn's *Budawanny* (1987) and *The Bishop's Story* (1994) dealt with the theme of illicit sexual relations and paternity among the clergy and the hierarchy. *Budawanny* contains these prescient lines delivered by a priest from the pulpit: 'From now on, you'll have another reason to call me father.'

These films were advance warnings, at a time when the hegemony of the church still held sway, of the crisis that was to engulf the clergy and church–state relations in the 1990s. Much as Australian cinema has drawn attention to the plight of the 'stolen generation' of Aboriginal children, so film and television have relentlessly exposed the secrets of institutional violence and sexual abuse stifled under the bureaucracy of the Catholic church in Ireland. The controversial television documentaries

Dear Daughter (Louis Lentin, 1998) and *States of Fear* (Mary Raftery, 2000), dealt with the hideous treatment of young girls in orphanages and institutions for 'fallen women', were followed by the television drama *Sinners* (Aisling Walsh, 2002), and the feature film *The Magdalene Sisters* (Peter Mullan, 2002), which received the Golden Bear at Venice while also incurring the wrath of the Vatican, and by *Song for a Raggy Boy* (Aisling Walsh, 2003).

Confirming the early perception that it was competing for the same psychic territory as the Catholic church, cinema in Ireland often functioned as the return of the repressed, bringing to the screen many of the hidden injuries and silences buried under decades of film censorship. In some cases, films have dealt with identifiable events or institutions, as in *A Love Divided* (Sidney Macartney, 1999), the story of a mixed-religion couple hounded out of an Irish town in the 1950s. For the most part, however, they chart the stultifying moral and emotional climate of those decades, as in *Philadelphia, Here I Come* (John Quested, 1974), *Circle of Friends* (Pat O'Connor, 1993), *Dancing at Lunaghasa* (Pat O'Connor, 1998), *Korea* (Cathal Black, 1996) and *Country* (Kevin Liddy, 2000). In Neil Jordan's *The Butcher Boy* (1998), set in small-town Ireland of the early 1960s, devotion to the church, and particularly the Virgin Mary, is intercepted in the impressionable mind of a young boy, Francie Brady (Eamonn Owens) by media fantasies drawn from comics, film and television, and the impending Armageddon of the Cuban crisis. Caught between the forces of church, state and a dysfunctional family, Frankie gradually descends into a small-town Raskolnikov, as if the extremities of life charted by Dostoyevsky have found their way to the mediocrity of the Irish midlands. In Kirsten Sheridan's *Disco Pigs* (2001), the warped mentality of Francie's pig-like condition is extended into teenage years as Pig (Cillian Walsh) and his childhood sweetheart Runt (Elaine Cassidy) go on a Badlands-type rampage through the Irish countryside.

More than any part of the social landscape, the faultlines in the traditional Irish family, as idealised in romantic conceptions of faith and fatherland, have been exposed on the cinema screen. Almost every variation of family life has been explored as cinematic representations of women cut across the conventional images of 'Mother Ireland' or the virgin mother ideal. Outcast, widowed or defiant single mothers feature in *Reefer and the Model, Joyriders* (Aisling Walsh, 1988), *Hush-a-Bye-Baby* (Margo Harkin, 1989), *December Bride* (Thaddeus O'Sullivan, 1990), *The Snapper, The Playboys* (Gilles MacKinnon, 1992), *Widows' Peak*

(John Irvin, 1994), the marvellous short film *After '68* (Stephen Burke, 1994), *The Sun, the Moon and the Stars* (Geraldine Creed, 1996), *A Love Divided* (Sydney Macartney, 1999). Children with missing mothers, absent fathers or indeed with two fathers feature in *Traveller*, *December Bride*, *Into the West* (Mike Newell, 1994), *The Miracle* (Neil Jordan, 1989) and *The Secret of Roan Inish* (John Sayles, 1996).

In many of these films, as the director Jim Sheridan has remarked, fathers have had a bad press and, as if to compensate for this, the 1990s witnessed the emergence of the 'good father'. Hence the gallant Dessie Curley (Colm Meaney) in *The Snapper*, who ends up reading gynaecology books to help his daughter, Sharon (Tina Kelleher), through her pregnancy, and the sensitive stoicism of Guiseppe Conlon (Pete Postlethwaite) in *In the Name of the Father* (1999). Male sexuality is depicted in a different light in a number of films that explore parodic or dissident versions of the family. 'Maybe we should settle down', jokes Michael Collins (Liam Neeson) to his soul (and bed) mate Harry Boland (Aidan Quinn) in *Michael Collins*, when they encounter a rural wedding. 'Just the two of us', replies Boland. The theme of homoerotic bonding underlies *Michael Collins*, *Pigs* and *I Went Down* (Paddy Breathnach, 1998), and is given more overt expression in *Reefer and the Model*, *The Crying Game* and Jimmy Smallhorn's visually powerful *2 by 4* (1998). The narrative and emotional complexity of Jordan's *The Crying Game* may be due in no small part to the startling manner in which it juxtaposed images of the new Ireland – related to questions of race, transgressive sexuality and masquerade – with the legacy of the colonial past represented by Northern Ireland. Whether depicting the changing attitudes towards male or female sexuality, one of the recurrent trends in Irish films is a constant blurring of the boundaries between the private and public spheres, the personal and the political. On the Irish screen, love stories are where problems begin rather than end.

Behind these seemingly endless transgressions of the family lies another series of real-life episodes, the traumatic fall-out from the divisive abortion and divorce referenda of the 1980s. Not least of the damaging consequences of these referenda was the muting on radio and television of the voices of women who had experienced abortion, or the anguish of unwanted pregnancies. As if picking up where current affairs left off, Irish cinema has returned to these traumatic episodes, discharging the excess that could not be accommodated within the language of broadcasting, journalism or indeed the courtroom. More than any other film, Margo Harkin's *Hush-a-Bye-Baby* captures the underlying fears and anxieties of this repressive climate as they impinge on the crisis pregnancy of a schoolgirl, Goretti (Emer MacCourt), from a nationalist community in Derry. At one point in the film, an anti-abortion campaigner intones 'pro-life' sentiments on a background radio programme as Goretti struggles to come to terms with her pregnancy, and is hardly reassured when another speaker on the radio recalls the fate of Anne Lovett, a 15-year-old school-girl who died giving birth at a shrine to the Virgin Mary in a midlands town, immediately after the referendum. In a later sequence, Goretti is filmed staring at the sea on a beach as if attempting to discover herself, in time-honoured romantic fashion, through communion with nature. The sequence opens, however, on a jarring note: in a momentary, seemingly desultory shot, a blue fertiliser bag is washed up on the beach. For Irish viewers – and for Goretti – this recalls the story of 'The Kerry Babies' that convulsed the nation after the abortion referendum. In the course of this sensational legal case, an unmarried mother, Joanne Hayes, was prosecuted for the murder of two separate babies, one of which was found in a fertiliser bag on the seashore. As in the case of Joyce's aesthetic, it is the throwaway details, and the incidental background allusions, that carry the emotional freight, acting as painful, elliptical reminders of the innermost recesses of communal experience.

Narratives of the nation

It is in this sense that cultural memory and local knowledge, even of a fugitive, endangered kind, operate as shadow texts in Irish cinema, allowing a culture to look at itself, as it were, through a glass darkly. The manner in which the past throws a shadow over the present in Irish nationalism is displayed to telling effect in Cathal Black's *Korea* (1996), in which bitter recriminations over the Irish civil war (1922–23) are visited upon the next generation in the 1950s. That the animosities of the civil war extended into the era of the 'Celtic Tiger' was made abundantly clear by the national furore over the release of Neil Jordan's *Michael Collins* in late 1996. Michael Collins was the tarnished hero who accepted (however reluctantly) the Partition of Ireland, and his rehabilitation in an historical epic was interpreted as signalling the belated end not only of the civil war, but of Irish nationalism itself. Other critics of *Michael Collins* were not so optimistic, however, and viewed the film as a thinly disguised allegory of the unresolved contemporary conflict in Northern Ireland. Collins's tragic death in the final scenes of the film – with its powerful

dirge-like accompaniment of Sinead O'Connor's rendering of the traditional ballad 'She Moved Through the Fair' – removed any trace of an
upbeat Hollywood ending. The lack of closure was augmented by the use
of actuality footage of Collins's funeral in the final scenes. On this reading, it is as if history itself has the last word. The problem for international audiences, however, was that this conclusion itself required some
knowledge of Irish history, a prerequisite out of keeping with the use
of historical epics as vehicles for stargazing or lavish spectacle. 'Don't
look for happy endings', the character (Frankie McGuire) played by Brad
Pitt remarks in the not dissimilar plot line of the *The Devil's Own* (Alan J.
Pakula, 1997): 'It's not an American story, it's an Irish one.'

Early twentieth-century Ireland was featured in a different light in
Edward Bennet's *Ascendancy* (1983) and Thaddeus O'Sullivan's *December
Bride* (1990), both of which offered fresh perspectives on Protestant and
Unionist culture in Northern Ireland. Much as hostilities in the Vietnam
war had to cease before Hollywood addressed the war, however, so representations of the conflict in Northern Ireland had to await the peace process in Northern Ireland for the full horror to appear on the screen. The
depravity of the Shankhill Butchers, the loyalist murder gang that fused
Hannibal Lecter with Alex and the Droogs from *A Clockwork Orange*, was
the subject of two of the darkest films on the Troubles, *Nothing Personal*
(Thaddeus O'Sullivan, 1996), and *Resurrection Man* (Marc Evans, 1997).

Political debate on the Northern conflict had been stifled on the airwaves for several decades under Section 31 of the Irish Republic's Broadcasting Act, so it was not surprising that this conspiracy of silence should
also have proved inhospitable to the production of major films on 'the
Troubles'. This was particularly the case with the two main events that
plunged Northern Ireland into deeper levels of violence: Bloody Sunday,
1972, in which thirteen civilians were shot dead by the British army on
a march in Derry, and the hunger-strikes in the H Blocks in 1981. Two
films about Bloody Sunday, *Bloody Sunday* (Paul Greengrass, 2002) and
Sunday (Jimmy McGovern (2002)) eventually reached the screen in 2002,
reviews of the films competing in the newspapers with sensational rev-
elations from the ongoing government inquiry into the shootings. The
first major film about the hunger strikes, *Some Mother's Son* (Terry George),
was screened in 1996, but its 'human interest' ending, in which a mother
opts out of political involvement by signing her son off the hunger strike,
owed more to Hollywood formulas than to the events themselves. By
contrast, Tom Collins's *Bogwoman* (1998) made on a much smaller budget,
moved in the opposite direction – a young mother (Rachael Dowling)

who has kept her distance from the strife finally showing her personal resolve by taking her place on the street with other women during a riot in Derry's Bogside, a dedication to political struggle that reached its grim culmination in the 'dirty protest' of the women political prisoners in Armagh jail, the subject of *Silent Grace* (Maeve Murphy, 2001). *H3* (Les Blair, 2001), scripted by a survivor of the hunger-strikes, Lawrence McKeown, brought a vivid, naturalistic treatment to the struggles in the H Block, questioning the coherence of narrative itself as a means of depicting the pain of a slowly disintegrating body.

The extent to which even well-plotted narratives, with different degrees of suspense, fail to offer protection from the incursions of politics and history is clear from the hostile reception accorded to two of the most controversial films released before the ceasefire in 1994, Ken Loach's *Hidden Agenda* (1991), which exposes corruption and dirty tricks within the British security establishment, and Jim Sheridan's *In the Name of the Father* (1994), a prison and courtroom drama dealing with the attempts of Gerry Conlon (Daniel Day-Lewis) to clear the names of the Guildford Four after fifteen years of false imprisonment for bombings in Britain. Bearing out Siegfried Kracauer's hope that, however compromised by the entertainment industry, cinema could act as an alternative public sphere,[8] both films were treated as if they were direct interventions in journalism and current affairs, although the specific events they covered had long since moved off the front page.

Cinema and the Celtic Tiger

In keeping with the unprecedented growth of the Celtic Tiger economy and the cultural buoyancy in the 1990s, images of urban realism, youthful energy and (relatively) uninhibited sexuality came to feature more prominently in films as diverse as the highly acclaimed Roddy Doyle trilogy *The Commitments*, *The Snapper* and *The Van*, *The Miracle* (Neil Jordan, 1990), *The Last of the High Kings* (David Keating, 1997), *The Disappearance of Finbar* (Sue Clayton, 1997), *Snakes and Ladders* (Trish McAdam, 1997), Paddy Breathnach's Krzysztof Kieslowski-like *Ailsa* (1995), and his very different Irish appropriation of both the gangster and the road movie, *I Went Down* (1998). Though there may have been a temptation to present the bright lights of the city as the 'cure' for the unremitting bleakness of rural realism, the ravages of drug abuse, alcoholism and domestic violence reappear in urban or suburban settings as the collateral damage of modernity, rather than the residues of faith or fatherland. Hence the visceral domestic violence of the Roddy Doyle and Mike Winterbottom television drama series, *Family* (1994), set in a run-down working-class estate, the anomie of the traveller community in *Into the West*, the middle-class ennui of Alan Gilsenan's *All Souls' Day* (1997) and Fintan Connolly's *Flick* (2000). That domestic violence is not simply a destructive element in working-class culture is clear from the reign of terror in Gerry Stembridge's *Guiltrip* (1996), in which a misogynist army officer carries his military and macho persona into the home.

Traditional stereotypes of the violent Irish did not cease with the Peace Process. No sooner had the ceasefire taken effect than the psychotic violence of the Northern conflict was transferred to more mundane Dublin settings in the urban gangster film. Three films were based on the life of the notorious gangleader and art thief Martin Cahill: *The General* (John Boorman, 1998), *Ordinary Decent Criminal* (Thaddeus O'Sullivan, 1999) and the excellent BBC drama *Vicious Circle* (1999). Two further films were based on the life of the high profile crime journalist Veronica Guerin, murdered by drug barons in 1996: the lack-lustre *When the Sky Falls* (Jerry Bruckheimer, 2000) and the high budget *Veronica Guerin* (Joel Schumacher, 2002), starring Cate Blanchett.

The more upbeat version of the Celtic Tiger – and its local habitation, the Temple Bar district of Dublin – found its way onto the cinema screen in 2001 with the Roddy Doyle-scripted *When Brendan Met Trudy* (Kieran J. Walsh) and *About Adam* (Gerry Stembridge). *About Adam* deals with a philandering young man about town, Adam (Stuart Townshend), who keeps affairs going with three sisters (and perhaps even their brother and mother), while ostensibly conducting a normal relationship with one of the sisters, Lucy (Kate Hudson). Adam's exploits are shot from the shifting perspectives of each of his lovers, but never from his own viewpoint, still less using objective or 'omniscient' narration. The most striking aspect of the reception of *About Adam* was the repeated pronouncement that, though set in Ireland and dealing with modern themes, these were truly international films that bore no visible traces of Irishness. As one critic, Tom Humphries, commented:

> Dublin looks suddenly gloss-finished and prosperous and its
> populace briefly forgetful of their history as the most-oppressed
> people ever . . . Almost uniquely, too, it is an Irish film which could
> have been made anywhere. There are no dying patriots, no visual
> clichés, no oppressed peasants.

But having noted this new look Dublin, Humphries adds: 'The Irishness comes through in the characterizations and the speech. Stembridge set out to show Irishness in the day-to-day way we live, not through cinematic shorthand.'[9] It is precisely at this level of story-telling that the cultural specificity of the film is relayed, especially in its use of recognisable locations, idiomatic register and *Rashomon* (or Theatre of the Oppressed) techniques. Films like *About Adam* draw on disjointed narrative styles that have characterised the most innovative Irish fiction from Bram Stoker and Joyce through to Roddy Doyle, and which, as we have noted above, were already part of early Irish cinema.

Roddy Doyle himself brings this kind of reflexive story-telling to bear on *When Brendan Met Trudy*, in which a conscientious young teacher, choir-member and film buff, Brendan (Peter MacDonald), meets up with the vivacious Trudy (Flora Montgomery), who happens to be a cat-burglar by night. As in the case of Francie Brady in *The Butcher Boy*, legacies of traditional Ireland – choir practice, John McCormack's singing of 'Panis Angelicus' at the 1932 Eucharistic Congress in Dublin – are intercut in Brendan's imagination with flashbacks to classic Hollywood films. A visit to a miniature Famine village, fabricated by the heritage industry, suggests that cultural memory has indeed been one of the casualties of the Celtic Tiger. One of the subplots involving the deportation of a Nigerian refugee Edgar (Maynard Eziashi) from Dublin shows that the erasure of memory has direct consequences for the present, removing some of the gloss of the success story of the Celtic Tiger. As the director, Kieran J. Walsh, observed, contrasting his film to Stembridge's *About Adam*:

> I gather Gerry Stembridge's intention was to depict a new Dublin and a contemporary Ireland that was on a par with any good place to live. I didn't have that in mind at all. There's a backdrop of things in this film that are very specifically Irish. It wasn't Roddy's intention or mine to sell Dublin as a great place to live.[10]

As if taking these comments on board, Stembridge confronts the issues of immigration and refugees head-on in his television drama, *Black Day at Blackrock* (2001), which deals with attempts to stir up resentments to the placement of African asylum seekers in a rural town. As the animosities build up, it becomes clear that the government officials behind the scheme are no better disposed towards the new arrivals than the most belligerent townspeople. They are singularly unimpressed when the local history-teacher informs them of his efforts to evoke sympathy in his classroom for the refugees by drawing analogies with the plight of the Irish diaspora after the Famine. At a tense town-hall meeting, the teacher reads out a letter home from a Famine emigrant whose anxieties and fears in a strange land could equally have been expressed by a contemporary refugee in Ireland.

The narrative device of the history teacher attempting to compensate for the loss of cultural memory is also apparent in Paul Quinn's *This Is My Father* (1999). In this case, the teacher is an Irish-American, Kieran Johnston (James Caan), who is facing burn-out in his school at Aurora, Illinois, where assimilation into the melting pot has succeeded all too well in severing his delinquent pupils from any connection with their communal or ethnic pasts. The amnesia which surrounds even family history is revealed when one student traces her ancestry to Eric the Red. That a similar historical void has brought Kieran's own life to a standstill becomes clear when a chance discovery of a tattered photograph leads him back to Ireland. The family past he uncovers is not the nostalgic world of *The Quiet Man*, but a community whose internecine hatreds bring about the suicide of a father he had never known, and the flight of his ostracised, expectant mother to America. There is no happy ending, other than a final scene back in Kieran's classroom in which students pass around the tattered photograph of their history teacher's ill-fated parents. Such resolution as the film achieves rests on the implication that any one of the socially disconnected students may have such stories secreted in their own pasts. It is as if the kind of knowledge that audiences once brought to early cinema, but which was dispensed with under the classic Hollywood system, has now come back to haunt American culture. In this form of vernacular modernism, it is not only Ireland but Hollywood itself that has to come to terms with its own buried pasts.

Notes

1. Robert Sklar, *Movie-Made America: A Cultural History of the American Movies* (New York: Vintage, 1994).
2. On vernacular modernism, see Homi Bhabha, *The Location of Culture* (London: Routledge, 1994), ch. 12, and, in relation to cinema, Miriam Hansen, 'The mass production of the senses: classical cinema as vernacular modernism', in *Reinventing Film Studies*, ed. Christine Gledhill and Linda Williams (London: Arnold, 2000), pp. 332–50.
3. Miriam Hansen, *From Babel to Babylon: Spectatorship in American Silent Film* (Cambridge, MA: Harvard University Press, 1991).

4. I am indebted to Professor Jeffrey Chown, Northern Illinois University at De Kalb, for this information.

5. 'Far Afield', *New York Daily Mirror* (2 November 1910) cited in Eileeen Bowser, *The Transformation of Cinema: 1907–1915* (Berkeley: University of California Press, 1994), p. 153.

6. Kevin Rockett, *The Irish Filmography* (Dublin: Red Mountain Media, 1996), p. 250.

7. For a persuasive feminist reading of *The Quiet Man*, see Brandon French, 'The joys of marriage: *The Quiet Man*', in *On the Verge of Revolt: Women in American Films of the 50s* (New York: Frederick Ungar, 1978), pp. 13–22.

8. Siegfried Kracauer, 'The cult of distraction', in *The Mass Ornament: Weimar Essays* (Cambridge, MA: Harvard University Press, 1995).

9. Tom Humphries, 'Sultan of satire', *Irish Times*, 20 January (2001).

10. Kieran J. Walsh in interview with Hugh Linehan, *The Ticket*, supplement to *The Irish Times*, 7 March (2001).

Further reading

Kevin Barry, *The Dead* (Cork: Cork University Press, 2001)

Ruth Barton, *Irish National Cinema* (London, 2004)

Ruth Barton, *Jim Sheridan* (Dublin, 2002)

Joseph Curran, *Hibernian Green on the Silver Screen: The Irish and American Movies* (New York: Greenwood Press, 1989)

Luke Gibbons, *Transformations in Irish Culture* (Cork: Cork University Press, 1996)
    The Quiet Man (Cork: Cork University Press, 2002)

Debbie Ging, 'Screening the green: cinema under the Celtic Tiger', in *Reinventing Ireland: Culture, Society and the Global Economy*, ed. Peadar Kirby, Luke Gibbons and Michael Cronin (London: Pluto, 2002), pp. 177–95

Brian McIlroy, *Shooting to Kill: Filmmaking and the 'Troubles' in Northern Ireland* (Trowbridge, 1998)

James MacKillop (ed.), *Contemporary Irish Cinema: From the Quiet Man to Dancing at Lunaghasa* (Syracuse: Syracuse University Press, 1999)

Martin McLoone, *Irish Film: The Emergence of a Contemporary Cinema* (London: British Film Institute, 2001)

Lance Pettitt, *Screening Ireland* (Manchester: Manchester University Press, 2000)

Kevin Rockett, *The Irish Filmography* (Dublin: Red Mountain Books, 1996)

Kevin Rockett, Luke Gibbons and John Hill, *Cinema and Ireland* (London: Routledge, 1988)

13

Folk culture

Introduction

This chapter surveys current and past definitions and theories of Irish folklore. It relates our understanding of folklore and folklife to the ways in which these knowledges have developed and become institutionalised and argues for the special place of folklore studies in our understanding of Irish subaltern culture more generally.

In practice, 'folk culture' usually distinguishes those aspects of popular culture which have long been established in agrarian society and are associated with a particular way of life – especially that of peasants – from more recent and non-rural forms. The latter, of course, may be traditional too, but are usually seen as being a product of modern rather than traditional society. Folk culture in another sense refers to an ideal of authenticity, as in the attribution by the Romantic thinker Jean-Jacques Rousseau to nature of various social phenomena supposedly uncorrupted by culture: the 'noble savage' and then the peasant challenged the decadence of aristocratic society. Johann Gottfried von Herder explicitly contrasted natural writing (*Naturpoesie*) with the artifice of civilisation (*Kunstdichtung*). Ireland in the same period saw a heated Irish controversy over James Macpherson's appropriation of the common Gaelic Ossianic poems. The Ossian poems prefigured European romanticism with their wild native energy. To Herder these poems, along with *Reliques of Ancient English Poetry* (1765) by Bishop Percy (a friend and mentor to the pioneering editor and translator of Irish poetry, Charlotte Brooke), were the epitome of *Naturpoesie*. Herder was the first to break with the notion of culture as a singular process leading to the formation of the cultivated individual. He insisted on the plurality of cultures. The

Enlightenment, by emphasising the equality and universality of individuals and of communities, had implied their sameness. Breaking with this, Herder insisted that every culture had to be valued on its own terms. The authentic ideal was of belonging to and being true to a specific national tradition, hence the *Volksgeist*, the spirit or genius unique to each people. The Romantic movement across Europe followed Herder in emphasising the singularity and the specificity of individuals and communities.

According to Han Vermeulen, 'the discipline of ethnology or ethnography, as the Greek neologisms of the German concepts *Völkerkunde* and *Volkskunde*, was conceptualized in the years 1771–87 as part of the Enlightenment endeavour to create some order in the growing body of data on peoples, nations or *Völker* in the world of that era . . .'.[1] In German and other languages, 'national' and 'popular' are synonymous, or nearly so; hence *Kultur des Volkes* has connotations of the national culture as well as of 'popular culture'.

The development of folklore studies

Ernest Gellner argues that in the development of the modern nation-state the options for folk culture were either 'induced oblivion' or 'created memory'.[2] Dynastic religious states, such as England and France, that developed into modern nation-states under an existing ethnic high culture, obliterated folk traditions along the way. In the case of ethnic groups dominated by a ruling class of foreign origin and lacking a continuous high culture, such as Finland or Ireland, a modern high culture had to be created from existing folk traditions.[3] Romanticism was of great importance in the latter situation. It rhetorically opposed modernity but in fact helped to nationalise it. 'The mental world of romantic nationalism', concludes Perry Anderson, 'was no longer cosmopolitan, but in valuing cultural diversity as such, it tacitly defended a kind of differentiated universalism.'[4]

The success of the late nineteenth-century cultural revivals in Ireland was due in large part to their national-popular dimension, successfully eliding the temporal and social distance between the aristocratic 'national' Gaelic past and the peasant Gaelic present. The concept of folklore was crucial. 'Folk-lore' was coined by the antiquary William John Thoms in 1846, to replace 'popular antiquities' or 'popular literature'. 'Folk-song' first appeared in 1870, and came to be limited to the pre-industrial, pre-urban, pre-literate world. Raymond Williams sees the genesis of these 'folk' terms in the context of the new industrial and urban society. They had the effect of 'backdating all elements of popular culture', in contradistinction to modern forms, 'either of a radical and working-class or of a commercial kind'.[5] The term *folkliv* was used in Sweden from the mid-nineteenth century and is probably the source of 'folklife' in English, due perhaps to the influence of Sigurd Erixon. Irish *béaloideas*, well documented since the seventeenth century with the connotation of 'oral instruction', was used as the equivalent of 'folklore' possibly from the turn of the nineteenth century and certainly from the late 1920s.

Jacob Grimm was the founder of comparative research on the folktale and the foremost folklorist of the first half of the nineteenth century. His use of antiquities, philology and oral traditions created a long-lasting methodological model for the new discipline of folklore. *Kinder und Hausmärchen (Grimm's Fairy Tales*, 1812), the folktale collection recorded and edited by Jacob and his brother Wilhelm, inspired folktale collections throughout Europe, not least the pioneering Irish collection by Thomas Crofton Croker in 1824. Various theories of the origin of folktales informed scholarship in the nineteenth century, beginning with Wilhelm Grimm's idea – deriving from contemporary developments in comparative philology – that folktales were a common Indo-European inheritance. A major influence on folklorists was Edward Tylor's *Primitive Culture* (1871), which interpreted arcane peasant customs in evolutionary terms as 'survivals', historical evidence of primitive mentalities.

A broad and relatively undifferentiated study of culture in the early nineteenth century later broke up into separate disciplines. While the large colonial powers developed anthropology to study their subject peoples, other European countries developed a 'domestic anthropology' to study their own peasantry.[6] Though the Folk-Lore Society was founded in London in 1878 and the first international folklore congress held in Paris in 1889, within metropolitan countries folklore studies flowered on the internal periphery – Ireland, Brittany, Catalonia – and were closely linked to the question of regional or national identity. They largely remained the preserve of amateurs in England and France in the nineteenth century, a 'middle-brow science, in the shadow of the legitimate disciplines', as Renato Ortiz puts it, flowering instead as a product of the association of the national and the popular on the European periphery.[7]

Indeed, the most influential folklore theory, the diffusionist historical-geographical method that dominated scholarship until the 1960s, had its origins in late nineteenth-century Finland and had one of its bastions in Ireland. The interest of the state was important in the development of folk culture studies, as can be seen from the 1930s in the Irish Free State and in Northern Ireland from the late 1950s. The most important national folklore archives were assembled in Finland, Estonia and Ireland.

A key factor in the development of the field was late industrialisation and late urbanisation, and hence the survival of folk culture. The Romantics greeted the industrial era with apprehension and strongly influenced intellectual responses to it. The death of traditional rural society was experienced both as national cultural disaster (by Douglas Hyde, for example) and as the inevitable march of progress (the more common metropolitan and socialist view). Traditional élites threatened by the rise both of the bourgeoisie and of the industrial proletariat glimpsed their own fate in that of folk society and bemoaned the undoing of the two poles of an idealised social order: this is evident in the writings of the Anglo-Irish literary revival. Observers as diverse as folklorists and the critical philosophers of the Frankfurt School complained of 'the crisis of "authentic" cultures (the classical and the folkloric)' lamenting 'that it is the intermediary that is most alive: urban popular culture and mass culture'.[8]

While folklorists dealt with notions of folklore, folk culture or traditional culture, the term 'folk society' was introduced into anthropology by Robert Redfield around 1930.[9] Peasant society corresponds in broad terms to this notion of 'folk society', emphasising small communities of family-based, rather than entrepreneurial, rural cultivators in which kinship and religion are very important. There is little economic differentiation and simple technologies are used. Part of the community's surplus is appropriated by dominant groups into a wider economic system. Hence peasants have an unequal relationship with élites, market towns and the state. Most of the Irish field studies by anthropologists (beginning with Conrad Arensberg in the 1930s) exemplify this perspective. The folklife scholar E. Estyn Evans also worked with the concept, seeing Ireland as essentially a peasant society.

National research traditions were strong in the field of folk culture studies in Europe and publication in national languages, including Irish, predominated (and still do), but international cooperation and collaboration nevertheless were the norm, leading to the partial acceptance of new terms for the research field: 'regional ethnology', associated with Sigurd Erixon, and 'European ethnology' (both in contrast to general ethnology or anthropology), the latter proposed in 1955 and since become fairly widespread in the nomenclature of university departments. Today most university departments are either of folkloristics, with their roots in philology, or of (European) ethnology, originating in folklife study. From the 1960s the influence of socio-linguistics and of field studies shifted the emphasis from text to performance as a key concept in folkloristics. From the 1960s structuralism and semiotics had a similar influence. Feminist readings began to inform folklore studies from the 1970s, critiquing research traditions as well as opening up new research areas. Ethnology began a sustained engagement with anthropology and sociology and in some countries largely turned its back on studies of folk culture in favour of contemporary urban society.

A subaltern culture?

All of native Irish culture is subaltern from the seventeenth century, but it is 'Irish' rather than 'popular' until the twentieth century when the new social order is consolidated. From the eighteenth century the popular was being noted by the churches in the form of the errors of the common people, or of Catholics, by travel writers who were particularly fascinated by popular Catholic rituals such as wakes and 'patterns', by writers of fiction using popular themes, by improvers and surveyors and by antiquarian scholars. General Charles Vallancey, a military engineer who came to Ireland in 1762, devoted part of volume 12 of *Collectanea de rebus Hibernicis* (1770–1804; 1783) to the festivals of *Lúnasa* and *Samhain*, and has been called 'the first practitioner of ethnology in Ireland'.[10] The general subaltern status of Gaelic culture brought learned and oral materials together in such pioneering works as Charlotte Brooke's *Reliques of Irish Poetry* (1789), a bilingual anthology of learned and oral Gaelic poetry. Brooke, born to a landed family in Co. Cavan, was influenced by *Ossian* and encouraged by Bishop Percy among others. She was associated with a first Gaelic revival, concentrated in late eighteenth-century Belfast and benefiting particularly from the support of the largely Presbyterian middle class and partly overlapping with radical politics (the McCracken family exemplify this overlap). In July 1792, the Belfast Harpers' Festival was held in the Assembly Rooms in Belfast, bringing together ten mostly elderly harpers, part of a dwindling number of wandering musicians playing a repertoire by then mostly composed of folk music.[11]

In 1795, a magazine, *Bolg an Tsolair* or the *Gaelic Magazine*, appeared in Belfast, published from the offices of the *Northern Star*, the newspaper of the United Irishmen. Including an Ossianic poem and folksongs translated by Brooke, the publication offered itself to the public 'hoping to afford a pleasing retrospect to every Irishman, who respects the traditions, or considers the language and composition of our early ancestors, as a matter of curiosity or importance'.[12] It was to be the first and only issue. The printing presses of the *Northern Star* were destroyed in a raid by the Monaghan Militia in 1797. Bunting had been asked to transcribe the music at the harpers' festival and immediately afterwards set off, collecting music in Derry, Tyrone and Connacht. He published a first collection in 1796, *A General Collection of the Ancient Music of Ireland*. At the McCrackens' expense, Patrick Lynch, a Gaelic scholar and the compiler of *Bolg an Tsolair*, was sent to collect the words of the songs. The collecting work was coordinated from the McCrackens's house, and Lynch's letters to Mary Ann give a vivid account of the fieldwork. Political events, in the form of the rebellions of 1798 and 1803 and their repression, had a profound impact on these activities, both on the lives of the key figures and on attitudes to Gaelic culture.[13]

The businessman Robert S. Mac Adam was a central figure in the cultivation of Irish folklore studies in the nineteenth century. He travelled Ulster selling the family's wares, taking advantage of his travels to collect Irish manuscripts and record oral traditions. His collections consisted of tales, proverbs, verses and songs – 'the first collection of folklore from the Gaeltacht'.[14] Mac Adam also made the largest collection of proverbs in Ireland, published in the journal which he had founded and of which he was the first editor, *The Ulster Journal of Archaeology*, between 1853 and 1862.

The Corkman, Thomas Crofton Croker, an admiralty clerk in London, was an admirer of the Grimm Brothers. His *Fairy Legends and Traditions of the South of Ireland* (1825) was translated by them and published as *Irisches Elfenmärchen*, with their own scholarly introduction. It was also admired by Walter Scott, and Croker dedicated a further two volumes respectively to Scott and to the Grimms. Croker's first work was a useful antiquarian sketchbook, *Researches in the South of Ireland, Illustrative of the Scenery, Architectural Remains, and the Manners and Superstitions of the Peasantry* (1824). He published several more collections, of tales and of songs, as well as

The Keen of the South of Ireland (1844). Faulted both for his unaccredited use of the work of others and as an exploiter of Irish material 'spiced' for an English audience as Douglas Hyde put it, with 'stage-Irish' caricatures that became a commonplace in the genre, he nonetheless reflected a typical perspective on the Irish peasantry from the standpoint of the Protestant ascendancy.

The subject of such books as Croker's was – for the first time – the peasantry. Many subsequent authors, also mostly ignorant of Irish, saw their work as engaging with the research field established by the Grimms. Among the more important was the Dublin bookseller Patrick Kennedy, originally from Wexford. The most significant of his several books, which covered both folktale and legend, although written in the whimsical Croker style, was *Legendary Fictions of the Irish Celts* (1866). Jeremiah Curtin, born to Irish parents in Wisconsin, was a gifted linguist and studied under the famous ballad scholar Francis James Child in Harvard. He recorded and published Russian and Eastern European tales as well as Native American myths. Coming to Ireland in search of myths in 1887, the first of three visits, he met Irish scholars before going on to Kerry, Galway and Donegal. He knew some Irish, but depended mainly on interpreters. He published three important collections: *Myths and Folklore of Ireland* (1890), *Hero-Tales of Ireland* (1894) and *Tales of the Fairies and of the Ghost World* (1895). William Larminie, a civil servant in the India Office in London, under Hyde's influence learnt Irish in his native Co. Mayo and from 1884 recorded tales in Mayo, Galway and Donegal. He published them in the scrupulous collection, *West Irish Folk-tales and Romances* (1893), giving names and some biographical details of his informants.

The vibrant traditional world that drew many writers like Croker to it in the course of the century was dealt a devastating blow by the Great Famine of 1845–48. Sir William Wilde (father of the writer Oscar Wilde) attributed the decline of popular tradition as much to modernity itself as to the catastrophic years of 1845–48. He made substantial collections of folklore, including *Irish Popular Superstitions* (1852), and these were to form the basis for the anthologies – *Ancient Legends, Mystic Charms and Superstitions of Ireland* (1887) and *Ancient Cures, Charms and Usages of Ireland* (1890) – published by his wife, Lady Jane Wilde and greatly admired by Yeats. Many collections of tales derived from the popular tradition appeared in the course of the nineteenth century, but few of these, at least until the beginning of the language revival movement, are of major interest to folklore studies today.

Cultural nationalism was largely introduced from the 1840s *via* the Young Irelanders. The popular tradition came to be seen as a cultural asset, both the proof of continuity from the ancient Gaelic past and an artistic resource. The Anglo-Irish literary revival was rooted in previous antiquarian study, popular nationalist literature and folklore. W. B. Yeats, well read in contemporary folklore scholarship and influenced by Ernest Renan's Celticism, published two anthologies of folktales and legends, *Fairy and Folk Tales of the Irish Peasantry* (1888) and *Irish Fairy Tales* (1892) as well as *The Celtic Twilight* (1893), a mixture of oral traditions, his own spiritual experiences and his observations. His interest in folklore overlapped with spiritualism and occultism. For him, the value of a living folk tradition was artistic rather than scientific; it offered a model opposed to the rationalism and materialism of the modern world.

For Lady Gregory with her ascendancy background, the discovery of traditional culture at her doorstep was a revelation. She learned Irish, though, like Curtin, she needed the assistance of an interpreter to work with Irish-speaking informants. The result of her extensive fieldwork was four volumes, consisting of a range of genres from songs, folktales and legends to the type of supernatural belief narrative called 'memorate' by folklorists: *Poets and Dreamers: Studies and Translations from the Irish* (1903), *The Kiltartan History Book* (1909), *The Kiltartan Wonder Book* (1910) and, most importantly, *Visions and Beliefs in the West of Ireland* (1920). The last work in particular is an important collection of supernatural traditions, and with the most equitable representation of female informants, grossly underrepresented in most collections.[15]

John Millington Synge's literary work, like Yeats's and Gregory's, was informed by an engagement with folk culture as an artistic resource. For him, too, Hyde's *Love Songs of Connacht* was a major influence, and he read widely in folklore scholarship. He first visited the Aran Islands in 1898, at Yeats's suggestion, and made several more visits between then and 1902, learning Irish well and recording oral traditions. *The Aran Islands* (1907) gives translations of some of the tales and poems he heard and his photographs of local life. It is travelogue, memoir and even, arguably, an anthropological study based on what later would be called participant-observation.

Maurice Goldring has argued that the anglophone revivalists – Yeats and Gregory, and to a lesser extent, John Millington Synge – carried on no dialogue with the folk world but egoistically used the poetic spectacle the peasant offered: 'Misery for them was never poverty, and transformed itself into rich tapestries.'[16] If Lady Gregory's 'three happy afternoons' recording folktales in a workhouse left her moved by the contrast 'between the poverty of the tellers and the splendour of the tales', our own unease to a large extent derives from the splendour of her status and the poverty of theirs.[17] Still, Máirtín Ó Cadhain, himself from a humble Irish-speaking family of storytellers, admired Gregory and Yeats for their imaginative use of folklore, transcending the dead 'paradigms and glosses' and the cultural pessimism of the Irish Folklore Commission.[18]

The two bilingual folklore collections of Douglas Hyde, *Beside the Fire* (1890) and *Love-Songs of Connacht* (1893), were scholarly works whose influential literary style made them extraordinarily influential and an important part of the fiction of the revival.[19] As a folklorist, Hyde brought new scholarly dimensions to the field. He was publishing folktales in Irish from 1889, with the appearance of *Leabhar Sgéaluigheachta*, part of which appeared in translation in 1890 in *Beside the Fire*. Most of the stories were recorded from Proinsias Ó Conchubhair, an inmate of the Athlone workhouse, more of whose stories appeared in *Sgéulauidhe Fíor na Seachtmhaine* (1909). *Beside the Fire* gave an extended overview and evaluation of the works of earlier folklorists and a state of play in the field at the time, advice on what needed to be done and practical instructions to folklore collectors. Other works of his dealing with the oral tradition include *Songs Ascribed to Raftery* (1903), *Religious Songs of Connacht* (1905–6), *Legends of Saints and Sinners* (1915), *Ocht Sgéalta ó Choillte Mághach* (1936) and *Sgéalta Thomáis Uí Chathasaigh/Mayo Stories Told by Thomas Casey* (1939).

Hyde is the key link between the artistic use of the oral tradition and scholarly study of it and between the literary revivals in English and in Irish. He set the agenda for cultural nationalism within which folk culture, and especially Gaelic folk culture, would have an important place. His 1892 lecture on 'The Necessity for De-Anglicising Ireland' was informed by the idea that unless Ireland rediscovered its *Volksgeist*, it would be incapable of any worthwhile artistic production. The Gaelic League was founded in 1893 with the aim of reviving Irish as a spoken and as a literary language. Hyde was elected president. It published volumes of folklore that helped to fill the gap for reading materials and thus provided an oral model for prose fiction in Irish.[20] Competitions and prizes for storytelling, singing, dance, and for collections of folklore were held.[21] The League struck a blow for the legitimacy of the Irish language, until then associated largely with an oppressed, impoverished, illiterate and declining minority. It was an important part of the struggle for the widening of political and cultural citizenship in Ireland.

The nineteenth-century development of Old Irish philology on the continent led to the study of modern Irish dialects, storytellers often providing outstanding informants and folklore convenient texts for scholars such as F. N. Finck, who spent four months in Aran in 1894–95 and published the first monograph on an Irish dialect (*Die araner Mundart* 1899), and Holger Pedersen, who spent a similar period there in 1895–96. Both studied Irish with the storyteller Máirtín Ó Conghaile (Pedersen's collection of his tales was published as *Scéalta Mháirtín Neile* in 1894), as did Synge, while Curtin recorded from him. The influence of visiting scholars – Carl Marstrander, Robin Flower, Bryan Kelly, George Thomson – was crucial to the emergence of the literature of the Great Blasket Island. Many more such peasant autobiographies – written or dictated – were published in Irish, and they form an important part of Irish ethnological writing.

In 1927 several members of the Gaelic League founded the Folklore of Ireland Society with the aim of collecting, publishing and preserving the folklore of Ireland. Pádraig Ó Siochfhradha was elected president, Hyde treasurer and J. H. Delargy (Séamus Ó Duilearga) librarian and editor of the society's journal, *Béaloideas*, the first number of which appeared the same year. In 1930, the government established the Irish Folklore Institute, to be replaced in 1935 by the Irish Folklore Commission, attached to the Department of Education with Delargy as director (on secondment from his lectureship in University College Dublin) and Seán Ó Súilleabháin as archivist. Its task was to record, catalogue and publish Irish folklore, its remit covering all of Ireland.

A number of full-time fieldworkers ('collectors'), all male and mostly native speakers of Irish, were recruited and were sent generally to their home districts. Their work was supplemented by the voluntary contributions eventually of thousands of others, including in 1937–38 senior pupils from primary schools in a scheme carried out with the cooperation of the Department of Education and the Irish National Teachers Organization. The Irish Folklore Commission's understanding of folk culture as well as the contents of its archives can be gauged by the fieldworkers' manuals prepared by Ó Súilleabháin, *Láimhleabhar Béaloideasa* (1937) and *A Handbook of Irish Folklore* (1942). The latter is arranged thematically according to the following categories: 'Settlement and Dwelling',

'Livelihood and Household Support', 'Communication and Trade', 'The Community', 'Human Life', 'Nature', 'Folk Medicine', 'Time', 'Principles and Rules of Popular Belief and Practice', 'Mythological Tradition', 'Historical Tradition', 'Religious Traditions', 'Popular Oral Literature' and 'Sports and Pastimes'. Nordic models were to the fore in folklore research. The Swedish folklorist C. W. Von Sydow's encouragment was behind Delargy's extended visits to the universities of Lund and Uppsala in 1928. The Norwegian folklorist Reidar Th. Christiansen, like von Sydow an Irish-speaker, was influential in the establishment of the Folklore of Ireland Society. Ó Súilleabháin spent three months in Sweden in 1935 and applied the methods of Uppsala's folklore and dialect archives to the Irish Folklore Commission. Ó Súilleabháin and Christiansen together prepared *Types of the Irish Folktale* (1963), which gave references to the 43,000 or so folktale variants recorded in Ireland up to the end of 1956. The close links between philology and folklore facilitated contacts with the Nordic countries and with Germany – Kevin Danaher, the foremost folklife specialist in the Irish Folklore Commission, studied there – and also with Scotland, where there has also been an overlap between Gaelic philology and folklore. Delargy was strongly interested in the pan-Gaelic dimension of folklore. The Irish Folklore Commission was abolished in 1970, its staff transferred to the new Department of Irish Folklore in University College Dublin, headed by a graduate of Uppsala, Bo Almqvist. By that time the archives had at least 2 million pages, plus some 25,000 photographs and thousands of hours of sound recordings.

The enormity of the task the Irish Folklore Commission set itself and the precarious situation of the Irish language meant that the recording and cataloguing of materials – clearly understood as an eleventh-hour mission – usually took precedence over analytical research, though at least one major analytical work was published by a member of the Irish Folklore Commission: Máire Mac Neill's *The Festival of Lughnasa* (1962). Contemporary understandings of folklore led to a philological orientation, a neglect of new cultural forms and a certain cultural pessimism. Female traditions were undervalued. The Irish Folklore Commission's full-time collectors were all male, and so too were seven-eighths of the other collectors to the main collection and more than five-sixths of the informants.[22] International folklore research was largely preoccupied with the *Märchen*, a magic tale usually with a male protagonist and told by a male storyteller. This was even more the case with the Gaelic hero tales of which the Ossianic or Fenian tales are the best known. The institution of night visiting to tell folktales has been well described, but generally involved men. Clodagh Brennan Harvey was among the first to point to the lack of evidence about female storytelling in Ireland, and she has been followed by others.[23] The fourth volume of *The Field Day Anthology of Irish Writing* (2002), which includes a comprehensive discussion and a large anthology of women's oral traditions, makes up for much of the under-representation in the published record.[24]

The Irish Folklore Commission's folklore collection was one of the most important cultural projects in Irish history. The influence of J. H. Delargy, the key figure in Irish folklore studies for half a century, is crucial, both from his formal position and from his charismatic personality. Born in the Glens of Antrim, he moved to Dublin as a child. Developing an interest in the Irish language, he recorded his first folktales on holidays in Antrim. He took Celtic Studies in University College Dublin and in 1923 was appointed assistant to Hyde (professor of Modern Irish since 1909), and lecturer in folklore in 1934 (though on secondment to the Irish Folklore Commission from 1935). He held a chair of folklore from 1946 to 1969. With a knowledge of many European languages, he was well versed in international folklore and philological scholarship and his contacts with other countries were extensive. His published works included the influential lecture, 'The Gaelic Storyteller' and *Leabhar Sheáin Í Chonaill* (1948), the first complete edition of the repertoire of an Irish storyteller, and he edited *Béaloideas* from 1927 until 1970. The cultural pessimism of Ernst Renan, W. B. Yeats and Robin Flower regarding the future of Gaelic culture informs much of his work, and he was preoccupied with rescuing the remnants of the Gaelic past. He underlined the pressing need to record the world's folklore because soon 'the sources of tradition will have dried up in the shifting sands of progress, and the voice of the storyteller and the tradition-bearer will be stilled for ever'.[25]

To a large extent this view was characteristic of folklorists until the 1960s when changing paradigms opened up new perspectives. Since then, two university departments have developed in Ireland, the Department of Irish Folklore in University College Dublin out of the Irish Folklore Commission, and the Department of Folklore and Ethnology in University College Cork (2000, although the study of folklore was introduced in 1977 by an anthropologist and folklorist, Gearóid Ó Crualaoich), and courses in folklore are taught elsewhere. Interdisciplinary approaches now characterise a great deal of the work done in the field, exemplified by Angela Bourke's *The Burning of Bridget Cleary* (1999), the most widely read scholarly book dealing with Irish folk tradition in several decades. Folklife studies were part of the brief of the Irish Folklore Commission. From the late 1920s the National Museum under Adolf Mahr set about assembling a folklife collection based on previous holdings and later cooperating with the Irish Folklore Commission and with the Irish Countrywomen's Association, which had surveyed craftworkers. Still photography and film along with field surveys, such as those of the Swedish ethnologists Åke Campbell and Albert Nilsson (Eskeröd) in the 1930s and the village surveys by the School of Architecture, University College Dublin, in the 1940s, added further documentation. The first major exhibition of folklife material was displayed in 1937 and a permanent exhibition from 1950. A. T. Lucas, later director of the National Museum, was put in charge in 1947, the first full-time appointment, though the material was part of the Irish Antiquities Division until 1974, when a separate Irish Folklife Division was created.[26] After decades of neglect, the collection – the largest in Ireland and amounting to some 50,000 artifacts – got a permanent home when the Museum of Irish Country Life was opened in 2001 at Turlough House, a few miles from Castlebar, Co. Mayo. It is an indoor museum, with a new purpose-built gallery and the lower floor of the Victorian mansion for the exhibits, while the upper floor of the mansion is used for administration. Unlike the Ulster Folk Museum, whose location was intended to draw on the largest local concentration of population, the Museum of Country Life was established in the west for essentially political reasons. Its name is misleading since its holdings are not representative of rural life as a whole, but rather of folk culture. It is a new institution, winner of the museum of the year award in 2001, and already has been very successful in attracting visitors.

The belated recognition of folklife can be explained by the fact that its artifacts unavoidably link it to the peasant condition and to popular culture. The intangible nature of folklore, on the other hand, lent itself to the national-popular, where traditions recorded from peasants nevertheless transcended their social condition and were used to assert the continuation of a national tradition. Delargy and others stressed the preservation of elements of Gaelic high culture by peasants who absorbed them into their popular tradition and he referred to himself and his staff as 'literary executors of earlier generations'.[27] Folklore was raw material for national culture, as Yeats and Hyde and the writers of the Anglo-Irish and Gaelic revivals averred. Folklife developed as a research field in a low key, far removed from cultural revolutions since it did not challenge any existing hegemony. It could be read in evolutionary terms as primitive survival, as Estyn Evans did following Tylor, and not the remnants of a vanishing glory, as cultural nationalists read folklore.

Emyr Estyn Evans was the key figure in the development of folk life studies in Northern Ireland. Born on the Welsh borders, he studied geography and anthropology in Aberystwyth under Professor H. J. Fleure, another of whose students, Iorwerth Peate, curated the Welsh Folk Museum from its foundation in 1946. Tuberculosis prevented Evans from taking up postgraduate studies in archaeology, though this interest was sharpened during his convalescence. He arrived in Queen's University, Belfast in 1928 to set up a department of geography. Co-organiser of an archaeological field survey of Northern Ireland, he also carried out excavations and revived the *Ulster Journal of Archaeology* in 1938. As a student he had visited Scandinavia and seen Skansen, the first open-air folk museum (founded in Stockholm as part of the Nordic Museum by Artur Hazelius in 1891). He conceived the idea for such a museum in Northern Ireland. According to Gwyneth Evans, his wife, he felt that Ireland, 'which had escaped the industrial revolution and the worst of repressive Puritanism, was a treasure-house of old ways, and so, excluding the more recent crafts which were already documented, he wrote of archaic practices and outdated tools that were still used'.[28] He published the first major book in the field of Irish folklife in 1942, *Irish Heritage*. By 1955, he had established the journal *Ulster Folklife*, and pushed for the creation of a folk museum. In 1961 the Ulster Folklife Society was founded. Evans also campaigned for the teaching of anthropology in Queen's University, Belfast.

Evans's books were widely read, especially *Irish Folk Ways* (1957), which gives a perspective of thousands of years on Irish folk culture, beginning with the geographical and prehistoric context. The title of the first chapter, 'Ireland the Outpost', sums up his perspective on the country as a periphery in which prehistoric and medieval relics have survived: 'The study of both the material and spiritual folk-life of Ireland and the oceanic fringes of Europe can throw light on the past and on the evolution of society in Britain and western Europe generally.'[29] Evans saw the fact that Ireland was in essence a peasant society as being crucial to the retention of Irish folk ways. He emphasised the importance of kinship, the prioritisation of the 'maintenance and continuity of society' over economic concerns, the valuing of large families, a superstitious attitude to life, limited contact with the world of money and being permanently linked to the soil.[30] He saw the province of Ulster as differing both from the rest of Ireland and from Britain in its geography, pre-history and history,[31] but at the same time Ireland's folk life was a heritage common to all the people of the island.

An Ulster Folk Museum finally emerged as part of a post-war movement in museums of everyday life in the United Kingdom, and was founded in 1958. Following the Skansen model, it consists of representative vernacular buildings re-erected on the museum site, furnished and decorated as they would have been around 1900, and provides demonstrations of traditional arts and crafts. The region covered is the nine-county province of Ulster rather than the six-county entity of Northern Ireland, perhaps due to Evans's belief in Ulster's difference from the rest of Ireland, or to the fact that the Ulster Plantation also included Donegal and Cavan while Monaghan had a large and historically significant Protestant population. The period reflected in the presentation of the buildings, as Alan Gailey has pointed out, 'is the earliest period for which a sufficiently complete inventory can be gathered together'[32] and presumably the latest period before the widespread replacement of this inventory. This reflects practice in other countries. The centre of the complex of buildings is Cultra Manor, in which the museum's administration is based, and there are exhibition centres for the display of traditional artifacts. Merged with the Belfast Transport Museum to form the Ulster Folk and Transport Museum in 1967, it was recently amalgamated with other heritage institutions in the umbrella grouping of the National Museums and Galleries of Northern Ireland. Its first two directors, George B. Thompson and Alan Gailey, were both geographers by training and former students of Evans's, while at the time of writing in 2004 it is headed by Jonathan Bell, an anthropologist. With a large staff of curators and researchers, it is the major centre for folk life research in Ireland.

The Ulster Folk and Transport Museum was established under the Stormont government, and its creation can be seen as 'indicative of a confidence in the regional status of Northern Ireland within the United Kingdom',[33] but the act establishing it specified its mission as 'illustrating the way of life, past and present, and the traditions of the people of Northern Ireland'. Such museums were intended to be both modern and national/regional; there may be 2,000 of them in Europe today.[34] Undoubtedly the folk museum (and by extension almost any museum) by its microcosmic nature asserts an underlying unity behind the surface diversity of the region or nation, and intimates too the fate of regional cultures synthesised into national culture. It is true too that there is an unfortunate symbolism in the administrative centre of the museum being located in the manor (to a degree also applying to the Museum of Country Life): 'the museum's controlling ideological centre, a bourgeois country house under whose controlling gaze there is organized a harmonious set of relationships – between town and country, agriculture and industry, for example, as well as between classes . . .', as Tony Bennett writes of a comparable institution in England.[35] The Ulster Folk Museum and the Museum of Country Life nevertheless were shaped first and foremost by the dominant international ethnological and museological discourses, by the physical constraints of their sites and by the need to display their collections.

Conrad Arensberg's *The Irish Countryman* (1937) and Arensberg and Solon Kimball's *Family and Community in Ireland* (1940) were the first anthropological community studies in Europe, the latter in particular acting as a benchmark for anthropological studies of rural society in Ireland. Both works originated in the Harvard Irish Study of 1931–36.[36] Most studies, to the 1970s at least, focused on West of Ireland communities, concentrating on tradition, family and kinship, many of them depicting a dying traditional society. Though folklorists and anthropologists were aware of each other and worked in the same regions, the lack of common interest tended to militate against any engagement with one another until the 1970s. The folklorists have been mostly Irish and Irish-based, with some important exceptions, mostly Scandinavian or American. The anthropologists until recently were American or British and based abroad. Irish anthropology departments are young: that of Queen's University, Belfast, was founded in 1973 and that of the National University of Ireland, Maynooth, in 1983.

The future of folklore

In the 1930s Antonio Gramsci observed that 'the folkloric comes close to the "provincial" in all senses, whether in the sense of "particularistic", or in the sense of anachronistic, or in the sense of proper to a class deprived of universal (or at least European) characteristics'.[37] Post-modernity suggests the displacing of universalism: 'the great stories of modernity . . . are disintegrating under our eyes and give way to a multitude of heterogeneous and local "petites histoires" . . .'[38] The story of folklore studies has always been one of *petites histoires*. Folklore never developed as a unitary discipline and arguably never had a metanarrative, shaped as it was by the ideas of Herder and the Romantics, valorising linguistic diversity and cultural specificity. Isac Chiva perhaps misses one of its strengths when he laments the fact that it produces work in a large number of different languages and is deprived of a lingua franca and hence 'of a common language, definitions and analytical concepts' as well as lacking a common denomination.[39]

The death of peasant society, the decline of the industrial working class, the growth of a tertiary employment sector and the dominance of the culture industries to the extent that their products are now consumed by the majority of all social classes in the West – these factors have problematised definitions of the folk and of the popular today. Consumption has cut across traditional divides between high and popular culture. Folk culture is being reconfigured by producers such as artisans working for the tourist or fine arts market, by middlemen such as dealers in country furniture for the antiques market and above all by the culture industries. Broadcasters, record producers and concert promotors have placed Irish folk music in a prominent place within national and global ('World Music') markets. The folk and the popular have been transformed, fulfilling new functions in a process that Lauri Honko has called 'the second life of folklore' and García Canclini terms 'cultural reconversion'.[40] At the same time post-modernism has embraced cultural diversity and defended the validity of other systems of knowledge.

Stuart Hall has pointed out that in every period the cultural process involves drawing a line 'as to what is to be incorporated into "the great tradition" and what is not'.[41] García Canclini concludes that cultural heritage can be a resource for reproducing social differences since it is the dominant groups that determine which elements are superior and worthy of being preserved. Popular groups can achieve a high aesthetic value in their artistic creations, he points out, but they 'have less possibility of carrying out various operations that are indispensable for converting those products into a generalized and widely recognized patrimony'.[42] Gayatri Chakravorti Spivak, commenting on the work of the Subaltern Studies historians who wished to rescue the voices of Indian peasant insurgents from both colonial and nationalist discourses, asked whether the subaltern can ever speak since its position by definition precludes communication between equals.[43] If taken literally, of course, the question can only lead to paralysis. No documents from the past can be understood purely at face value. Folklorists and folklife specialists nevertheless have assembled by far the largest record of Irish subaltern culture, one of the largest such records in the world, and one which deserves a more visible place within contemporary Irish Studies.

Notes

1. Han F. Vermeulen, 'Origins and institutionalization of ethnography and ethnology in Europe and the USA, 1771–1845', in *Fieldwork and Footnotes: Studies in the History of European Anthropology*, ed. Han F. Vermeulen and Arturo Alvarez Roldán (London and New York: Routledge, 1995), pp. 39–40.
2. Ernest Gellner, 'The coming of nationalism and its interpretation: the myths of nation and class', in *Mapping the Nation*, ed. Gopal Balakrishnan (London and New York: Verso, 1996), p. 139.
3. Miroslav Hroch, 'From national movement to fully-formed nation', in Balakrishnan, *Mapping the Nation*, p. 80; Anne-Marie Thiesse, *La Création des Identités Nationales: Europe XVIIIe–XXe siècle* (Paris: Éditions du Seuil, 1999).
4. Perry Anderson, 'Internationalism: a breviary', *New Left Review* (March–April 2002), 9.
5. Raymond Williams, *Keywords: A Vocabulary of Culture and Society* (London: Fontana, 1988), pp. 136–7.
6. Billy Ehn and Orvar Löfgren, *Vardagslivets Etnologie: Reflektioner Kring en Kulturvetenskap* (Stockholm: Natur och Kultur, 1996), pp. 23–4.
7. Renato Ortiz, *Românticos e Folcloristas. Cultura Popular* (São Paulo: Olha d'Água, 1992), pp. 65–7.
8. José Jorge de Carvalho, 'O Lugar da Cultura Tradicional na Sociedade Moderna', in *Série Encontros e Estudos 1: Seminário Folclore e Cultura Popular* (Rio de Janeiro, 1992), pp. 27, 29.
9. Michael Kearney, *Reconceptualizing the Peasantry: Anthropology in Global Perspective* (Boulder, CO, and Oxford: Westview Press, 1996), p. 78.
10. Caoimhín Ó Danachair, 'The progress of Irish ethnology, 1783–1982', *Ulster Folklife* 29 (1983), 4.
11. Breandán Ó Buachalla, *I mBéal Feirste Cois Cuain* (Dublin: An Clóchomhar, 1968), p. 23.
12. Ibid., p. 33
13. Ibid., pp. 23, 28–9, 37–44.
14. Ibid., pp. 69.
15. Patricia Lysaght, 'Perspectives on narrative communication and gender: Lady Augusta Gregory's visions and beliefs in the west of Ireland (1920)', *Fabula* 39, 3–4 (1998), 267.
16. Maurice Goldring, *Irlande: Idéologie d'une révolution nationale* (Paris: Éditions Sociales, 1975), p. 82.

17. Lady Augusta Gregory, *Poets and Dreamers. Studies and Translations from the Irish* (Dublin and London: Hodges, Figgis, and Co. and John Murray, 1903), pp. 129–30.

18. Seán Ó Laighin (ed.), *Ó Cadhain i bhFeasta* (Dublin: Clódhanna Teoranta, 1990), p. 158.

19. John Wilson Foster, *Fictions of the Irish Literary Revival: A Changeling Art* (Syracuse, NY: Syracuse University Press, 1987), p. 221.

20. Philip O'Leary, *The Prose Literature of the Gaelic Revival, 1881–1921* (University Park, PA: Pennsylvania State University Press, 1994).

21. Donncha Ó Súilleabháin, *Scéal an Oireachtais 1897–1924* (Dublin: An Clóchomhar Tta, 1984).

22. Fionnuala Nic Suibhne, ' "On the straw" and other aspects of pregnancy and child-birth from the oral tradition of women in Ulster', *Ulster Folklife* 38 (1992), 12.

23. Clodagh Brennan Harvey, 'Some Irish women storytellers and reflections on the role of women in the storytelling tradition', *Western Folklore* 48 (1989), 109–28; Clodagh Brennan Harvey, *Contemporary Irish Traditional Narrative: The English Language Tradition* (Berkeley, Los Angeles, Oxford: University of California Press, 1992), pp. 12–13, 47–8.

24. Angela Bourke, 'Oral traditions', in *The Field Day Anthology of Irish Writing: Irish Women's Writing and Traditions* (Cork: Cork University Press, in Association with Field Day, 2002), vol. IV, pp. 1191–458.

25. J. H. Delargy, 'The Gaelic storyteller', *Proceedings of the British Academy* 31 (1945), 46–7.

26. See A. T. Lucas, 'The National Folklife Collection' and Breandán Ó Ríordáin, 'The National Museum contribution', both in Patricia Lysaght, Anne O'Dowd and Bairbre O'Flynn (eds.), *A Folk Museum for Ireland* (unpaginated). Proceedings of a one-day conference held in the Conversation Room at the Royal Dublin Show-grounds, Dublin, 9 June 1984 (Dublin: no publisher, 1984).

27. Séamus Ó Duilearga, 'Volkskundliche Arbeit in Irland von 1850 bis zur Gegenen-wart mit besonderer Berücksichtigung der "Irischen Volkskunde-Kommission"', *Zeitschrift für Keltische Philologie und Volksforschung* 23, 1–38 (1943), 13.

28. Gwyneth Evans, 'Estyn: a biographical memoir', in E. Estyn Evans, *Ireland and the Atlantic Heritage: Selected Writings* (Dublin: Lilliput, 1996), p. 11.

29. E. Estyn Evans, *Irish Folk Ways* (London: Routledge and Kegan Paul, 1957), p. 3.

30. E. Estyn Evans, *Irish Heritage* (Dundalk: Dundalgan Press, 1942), p. 11; Evans, *Folk Ways*, pp. 10–11; see also Megan McManus, 'Some notions of folklore, history and museum interpretation', in Trefor M. Owen (ed.), *From Corrib to Cultra: Folklife Essays in Honour of Alan Gailey* (Belfast and Cultra: Institute of Irish Studies, Queen's University Belfast in Association with the Ulster Folk and Transport Museum, 2000), p. 20.

31. E. Estyn Evans, *Ulster: The Common Ground* (Gigginstown, Mullingar: The Lilliput Press, 1984), p. 8.

32. Alan Gailey, 'Cultra – From manor land to open air museum', in Lysaght *et al.* (eds.), *Folk Museum* (unpaginated).

33. Richard Kirkland, *Literature and Culture in Northern Ireland since 1965: Moments of Danger* (London and New York: Longman, 2000), p. 136.

34. Alan Gailey, 'Deeply domestic realms: origins, development and criticisms of open-air museums', *Ulster Folklife* 44 (1998), 20.

35. Tony Bennett, *The Birth of the Museum* (London and New York: Routledge, 1995), pp. 113–14.

244 Diarmuid Ó Giolláin

36. Anne Byrne, Ricca Edmondson and Tony Varley, 'Introduction to the third edition', in Conrad M. Arensberg and Solon T. Kimball, *Family and Community in Ireland* (Ennis, Co. Clare: Clasp Press, 2001), pp. xli, lii, lxiv.
37. Antonio Gramsci, *Letteratura e vita nazionale* (Rome: Editori Riuniti, 1996), p. 44.
38. Matei Calinescu, *Five Faces of Modernity* (Durham, NC: Duke University Press, 1987), p. 275.
39. Isac Chiva, 'Les Revues Ethnologique en Europe', in Christiane Amiel, Jean-Pierre Piniès and René Piniès (eds.), *Au Miroir des Revues: Ethnologie de l'Europe du Sud* (Carcassonne and Paris: Garae/Hesiode and Ent'revues, 1991), pp. 203–4.
40. Lauri Honko, 'The folklore process', in *Folklore Fellows' Summer School Programme* (Turku: Folklore Fellows' Summer School, 1991), p. 42; Néstor García Canclini, 'Cultural reconversion', in *On Edge: The Crisis of Contemporary Latin American Culture*, ed. George Yúdice, Jean Franco and Juan Flores (Minneapolis and London: University of Minnesota Press, 1992), pp. 29–43.
41. Stuart Hall, 'Notes on deconstructing "the popular"', in *People's History and Socialist Theory*, ed. Raphael Samuel (London: Routledge and Kegan Paul, 1981), p. 236.
42. García Canclini, *Hybrid Cultures*, p. 137.
43. Gayatri Chakravorti Spivak (1995), pp. 24–8.

Further reading

Conrad M. Arensberg and Solon T. Kimball, *Family and Community in Ireland* (Ennis, Co. Clare: Clasp Press, 2002)
Angela Bourke (ed.), 'Oral traditions', in *The Field Day Anthology of Irish Writing: Irish Women's Writing and Traditions* (Cork: Cork University Press, in Association with Field Day, 2002), vol. IV, pp. 1191–458
J. H. Delargy, 'The Gaelic storyteller', *Proceedings of the British Academy* 31 (1945), 177–221
E. Estyn Evans, *Irish Folk Ways* (London: Routledge and Kegan Paul, 1957)
Diarmuid Ó Giolláin, *Locating Irish Folklore: Tradition, Modernity, Identity* (Cork: Cork University Press, 2000)
Seán Ó Súilleabháin, *Irish Folk Custom and Belief* (Cork: Mercier Press, 1977)
Seán O'Sullivan, *Folktales of Ireland* (Chicago, IL and London: University of Chicago Press, 1968)
Georges Denis Zimmermann, *The Irish Storyteller* (Dublin: Four Courts, 2001)

14

Irish prose fiction

Introduction

The novel, the dominant narrative form in the English-speaking world for the period treated in this volume, is not an indigenous Irish form. When novels did come to be written in and about Ireland (from the late eighteenth century), English was the language of expression and the influence of Irish-language narratives on these new productions was not obvious. Nonetheless, writers in English from the time of Maria Edgeworth's *Castle Rackrent* (1800) have been at least intermittently and selectively responsive to Irish-language materials, particularly the largely oral story-telling tradition. When an important Irish-language tradition of prose fiction did emerge, at the beginning of the twentieth century, it drew energy from both the revival of indigenous forms and English-language influences. Thus, it is no longer possible to insist with some of the older cultural nationalists that prose fiction in Irish owes nothing to Irish prose fiction in English. Much scholarly work remains to be done, however, in investigating the two bodies of writing and in establishing points of contact. This chapter treats the two traditions of novel writing in separate sections, but aims to offer readers a rich sense of the Irish novel as it developed across a range of voices, forms and languages.

Prose fiction in Irish

The history of prose literature in Irish since 1800 inevitably reflects the shifting state of the Irish language itself during that period, from its cataclysmic decline in the nineteenth century and its revival at the end of that century and on to its continuing survival today.

The linguistic background

Irish had been losing ground to English since the early sixteenth century when a new English-speaking landed class began to emerge following the Tudor and Stuart plantations and settlements. The seventeenth century witnessed a major change in land ownership and a consequent shift of power from native to settler and is generally regarded as a watershed in the history of the Irish language and native culture. While Irish continued to be widely spoken, by the eighteenth century its status was considerably inferior to that of English, which had effectively become the language of government and administration. Despite an unprecedented increase in the Irish-speaking population in the following century, English retained its superior status as the language associated with property and power. This situation was further reinforced by the passing of the Act of Union in 1801. The massive language shift which occurred in the second half of the nineteenth century was, however, unparalleled and while this catastrophe can be attributed to a number of causes the single most significant cause was, unquestionably, the Great Famine of the 1840s, which resulted in the deaths of 1 million people and the further loss of 2 million in the wave of emigration that followed. These losses were particularly high amongst the Irish-speaking population. Furthermore, the perception of English, not only as the language associated with power at home in Ireland but now, also, as the language associated with success in the New World, provided the survivors who remained at home with a strong psychological motive for ensuring that the next generation would reject Irish in favour of English. Thus, by 1891, according to the data collected in the census of that year, a mere 8 in every 1,000 of the population were Irish-speaking monoglots, 145 in every 1,000 claimed to be bilingual and 855 in every 1,000 were unable to speak any Irish. Most of those who could speak the language could not read or write it. Two years later the Gaelic League, the Irish language revival organisation, was founded.

As the status of Irish waned, so did literary activity in the language, with the result that the eighteenth century has been described by one eminent scholar as 'the end of a tradition.'[1] Although an important oral story-telling tradition survived and some scribal activity continued, the nineteenth century was, effectively, 'a blank sheet' as far as Irish fiction was concerned. A small number of isolated original works however were produced. Most notable amongst these were *Cinnlae Amhlaoibh Uí*

Shúilleabháin/The Diary of Humphrey O'Sullivan, written between 1827 and 1835 and *Fealsúnacht Aodha Mhic Dhomhnaill/The Philosophy of Hugh Mac Donald*, written between 1849 and 1853; the former was not published until 1912 and the latter until 1967. When the movement to revive the language began towards the end of the century, the initiators of the revival had as one of their aspirations the creation of a modern literature in the Irish language. Given that the dominant narrative forms of the period were the novel and short story, the fact that Irish was by now a predominantly oral language which had evolved very little as an urban medium represented a major challenge to such literary aspirations. The increasing dominance of English in the everyday life of the country represented an even greater challenge. Nevertheless, the twentieth century produced a significant corpus of fiction in Irish which responded, with varying degrees of success, to those challenges.

Literature of the revival

Virtually all of the literature written in Irish since the revival has been ideologically motivated. Despite the increase in the number of people claiming an ability to read Irish since the beginning of the last century, the Irish language writer could be certain not only that his/her readers were as competent in English as they were in Irish, but were often *more* competent in English than in Irish. In certain cases, the latter may even be true of the writer him/herself. Thus, those writers who decided to write through the medium of Irish made a deliberate choice and in so doing, foregrounded the medium itself in such a way that, in many cases, it could almost be regarded as the subject. The significance of this choice became more apparent in the second half of the twentieth century, as the language itself evolved in response to an increasingly modern, urban and cosmopolitan Ireland.

The narrative fiction of the past one hundred-odd years falls into three distinct phases, reflecting the three generations of writers that emerged during the period. The first generation, that is the so-called revival writers, whose work was produced during the first twenty years of the last century, were responding to a need for reading material created by the large numbers of language learners attending the Gaelic League classes in the initial years of the revival. Four years after its establishment, the Gaelic League initiated an annual literary competition, the *Oireachtas* (1897), for the purpose of encouraging new writing in the language. Its short-story category was particularly successful in attracting writers of literary potential, most notably, the Galway-born Pádraic Ó Conaire, who was living in London at the time. Some of Ó Conaire's best-known short stories deal with contemporary life in the west of Ireland, although what is probably his best collection, *An Chéad Chloch/The First Stone* (1914), contains four stories based on characters from the New Testament and four dealing with a mythical oriental tribe. *Seacht mBua an Éirí Amach/The Seven Victories of the Rising* (1918) consists of seven stories about individuals whose lives were affected by the 1916 rebellion. Ó Conaire's simple style made his stories immediately accessible to a wide readership but this ostensible simplicity masked a highly sophisticated treatment of psychological issues. His one novel, *Deoraíocht/Exile* (1910), is purportedly set in London. However, this 'London' is not any identifiable geographical location but simply the obverse of a paradise lost which is the narrator's native Galway. Resembling a nightmare scenario rather than a physical city, Ó Conaire's London is synonymous with psychological alienation. Exile is a dominant theme of the author's work. The state or place from which the narrator of *Deoraíocht* is psychologically exiled, and to which he cannot return, is Irish-speaking Ireland. This extraordinary novel, with its surreal setting and cast of grotesque characters, has been subjected to numerous interpretations but it seems more than plausible to read it as a metaphor for the trauma that followed the demise of the Irish language and the imposition, in its place, of English.

Ó Conaire probably owes his success as a writer to Patrick Pearse, who, in his role as secretary of the Gaelic League's Publication Committee and as editor of the organisation's weekly paper, *An Claidheamh Soluis*, offered valuable advice to the young writer. Pearse was one of the most enlightened figures associated with the language revival. His editorial influence was extremely important; Pearse exhorted potential writers to adopt contemporary literary models from other European languages but also emphasised the importance of maintaining continuity with the Irish literary past. Pearse's own short stories present an idealised picture of the people of Connemara, particularly of the women and children. Although the subject matter can be limited, the stories were skilfully constructed and demonstrated the difference between the modern short story and the traditional tale. This distinction was not universally appreciated at the time and the title story from his first collection, *Íosagán agus Scéalta Eile/Child Jesus and Other Stories* (1907) provoked much negative reaction because it had rejected the traditional opening formula

'Once upon a time . . .' in favour of the modern or so-called 'explosive' opening.

Father Peter O'Leary (known in Irish as an tAthair Peadar Ó Laoghaire) is credited with establishing *caint na ndaoine* (the spoken language) as an acceptable literary medium. The publication, in 1904, of his highly acclaimed folk novel, *Séadna*, demonstrated the error of those who maintained that modern Irish literature could not be written in the allegedly unrefined living language but who advocated, instead, a return to the classical language of seventeenth-century literature. Based on the Faust legend, *Séadna*, the story of a poor shoemaker who makes a pact with the devil and then sets about redeeming himself, takes place in an imaginary Irish-speaking world where the natural and the supernatural cohabit. Purportedly narrated by a young woman to a group of children, this is basically a moral tale about the triumph of good over evil and although the narrator closely resembles a *seanchaí* or traditional storyteller the occasional short passages of explanatory dialogue between her and her purported audience provide the oral narrative with a literary frame. The ending is flawed, probably because *Séadna* was not originally conceived as a book but was serialised over a lengthy period in a number of newspapers and suffered, ultimately, from poor editing. In spite of the outstanding narrative skills to which this book attests, the author produced no other fiction of lasting value.

It is noteworthy that all three of the writers discussed were extremely competent English-speakers yet no knowledge of English is required in order to comprehend their work. The literary world which they created is one in which English plays no part except as an aberration from the norm. In this respect, all three reflect the ideological position of the cultural revolution of the time, which had as its ultimate aim the replacement of English by Irish.

The Blasket autobiographies

At the end of the 1920s, the language revival brought a number of philologists to the Blasket Islands, in West Kerry, in order to learn Irish. The unintended consequence was an important literary phenomenon, namely, the appearance of a group of memoirs written in Irish and collectively known as 'The Blasket autobiographies'. Each of the three main books of this group, Tomás Ó Criomhthain's *An tOileánach/The Islandman* (1929), Muiris Ó Súilleabháin's *Fiche Blian ag Fás/Twenty Years a-Growing* (1933) and Peig Sayers's *Peig* (1936), was written at the suggestion of one of the scholars visiting the Blaskets who recognised the narrative potential of the respective authors, and each told the story of life on the small Irish-speaking island during the second half of the nineteenth century and up to the end of the 1920s. Although unaware that they were providing 'an account of Neolithic civilisation from the inside'[2] or that the society they were describing had many features in common with that described by Homer,[3] all three of the authors seem to have been aware that, in recounting their own experience of everyday events on the Great Blasket, they were, in fact, telling the story of an ancient civilisation in the process of disappearing. When they were first published, in the early days of the newly independent Irish Free State (founded in 1922), these books depicted a society which embodied the ideal Ireland imagined by the founders of the state, a society which was not tainted by materialism, which was essentially rural, strongly traditional, virtually self-sufficient, heroic and Irish-speaking. Moreover, these were not works of fiction but autobiographical narratives and, as such, all written in the past tense. They constituted the perfect literary achievement and, as a result, became a linguistic and stylistic model for a great deal of subsequent writing in Irish, including fiction. Ó Criomhthain's statement, *ní bheidh ár leithéidí arís ann* ('the likes of us will never be again') became a catchphrase in the language and was taken up by Myles na gCopaleen (Brian O'Nolan) in his satire on the more fanatical and unenlightened aspects of the Irish Revival movement, *An Béal Bocht/The Poor Mouth* (1941), in which he parodied the Blasket books and some of their overly sentimental derivatives. (*An Béal Bocht/The Poor Mouth* is the only novel in Irish by this author, who is better known for his work in English, discussed below.)

Emigration had figured prominently in all of the Blasket autobiographies and the experience continued to be a feature of Irish life. By the late 1930s, however, a new kind of migration had begun which, to a certain extent, informed the next phase of Irish writing. This migration was internal, from rural Ireland to the cities and bigger towns. Following the foundation of the state in 1922, teachers, members of the native police force and civil servants were required to have a knowledge of the language and many educated young people from the Irish-speaking areas in the West availed themselves of the new employment opportunities which this represented. Some of the most successful writers of modern Irish were such internal migrants and their writings mainly document the experience of a generation linguistically and culturally uprooted.

The 1940s saw a flowering of writing in Irish, particularly of the short story. The proliferation of literary periodicals at this time was a contributory factor as was the re-establishment, in 1939, of the *Oireachtas* literary competition, which had been discontinued in the 1920s. Writers such as Donncha Ó Céileachair from the West Cork Gaeltacht (Irish-speaking area), Séamus Ó Grianna and his brother, Seosamh, from the Donegal Gaeltacht, Máirtín Ó Cadhain from the Connemara Gaeltacht and Liam Ó Flaithearta/Liam O'Flaherty from the Aran Islands (better known for his English writings) all had collections of short stories published in this period. All of these writers had monoglot, or virtually monoglot, parents and had grown up in a linguistic environment in which Irish was the first language. Unlike their parents, however, they had all had a formal education in the course of which they had been exposed to English at primary, secondary or third level and had settled, as adults, in English-speaking Dublin. These writers could be said to represent the last generation who straddled a monoglot-Irish and a mainly English-speaking world – a fact which is reflected in their writing. Apart from O'Flaherty, whose Irish writing is virtually free from traditional influence, all consciously drew on oral storytelling techniques. Because of the author's untimely death, the corpus of Ó Céileachair's work is very small; it is, however, significant, representing a masterful blending of two distinct narrative forms – the traditional oral hero tale and the modern short story. His stories deal with a world that is undergoing a radical transformation, from a traditional rural society to a modern urban society, from an Irish-speaking society to an English-speaking society and the process of change is portrayed as a conflict which replicates the traditional conflict between hero and villain.

Ó Cadhain, author of six collections of short stories and two novels, was probably the most innovative writer of the whole period. The earlier part of his work is almost entirely set in the Connemara Gaeltacht but his later, more experimental work is set in Dublin, reflecting the pattern of his own life. The Connemara stories deal mainly with the plight of women who are trapped in traditional roles in a conservative and unsympathetic society; the Dublin stories deal mainly with men, trapped in an equally unsympathetic urban situation. The Connemara stories contain little humour but the urban stories are generally satirical in tone, with a strong tendency towards surreal black comedy. His first novel, *Cré na Cille/Churchyard Clay* (1949) consists wholly of dialogue between the corpses interred in the graveyard – a metaphor for contemporary Ireland, whose most prominent institutions the book satirises brilliantly. An Irish writer *engagé*, Ó Cadhain was passionately committed to the language and, like Ó Céileachair, he deliberately exploited the conflict caused by the cohabitation of English and Irish for literary effect. Both writers acknowledged the existence of the English language as part of contemporary reality and, unlike the previous generation, they depicted English in their writings, not as something marginal or as something that could be excluded completely but rather as an important source of conflict and even as a threat to the survival of Irish.

The threat notwithstanding, Irish has continued to survive and while the cohabitation of the two languages has, inevitably, resulted in considerable contamination of the weaker language, there have been positive consequences also. The writings of the post-1960s generation reflect these consequences.

The writers from this latter group would not have had an Irish-speaking monoglot parent. They grew up in an Ireland which had conceded that the radical aims of the early revivalists were more idealistic than realistic. Probably the most significant characteristic of the language itself since the 1960s has been its increasing urbanisation. In the work of writers like Eoghan Ó Tuairisc, Diarmaid Ó Súilleabháin and later, Alan Titley, Seán Mac Mathúna, Séamus Mac Annaidh, Pádraig Ó Cíobháin and Mícheál Ó Conghaile, the evolution of the language and its relationship to English have been exploited for literary purposes with considerable success. With the exception of Mac Mathúna, all of these writers have produced both short stories and novels and it is interesting to note that the shorter form is giving way, gradually, to the longer one as the writers become increasingly experimental both in their use of the language and in their approach to the novel itself. Éilís Ní Dhuibhne has written both short stories and novels, in Irish and in English. Two of her novels, *The Dancers Dancing* (1999) and *Cailíní Beaga Ghleann na mBláth*/The Little Girls of Gleann na mBláth (2003), each of which could be described as a *Bildungsroman*, document the experiences of young girls attending an Irish language summer course. Although set in an Irish-speaking environment, both novels are narrated from an English-speaking perspective. Ní Dhuibhne's English-medium novel is, however, more stylistically assured and more convincing than her novel in Irish.

A recent novel by one of these authors, *Sna Fir* (1999), by Mícheál Ó Conghaile, exemplifies the linguistic iconoclasm which characterises much of the recent fiction in Irish. The title, which literally means, 'in the men', more usually means, in Connemara Irish, 'having attained adulthood'. The ambiguity is deliberate as this is a gay *Bildungsroman*. The narrator, John Paul MacDonagh (so called because he was born in 1979, the year the Pope came to Ireland) recounts a year of his life. Echoes of Ó Súilleabháin's *Twenty Years a-Growing* are apparent throughout, while the setting – Connemara, Dublin and London – recalls Ó Conaire's *Deoraíocht*. Probably Ó Conghaile's most notable achievement, this book is as much about the Irish language at the end of the twentieth century as it is the story of John Paul MacDonagh (or alternatively, Eoin Pól Mac Donnchadha). Early in the book, the tension between the traditional ways of the older Gaeltacht people and the modern world of the young is conveyed by interspersing one of the great symbols of the tradition, a *sean-nós* (traditional unaccompanied) song, rendered by an elderly local practitioner of the form, with a commentary in crude, inarticulate English by some local youths who are watching an English football match on the public house television. Different registers of Irish and mixtures of Irish and English are used throughout to excellent effect, reflecting the varieties of language spoken both in the *Gaeltacht* and in the rest of Ireland today, from the pure, relatively uncorrupted Irish of the older speakers to the anglicised, urbanised Irish of the sophisticated younger speakers, with interesting intermediate varieties of slang, special jargon, pidgin and creole, as well as literary language itself. Ó Conghaile's book could justifiably be called *Seventy Years a-Growing* after Ó Súilleabháin's autobiographical *Bildungsroman*. In Ó Conghaile's case, though, the subject is not only the boy who becomes a man but the Irish language itself, whose evolution over the past seventy years it chronicles. *Sna Fir* is not just a novel written in Irish; it is a novel about Irish and about the relationship between Irish and English in contemporary Ireland. Furthermore, it is a novel which could only have been written in the Irish language and, as such, defines the place of Irish narrative literature today.

Prose fiction in English

The novel and the short story – English, European and American rather than specifically Irish literary forms – emerge as increasingly important and distinctive modes of writing within the English-speaking world in the course of the nineteenth century. But fiction has had different significance at different times in Ireland, sometimes attracting less public interest than poetry, plays or political journalism. James Joyce is the leading Irish novelist, but Irish literary history before Joyce has paid relatively little attention to novels because formative episodes – the United Irishmen's rebellion of 1798 and its cultural aftermath, Young Ireland in the 1840s, the literary revival of 1890 to 1914 or so – were dominated by other literary forms. Poets responded sooner and more effectively than novelists to the political troubles of Northern Ireland since 1968. Ireland's national writer before Yeats was the romantic, decorously patriotic poet Thomas Moore rather than any novelist, and although some of Moore's controversial, more or less fictional prose such as *Memoirs of Captain Rock* (1824) or *Travels of an Irish Gentleman in Search of a Religion* (1833) still repays attention, it has been overshadowed by his musical verse. English as much as Irish cultural history provides rough, overlapping categories for the consideration of Irish fiction in English. It is variously romantic, Victorian, modernist, realist (or neorealist) and contemporary. But the chronology is not straightforward: romantic concerns persist into the late Victorian period and beyond, while bleakly realist writing in the 1920s and 1930s can come out of a disillusioned and deeply chastened romanticism, and contemporary writing can still pursue modernist or realist agendas.

Romanticism and fiction

If the Irish novel in English owes little to Irish-language antecedents, at least in the first instance, it owes a great deal to other forms of Irish writing, including travel narratives, the drama (with the stage Irishman), published sermons and political speeches, and topographical and historical or antiquarian studies. There were eighteenth-century Irish novelists such as Henry Brooke, author of the once-popular *Fool of Quality* (1766–72), whose matter was specifically and obviously Irish. A new departure was signalled by Maria Edgeworth's *Castle Rackrent* (1800). This satire on irresponsible Irish landlordism, with an unreliable servant-narrator, coincides with the ambiguous new beginnings signalled by the Act of Union between Britain and Ireland which was passed later the same year, and it is usually regarded as the first Irish novel. It was perhaps a pre-romantic rather than a romantic text, but by using non-standard English to give a voice to non-metropolitan concerns it had enormous influence on subsequent writers, including the supreme romantic novelist Sir Walter Scott. Edgeworth and her father Richard Lovell Edgeworth were didactic rationalists already noted for *Practical Education* (1798), and their sophisticated anthropological exercise, *Essay on Irish Bulls*, appeared in 1802. *Castle Rackrent* is, among other things, itself an exercise in anthropology, describing the manners of the Irish, incorporating a glossary in later editions, and linking itself with travel narratives reporting on Irish matters such as Arthur Young's *Tour in Ireland* (1780).

The sense of Ireland as difficult and unfamiliar matter for report, a set of socioeconomic problems requiring solution, is even stronger in Edgeworth's subsequent Irish novels such as *Ennui* (1809) and *The Absentee* (1812), in which reader and protagonist alike need to learn about the 'real' Ireland rather quickly. The subject matter is near-contemporary, though there are still traces of an older Ireland represented for example by the traditional harper Arthur O'Neill (a real person, known to the Edgeworths) in *The Absentee*. O'Neill plays at the wedding of the previously absentee landlord's son with the authentically Irish Grace Nugent, a symbolic resolution of endemic tensions between Anglo-Irish and native elements which provides a pattern for many subsequent Irish fictions. The assumed readership is English and metropolitan rather than Irish. Although there were short-lived Irish journals such as the Cork-based *Bolster's Quarterly Magazine* (1826–27) and the *Dublin Monthly Magazine* (1830) which carried fictional pieces, and the more successful *Dublin University Magazine* (1833–77) which published novels in serial form, the domestic market for works of fiction, a relatively expensive luxury in a poor country, was severely limited. On the other hand, Gothic fictions set in Ireland fed a post-classical European taste for romantic primitivism and exotic extremity of landscape and behaviour. Audiences that already idolised 'Ossian' (as much Irish as Scottish in origin) and celebrated traditional Irish harp music (collected and publicised after the Belfast Harp Festival of 1792) provided an overseas market for Irish material (translated if necessary) which continued until at least mid-century.

The market-conscious Sydney Owenson, Lady Morgan, exploited the picturesque and musical as well as literary tastes of her time. The biographer of the Italian landscape painter Salvator Rosa (1824), Owenson was sensitive to Ireland's visual appeal as well as being a singer who could accompany herself on the harp. In 1805 she published *Twelve Original Irish Melodies*, lyrics in English set to Irish tunes. A sentimental nationalist sense of the ancient dignity of a partly suppressed culture in a country now subject to the Act of Union pervades her writing. Dreams of a harmonious national future, anticipated in romantic marriages between

Celt and Saxon, draw on recent memories of the United Irishmen and the stirring speeches of patriotic orators such as John Philpot Curran which were available in published collections. Self-dramatising (she was the daughter of an actor-manager), Owenson had seen different parts of Ireland on tour with her father and was able to report on its people and landscapes in novels such as the proto-feminist *The Wild Irish Girl* (1806), *O'Donnel* (1814) and *The O'Briens and the O'Flaherties* (1827). Owenson's novels are littered with footnotes to learned topographical and antiquarian research which had recently become fashionable, encouraged by the Royal Irish Academy (founded in 1785).

The success of *The Wild Irish Girl* encouraged the penniless and extravagantly theatrical clergyman Charles Maturin to try his hand at fictions such as *The Wild Irish Boy* (1808) as well as Gothic melodramas for the stage such as *Bertram* (1816). His gifts for melodramatic narrative and perfervid emotional intensity, evident in the lurid anti-Catholicism of some of his published sermons, came into their own in the interwoven tales of *Melmoth the Wanderer* (1820), which is both the longest and best Irish Gothic novel and, since it ranges over some 150 years, one of the earliest examples of Irish historical fiction.

Ireland's troubled history, up to and including the horror and heroism associated with the United Irishmen in 1798, and the example of Sir Walter Scott, encouraged Irish writers to attempt historical novels. *Rory O'More* (1837), a tale of 1798 by Samuel Lover, was an entertainment by an entertainer, but among the more serious and successful historical novelists were the Banim brothers, John and Michael, who first collaborated in a series of national tales published as *Tales of the O'Hara Family* (1825). History is notoriously written by the victors, usually Protestants in eighteenth and nineteenth-century Ireland, but works such as *The Boyne Water* (1826) and *The Croppy* (1828), revisiting the battles of 1690 and 1798 respectively, explored old wounds and imagined possible healing from a Catholic point of view.

If the Banims were Ireland's first serious Catholic novelists they were soon followed by Gerald Griffin whose best novel *The Collegians* (1829), a melodramatic narrative based on a famous murder case, romantically draws on Griffin's Limerick childhood to present a range of Irish character-types. Its inherent theatricality encouraged Dion Boucicault to adapt it for the stage as *The Colleen Bawn* (1860).

William Carleton, Catholic born but a convert to Protestantism, made his name with the early short stories collected as *Traits and Stories of the*

Irish Peasantry which provide a graphic, serio-comic panorama of rascals and pedants, wakes and weddings in traditional rural society before the Famine. The bleakness of earlier famine experiences contributes to the grotesque, atmospheric harshness of his best full-length novel *The Black Prophet* (1847) which appeared during the Famine. A poor man, largely self-educated and without the family connections that might have ensured material success, Carleton had to write for money. Like other Irish writers of the time, he found it difficult to make a living, despite catchpenny didactic fictions such as *Art Maguire* and *Parra Sastha*, both published in 1845 in the nationalist Library of Ireland series in which fiction seldom featured.

Victorian Ireland

The political divisions of Victorian Ireland between more or less separatist nationalists and unionist conservatives were reflected in different strands of fiction, but the differences were less extreme than one might have expected. The conservative *Dublin University Magazine*, which disapproved of the Library of Ireland, published work by Charles Lever who briefly edited the magazine (1842–45). Lever's novels included not just light-hearted apolitical chronicles of horsemanship and military life such as *Charles O'Malley* (1841) but later, more serious fictions such as *Lord Kilgobbin* (1872) which satirises the English administration of Ireland and includes a fairly sympathetic portrait of a Fenian leader on the run. A subsequent editor, and for a time proprietor, of the *Dublin University Magazine*, Sheridan Le Fanu, a romantic survivor into the Victorian era, first published many of his ghost stories and Gothic novels in the magazine, including the best known, *Uncle Silas* (1864), set in England but in some ways a coded account of the perennial tensions associated with Irish land ownership. Similar claims have been made for *Dracula* (1897), an even more blood-curdling narrative of sexual terror and abuse of hereditary power, by the former Irish civil servant and man of the theatre Bram Stoker.

The problems of landlord and tenant in Ireland, particularly acute in the Famine years, highlighted rather than resolved by Gladstone's first Land Act of 1870, were reflected in the famous *Knocknagow, or the Homes of Tipperary* (1879), a nationalist classic by the Fenian journalist Charles Kickham, answered in a sense by the Unionist Emily Lawless in her novel *Hurrish* (1886), which seems to advocate abandoning politics, that is, the politics of violence and insurrection, in favour of the indigenous virtue of the Irish people. Rosa Mulholland (Lady Gilbert), a well-to-do Catholic novelist, addresses the same problem in her novel of the Land War, *Mary O'Murrough* (1908), looking to the new Catholic gentry to assume leadership. Her earlier, more romantic *Wild Birds of Killeevy* (1883) shows Irish people finding success in continental Europe.

While poets and dramatists, philologists and folklorists were busy rediscovering the Celtic past and contributing to the literary revival, most of the late-Victorian and Edwardian novelists either continued to address some of the economic, social and political problems of contemporary Irish society or, like Oscar Wilde in *The Picture of Dorian Gray* (1891), took refuge in a more or less decadent aestheticism. Aesthetic dreaming and sensitive recreation of boyhood experience as an escape from industrial Belfast characterise the fiction of Forrest Reid as late as the 1930s and 1940s. 'Somerville and Ross', Edith Somerville and her cousin Violet Martin, came from and wrote about the decaying Anglo-Irish gentry. The humour of their immensely popular 'Irish RM' hunting stories (1899–1915) is balanced by the sombre economic realism of *The Real Charlotte* (1894), a study in amoral survival.

Book-production, now mechanised, had become much cheaper, and improved standards of literacy in Ireland as in England had expanded the reading public. For writers such as George Moore, from a Catholic landed family but in reduced circumstances, writing novels was actually a way of making money. Cosmopolitan, a Wagnerian, aesthete and realist by turns, writing from and for both Ireland and England, Moore's successes include the realist, feminist novels *A Drama in Muslin* (1886), set in Ireland and London, and *Esther Waters* (1894), concerning an unmarried mother, set in England. His iconoclastic short stories, collected in *The Untilled Field* (1903), were originally written for translation into Irish to help the Gaelic League, and these and some of his experiments with interior monologue probably influenced the young James Joyce and the development of literary modernism.

Modernist fiction

James Joyce is both the supreme Irish Catholic novelist and the supreme Catholic rebel. Educated into habits of intellectual and aesthetic if not spiritual discipline by the Jesuits but impatient of the religion and of the Celtic revivalist sentimentality and the rhetorical politics with which ıe had grown up, he could neither live in Ireland nor write without it. The long-meditated short stories collected as *Dubliners* (1914) are spare, almost meagre masterpieces describing failure, frustration and a kind of moral paralysis. They have continued to influence generations of laconic Irish short-story writers from Sean O'Faolain to William Trevor. The shifting styles and perspectives of *Portrait of the Artist as a Young Man* (1916), a partly ironic account of the aesthetic education of the Joycean alter ego and aspiring writer Stephen Dedalus, draw on nineteenth-century realism and the dedication to 'art for art's sake' pursued by Oscar Wilde but pass beyond them to self-conscious exploration of the language of consciousness itself. This exploration continues in his most important novel *Ulysses*, published in Paris in 1922. The flux and shapelessness of everyday consciousness is always likely to present its narrator with problems of literary form. Joyce's solution was to pattern his modernist epic, based on the awareness of three characters on a single day in Dublin in 1904, on episodes in Homer's *Odyssey*. His hero, corresponding to Odysseus (also known as Ulysses), is the ordinarily decent but not obviously heroic Leopold Bloom who nevertheless provides access to a wide range of human experience. It is not certain that *Finnegans Wake* (1939), Joyce's last and most ambitious work, can properly be described as either a novel or as prose in English. Its title alludes among other things to an Irish ballad about a man who came back to life at his own wake, and much of the incidental detail is Irish, but its aspirations and range of reference are universal. Almost everything, from Fall narratives, whether of Humpty Dumpty or in the Garden of Eden, to the Egyptian Book of the Dead, has gone into its making. A vast dream-vision written in a style which incorporates endless multilingual puns sponsoring multiple simultaneous meanings, it incorporates narrative elements which do not quite amount to conventional stories and shadowy, unstable identities which are hardly characters in any conventionally fictional sense. Drawing systematically on cyclical theories of history, Joyce ensures that the sense of the book's closing words is completed only by going right back to the beginning again. Baffling, fascinating, endlessly discussed and explained without being exhausted, *Finnegans Wake* is a unique achievement which celebrates the inextinguishable vitality of language itself.

Unsurprisingly, *Finnegans Wake* has had no imitators, though it has attracted some heroic and ingenious translators. Arguably, Irish modernism has persisted and developed more in poetry than in prose. The young Samuel Beckett met Joyce in Paris and wrote out some of

Finnegans Wake to Joyce's dictation. But, despite a common commitment to innovative fiction and a common admiration for Dante, Joyce and Beckett really represent different kinds of modernism. Joyce wrote some short fiction, but, in a sense, not just the short stories in *More Pricks than Kicks* (1934) but all Beckett's narratives are short fictions, ironic, bleakly funny exercises in minimalism which contrast both with the exuberantly rhetorical tradition of Irish talk and the endlessly accumulating detail of Joyce's longer fiction. Even more than Joyce, Beckett wanted to get away from Ireland. His first novel, *Murphy* (1938), has some Irish scenes and characters but Murphy himself lives and dies in London. Later novels such as *Molloy* and *Malone Dies* (1951), originally written in French, have protagonists with Irish names but there is little else which is obviously Irish in either work.

Perhaps only Brian Nolan, better known as Flann O'Brien or Myles Na Gopaleen, well versed in traditions of Irish-language writing, as we have seen above, has managed to combine Joycean exuberance, Gaelic culture and modernist innovation in an Irish context, particularly in his first novel *At Swim-Two-Birds* (1939). O'Brien's language is more conventional and accessible than that of the later Joyce, but he offers not so much a straightforward narrative as a whole series of interwoven narratives constituting an obviously fictive fiction about the creation of fiction. Ancient stories from the Irish tradition about Mad Sweeney or Finn MacCool, Wild West yarns and contemporary life are all mingled together and characters rebel inconveniently against the tyranny of the author. O'Brien's subsequent novels, of which the best is probably *The Third Policeman*, written in 1940 but not published until 1967, are fantastic, grotesque, unnerving and satirical by turns, challenging the 'normal' notions of time, matter and identity which characterise more conventional narratives.

Modernist experiment, articulating destabilising challenges to our habitual understanding or construction of the world, has continued intermittently in more recent Irish novels. The Belfast-born writer Brian Moore wrote ostensibly realist fictions such as *Fergus* (1970) or *The Great Victorian Collection* (1975), which are nevertheless complicated by games or tricks played with reality, animated or interrogated by ghostly presences or, as in the earlier novel *The Feast of Lupercal* (1957), assimilated to strange ritual patterns. In his autobiographical fiction *Blacklist, Section H*, eventually published to great acclaim in 1971, Francis Stuart reviewed the strangeness and difficulty of his own life and times, including wartime broadcasts from Berlin which assisted the Nazi propaganda offensive, transforming his controversial journalism into a complex vindication of living dangerously as part of the artist's training. Subsequent novels such as *High Consistory* (1981) or *Faillandia* (1985) were even more innovative and experimental but less successful. John Banville has taken as his starting point episodes in the history of science (*Doctor Copernicus* (1976), *Kepler* (1981)) or contemporary news stories (*The Book of Evidence* (1989), *The Untouchable* (1997)) and demonstrated how language, narrative and intellectual construction can confer or create meaning and significance, a kind of 'reality' which may be illusory. These ambitious fictions challenge the confidence of the realist writer of the nineteenth and the earlier twentieth centuries that it is possible to penetrate veils of sentiment or mystification and render the world reliably, as it 'really' is.

The new realism

Celtic revivalism and militant nationalism alike fed on romantic nostalgia, dreams of nationhood and quasi-religious enthusiasm for the lost soul of Ireland, enshrined in the dying Irish language, held in durance vile by English cultural and political dominance. But the struggle and the bloodshed of Easter Week, 1916, of the War of Independence (1918–21) and of the Civil War (1922–23) damaged romantic ideals by exposing them to incidental chaos and brutality, brought in a new and in some ways repressive political order and left it unclear whether the country one had been fighting for was going to be worth living in. Novelists and short-story writers who had been combatants had the opportunity to register post-romantic disillusionment and psychic trauma in the 1920s and the 1930s. Among the most distinguished were Sean O'Faolain, author of *Midsummer Madness and Other Stories* (1932), and Frank O'Connor, author of *Guests of the Nation* (1931), the title story of which was later filmed, for whom the concentrated economy of the short story as it had been developed by Joyce was a more appropriate medium than the more extended form of the novel. Studies of war-induced psychological tension and disorder by Liam O'Flaherty, less prominent in his short stories than in novels such as *Black Soul* (1924) and *The Informer* (1925), draw on painful personal experience. *The Puritan* (1931) conveys his savage hostility to the new Irish Free State which surrendered to narrow-mindedness and shackled its writers with a literary censorship in 1929.

For other writers of the period, fantasy and satire rather than realist fiction seemed the most appropriate mode of moral resistance to the new nation with its official ideology of romantic ruralism, its stagnant economy and oppressively Catholic puritanism. Eimar O'Duffy constructed a dystopian fable in *King Goshawk and the Birds* (1926) and a sexually enlightened utopia in *The Spacious Man in the Street* (1928) to embody a radical critique of the capitalist economic order and the restrictiveness of modern Ireland. Mervyn Wall's 'Fursey' novels of the 1940s revisit the famous ancient monastery of Clonmacnoise, not out of reverence for the austere traditions of Irish monasticism but in the interests of comic subversion, giving the devil considerably more than his due.

Irish Catholicism, increasingly vigorous, even triumphalist, since the later nineteenth century, was the religion of the vast majority of Irish people in the post-independence state, all the more because the mainly Protestant north-eastern counties, present-day Northern Ireland, had been separated off by Partition. But the new Catholic ascendancy was conservative and dominated by male priests and politicians. The new Catholic professional middle class, including women as well as men, was better educated and more affluent than parents or grandparents had been. Its problems and tensions, sexual as well as social, are explored with great sensitivity and insight in the feminist fictions of Kate O'Brien, notably in *Mary Lavelle* (1936) and *Land of Spices* (1941), some of the best though still undervalued novels of the period.

The literary critique of the new order coincided with complicated responses to the passing of the old, the Anglo-Irish milieu of big houses and tennis parties. In *The Last September* (1929) Elizabeth Bowen, of Bowen's Court, Co. Cork, vividly recreated this world in a distinctive, concentrated style which continues to fascinate modern readers. She juxtaposed the country house with the new revolutionary 'business of Ireland' which led to the burning of so many big houses and the eclipse, for better or worse, of a doomed way of life. This elegiac theme, often complicated by ironic interrogation of the kind of life that was lost, has continued in the contemporary fictions of Molly Keane (*Good Behaviour*, 1981) and William Trevor (*Fools of Fortune*, 1983 and *The Story of Lucy Gault*, 2002).

Contemporary fiction

Somewhere in the 1960s Ireland – arguably – evolved into a modern nation. North and south of the border, traditionally minded politicians were replaced by cautious reformers and modernisers. Insularity yielded to increasingly European perspectives; poverty slowly yielded to modest prosperity. The sexual revolution and the new feminism in England and the United States eventually had an impact in Ireland, first reflected in Edna O'Brien's *The Country Girls* (1960) and its sequels about Irish girls seeking new possibilities in Dublin and London.

Despite the conservative squeamishness which caused John McGahern to lose his job as a teacher after the publication of his second novel *The Dark* (1965), a disturbing account of the difficult coming of age of a motherless boy in a dysfunctional Catholic family, a new frankness in sexual matters became acceptable. McGahern's *Amongst Women* (1990), perhaps his finest novel, signals the coming of age of Irish society and the eclipse of old-fashioned patriarchy as the energies of a once-famous IRA leader of the 1920s pass to his daughters.

The 'backward look' which Frank O'Connor had noted as endemic in Irish culture has continued as a theme in Irish fiction, notably in *The Captains and the Kings* (1972) and other works by Jennifer Johnston. But younger novelists such as Colm Tóibín in *The South* (1990) and *The Heather Blazing* (1992) have explored narrative and imaginative links between past and present, rebel tradition and contemporary experience. Dermot Bolger, grim and gritty chronicler of contemporary Ireland as Europeanised nightmare in *The Journey Home* (1990), has explored the antecedents of the present in *A Second Life* (1994) in which the protagonist starts to find out about his mother. The sharp dialogue and humane tolerance of the Barrytown Trilogy by Roddy Doyle, narratives of working-class life in the new north Dublin housing estates, have attracted attention partly because of the popularity of the film version of *The Commitments* (1989), but Doyle has moved from realism to magic realism and from present to past in his ambitious novel of 1916, *A Star Called Henry* (1999).

There have been challenging constructions of both past and present in recent women's fiction, often thematically and formally innovative, which have both stimulated and drawn stimulus from Ireland's late-flowering women's movement. Women's sense of contemporary Ireland as a site of confusion and change is enterprisingly confronted in Éilís Ní Dhuibhne's short stories in Irish and English, particularly *Blood and Water* (1988), and in her linguistically innovative novel *Dancers Dancing* (1999), which captures the complex bilingual experience of life in the Donegal *Gaeltacht*. Set in Dublin and Donegal in 1972, the novel shows how a group of adolescent girls are effected by a range of diverse phenomena – weight loss, fashion and teenage crushes side by side with Partition, infanticide and urban poverty – that are woven together in the texture of their young lives. Anne Enright's ambitiously structured novel *What Are You Like?* (2000) confronts issues of identity through the lives of separated twins, while her later novel *The Pleasure of Eliza Lynch* (2002) boldly draws on the true history of a nineteenth-century Irish courtesan in Latin America. Lesbian desire has been explored in the scholarly as well as creative work of Emma Donoghue, particularly her novel *Stir-Fry* (1994), and in Mary Dorcey's stories *A Noise from the Woodshed* (1989) along with her first novel *Biography of Desire* (1997). A recurring sense that individual life and hope were stifled and restricted even among those close to the 'freedom fighters', was confirmed by *The Killeen* (1985), Mary Leland's sombre narrative of three related lives in the 1930s. Less glumly, *The Largest Baby in Ireland after the Famine* (2000), Anne Barnett's spare novel of rural Ulster during the Great War, features the splendid Sarah-Ann O'Malloran, a free spirit who wears purple and serves as a reminder that there have always been strong independent women, even in the most traditional parts of patriarchal Ireland. There is a new boldness too in *The Judas Cloth* (1992), Julia O'Faolain's exploration of hypocrisy and nineteenth-century clerical politics in the Rome of Pio Nono. O'Faolain has also explored female vocation, fanaticism, passion and guilt in the more remote past of sixth-century Gaul in *Women in the Wall* (1973), deploying varying points of view and narrative modes with great technical skill. O'Faolain's work, like Mary Morrissey's *The Pretender* (2000) about the alleged Anastasia, claiming to be the last of the Romanovs, registers a sense that Irish women writers and Irish fictional treatments of universal issues have now been liberated to have their being beyond Ireland and the matter of Ireland. This is apparent also in some of the best work of Deirdre Madden, whose vivid and exact visual sense gives luminous particularity to *Remembering Light and Stone* (1992), set partly in Italy, and *Authenticity* (2002), based on the intertwined lives of three artists.

The increasingly separate development of Northern and Southern Ireland after Partition in 1921 has led to different fictional agendas. Protestant rather than Catholic obstacles to personal and communal fulfilment feature in the Ulster novels of Sam Hanna Bell from *December Bride* (1951) to *A Man Flourishing* (1973). Violence and sudden death in the Ulster Troubles since the late 1960s, of little interest to most Southern writers, have presented an opportunity and a challenge for Northern realists. The results have been mixed. Colin Bateman's best-selling *Divorcing Jack* (1995), later filmed, managed to distill black comedy from horror. Bernard MacLaverty's *Cal* (1983), also filmed, and the later *Grace Notes* (1997), look to personal and artistically creative healing beyond a violence which victimises its agents. But other 'Troubles' novels such as Eoin McNamee's *Resurrection Man* (1994) have been less effective. The most impressive contemporary Irish novel about violence and insanity, *The Butcher Boy* (1992) by Patrick McCabe, is not actually about the Troubles at all, and some of the best recent Ulster fiction, such as Robert McLiam Wilson's stylistically exuberant tramp-narrative *Ripley Bogle* (1989) or Glen Patterson's *The International* (1999), set in a Belfast hotel in the 1960s, is about life, language and personal identity rather than violent death. Perhaps that is the way forward for Irish fiction in general.

Notes

1. R. A. Breatnach, 'The end of a tradition: a survey of eighteenth century Gaelic literature', *Studia Hibernica* 1 (1961), 128–50.
2. E. M. Forster, 'Introductory note', in Maurice O'Sullivan, *Twenty Years a-Growing* (Oxford: Oxford University Press, 1933).
3. J. V. Luce, 'Homeric qualities in the life and literature of the Great Blasket Island', *Greece and Rome* 16 (1969), 151–67.

Further reading

Prose fiction in Irish

John Jordan (ed.), *The Pleasures of Gaelic Literature* (Cork and Dublin: Mercier Press, 1977)

Proinsias Mac Cana, *Literature in Irish: Aspects of Ireland*, 8 (Dublin: Government of Ireland, 1980)

Brian Ó Cuív (ed.), *A View of the Irish Language* (Dublin: Stationary Office, 1969)

Eoghan Ó hAnluain, 'The twentieth century: prose and verse', in *Gaelic Literature Surveyed*, ed. Aodh de Blacam (Dublin: Talbot Press, 1973), pp. 387–405

Philip O'Leary, *The Prose Literature of the Gaelic Revival, 1881–1921, Ideology and Innovation* (Philadelphia, PA: Pennsylvania State University Press, 1994)

Máirtín Ó Murchú, *The Irish Language: Aspects of Ireland, 10* (Dublin: Government of Ireland, 1985)

Seán Ó Tuama, *Repossessions: Selected Essays on the Irish Literary Heritage* (Cork: Cork University Press, 1995)

J. E. Caerwyn Williams and Patrick K. Ford, *The Irish Literary Tradition* (Cardiff: University of Wales Press, 1992)

Prose fiction in English

James M. Cahalan, *The Irish Novel: A Critical History* (Dublin: Gill and Macmillan, 1988)

John Cronin, *The Anglo-Irish Novel*, 2 vols. (Belfast: Appletree Press, 1980, 1992)

Seamus Deane, *A Short History of Irish Literature* (London: Hutchinson, 1986)

John Wilson Foster, *Forces and Themes in Ulster Fiction* (Dublin: Gill and Macmillan, 1974)

Fictions of the Irish Literary Revival: A Changeling Art (Syracuse, NY: Syracuse University Press, 1987)

Liam Harte and Michael Parker (eds.), *Contemporary Irish Fiction: Themes, Tropes, Theories* (Basingstoke: Macmillan, 2000)

Rudiger Imhof, *The Modern Irish Novel: Irish Novelists after 1945* (Dublin: Wolfhound, 2002)

Otto Rauchbauer (ed.), *Ancestral Voices: The Big House in Anglo-Irish Literature* (Dublin: Lilliput, 1992)

Gerry Smyth, *The Novel and the Nation: Studies in the New Irish Fiction* (London: Pluto, 1997)

15

Irish music

Music in Ireland in the modern period reflected the changing socioeconomic strata of the society in which it was produced and consumed. Professional performances by popular European composers were put on in theatres for well-off audiences. A burgeoning print culture produced broadsides and pamphlets of songs and ballads disseminating radical republican ideas, coexisting with an older, Irish-language tradition, where anonymous love songs, drinking songs, laments and other songs by literate poets abounded.[1] Professional traditional musicians, harpers, fiddlers and pipers plied their trades and tailored their repertoires to suit their patrons, so that, depending on opportunity, their playing could range across the available gamut of contemporary musical genres. This chapter shows how an outline of the changing political climate is crucial for an understanding of the emergence of a canon of 'Irish music' as a distinct category. Developments in the formation of that canon, marking changing material realities and cultural tastes will also be discussed, and some account will be given of the enduring controversies that are integral to the ways in which 'Irish music' has been imagined.

Our modern understanding of Irish music begins in Scotland. From the mid-eighteenth century, James Macpherson's 'epics', loosely based on Gaelic heroic poetry, centring upon the legendary hero Ossian (or Oisín), enjoyed huge success, part of a growing and fashionable interest in the culture of the marginalised 'Celtic' periphery. These poems were popular in a climate marked by the effective defeat of the Jacobite forces at Culloden in 1746, and rode a wave of romanticism for a cause which had recently been a source of real danger to the peace and stability of the existing polity of the islands.

Ireland was centrally involved in debates that arose surrounding the authenticity of these creations. Macpherson was dismissive of Irish Gaelic claims on Ossian, and scholars like the Catholic historian, Charles O'Conor, took it upon themselves to correct him. Such lively debate belonged to a cultural climate in which an interest in history and antiquities flourished as part of a new patriotism among the ascendancy class. As the century progressed, this atmosphere became reenergised by events in mainland Europe. The French Revolution of 1789, and publications like Thomas Paine's *The Rights of Man* (1791), influenced the increasingly radical political mood on the island. Music partook of this mood and also helped incite it. From 1791, the Society of United Irishmen's programme for a non-sectarian, inclusive and democratic politics, following classic Enlightenment thought, stressed the enabling aspects of history and avoided divisive issues. Their internationalist gaze was oriented towards modernity and a future of rationality and progress, deliberately downplaying the excesses of the past. The United Irishmen aimed at politicising ordinary people by educating them about Enlightenment ideals through popular culture. A few of their number, however, were familiar with, or became absorbed in the Gaelic cultural heritage through antiquarian study, and sought to celebrate its regional uniqueness and specificity. This proto-Romantic nationalism, part of a wider European reaction to the Enlightenment, was to emerge as a powerful vector influencing the development of musical culture in Ireland, destabilising the preoccupation with the future by valorising the past.[2]

Many of those involved in the organisation of the Belfast Harp Festival in July 1792, held during the third anniversary of the revolution, were active in the United Irishmen. Theobald Wolfe Tone himself, later to lead a French-assisted armed uprising in 1798, attended some of the performances in the Exchange Rooms. Unimpressed by what he heard, however, he recorded the following caustic remarks in his diary: 'All go to Harpers at one; poor enough; ten performers; seven execrable, three good . . . the Harpers again, strum, strum and be hanged . . .'[3] Gatherings of harpers had previously occurred at the 'Granard Balls' of 1781, 1782 and 1785, sponsored by James Duncan, a merchant resident in Copenhagen. They were competitive events, with the same performers taking the prizes every year, causing such acrimony among the remainder that Duncan withdrew his support. The Belfast event was directly influenced by these balls and took pains to avoid any bitterness over prize money. All competitors were to be given 'some premium' and the amounts were cept secret, in an attempt to allay any potential jealousy.[4] Another major difference between the Belfast event and its predecessors was the explicit link to the United Irishmen, whose crest, a harp, bore the motto, 'It is new strung and shall be heard.' Thus, patriotic politics, metaphorically interpreted as harp-playing, specifically linked the imagined, historical Gaelic past with direct activism in a politically sensitised popular culture of the present.

Harpers, as professional musicians, were subject to the demands of their patrons. Consequently, most of the ten who attended knew items fashionable at the time, which might not have been regarded as particularly Irish. Some, indeed, may not have played Gaelic material regularly. To counter this, the festival organisers decreed specifically that only Irish music, understood as Gaelic harp music and folk music, was to be played, officially recognising 'Irish music' as a specific category, which conferred upon it a special status, serving to bracket it off from a more general repertoire of 'music played in Ireland'.

Uniquely in Belfast, preservation was a chief aim. Several experts, including a Gaelic scholar, were engaged to write down both music and words of the songs, although the only one to appear was Edward Bunting, a young organist from Armagh, and a protégé of the McCracken family who were active in the United Irishmen. Bunting notated tunes from the musicians over the three days of the festival, a singular achievement. Deeply impressed by his experiences, he devoted much of the rest of his life to the collection and publication of Irish music. He made countrywide collecting trips later in 1792, in 1800 and 1802, and visited Arthur O'Neill, Daniel Black and Denis Hempson (the oldest of the harpers), collecting from them almost the only extant information about the playing technique of the Gaelic wire-strung harp. From this material, he published collections in 1796, in 1809 and in 1840 respectively. His manuscripts, held in the library of the Queen's University of Belfast, remain an important source regarding music in eighteenth- and nineteenth-century Ireland.

Bunting was trained in the major and minor system of keys which had emerged in the eighteenth century. Consequently, the modal character of much of the music may have eluded him and he often deliberately altered tunes to suit the conventions of his time. A re-emphasis of the link between medieval church modes and folk music, emerging around the turn of the twentieth century, led to criticism of Bunting's editorial methods, so that his work is now approached with caution. Nevertheless, the Belfast Harp Festival marks the known beginning of the collection of music in Ireland from practising musicians, and the establishment of a tradition of scholarship concerning Irish music. Issues emerging from its Romantic impulses (notably the fear of extinction), the drive towards active transmission and performance, and the concern for purity and authenticity became established discourses within that scholarship and have remained influential factors in the direction of 'Irish music'.

In 1809, the Dublin Harp Society proposed to halt the decline of the harp, following the Belfast Harp Society, established the previous year, which also continued the ideals underpinning the festival. Financial troubles dogged the Belfast society from the beginning. Arthur O'Neill, appointed as teacher, died in penury in 1814. A revival in 1819 allowed it to limp on until 1840. One performer of note emerged, Patrick Byrne, who toured extensively until his death in 1863. The tradition of the wire-strung harp thus ended in the nineteenth century, as modern lightweight gut-strung instruments replaced it. Its identification as a nationalist symbol arguably contributed to this, but there was also a growing fashion for piano playing which overtook the harp as a drawing room accomplishment for young ladies.

Harp imagery is central in the work of Thomas Moore, a major musical and literary figure of this period. Born in Dublin, and encouraged by his mother to perform at social gatherings from an early age, he became an accomplished musician and singer. He entered Trinity College, then only recently made accessible to Catholics, and published his translation of the Odes of Anacreon in 1800 to instant acclaim. Although closely associated with a number of those active in the 1798 uprising, notably with the rebellious Robert Emmet, he was opposed to violence. He left Ireland in 1799 probably because of a genuine fear of arrest, although he remained committed to Ireland's welfare. His *Irish Melodies*, published in ten volumes between 1808 and 1834, form his most lasting legacy to both music and literature, gaining him the popular title of 'Ireland's National Poet' and earning him huge recognition across the nineteenth-century English-speaking world.

In Britain, Moore's achievement can be partly attributed to great personal charm and a gift for performance that ensured him a place in fashionable society.[5] His formidable lyrical facility and the sweet dreamy romanticism of his verses, wedded to appealing Gaelic melodies borrowed from Bunting and others, further enhanced his appeal. Their reception in polite salons as lamentations for a defeated culture added another winning dimension. William Hazlitt, the renowned Romantic essayist, unimpressed by Moore's poetic style, famously remarked that he had turned the wild Irish harp into a 'musical snuff box'.[6] However, despite the superficially frivolous aural impression, Moore's musical box contained more incendiary materials. His tremendous popularity allowed the Catholic middle classes, gathering confidence after the repeal of most of the Penal statutes, to appropriate his work as an important element in a respectable and newly emergent English-speaking Irish national identity, instantly recognisable to all anglophones as Irish. Through his prudent foregrounding of melodic attractiveness and muting of aspects unpalatable to the colonial status quo, Irish audiences could hear claims to a national identity distinctly, if softly, voiced in his songs. His work, then, indicates the close but always ambivalent connection between nationalism, poetry and music.[7]

Moore's relationship with Edward Bunting can be regarded as the first significant instance of still current debates concerning tradition and innovation. Moore has been described variously as a mediator and a translator. Although Bunting produced his work in similar ways, he regarded himself as a preserver of the music's authentic character. Moore's offer of his services as a lyricist for Bunting's 1808 volume had been rejected. Because of Moore's subsequent celebrity, however, it is likely that Bunting regretted his rebuff. Although he praised Moore's lyrics, he alleged that his musical arrangements were compromised. Moore countered that by changing the songs he had popularised them, without which they would have remained sleeping in their 'authentic dross'.[8] The burden of authenticity and the commercial rewards of popular success were the issues at stake. Bunting represented the closest thing to faithful transcriptions in the field. Moore's melodic adaptations, conversely, prioritised his own lyrical requirements in a conscious strategy of communicative translation. Notwithstanding Bunting's objections, he certainly envied Moore's celebrity, and felt cheated of an acclaim that was rightly his.

Gaelic poets and singers also continued an ancient link between poetry and music. Although some came under United Irish influence, calling for the establishment of *dlí na Fraince* (the law of France), others invoked seventeenth-century traditions of bitter invective against the colonial presence. Pádraig Cundún, Máire Bhuí Ní Laoghaire and Tomás Rua Ó Súilleabháin in Munster, and Raiftearaí (Raftery) in east Galway made songs on many subjects. They combined older motifs with the prophecies of 'Pastorini' in anticipation of the overthrow of the *Gaill* (foreigners), providing a stark contrast to Moore's delicate verse. Máire Bhuí's '*Cath Chéim an Fhia*' is a musical and poetic classic of the genre. Love was also a theme, as were laments about local catastrophes, such as Raftery's graphic '*Eanach Dhúin*', commemorating nineteen people who drowned as they boated down the Corrib to a fair in Galway. Ó Súilleabháin's '*Amhrán na Leabhar*' is another highlight, a moving lament for the loss of his books in a fire aboard ship. The poet-singers' audiences were their Irish-speaking neighbours, whose concerns they shared. Their work remained locally popular, surviving the Famine, but, because of their lack of wide access to print culture, was largely unknown outside their own communities until the later Gaelic revival at the end of the century.

Many belonged to a popular vernacular culture in which musical performance, dancing and singing were essential social skills, the festive hallmarks of most important events. Wakes and funerals were occasions for such conspicuous merriment and consumption, often in the face of dire want. A separate women's tradition of keening formed a significant part in these practices, and is discussed in chapter 8 of this volume. When instrumentalists were unavailable, skilled individuals (often women) provided music for dancers by *portaireacht* (lilting or 'puss' music). Travelling dancing masters were in demand, teaching the steps of intricate jigs, reels and hornpipes among other solo and popular group dances. The Catholic clergy had waged a sustained and organised campaign against such popular entertainment from the late eighteenth century, seeking to control profane practices integral to festivals such as *laethanta patrúin* ('pattern' days), celebrated at Holy Wells dedicated to local saints. Although encompassing pilgrimages and other sincerely observed devotional practices, they also featured music, dancing, singing, courting, drinking and fighting.

Such a mingling of sacred and secular, the simultaneous celebration of the spiritual and the corporeal, both scandalised and fascinated the 'civilised' assumptions of nineteenth-century observers. In the aftermath of the Great Famine, beliefs in the fairy otherworld and similar phenomena, regarded as characteristically Irish, were rapidly being abandoned. As these aspects of life disappeared or went underground, attitudes towards them changed. Viewed with fear and suspicion by the educated in their heyday, they became increasingly valued as another manifestation of old Gaelic culture threatened by advancing modernity as they declined.

The 'devotional revolution' gathered pace from 1850 with the appointment of Paul Cullen as archbishop of Armagh. His romanising of the Catholic church included musical reform. He introduced and promoted chant in the Palestrina style, then popular in Europe, to the exclusion of all other forms of music. A large body of vernacular hymns, maintained largely by women, many focusing on Christ's Passion and upon Mary as *bean chaointe* (keening woman), were anathema to this programme, and their use decreased.

Such cultural obsolescence was of grave concern to individuals like George Petrie, the inheritor of Bunting's mantle. A painter by profession, and also a violinist, he became a leading antiquary and was involved in the Ordnance Survey (1824–46) and the Royal Irish Academy, which brought him into contact with the Gaelic scholars John O'Donovan and Eugene O'Curry. The latter in particular shared Petrie's interest in music and provided him with many songs and information about them. Petrie regarded O'Curry as the essential embodiment of the purity and truth characteristic of the best of Gaelic culture, reflecting his conviction that the Gaelic component represented the most significantly Irish element of the musical repertoire. He collected from his youth and passed on material to more leading figures in the music world, particularly to Bunting, and to Moore between 1807 and 1808. Petrie published on Irish music from the 1820s, becoming more prominent after Bunting's death. In 1851, he was among the founders of the Society for the Preservation and Publication of the Melodies of Ireland, and also became its president. The concerns of the society centred, as earlier in Belfast, on the disappearance of Irish music and the need for collection and preservation. Petrie's work gained a new impetus after the Great Famine, which had reduced the population of Ireland by an estimated 1.7 million in the space of ten years, and was believed to have catastrophically affected the popular musical culture that provided the sources for the collectors' melodies. Despite the devastation, Petrie collected with O'Curry on Aran in 1857 and recovered excellent material, testifying to an uneven distribution of such change.

In 1855, the society published Volume 1 of *The Petrie Collection of the Ancient Music of Ireland*. This ambitious project was soon disbanded, although a partially complete second volume appeared posthumously in 1882. Other publications associated with him include *Ancient Music of*

Ireland from the Petrie Collection and Sir Charles Stanford's *The Complete Collection of Irish Music as Noted by George Petrie*, published in three volumes between 1902 and 1905. Petrie critiqued Bunting's ideas, recognising melodic variation despite Bunting's claims to the contrary. He was committed to discovering the 'best' versions and believed in the existence of originals, sometimes applying rather subjective criteria. His musical approach seemed to embody a conflict between his romantic view of the Gaelic past and his commitment to scientific study. He published both Gaelic and English words to his songs, and gave detailed commentaries regarding their origins and structures, building upon Bunting's work. His conviction that the best versions of melodies were collected from singers, explicitly foregrounded singing as a mainstay of authenticity in the developing canon.

Thomas Moore had his musical heirs in the Young Ireland movement (1842–48). Due to growing literacy among the population, transmission from printed sources increased accordingly. Broadsheet ballads were hawked at fairs by wandering singers or underemployed labourers as a supplement to their income, seditious ballads apparently forming the most popular genre. Thomas Davis, whose ideas were influenced by Johann Gottfried Herder, the German nationalist philosopher, was a central figure and a seminal influence on the cultural nationalism of Young Ireland. Like the United Irishmen, this group recognised the excellent propagandising properties of the ballad and printed many in *The Nation*, established in 1842. They were published in *The Spirit of the Nation* (1845), reprinted fifty-eight times until 1934. Although more literary than the street ballads, and sometimes not strictly regarded as 'traditional', some of them ('A Nation Once Again' and 'The West's Awake') remain staples of the popular repertoire.

P. W. Joyce, from the Ballyhoura region of Limerick, came to Dublin where he met George Petrie, who encouraged him to write down songs and tunes from memory. He published three collections, *Ancient Irish Music* (1873), *Irish Music and Song* (1888) and his largest and most influential book, *Old Irish Folk Music and Songs* (1909), which drew from manuscript sources as well as from his own collecting. Joyce's lifetime saw the interest in Gaelic subjects reach a zenith in Ireland and the re-emergence of an interest in all things Celtic. It is also worth pointing out, however, that the rage for Celticism coincided with a crisis in Irish rural culture, exacerbated by emigration, a precarious economy and the demise of the great mass of the rural poor.

Interest led to the formation of societies to promote aspects of Gaelic culture, such as the Society for the Preservation of the Irish Language (1876), the Gaelic Athletic Association (1884) and most importantly, perhaps, the Gaelic League (1893). The year previous to the foundation of the League, Douglas Hyde, the son of a Roscommon minister interested in the Irish language and in folklore, delivered his epoch-making address, 'The Necessity for De-Anglicising Ireland', addressing many of the same concerns as his predecessors. He focused on 'Irish music' as a close second to the Irish language in cultural importance. Taking up a familiar refrain, he noted that modern popular music was fast replacing old native airs, which, he insisted, were vastly superior. 'Irish Music' must be protected from encroachment and preserved at all costs. Adherents of the new cultural nationalism, of which the Gaelic League was emblematic, focused on rural dwellers in the west in ways practically unthinkable to most of their predecessors only a generation earlier. Irish-speakers were actively sought out, as urban dwellers began to learn and speak the Irish language, in line with Gaelic League ideas of revitalisation.

Fascination with folk music and song grew apace with the developing discipline of folklore. Echoing the Belfast Harp Festival of 1792, exponents emphasised living orally transmitted culture found in rural communities as an expression of national identity. Hyde explicitly linked the study of folklore with learning the Irish language. The Folk Song Movement was highly influential and assisted the formation of a new performance aesthetic based on principles outlined in Cecil Sharp's book, *English Folksong* (1907). The modal similarity of Gaelic airs and singing styles to plainchant also contributed to this new development, and Hyde's *Abhráin Ghrádh Chúige Chonnacht* (*The Love-Songs of Connacht*, 1893) was important in identifying a canon of verse which stimulated other similar publications.

Strong proponents of nativism were often at loggerheads with progressive cultural advocates. The 'old Irish style' of singing, soon to be called *sean-nós* (solo, unaccompanied and sometimes cacophonous to metropolitan ears) was touted by nativists at the expense of harmonised choral versions of Gaelic songs, alienating many urban singers. Harmonic arrangements and choral performance could be condemned as a pollution of the pure, authentic state of the music as collected from the people, in what amounted to an aesthetics of opposition. These issues can be regarded as extreme cases of the concerns addressed by Petrie's work, and also as a continuation of the debate between Bunting and Moore.

The union or uilleann pipes, a bellows-blown instrument with a chanter, three drones and keyed melody pipes capable of harmonic effects, which had first emerged at the beginning of the nineteenth century, also became the focus of attention. Steps taken at this time ensured an intermittent revival in the instruments' fortunes, until 1966, when *Na Píobairí Uilleann* (NPU) with offices at Henrietta St., Dublin, came to serve as an umbrella organisation for increasing numbers of pipers. Sets of quadrilles, however, having enjoyed their first wave of popularity in the 1820s were ostracised by the Gaelic League, which ousted them in favour of their own Scottish-influenced inventions. By the 1980s the style and the repertoire were back in vogue and are now considered by fervent advocates to be more authentically traditional than *céilí* dancing.

The extremism that characterised much of the controversy of the Revival was reflected in a regrettable trend towards political entrenchment, which was to continue for many years. The new 'authenticity', perceived as more masculine, accompanied a waning of Thomas Moore's star as a musician, since his lyrical and musical approach were now considered an embarrassment.[9] In fact, his success in England could now be repudiated, causing him to be branded, in the words of one irascible commentator, a 'half-fledged pervert' who pandered to the colonial élite.[10] Such extreme nationalist viewpoints also led to the rejection of the composer Charles Villiers Stanford (1852–1924) as a unionist, although he knew the repertoire of Irish tunes well and combined it with German influences in his work, creating a distinctive voice, now claimed as 'English'.[11]

Emphasis on the preservation and publication of 'Irish Music' had focused primarily on song until now, since it was perceived as the crucial linguistic link to the aristocratic Gaelic past represented by the harpers. Jigs, reels, hornpipes and other instrumental dance tunes had not received the same attention, despite their huge popularity. It was probably no accident that the impetus for redressing this imbalance came from a musician resident outside Ireland. 'Chief' Francis O' Neill from Bantry, with his unrelated collaborator, Sergeant James O' Neill, compiled a prolific music collection in Chicago, from memory and from the playing of other emigrants. Among many publications, his most influential was *The Dance Music of Ireland* (1907). Known among musicians simply as 'The Book', it ran to four editions and became the most popular reference work for practising traditional instrumentalists until it was superseded by Breandán Breathnach's first volume of *Ceol Rince na hÉireann* (1963). O'Neill was sometimes criticised for including material that was not 'Irish', such as the song 'Killarney' by Michael Balfe, although this item circulated in oral tradition. Such criticism highlights the selective nature of what was considered Irish, excluding elements that did not fit a particular prescriptive model. O'Neill's work also heralded the significance of the United States in Irish traditional music, a trend that continues to grow in the third millennium.

The establishment of two states coincided with the advent of radio on the island in 1921, and a period when extremist prescriptions became more marked. 2BE (now BBC Radio Ulster) began broadcasting in Belfast from 1922. By 1926, 2RN, a national radio channel, had been established in Dublin under the directorship of Séamus Clandillon. A prominent Gaelic Leaguer, singer and collector of Irish music, his leadership ensured that Gaelic song and traditional music were programmed regularly. Later, in 1951, outside broadcasters collected traditional music in the field, which led to successful series such as *A Job of Journey Work* and *The Long Note*. In Northern Ireland, on the other hand, in 'a society devoid of consensus',[12] music repeatedly proved to be a contentious issue drawing criticism from both sides of the political divide. Although, in Britain, it was hard to see that such matters could be contentious, society in the North became acutely sensitive to the least tweaking of political and cultural identities on the airwaves. Under the directorship of George Marshall, the station attempted to avoid material that might be critical of the Northern government. Music was an accurate barometer of such tensions, where songs such as 'The Minstrel Boy' and 'The Boyne Water' were guaranteed to offend Orange and Green sensibilities respectively.[13] Marshall also attempted to stop the broadcast of 'The Soldier's Song', the national anthem of the Republic, and was supremely reactive to Southern claims on the word 'Irish'. Sensitivities ran both ways. When the BBC attempted to mount a programme entitled 'County *Ceilidhe*' from Armagh in 1946, it drew the ire of the local Gaelic League, which regarded the attempt as a 'travesty of all that is commonly understood by *ceilidhe*'.[14]

Matters improved with the appointment of Andrew Stewart in 1948, a seasoned BBC broadcaster, who oversaw the broadcast of the legendary series 'As I Roved Out' in 1951. By 1967, when a Clancy Brothers' concert heralding the arrival of BBC2 was held in the Ulster

Hall, the reception was unanimously enthusiastic, leading to a series with the group. Although classical music was broadcast by both stations, many technical and logistical difficulties had to be overcome to bring standards to an acceptable level.

The political upheavals of the twenties caused great disruption to musical activities in Ireland. The *Oireachtas*, since 1897 Ireland's first annual festival for literary and performing arts, was not held from 1924 until 1939. Although it remains an important platform for traditional singing in Irish, as a forum for instrumental music and English song, it has been supplanted by the *Fleadhanna* of *Comhaltas Ceoltóirí Éireann*. Dancing was also under attack in the 1920s from the clergy. Both they and conservative Gaelic League elements tried to suppress popular music and dance, the League favouring its own *céilí* dances instead. The Dance Halls Act (1935) attempted to regulate dancing, and probably contributed to the decline of the house dance. Conversely, however, it stimulated the formation of larger music ensembles, known as the *céilí* bands (sometimes including saxophones), whose heyday lasted into the showband era of the sixties. Full-time collectors hired by the Irish Folklore Commission from 1935 ensured that many excellent musicians and singers were recorded, initially on paper only, with sound recordings following gradually.

Despite such developments, traditional music was still seen as a threatened part of native culture. *Comhaltas Ceoltóirí Éireann* (literally, a gathering of Ireland's musicians) was established in 1951, coincidentally the same year as the Wexford Opera Festival was founded, and has since proliferated into the largest organisation promoting Irish music today, with 'provinces' in Britain, the United States, Canada and Australia. It places great emphasis on the transmission of musical skills to the young, claiming some 600 classes in 1999. Its competitive *Fleadhanna*, organised at county, provincial and international level, have raised playing standards across all instruments, leading also to a certain homogenisation of styles. *Fleadh Cheoil na hÉireann*, the culmination of the year's competitions, is held annually in Ireland and continues to attract up to 200,000 people. With a democratic political structure, *CCÉ*'s membership covers a wide spectrum of opinion. Some of its social and political interventions were controversial, such as the cancellation of the 1971 *Fleadh* in protest against internment in Northern Ireland, and, in 1983, the adoption of a position in the national referendum on abortion. Lifetime (appointed 1968) Director General Labhrás Ó Murchú's government report on traditional music in 1998 was widely criticised for its failure to consult organisations other than *Comhaltas* involved in traditional music. The 2002 Arts Bill was resisted also because it contained a proposal, supported by CCÉ, recommending the establishment of a standing committee that would advise the Arts Council on the new category of 'Traditional Arts'.

In classical music, English composers of the twenties and thirties, such as Philip Heseltine (Peter Warlock), Sir Arnold Bax and Ralph Vaughan Williams produced works that revealed some engagement with Irish culture. Seán Ó Riada is widely regarded as one of the most influential figures in Irish music in the second half of the twentieth century in terms of public appeal. Following such composers as the gifted but stricken progressive Frederick May and the prolific nativist Éamonn Ó Gallchobhair, his career has addressed the disjunctures between the European and the native repertoires.

Deeply familiar with mainstream European literature and music, Ó Riada was initially attracted by modernism. His interest in traditional music was stimulated by his association with figures in the organisation *Gael-Linn* and RTÉ. In a radio series in 1962, entitled 'Our Musical Heritage', he revealed ideas about Irish music that were considered ground-breaking and original in a modernising Ireland, inclined to view that music as part and parcel of a legacy of poverty and backwardness. Ó Riada's aesthetic strategy deliberately made links beyond European music with Indian classical music, emphasising its circularity and variational qualities. By invoking a more global context, Ó Riada's orientalising imagining of Irish music succeeded in making traditional culture interesting to many who had previously rejected it. He experimented widely with the forms of traditional music, using orchestral arrangements of Gaelic airs in the film scores for *Mise Éire*, *Saoirse* and *An Tine Bheo*. These scores (particularly that for *Mise Éire*) were highly acclaimed, and made welcome within the climate of nationalistic fervour preceding the commemoration of the fiftieth anniversary of the 1916 rising. Musically, however, they remain some of the most interesting experiments attempted with the traditional repertoire. The incongruity of creating a nineteenth-century symphonic soundscape as an accompaniment to a distinctly modern twentieth-century genre, commemorating Ireland's struggle for independence, clearly illustrates Ó Riada's formidable imaginative capability. These compositions almost seemed to fill the gap that existed in nineteenth-century musical development in Ireland, and yet also stand as a modern phenomenon, encapsulating the way in which past, present and future have never existed in some tidy, linear schematic sequence. Ó Riada's Mass, created in conjunction with the male unison choral group, *Cór Chúil Aodha*, drawn from the congregation in the west Cork village in which he had settled in 1963, also validated interest in traditional song. Ó Riada's popular appeal tended to overshadow other important composers among his predecessors and contemporaries.

Yet another experiment was the establishment of *Ceoltóirí Chualann* in the late fifties. Ó Riada assembled some of Ireland's most accomplished virtuoso players and formed them into an ensemble along classical lines, adding what some regarded as an unprecedented finesse to traditional music performance. His use of the singer Seán Ó Sé, whose excellent command of Irish and powerful tenor voice could be regarded as an attempt to reconcile *sean-nós* style with that of the 'trained' singer is a case in point. Above all, the evening wear adopted by *Ceoltóirí Chualann* for *Ó Riada sa Gaiety* in 1969 transmitted a message that amplified Ó Riada's musical innovations. This was serious music that demanded respect.

Paddy Moloney, the ensemble's piper, convened a group of his fellow members to record for Claddagh Records in 1963, eventually forming a new band which began to develop Ó Riada's ideas. Since they went fully professional in 1975, The Chieftains have become one of the most commercially successful Irish traditional groups ever, paving the way for others.

Nor did the rich musical effloresence end there. The Dubliners, whose powerful singing and playing represented many people's first contact with traditional music, emerged as a powerful force. Their performances of more earthy and ribald material gained recognition for street ballads, previously excluded from the officially prescribed canon as uncouth. The Clancy Brothers and Tommy Makem, taking advantage of the folk revival in the United States, sporting Aran sweaters and singing rousing ballads, also became stars and spawned a myriad of imitators, some of whom were captured on celluloid by RTÉ, which had begun television broadcasting in 1961. Soon after came Sweeney's Men and the Johnstons. In 1974, another group, known as *Seachtar*, reformed as The Bothy Band. Named for the huts that had housed Irish migratory labourers in Scotland, the band created another kind of sound, influenced by rock music of the period, characterised by a unique drive, energy and virtuosic playing. Their style remains influential upon all traditional bands who have subsequently emerged. Groups such as Planxty, De Danann, Clannad,

Horslips and later, Moving Hearts and Altan, created their own sonic musical worlds and prefigured the rapid diversification that has now become an established pattern. The era also produced Them, a blues/rock group, that although itself short-lived, led to the emergence of lead-singer Van Morrison as a major international star. Rory Gallagher also achieved acclaim as a major blues guitarist and Thin Lizzy began a suc-cessful career with a rock version of a ballad on 'Top of the Pops'. The New Wave and Punk era also produced The Boomtown Rats and in Britain, Johnny Rotten and the Sex Pistols. Later, Boy George, The Smiths and the Pogues also explored the Irishness of the 'Plastic Paddy' phenomenon.[15]

'Irish music', imagined in different ways since 1792, was now on the way to becoming a marketable international commodity, a trend that has escalated since the seventies. The success of U2, Sinéad O' Connor, the Cranberries and Enya in the eighties and nineties has made it easier for Irish musicians of all genres to gain recognition in a global market. Country music has also flourished in a distinctively Irish form since the fifties – Daniel O' Donnell is, perhaps, its most popular exponent today. Like Thomas Moore, many musicians have successfully set forth to seek their fortune abroad, adapting and packaging 'Irish' music in arrange-ments attractive to audiences worldwide. 'Irish music' and the more eth-ereal 'Celtic' music have been transformed by this expansion to medi-ate with other musics across many genres. The phenomenal commer-cial success of Bill Whelan's *Riverdance*, with its innovative use of Balkan rhythms and its chorus lines of dancers, is perhaps the most spectacular example of the kind of melding of styles which is now occurring. This has caused unease among conservatives, sparking the old debate, famil-iar from Bunting and Moore's disagreements, about the 'real' meaning of 'tradition'. Such a debate provided the main theme for the Crossroads Conference, in Dublin (1996), where 'traditionalists' and 'innovationists' met to discuss Irish music, giving rise to heated arguments about authen-ticity, maintenance, direction, change and commercialisation.

Old barriers continue to be breached in ways inconceivable even twenty years ago. In 1996, at the Merriman Summer School, five of Ire-land's most prominent musicians shared the stage in a one-off gala con-cert: Hugh Tinney (piano), Louis Stewart (jazz guitar), Joe and Anne Burke (accordian) and Áine Uí Cheallaigh (song). This may be read as an unprecedented official acceptance of a musically heteroglossic island.

One consequence of continuing globalisation and commodification of 'Irish music' as a 'world' genre has been to exacerbate debates about

copyright. Although three organisations collect and administer musicians' copyright dues, dissatisfaction with their rationale is widespread.
'Irish music', until recently regarded as common property has increasingly become 'enclosed' as individuals and organisations claim ownership in order to reap the financial rewards of commercialisation. Copyright is likely to be a cause of acute concern for traditional musicians
for some time to come. The recently established FACÉ (Filí Amhránaithe
agus Ceoltóirí Éireann) (2001) has emerged as an alternative body, aim-
ing to promote and defend the rights of many artists who are dissatisfied
with existing institutions.

The expansion of 'Irish music' means that its direction is ever more
difficult to control, and that it will increasingly mediate with newly
emerging popular music genres. Although programmes continue to be
broadcast on Radio 1 and on RTÉ's music and arts station, Lyric FM, *Raidió
na Gaeltachta*, broadcasting in the Irish language has become the main
state-sponsored forum for traditional music. Yet here too there are signs
of hybridity, since every night between ten and midnight, the acclaimed
An Taobh Tuathail (The Dark Side), broadcasts the latest worldbeat, ambi-
ent and techno dance rhythms from bands such as Hyperborea, alongside
world music and commentary in Irish.

Academic study has expanded since the seventies. Micheál Ó
Súilleabháin established traditional music as a core element of the
University College Cork music degree from the seventies and, on
founding the Irish World Music Centre at the University of Limerick,
has developed innovative programmes in many areas. Since 1996, the
post-primary music syllabus in the Republic of Ireland contains a core
element on traditional music, so that its longstanding neglect in the
educational system has been somewhat redressed. Only some 25 per cent
of second-level schools in the Republic offer music, however, an irony
in a state whose emblem is a harp. By contrast, in Northern Ireland,
where all schools are obliged to offer music, traditional music has been
available in the second level curriculum since 1988.

Research into traditional music has grown steadily, but more is
needed in the area of classical music. The publication of Harry White's
controversial *The Keeper's Recital* (1998) heralded a new departure in Irish
music scholarship. White's argument that nationalism and the dominance of literary forms had left music in an underdeveloped and static
condition in Ireland has been vigorously disputed. Debates arising from
this pessimistic view are likely to continue and, beneficially, to stimulate

much needed studies and histories of both 'Irish' music and 'music in Ireland'.

Notes

1. Colette Moloney, *The Irish Music Manuscripts of Edward Bunting* (Dublin: Irish Traditional Music Archive, 2000), pp. 145–50.
2. Kevin Whelan, 'The Republic in the village', in *The Tree of Liberty* (Cork: Cork University Press, 1996), pp. 59–98.
3. Gráinne Yeats, *The Belfast Harpers' Festival, 1792* (Dublin: Gael Linn, 1980), p. 23.
4. Ibid., p. 21.
5. Matthew Campbell, 'Thomas Moore's wild song: the 1821 Irish melodies', *Bullán* 4, 2 (Winter/Spring 1999–2000), 83–103.
6. William Hazlitt, *The Spirit of the Age* (1825; Oxford: Woodstock Books, 1989), p. 397.
7. Harry White, *The Keeper's Recital* (Cork: Cork University Press 1998), p. 50.
8. Wilfred S. Dowden, *The Journal of Thomas Moore* (Newark, NJ: University of Delaware Press, 1988), vol. v, p. 2141.
9. Liam de Paor, *Tom Moore and Contemporary Ireland*, Ó Riada Memorial Lecture 4 (Cork: Traditional Music Society, University College Cork, 1989), p. 7.
10. R. Pryor, *Irish National Music* (Dublin, 1886), p. 22. Quoted in Joseph J. Ryan, 'Assertions of distinction: the modal debate in Irish music', *Irish Musical Studies 2: Music and the Church*, ed. Harry White and Gerard Gillen (Dublin: Four Courts, 1996), p. 65.
11. Online: http://www.classical.net/music/comp.1st/acc/stanford.html. Date accessed: 30/10/02.
12. Rex Cathcart, *The Most Contrary Region: The BBC in Northern Ireland, 1924–1984* (Belfast: Blackstaff, 1984), p. 10.
13. Ibid., p. 114.
14. Ibid., p. 143.
15. Sean Campbell, 'Beyond the "Plastic Paddy": a re-examination of the second-generation Irish in England', *Immigrants and Minorities* 18, 2–3 (1999), 273–6.

Further reading

Philip Bohlman, *The Study of Folk Music in the Modern World* (Bloomington, IN: Indiana University Press, 1988)

Nicholas Carolan, *A Harvest Saved: Francis O'Neill and Irish Music in Chicago* (Cork: Ossian, 1997)

David Cooper (ed.), *The Petrie Collection of the Ancient Music of Ireland* (Cork: Cork University Press, 2002)

Leith Davis, 'Sequels of colonialism: Edward Bunting's *Ancient Irish Music*', *Nineteenth Century Contexts* 23 (2001), 29–57

Tom Dunne, ' "Tá Gaedhil bhocht cráidhte": memory, tradition and the politics of the poor in Gaelic poetry and song' in *Rebellion and Remembrance in Modern Ireland*, ed. Laurence M. Geary (Dublin: Four Courts Press, 2001), pp. 93–112

James W. Flannery, *Dear Harp of My Country: The Irish Melodies of Thomas Moore* (Nashville, TN: J. Sanders, 1997)

Bernard Harris and Grattan Freyer (eds.), *The Achievement of Seán Ó Riada* (Chester Springs, PA: Dufour Editions, 1981)

Joep Leersen, *Remembrance and Imagination* (Cork: Cork University Press, 1996)

Colette Moloney, *The Irish Music Manuscripts of Edward Bunting, 1773–1843: An Introduction and Catalogue* (Dublin: Irish Traditional Music Archive, 2000)

Maura Murphy, 'The ballad singer and the role of the seditious ballad in nineteenth-century Ireland: Dublin Castle's view', *Ulster Folklife* 25 (1979), 79–102

Tomás Ó Canainn, *Traditional Music in Ireland* (London: Routledge, 1978)

Tomás Ó Canainn and Gearóid Mac an Bhua, *Seán Ó Riada: A Shaol agus a Shaothar* (Dublin: Gartan, 1993)

Seán Ó Riada, *Our Musical Heritage* (Dublin: Dolmen, 1982)

Micheál Ó Súilleabháin, 'Irish music defined', *Crane Bag* 5, 2 (1981), 83–7

Mary Helen Thuente, *The Harp Re-Strung* (New York: Syracus University Press, 1994)

Fintan Vallely, *The Companion to Irish Traditional Music* (Cork: Cork University Press, 1999).

Harry White, *The Keeper's Recital* (Cork: Cork University Press, 1998).

Gráinne Yeats, *The Belfast Harp Festival, 1792* (Dublin: Gael-Linn, 1980)

Georges Denis Zimmerman, *Songs of Irish Rebellion* (1966; Dublin: Four Courts, 2002).

Patrick Zuk, 'Music and nationalism' (Part 1), *Journal of Music in Ireland* 2, 2 (2002), 5–10 'Music and nationalism' (Part 2), *Journal of Music in Ireland* 2, 3 (2002), 25–30

16

Modern architecture and national identity in Ireland

Nationalism and modernism: the twin imperatives

n 1939, the Irish architect Michael Scott brought his design for an Irish Pavilion to the New York World's Fair: 'A board of ten or twelve architects vetted every building for the World's Fair. I appeared before them with the model and explained the whole idea behind it. They thought it was marvellous, a wonderful building. They liked how I solved the problem of nationalism and made it modern at the same time.'[1] To the visitor the pavilion initially appeared as a sleek and sinuous form clad in concrete and glass, with a bright, airy interior (Fig. 16.1). Only from the air would it become clear that the building had a shamrock-shaped plan. If this device now seems somewhat corny or superficial, the challenge facing Scott – that of reconciling the imperatives of nationalism and of modernism within a single representative form – was evidently a substantial and enduring one. Indeed it seems possible to discuss the architecture of Ireland's modern era precisely in terms of this tension between the desire to be modern and the requirement to be representative of some idea of the 'national spirit'.

While this tension sometimes became the subject of deliberate theories and projects (as with Scott's pavilion), more often it simply formed the cultural climate within which Irish architecture was produced. Sometimes the two forces effectively cancelled each other out, resulting in architecture which was neither particularly modern nor particularly Irish. But at other times an architecture emerged which seemed, almost effortlessly, to be as much of its place as of its time. However, Michael Scott's claims that his pavilion had achieved this difficult balance do seem somewhat disingenuous, especially when compared with perhaps the

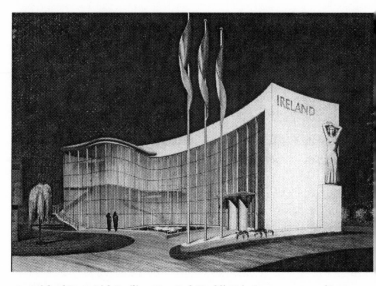

16.1 Michael Scott, Irish Pavilion, New York World's Fair. Image courtesy of Scott, Tallon and Walker

most fêted building at the 1939 World's Fair, Alvar Aalto's Finnish pavilion. In its layout, content and construction, and especially its central meandering timber exhibition wall, the pavilion managed to be richly suggestive of the pine forests and deep fjords of Aalto's native Finland while remaining resolutely contemporary. Whereas Scott's symbolism was simple in the extreme, Aalto submitted native forms, motifs and materials to a thoroughgoing reinvention. Conscious of the music of his contemporary Jean Sibelius, he wanted to create in his pavilion a 'total symphony' which perfectly conveyed the spirit of a proud, young independent nation.

Aalto's was only the latest in a long line of pavilions and exhibition pieces which, since the beginning of the twentieth century, had played an important role in the development of modern architecture. Projects such as Bruno Taut's glass pavilion at the 1914 Deutsches Werkbund Exhibition, Le Corbusier's Pavillon de l'Esprit Nouveau, exhibited in Paris in 1925, and the German Pavilion designed by Ludwig Mies van der Rohe for the Barcelona International Exposition of 1929 acquired an iconic importance far greater than their modest scale and limited lifespan might have suggested. Precisely because of its temporary nature and its freedom from the strictures of context and function, the pavilion was allowed to become a vehicle for the exploration of new technical, spatial and aesthetic possibilities. The expression of national identity – which was, after all, the supposed purpose of a pavilion – was not seen as being of great importance. Most architects sought, above all, to be true to the spirit of their time, rather than to that of their place. 'Building art [*baukunst*] is the will of the epoch translated into space … To create form out of the nature of the task with the means of our own time. That is our task', wrote Mies van der Rohe decisively in 1922, enunciating what became a persistent theme in writings of the period.[2] If Mies's Barcelona Pavilion was ostensibly about representing the Weimar Republic, it was in fact a concentrated formal essay in flowing space and material abstraction. So determinedly non-representational was the building that the German flag could only be inferred from the combination of a black carpet, a red velvet curtain and a gold onyx wall at its centre.

The overriding concern with the spirit of the age was also reflected in the earliest histories of modern architecture, such as Sigfried Giedion's *Space, Time and Architecture*, first published in 1941. The central thesis of this lengthy work was that the emerging new architectural language simply reflected the changing concepts of space and time ushered in by technological developments and by Einstein's theories of relativity.

> We are looking [wrote Giedion], for the reflection in architecture of the progress our own period has made toward consciousness of itself – of its special limitations and potentialities, needs and aims. Architecture can give us an insight into this process just because it is so bound up with the life of a period as a whole. Everything in it, from its fondness for certain shapes to the approaches to specific building problems which it finds most natural, reflects the conditions of the age from which it springs.[3]

The 'conditions of the age' were taken to be common to all nations, rather than being specific to any of them. Among architects and artists working in Holland, France, Germany, Czechoslovakia and Scandinavia, Giedion sought to find common cause. The new architecture was a universal language, neither inflected nor influenced by local circumstances. Anything that did not fit the thesis – such as the work of Hugo Häring and Hans Scharoun in Germany – was downplayed, or omitted entirely from the emerging modernist canon. The same emphasis on universal values had earlier been adumbrated by Henry Russell Hitchcock and Philip Johnson in their 1932 MOMA (Museum of

Modern Art) exhibition and catalogue *The International Style*. And while Giedion was at pains to explain the formal, aesthetic and political genesis of modernism, Hitchcock and Johnson were more interested in establishing and codifying the defining elements of the resulting language. But whether the focus was on end results or on root causes, there was a shared belief in the universality of modernism. Architecture was concerned chiefly with the manipulation of form, light, space and structure; any particular cultural expression would emerge naturally out of a general adherence to these precepts. And that cultural expression would reflect the spirit of the age: the *Zeitgeist*.

This emphasis on universality and on giving built expression to the epoch can be explained by the extent to which modern architecture was a reaction against the tendencies of the nineteenth century. For the modernists, the nineteenth century represented architecture's fall from grace. It was a period when the rational vision and classical order of the Enlightenment gave way to an overweening concern with surface and style. Buildings, it now seemed, might be dressed up in any number of different styles, in order to represent different values and convey different messages. This was as true of the modest houses depicted in J. C. Loudon's *Encyclopaedia* of 1834 in everything from English Castle to Swiss Cottage dress, as it was of the Gothic style of Charles Barry's Houses of Parliament.

In his essay 'Character and Composition', Colin Rowe discusses a shift in architectural thinking from enlightened abstraction to idiosyncratic singularity:

> The demand for expressed character as a prerequisite of good architecture was perhaps the principal agent in dissolving the hierarchy of value to which the academic system had been committed. The academic tradition had been preoccupied with the ideal and its physical embodiment as a visual norm; it had promulgated laws and had been indisposed to concern itself with exceptions to these; 'the whole beauty and grandeur of art consists in being able to get above all singular forms, local customs, particularities and details of every kind', says Sir Joshua Reynolds; but it was now precisely these 'singular forms', 'local customs', exceptions, those accidents of which Reynolds himself had inconsistently approved, which had become full of interest and 'character'.[4]

Nineteenth-century architecture was required, above all, to exhibit character and to be legible. For John Ruskin, the façade of a building, as in his beloved St Mark's in Venice, had to be capable of being read like a book. The demonstration of national identity was, for Ruskin, foremost among the tasks of architecture. Drawing on the work of Herder and Fichte who, in the late eighteenth century, had proposed that the soul of a people and a nation lay in its language and literature, Ruskin asserted an equivalent role for architecture, which would become a kind of built index of national character. 'The architecture of a nation', he wrote in *The Stones of Venice* in 1848, 'is great only when it is as universal and as established as its language.'[5] But, as Adrian Forty has observed, while it is one thing to find evidence of a nation's identity in its past architecture, it is another to devise new works of architecture to represent its present identity.'[6] Nonetheless, the widespread influence of Ruskin's work meant that in the second half of the nineteenth century architecture's primary role and responsibility was seen as being the representation of identity. In Ireland, where the politics of identity obviously had an added urgency, this requirement became even more pressing.

Nineteenth-century Irish architecture and the representation of identity

In nineteenth-century Ireland, where, in the aftermath of the Act of Union, the homogeneity of the ascendancy age had been replaced by a more splintered, heterogeneous political and cultural milieu, architecture was increasingly pressed into service as a means of expressing and strengthening the legitimacy of particular groups within society. In Dublin, the calm uniformity of the Georgian era was gradually supplanted by an urban architecture which instead emphasised variety and individuality. In the wake of emancipation, the extensive church-building programme of the Catholic church, which had begun with the symbolic establishment of the new pro-cathedral in what had previously been the heart of ascendancy power and privilege, culminated in such grandiloquent displays of power as St Augustine and John's church, which dominated the high ground of Thomas Street in Dublin. Although the Protestant church responded with the restoration of St Patrick's and Christ Church cathedrals, by the late nineteenth century its pre-eminence in the city had been usurped. And, whereas in the cities, the new Catholic churches often revived medieval monastic sites – as if summoning a long dormant presence back to glorious life – in towns around Ireland, the new buildings were often rude, insensitive insertions into the heart of the settlement (the church on the Mall in Westport, Co. Mayo, is a good example). The message of such siting was unambiguous: Catholics were in the majority, and were finally free to proclaim their presence.

But if siting was the principal means by which religious buildings gained pre-eminence, style and decoration also played an important role. What J. P. Mahaffy, writing in 1909, called a 'harlequinade of banks and insurance offices' gradually replaced the uniform eighteenth-century terraces of Dame Street and College Green, each building endeavouring at all costs to differentiate itself from its neighbours.[7] From being a harmonious composition of uniform streetscapes, the city had become much more a collection of discrete buildings, each with its own representational agenda. With the passing of the Irish Banking Act of 1824, the banking system became more open and competitive. Over the next 100 years, 819 branch libraries were built around Ireland, with each building trying to assert some sort of corporate identity, often bound up with broader political allegiances. As the century progressed, the expressive capacities of individual buildings were pushed further and further. While the National Irish Bank of 1842 was content to proclaim its individuality within the constraints of the existing street line and parapet height and to work with the warm yellow stone and the classical idiom of its immediate neighbours, the Hibernian Bank of 1871 broke completely with previous norms, establishing a corner entrance and employing a far more florid and thoroughgoing decorative scheme. A curious amalgam of French Gothic and Italian Romanesque styles, the building used a vocabulary of images and forms derived from Irish antiquity – the chevron, the harp, the spiral – to assert its nationalist credentials. In contemporary illustrations, the plain four-storey brick façades of its neighbours seem shrunken and pallid beside this confident, swaggering display. But when the Belfast Banking Company erected its Dublin branch alongside the Hibernian Bank in 1893, it, in turn, made every effort to outdo its neighbour, distinguishing itself through its use of a completely different style and massing and a contrasting red sandstone (Fig. 16.2).

The confidence and swagger which the Belfast Banking Company brought to Dublin reflected Belfast's rapid growth and industrialisation throughout the nineteenth century. Its population had increased from 20,000 to 250,000 between 1800 and 1890. In contrast to Dublin, which despite surface changes retained its eighteenth-century scale and grain, Belfast exhibited the sudden lurches in growth and the curious

6.2 Belfast Banking Company, College Green, Dublin. Photo by Hugh
Campbell, 2003

disjunctions in scale which characterised industrial cities in Britain such
as Manchester, Sheffield and Glasgow. Its trajectory of development was
also similar, from the 'shock city' produced by the early industrialists
to the 'civic gospel' propounded by the self-styled 'merchant princes' in
the latter half of the century.[8] However, the increasing Catholic population, and the resultant tensions for the unionist majority, seemed to
add another layer of urgency to the grand urban projects which followed
Belfast's achievement of city status in 1888. Thus the grandiloquent City
Hall, completed in 1905, could be interpreted as 'the corporate expression
of embattled unionism, and of an effort (perhaps largely unconscious) to
convert a brash and sprawling industrial centre into a politico-religious
capital city'.[9]

Across a range of political allegiances and differing contexts, there
was a shared belief in architecture's capacity to embody identity. Buildings might speak of identity through their siting and their very presence
(in the way the churches did) or through their language (in the way that
civic and commercial architecture did). And while the former might be
seen as a practically unconscious product of social and economic forces,

the latter was a very conscious architectural strategy. Buildings became concentrated statements of loyalties and lineages.

The nineteenth century saw an upsurge of interest in Irish antiquity with organisations such as the Royal Academy and the Royal Dublin Society sponsoring detailed enquiries into all aspects of Ireland's heritage. The origins and meanings of such uniquely Irish-built forms as the round towers became the subject of lengthy monographs and scholarly debate. As a result of such studies, and the popular exposure afforded by the Great Exhibitions of 1852 and 1853, the forms and decorative motifs of Irish antiquity came to be increasingly incorporated into the contemporary architectural language. In discussing Thomas Deane and Benjamin Woodward's Trinity College Museum, for instance (a building much admired by Ruskin), Eve Blau notes that while 'its monumentality, heaviness, and the thickness of the walls are characteristic of Romanesque architecture in general ... the round-arched windows, decorated piers, recessed voussoirs, and the profusion of geometric ornament are more specifically Celtic, indeed Irish, in origin'. 'The Celtic references in TCD', Blau concludes, 'are without a doubt consciously and purposefully made'.[10]

But instances of such imaginative use of Celtic reference were comparatively rare. (Deane and Woodward were certainly the most original and inventive Irish architects of the period.) In contrast to the complete renovation and reimagining of Ireland's past achieved by the poets and playwrights of the Celtic Revival, Irish architecture appeared to be less about reinterpreting the forms of the past, and more about simply reusing them. The Irish Industrial Village displayed at the Chicago Exposition of 1893 consisted in its entirety of quotations from what had by that stage become the familiar repertoire of Ireland's architectural heritage: the round tower, the tower house, the thatched cottage, the doorway of Cormac's chapel on the Rock of Cashel. Ireland's architectural identity was, it seemed, to be constructed entirely by reference to the past. Round towers and high crosses became popular as monuments in their own right (for instance, in Daniel O'Connell's memorial at Glasnevin) or as somewhat awkward appendages to churches (for instance, at Leighlinbridge in Carlow). Even as skilful an architect as William Scott, described as the 'architect by appointment to the Celtic Revival', seemed more comfortable renovating Yeats's Thoor Ballylee than in his attempts to generate a new 'Hiberno-Romanesque' language for his church at Spiddal, Co. Galway. Certainly, there was no real equivalent in Ireland to the English Arts and Crafts movement which had quite consciously been producing rchitecture that managed, in the words of Herman Muthesius, to be modern and at the same time wholly national'.[11]

Of course, it was always far more likely that the new cultural nationlism would initially find its fullest expression in scholarship and literature, rather than in architecture. Architecture, after all, required economic and political power to be implemented on any meaningful scale, and was not therefore the ideal weapon of a culture of opposition. But once independence had been gained, and nationalist culture gained political control, architecture would surely play a greater role in the construction of the new state.

The construction of the new state

Thus we come to the crucial problem confronting nations just rising from underdevelopment. In order to get on to the road toward modernisation, is it necessary to jettison the cultural past as *raison d'être* of the nation? Whence a paradox: on the one hand, the nation has to root itself in the soil of its past and forge a national spirit in the face of colonial censure and disparagement. But in order to become modern, it is necessary at the same time to take part in scientific, technical and political rationality, something that may require a jettisoning of the past. Not every culture can sustain and absorb the shock of modern civilisation. There is the dilemma: how to become modern and to return to sources, how to revive an old, dormant civilisation and take part in
universal civilisation.[12]

While it is debatable whether Ireland in the 1920s might be described as a nation 'rising from underdevelopment', Paul Ricoeur's discussion of nationhood and modernity encapsulates the challenges facing the new nation in every other respect. In the years leading up to independence, the central nationalist concern had been the promulgation of some potent vision of the nation: 'A nation', as W. B. Yeats wrote, 'cannot exist without a model of it in the minds of the people.'[13] But while the various versions of this vision all emphasised Ireland's future potential, they also sought to 'establish continuity with some suitable historic past'. Once independence had been achieved, the challenge was to make the model of the nation – what Edward Said calls its 'geographical identity' – a reality. The resultant tension between what the anthropologist Clifford Geertz has described as essentialism – namely, the adherence to some shared culture – versus epochalism – embracing the spirit of the age – became a defining characteristic of the new state.[14]

Initially, vacillation between historic certainty and projected ideals resulted largely in inaction. The Cumann na nGaedheal administration of the 1920s has been described by Joe Lee as 'a holding operation'. In the face of worldwide depression and continuing civil conflict, caution, rather than experiment, was the favoured policy. The only significant exception to this prevailing prudence was the building of a massive hydroelectric plant on the River Shannon at Ardnacrusha between 1925 and 1929. Initiated by an Irish engineer, T. A. McLaughlin, the project was designed and built by the German company Siemens, using a largely Irish workforce. It involved the diversion of the Shannon into a headrace canal at Parteen weir, which ran a distance of 12.6 kilometres to a huge dam that channelled the water into the turbine hall. The scale of earthmoving and construction involved was far greater than anything previously witnessed in Ireland.

The reinforced concrete buildings, bridges and dams on the Shannon were resolutely modern in appearance, but they also possessed a simple, elemental power, appearing almost to grow out of the surrounding landscape. In contemporary accounts, the inspiration for the Shannon scheme was traced back to Arthur Griffith, D. P. Moran and Patrick Pearse, all of whom had stressed the need for Ireland to exploit its natural resources in order to achieve an independent prosperity. 'A free Ireland', Pearse had promised, 'would drain the bogs, would harness the rivers, would plant the wastes … Ireland has resources to feed five times her population; a free Ireland will make these resources available.'[15] Throughout much of nineteenth-century Europe, modernisation had entailed a move away from rural culture. Progress and prosperity became associated with the city. In Ireland, by contrast, the most radical political and artistic achievements of the nineteenth century were rooted in rural areas. Ardnacrusha was able to translate a romantic idea about rural Ireland as the wellspring of nationhood into built reality. Firmly anchored in the popular mythology of Irishness, it was free to take a completely modern, functional form. Almost without trying, the Shannon project bridged the divide between the past and the future.

In the 1930s, architecture began to play a more substantial role in the making of the new state. The *Fianna Fáil* government which took power in 1932 under the leadership of Eamon De Valera instigated an ambitious and extensive building programme. While De Valera's vision

f the nation drew on familiar themes of rusticity, asceticism and spiri-
uality, he knew that in order to sustain itself, substantial improvements
needed to be made to the harsh realities of Irish rural life. Ireland's boglands began to be used to produce fuel and electricity, a renewed programme of school-building was initiated, and there was a proliferation
of new hospitals around the country. Between 1936 and 1940 twelve new
county hospitals and thirty smaller hospitals were built.

Vincent Kelly, the architect appointed to oversee the hospitals programme, was sent to study hospital buildings throughout Europe, particularly Alvar Aalto's recently completed Paimio Sanitorium in Finland.
But while his work at Nenagh and Portrane shows a thoroughly contemporary appreciation of the benefit to physical and mental health of a
clean, well-lit and ventilated environment, the buildings' plain surfaces
and organisational clarity could equally be seen to embody De Valera's
puritanical vision of Irish society. The more thoroughgoing functionalism of T. J. Cullen's Galway Central Hospital and Michael Scott's Port
Laoise Hospital invites a similar interpretation. These hospitals could be
read as a testament to enduring values as surely as they were symbols of
progress. They helped to stabilise De Valera's balancing of a sternly anti-
materialist philosophy and the pressing need for material progress. D. P.
Moran had previously diagnosed the need for 'making the people sober,
moderate, masculine and thereby paving the way for industrial advancement and economic reform'.[16] The stark, utilitarian hospitals, schools
and factories of the 1930s gave that prescription a built form.

But while it is certainly possible to find common ground between
the plain sobriety of this architecture and modernist pronouncements
such as Adolf Loos's famous equating of 'Ornament and Crime', it can
nonetheless be argued that Ireland was beguiled by the surface of modernism rather than by its substance. Modern architecture was a critical
practice, its aesthetic and forms emerging out of a sustained critique of
prevailing societal norms. Shorn of this critical apparatus, the new architecture was all too easily reducible either to a set of aesthetic motifs or to
an impoverished functionalism. As Alvar Aalto observed in the Finnish
context:

> The structures which were meant to create a new architecture have
> been wrested from us and turned into commercialised decorative
> ends in themselves with no inner value. There was a time when a
> misconstrued, lifeless traditionalism was the chief enemy of good

> architecture. Today its worst enemy is the superficial decorative
> misuse of the means acquired during the breakthrough . . . the
> contrast between deep social responsibility and decorative 'surface
> effects' is perhaps the oldest and certainly the most topical issue in
> the debate on architecture.[17]

So, just as Scott's New York Pavilion might be seen as superficial in its approach to national representation, so too can its version of modernism be criticised: more a case of style borrowed than an ethos embraced. Despite this, it is probably Michael Scott's name above all that is associated with the introduction of modern architecture to Ireland. Partly through his policy of employing the brightest of Ireland's young architects, his firm's work continued to be innovative, and gradually became more sophisticated and thoughtful in its embrace of modernism. His Central Bus Station for Dublin (Busarás), although dogged by difficulty and controversy during its construction, emerged as a building which fully understood the architectural language it was trying to speak. The opening of this building in 1953 marks the beginning of a period in which Irish architecture starts to become more confident and less self-conscious. In the process, and somewhat paradoxically, it also came to reflect more completely the nature of the society from which it emerged.

Conscious and unconscious Irishness

From the beginning of the 1960s, Ireland's economic fortunes began to improve dramatically. The annual growth rate averaged 4 per cent. The steady stream of emigrants began to slow down, with people finding employment in new industries and manufactories that were being attracted in from overseas. The key figures behind this transformation were T. K. Whittaker and Seán Lemass. Lemass took over from Eamon De Valera as leader of Fianna Fáil and *taoiseach* in 1957. Whittaker began a thirteen-year tenure as Secretary of the Department of Finance in 1958. In the same year, the First Programme of Economic Expansion was implemented, to be followed by a second in 1963 and a third in 1968. The rationale behind these programmes was spelled out by Whitaker in the government White Paper of 1957, *Economic Development*, which proposed a series of measures that would break with Ireland's previously isolationist economic policy and embrace international trends. These included a much greater involvement by the state in the investment in productive industry than had been thought wise in more prudent years, the employment of increased Central Bank power to direct investment by the commercial banks, and encouragement of foreign investment by packages of attractive incentives'.[18]

Lemass's leadership style was crucial in the implementation of this policy. Whereas Eamon De Valera's every decision was informed by his unshakeable attachment to a very simplified version of Irishness and his famous belief that to understand the people of Ireland he need only look into his own heart, Lemass, if no less patriotic, was far more objective and dispassionate. Joe Lee has highlighted his 'dedication to efficiency, his desire to remould the Irish Republic into a streamlined, functional corporate state which would allow decisions to be taken with a managerial dispatch . . . [and] his capacity to distinguish modernization from anglicization'.[19] This last point is crucial. No longer would Ireland have to package every modernising scheme in ultranationalist clothing for fear that it might otherwise be seen as a pernicious influence. It was now possible to be more straightforwardly aspirational. This was a feeling which permeated the population at large, as Terence Brown notes: 'most Irish people would still identify 1958–63 as the period when a new kind of Ireland began to come to life. Most associate the successes of those years with a renewed national self-confidence.'[20]

The new national mood found its perfect reflection in the architecture of Scott, Tallon and Walker, a partnership formed out of Michael Scott's office in 1959. Already, with Busaras, Michael Scott had begun to demonstrate how a modern architectural idiom might transform the nation's image of itself. Scott had employed Ove Arup and Varmings to provide the very best technical and structural advice on the new materials and new technologies employed. Whereas previously Ireland had sought to protect its identity by insulating itself from the world, it was now opening itself to the world marketplace. Part of that process was to embrace an architecture which spoke of internationalism, progress and serious-mindedness; an architecture that eschewed tradition and sentiment and celebrated rationalism and modernity. Scott, Tallon and Walker's clients from this period were typical of an expanding, modernising state: large-scale manufacturers like tobacco company Carrolls, state organisations like RTÉ (the national broadcasting agency), educational institutions like University College Galway and financial organisations like the Bank of Ireland. The scale and nature of the projects were

16.3 RTÉ Administration Building by Scott, Tallon and Walker. Photo by Hugh Campbell

new; thus, they demanded a new aesthetic. That aesthetic derived in large part from the American work of Mies van der Rohe (with whom Robin Walker had studied and worked in Chicago); a language of steel frame and curtain wall glazing, developed and refined through a series of iconic residential and office buildings. This was an architecture derived from a deep understanding of technology and materials. What William Jordy referred to as the 'laconic splendour' of Mies's buildings was the result of the patient, precise honing of a simple strategy and a very limited palette of materials.[21]

In a series of key projects – the Carrolls Factory in Dundalk, the early parts of the RTÉ campus in Donnybrook (Fig. 16.3), the Bank of Ireland headquarters in Baggot Street, Dublin – Scott Tallon and Walker translated the Miesian language for Ireland. And despite the fact that they derived from urban America, these projects resonated remarkably well with the Lemass ethos. For just as their machined reflective surfaces spoke of progress and modernity, their refined neutrality seemed to relate back to the Georgian fabric of cities and towns (a parallel explicitly drawn by Robin Walker). 'Architecture is a language having the discipline of a grammar', said Mies.[22] This was not a poetic language of rhetoric and imagery, but a structured, methodical prose. And yet by employing his mute language, Scott, Tallon and Walker's buildings managed to be eloquently expressive of their era. Importantly, these were projects which took ordinary functions and gave them dignity and presence. This concern for the ordinary is characteristic of the era: looking back over the prize-winning projects of the decade, the day-to-day equipment of a modern society – schools, offices and factories – dominates.

In the North, this engagement with the everyday took a somewhat different form. Whereas, in its early decades, architecture in Northern Ireland seemed even more hidebound by tradition and reluctant to experiment than in the South – the stern classicism of the parliament building at Stormont, completed in 1933, makes absolutely no concession to modernity – by the 1960s a new, more confident language had begun to emerge. Beginning with Francis Pym's extension to the Ulster Museum in 1965, a language of bold, sculptural forms in exposed concrete and brick was explored in a series of striking projects such as the Portadown Technical College by Shanks, Leighton, Kennedy and Fitzgerald. This work drew very directly on developments in England, where a 'brutalist' architecture that sought to 'drag a rough poetry' from the realities of mass-production society had been pioneered by Alison and Peter Smithson and championed by the historian and critic Reyner Banham. Translated to Northern Ireland, the language seemed to acquire some added resonances, both with the landscape and with the nineteenth-century industrial architecture.

By contrast the influence of brutalism appeared only rarely in the Republic, where, as the boom period of the sixties ended, architecture started to slip back into a blunt, impoverished functionalism, with little of the rigour or sophistication of Scott, Tallon and Walker's best work in evidence. During the seventies there was a world-wide reaction against what were seen as the excesses and insensitivities of modern architecture. With the advent of post-modernism, the benefits of an international, 'universal' architecture began to be questioned. In its place came a revival of interest in the historic city form and a renewed engagement with the particularities of place and culture. The historian Kenneth Frampton's famous championing of a 'critical regionalism' – an architecture deriving from its climate and context rather than from any universal norms – struck a chord in Ireland and led to a fresh exploration of native Irish urban and rural forms. In this context, Niall McCullough's book *A Lost Tradition* (1987) acted not only as a catalogue of indigenous Irish forms, but also as a polemical argument for the need to (once again) rediscover the past.[23]

This was a period of economic recession in Ireland, during which many architects went abroad to work. The combination of distance from home and exposure to architectural theory and practice in Europe, produced a strong desire to redefine what an Irish architecture might be. Irish architects of the twenties and thirties had largely rejected any calls for 'a national architecture', preferring buildings that were modern in style. In the fifties and sixties, they embraced a neutral, international architecture that had little to do with national particularities. But in the eighties an architecture consciously derived from its location was endorsed for the first time by the architectural élite. In part, this was a reflection of international trends as earlier tendencies; being regional and outside the mainstream of modernism was now seen as a badge of pride and a source of rich potential, rather than cause for embarrassment. The international renown which this generation of Irish architecture eventually began to attract in the 1990s was due precisely to its contextualism.

This contextualism manifested itself in both urban and rural settings. The loose affiliation of small firms which came together to form Group 91 demonstrated in their regeneration of the Temple Bar area of Dublin a profound respect for the historic city, and a determination to forge new architecture from a detailed engagement with the existing context. The rural architecture of these same firms was equally respectful of its context, drawing initially on a repertory of indigenous forms and types, but becoming increasingly inventive in its reinterpretation of the Irish rural tradition. Buildings such as O'Donnell and Tuomey's Blackwood Golf Centre (Fig. 16.4) and Letterfrack Furniture College manage to be both responsive and original; they fit in, not through mimicry and quotation, but through a fundamental reimagining of what an Irish vernacular might be. One of the first international exhibitions of this work was entitled 'figurative architecture', confirming that the mute, abstract architecture of the 1960s had given way to a far more expressive language, which in many ways harked back to the nineteenth century. Once again, buildings were seen as communicative objects, the bearers of potent messages about culture and identity. Unsurprisingly, this profound shift in Irish architectural culture happened at a time when Irish identity – both historical and contemporary – became the renewed focus of attention in the popular and academic arenas. What is perhaps more surprising is that

6.4 Blackwood Golf Centre by O'Donnell and Tuomey. Photograph by Christopher Hill

architecture in the North experienced no such thoroughgoing reinvention during this period. Northern architecture seemed content to mimic the various trends emerging in Britain, rather than engaging with the potentially divisive issues of context and identity.

Nonetheless, in the late twentieth-century reconstruction of Ireland's identity, architecture has certainly played a greater and more profound role than it had a century earlier, when the construction of the independent nation began. Solving the problem of nationalism and making it modern no longer seem such divergent goals as they had for Michael Scott in 1939. In part this is because architecture is now seen as a solid investment; it forms a vital component of the 'cultural capital' that all nations seem obliged to generate. And yet the self-conscious re-engagement with national identity which made this new architectural confidence possible may also be in danger of limiting its future potential. The Irishness of earlier, successful projects – from Ardnacrusha to the Bank of Ireland – was essentially a direct consequence of the conditions of their production rather than a consciously pursued objective. In a sense, it was their very indifference to issues of identity which allowed them to become potent expressions of their time and place. If Irish architecture is to move beyond the confines of its current position as a kind of élite calling card for Irish culture, it will need to become less self-conscious and more fully engrained in the fabric of everyday Irish life.

Notes

1. Dorothy Walker, *Michael Scott: Architect* (Kinsale: Gandon Editions, 1995), p. 96.
2. From 'Office Building', first published in *G*, 1 (July 1923), 3. Translated in Fritz Neumeyer, *The Artless Word: Mies van der Rohe on the Building Art* (Cambridge, MA: MIT Press, 1991), p. 241.
3. Sigfried Giedion, *Space, Time and Architecture* (1941; Cambridge, MA: MIT Press, 1963) pp. 19–20.
4. Colin Rowe, 'Character and composition', in *The Mathematics of the Ideal Villa and other Essays* (Cambridge, MA: MIT Press, 1982), pp. 60–87 (p. 67). Rowe is quoting from Sir Joshua Reynolds, *Discourse III, 1770: Literary Works* (London, 1835), vol. I, p. 333.
5. John Ruskin, *The Stones of Venice* (London: George Allen, 1912), vol. II. Quoted in Adrian Forty, '"Europe is no more than a nation made up of several others": thoughts on architecture and nationality prompted by the Taylor Institute and the Martyr's Memorial in Oxford', *AA Files* 32 (Autumn 1996), 26–37 (30).
6. Forty, '"Europe is no more than a nation made up of several others"', p. 30.
7. Article signed J. P. M., *Irish Times*, 8 June 1909.
8. On this typical pattern of growth see Asa Briggs, *Victorian Cities* (Harmondsworth: Penguin, 1990) and Burton Pike, *The Image of the City in Modern Literature* (Ann Arbor: University of Michigan Press, 1992).
9. C. E. B. Brett, *Buildings of Belfast, 1700–1914* (London: Weidenfeld and Nicolson, 1967), p. 54.
10. Eve Blau, *Ruskinian Gothic: The Architecture of Deane and Woodward, 1845–1861* (Princeton: Princeton University Press, 1982), p. 33.
11. Quoted in Forty, '"Europe is no more than a nation made up of several others"', p. 31.
12. From Paul Ricoeur, 'Universal civilisation and national cultures' [1961], quoted in Kenneth Frampton, *Modern Architecture: A Critical History* (London: Thames and Hudson, 1990), p. 313.
13. William Butler Yeats, *Autobiographies* (London: Macmillan, 1955), p. 493.
14. Clifford Geertz, 'After the revolution: the fate of nationalism in the new states', in *The Interpretation of Cultures* (London: Routledge and Kegan Paul, 1975), pp. 232–57 (234).
15. Quoted in Joseph Lee, *The Modernisation of Irish Society, 1848–1918* (Dublin: Gill and Macmillan, 1973), p. 147.
16. D. P. Moran, *The Philosophy of Irish Ireland* (Dublin, 1905), p. 45.
17. Alvar Aalto in an interview in the Swedish newspaper *Pages Nyheter* (1936), quoted in Goran Schildt, *Alvar Aalto: The Decisive Years* (New York: Rizzoli, 1986), pp. 202–3.
18. Joseph Lee, *Ireland 1912–1985* (Cambridge: Cambridge University Press, 1985), p. 242.
19. Ibid., p. 241.
20. Terence Brown, *Ireland: A Social and Cultural History, 1922–1985* (London: Fontana Press, 1990), p. 246.
21. William Jordy, *American Buildings and their Architects* (New York: Rizzoli, 1976), p. 225.
22. Quoted in *Mies in America*, ed. Phylis Lambert (New York: CCA & Whitney, 2001), p. 193.

3. Niall McCullough, *A Lost Tradition: The Nature of Architecture in Ireland* (Dublin: Gandon Editions, 1987).

Further reading

Annette Becker, John Olley and Wilfred Wang (eds.), *Twentieth-Century Architecture: Ireland* (Munich: Prestel, 1997)

Eve Blau, *Ruskinian Gothic: The Architecture of Deane and Woodward, 1845–1861* (Princeton: Princeton University Press, 1992)

Hugh Campbell, 'The emergence of modern Dublin: reality and representation', *Architectural Research Quarterly* 8 (1997), 44–53

David Evans, *An Introduction to Modern Ulster Architecture* (Belfast: Ulster Architectural Society, 1977)

Niall McCullough, *A Lost Tradition: The Nature of Architecture in Ireland* (Dublin: Gandon Editions, 1987)

Sean Rothery, *Ireland and the New Architecture 1900–1940* (Dublin: Lilliput Press, 1991)

Dorothy Walker, *Michael Scott: Architect* (Kinsale: Gandon Editions, 1995)

17

The visual arts in Ireland

Introduction

The history of the visual arts in Ireland in the nineteenth and twentieth centuries is the ongoing story of the relationship between a metropolitan culture (London) and a smaller, less economically sustainable environment (Dublin). The production of art is an expensive activity. Although all cultural media need patronage and financial assistance, the visual arts have the added burden of needing materials, be it oils and canvases or marble blocks or the latest innovations in information technology, so as to begin the process of visual communication. Finally, it needs forms of display to make it all accessible to an audience, be it private or public. For much of the period under discussion, 1800–2000, Ireland was very often not in a position to greatly assist its visual artists. In many ways an account of the visual arts in relation to Ireland in the modern period is a story of talent exported to London and in more recent times to other European cities and also to New York. In the nineteenth century London was the metropolis of empire while in the twentieth century it and other international locations have become convenient sites for artistic training, exhibition and sales. That economic dependency is vital to an understanding of the progress of the visual arts over the last two hundred years.

The nineteenth century

One of the key facts in discussing pre-twentieth-century Irish art is the dominant position of the British School. No native-born artists have had the cultural effect that John Constable, J. M. W. Turner or David Wilkie had in their native England or Scotland, while at the same time most rominent Irish artists of the period – from James Barry who died in 806 to Sir John Lavery who died in 1941 – are still staunchly included in 1ost reference books as British artists. The problem lies with the export f talent to London and the economic impossibility of making a living n Dublin or Ireland in general. Although, in Walter Strickland's incomarable *A Dictionary of Irish Artists*, published in 1913, Ireland boasts one f the most impressive accounts of artists' lives ever produced in these slands, the compiler's two-volume history is inevitably one of endless noves into exile and of feeding the London artistic market. An account f Irish nineteenth-century artists is thus a story of cultural assimilation nto the bigger world of the Royal Academy of Arts in London and other rtistic institutions.

The lack of impact of Irish artists on the state of the visual arts back 1ome is due to the fact that so few stayed for their whole careers. Irish 1ineteenth-century journals frequently list a litany of great achievers but his was more a case of wish fulfilment that effective influence. Barry, or example, left Dublin in the 1760s and never worked there again. His greatest single work is the series of murals in the Great Hall of the [Royal] iociety of Arts in central London. Similarly, that great mid-nineteenth-'entury star of 'British' art, the Cork-born Daniel Maclise, from the 1840s o the 1860s painted some of the most impressive murals in the newly lecorated Palace of Westminster. Finally, Lavery's international fame is nore for his late nineteenth-century canvases that recall James McNeill Vhistler than for his important series of Irish political portraits of the 920s.

Art institutions

t was invariably training and an unsure professional future that drove so nany into exile. Although Dublin had boasted a School of Drawing from 746, the nation as a whole did not have its own academy of arts until 1823, when Dublin was granted a royal charter to open the Royal Hibernian \cademy. Basing itself on London's Royal Academy established in the 760s, the RHA, throughout the nineteenth century, was an ill-run insti-:ution, endlessly troubled by internecine controversies. Instruction was given to students and annual exhibitions were held, yet it carried none)f the theoretical drive that distinguished the older academy in London. [n time, the Dublin Metropolitan School of Art was established in 1877, ioon followed by the Cork School of Art in 1885. Both were distinguished by their focus on design, the pioneering figure at both institutions being James Brenan who moved from Cork to Dublin in 1889.

As well as seeing the establishment of the Royal Hibernian Academy the nineteenth century also saw the setting up of the National Gallery of Ireland (1864), and the Crawford Gallery in Cork (1884) as well as the Belfast City Art Gallery (1890), which later became the Ulster Museum. Such developments in the visual arts might imply a healthy state of affairs and it can be argued that one can see mid-nineteenth-century Ireland as a nation following the comparable regional expansion then occurring in Britain with the establishment of museums and art galleries in such cities as Manchester and Birmingham in 1823 and 1867, respectively. The major difference in these comparisons is that most British regional collections formed in the nineteenth century focused their acquisition policy (if they had one) on contemporary or recent British art, while Dublin's National Gallery set out from the very beginning to collect old master paintings. Cork's collection was equally dominated, at least in its early years, by the legacy of a plaster cast collection of antique statuary given to the city by the Prince Regent (later George IV) in 1818. The irony of these examples is that as public collections developed in Ireland in the nineteenth century they were dominated by non-Irish art. While few would lament the fact that Henry Doyle, an early director of the National Gallery of Ireland, acquired a beautiful predella panel from Fra Angelico's *St Mark Altarpiece* in 1886 or Rembrandt's equally small *Rest on the Flight into Egypt* a few years earlier, the problem was that the establishment of the National Gallery did not greatly benefit nineteenth-century Irish art production.

Doyle did his best. One of his most important activities was an attempt to set up a national portrait collection comparable in range if not in scale to the then newly established National Portrait Gallery in London. In 1872 he applied to the Treasury for a grant to establish an Irish Portrait Gallery but was refused. Doyle wished to establish an inclusive collection, with images of 'eminent Irishmen and Irishwomen, but also statesmen and others who were politically or socially connected with Ireland, or whose lives serve in any way to illustrate her history, or throw light on her social or literary, or artistic records'. The Treasury's refusal to help Doyle set up an Irish National Portrait Gallery was because London was of the opinion that 'local, and not imperial, liberality is the proper source from which such collections should be created and maintained'. This imperial vision peripheralised Ireland and turned it into the 'local'. Writing to Doyle, a Treasury official stated that provision was already made by Parliament for a National Gallery of Portraits of distinguished personages where eminent Irishmen are represented indiscriminately with Englishmen and Scotchmen. It would materially lessen the importance and interest of this general and essentially National Collection if separate and competing Galleries were to be established in Dublin and Edinburgh, confined respectively to portraits of Irish and Scotch celebrities.[1]

Native versus imperial vision

This imbalance between Ireland's 'local' demands and its nineteenth-century imperial role is an aspect of the history of Irish visual production that has not been sufficiently discussed. A lot of attention has, understandably, been paid by scholars and gallery curators to the identification and persistence of Irish themes in late eighteenth-century and nineteenth-century artistic production. One can go back to the late 1770s and early 1780s and see James Barry including an Irishised Ossian at the apex of his mural *Eylsium and Tartarus or the State of Final Retribution* at the [Royal] Society of Arts in London. We can move forward to the mid-nineteenth century and acknowledge Maclise's inclusion of a rich array of archaeologically inspired trinkets in the foreground of his great *Marriage of Strongbow and Eva* (1854, Dublin: National Gallery of Ireland). Meanwhile, the century comes to a close with the burst of 'Celtic' creativity associated with the initiatives of the home art industries. All of these visual expressions of Irishness need discussion, but with every painting by Barry of St Patrick or a Maclise illustration to Tom Moore's *Melodies*, there exists a plethora of visual material produced and exhibited in nineteenth-century Ireland that supports and propagates what one can only call an imperial vision. The nineteenth century thus needs the kind of revisionist realignment that other disciplines in Irish Studies have received for the last two decades. Given the continued migration of Irish artists in the nineteenth century, as well as the widespread dissemination of English images due to the growth of exhibitions and the greater availability of engraved prints and developments in illustrated newspapers, one needs to look beyond demonstratively Irish representations such as Frederic William Burton's *The Aran Fisherman's Drowned Child* (1841; Fig. 17.1) and focus instead on the dominance of imperial visual material that was on show in Ireland during the first century of Union.

17.1 Frederic William Burton, *The Aran Fisherman's Drowned Child*, 1841, watercolour on paper, National Gallery of Ireland, Dublin

Burton's *Drowned Child* has entered the canon of Irish visual studies as an anthropologically intriguing study of life on the Atlantic seaboard in the mid nineteenth century. It can also be seen as a study in the romantic celebration of a stoic peasantry. In 1843 it was published as a print by the Royal Irish Art Union but that admirable commercial attempt to disseminate Irish images soon failed. The cause of such a failure was due to Ireland's status as an integral part of the United Kingdom and the fact that 'British' images either in oil or in print were more extensively available and usually cheaper in price. Starting with touring exhibitions of giant panoramas in 1801, telling the exciting stories of recent British victories in India, and moving through to the civic commissioning by the city of Dublin from London's most fashionable portrait painter,

ir Thomas Lawrence, of a royal portrait of the newly crowed George IV
1 1821 (now on display in Dublin's Mansion House), and on to touring
nglish paintings celebrating either Victoria or Protestantism, Ireland in
1e nineteenth century needs to be seen as the locus of constant colonial
1doctrination.

In 1801, James Barry sketched three pen drawings representing the
Jnion between Great Britain and Ireland (Fig. 17.2). For at least six
1onths of that same year, Dublin audiences thronged to a huge wooden
ower in College Green which displayed a panorama of the recent British
ictory at Seringapatam in Mysore, India. Barry's drawings were done
1 London and show the two sister countries joining hands above the
Jnion crown, while a recording angel (in the two British Museum ver-
ions) stands by, clasping the emblems of each island tightly to his breast.
arry's allegory is almost abstract in its classicism, and was originally pro-
uced as a visual statement of reconciliation and optimism in the face of
Villiam Pitt's dissolution of the Irish parliament. In the end, the drawing
ever materialised into a painting for the Society of Arts Great Room and
hus never became a fitting conclusion to Barry's great cycle 'The Progress
f Human Culture'. By contrast, the panorama that went on display in
)ublin was a wholly accessible and popular affair and can be read as a
nore appropriate visual indicator of the new relationship between the
slands in the light of the Act of Union.

The English artist Robert Ker Porter's huge panorama (120 feet in
ength covering 2,550 square feet of canvas; now destroyed) was exhib-
ted in Dublin for six months from July to December 1801 and then trav-
lled on to Cork and Belfast. It had already been seen in London and
ontinued its perambulations around the United Kingdom for many
nore years. Depicting the successful assault by British troops on the
alace of Tipú Sultan, its attractions for a Dublin audience (apart from
he spectacle of its display) was the fact that some 5,000 Irishmen joined
he East India Company army in the first decades of the nineteenth cen-
ury, with almost 900 coming from Dublin. A form of public display, the
otunda-shaped tower that exhibited Porter's panorama was actually the
nvention of an Irishman, Robert Barker, from Kells, Co. Meath, whose
wo sons went on to corner the market for the representation of such
najor 'national' events as the Battle of Waterloo and the Coronation of
George IV.

Sixty years later, the display in Belfast and Dublin of English paint-
ngs was still going on. Thomas Barker's *The Secret of England's Great-
ess*, or *Queen Victoria Presenting a Bible in the Audience Chamber at Windsor*

17.2 James Barry, *The Act of Union between Great Britain and Ireland*, 1801, pen and brown ink and grey wash over black chalk, Trustees of the British Museum

(*c*. 1863, London, National Portrait Gallery) is but one of many exam-ples of successful exhibitions that heightened visual awareness of not only the monarchy (in the figure of Victoria), but also the mores of the Established Church (in the symbolic handing over of the Bible to a kneel-ing African potentate). Interest in Barker's depiction of the civilising enefits of imperialism was such that it continued to appear as an engraving on the walls of Ulster homes well into the twentieth century. A similar popularity was associated with the display of William Holman Hunt's *he Shadow of Death* (Manchester City Art Galleries), an image of the oung Jesus foreshadowing his fate. This painting has subsequently been described as exhibiting a 'nationalistic Protestantism'[2] but it enjoyed uccess when on show in Dublin and Belfast in 1875. As such, imperial imagery had a longevity not matched by the dramatic action and he seeming authenticity of Burton's *Drowned Child* or the pathetic visualisation of famine disaster as seen in Daniel MacDonald's *The Discovry of the Potato Blight* (University College Dublin, Department of Irish 'olklore), which was exhibited at the British Institution in London in 847. An 1860s watercolour of an Irish colleen *Molly Macree* by Thomas Alfred Jones (Dublin, National Gallery of Ireland), president of the Royal Hibernian Academy from 1869 to his death in 1893, has recently been discussed as a post-Famine 'image of Ireland'.[3] With her comely smile and richly patterned shawl, it is indeed tempting to place iconic status n Jones's Irish girl but there is little evidence that such was the case with indigenous Irish imagery. Despite its popularity today as a postcard on ale at the National Gallery of Ireland, the provenance of the drawing is hrouded in mystery and it was out of circulation for nearly eighty years. By contrast, Barker's *Secret of England's Greatness* never had to suffer such a ustained act of visual disregard.

The imperial dimension in Irish visual culture continued into the wentieth century. In 1908, when Hugh Lane opened Dublin's new Municipal Gallery of Modern Art at 17 Harcourt Street, his catalogue isted three pages of 'Portraits of Contemporary Irishmen and Women', many of which were his own gift to the city. It perhaps comes as no surprise to know that John Butler Yeats contributed an oil of Douglas Hyde, co-founder and first president of the Gaelic League, another of playwright John Millington Synge as well as portraits of his son, W. B. Yeats and of the Abbey Theatre actor, W. G. Fay. The other main contributor of contemporary portraits was William Orpen, an artist of the next generation to Yeats *père* whose portraits of political figures included the radical Michael Davitt, 'Father of the Land League', as the catalogue put it, but also canvases of such figures as the Trinity don, the Reverend J. P. Mahaffy and Sir Anthony MacDonnell, like Davitt a native of Co. Mayo, but by contrast a former lieutenant-governor in India and under-secretary for Ireland since 1902.[4]

The twentieth century

It is often suggested that the move towards political freedom in Ireland is neatly echoed by an increase in nationalist art. The works of Seán Keating and Jack Yeats have been interpreted as celebrating a new cultural awakening. Yet, as Cyril Barrett wrote over a quarter of a century ago, 'the failure to produce a body of extreme nationalistic art was . . . because there was no public demand for it'.[5] David Lloyd's more recent discussion of the crisis of representation for the Irish novel in the nineteenth century offers us a solution to this reluctance to engage in Irish subject matter and the absence of a national art. Ireland's unstable middle class, Lloyd claims, did not 'furnish representative figures', a vital ingredient of so many realistic novels in the nineteenth century, resulting in a 'struggle for hegemony' amongst the people who would otherwise buy and read novels, just as they might buy or view art in either oils or engraved form. Lloyd's definition of the 'complex and shifting affiliations' of this class allows us to see parallels in the art-viewing public.[6]

That public demand did not even extend to non-nationalist art was proven by the prolonged saga of the Lane bequest to the city of Dublin of a group of French nineteenth-century paintings. As is well known, Dublin's slowness to house Lane's bequest led to the thirty-nine paintings, which included works by Manet, Degas and Renoir, being acquired by London's National Gallery. Following Lane's death at sea in 1915, the subsequent wrangling between Dublin and London over the fate of the paintings was as much a political squabble as it was a debate over the aesthetic worth of the canvases. That the plight of a number of late nineteenth-century French paintings was an issue for diplomatic concern is a wonderful irony given the Irish Free State's overall disinterest in the role of the visual arts. In 1939, even as the first Fianna Fáil government was continuing its argument with London over Lane's bequest, Caitlín Bean Uí Chléirigh, widow of Tom Clarke, a signatory of the 1916 proclamation of independence, was ordering the removal of Lawrence's fine portrait of George IV from Dublin's Mansion House.[7] Meanwhile, Irish-born artists, like their nineteenth-century predecessors, continued to emigrate. Jack Yeats was always an exception, both in what he produced and in his working practices. Having lived in England for much of his youth, he returned to Ireland in 1910 as he neared the age of forty and remained in Dublin until his death more than forty years later. But those who left and did not return include such names

s John Lavery and William Orpen, both of whom found success in
ondon.

Jack B. Yeats

n many ways, Jack Yeats is the key figure in Irish art in the first half of the
wentieth century. His move from humorous illustrator to urban commentator, and finally to a somewhat introverted expressionism, has been
well charted. He brings together one of the major artistic cunundrums
of the era, in that his work acknowledges the spread of modernist form
while continuously focusing on Irish themes. As such he acts as a balance
between the Parisian inspired experimentation of an artist like Mainie
ellett and the pictorial traditionalism of Seán Keating. In 1945, Ernie
)'Malley, a former republican revolutionary, usefully summed up Yeats's
ontribution in the catalogue that accompanied an exhibition at Dublin's
Jational College of Art:

> The memory of the dead makes for a tragic understanding in Ireland.
> It evokes a feeling of dead generations who served or had died for a
> common cause, their struggle echoed in each generation. The
> Batchelor's Walk incident is shown as a simple, but hieratic incident
> of a flower-girl who casts a flower outside a doorway where men have
> been shot down. There is a restrained dignity and grace in the
> movement of her hand and a tenderness that evokes a sense of pity . . .
> With him colour is an emotional force and his method of using it
> varies in regard to its substance as pigment and as texture. He may
> create a homogenous surface with his brush, improvise an absorbing
> study in chiaroscuro, or use the priming of the canvas to aid
> luminosity of light and shade.[8]

Iere O'Malley articulates Yeats's binary powers: he is an artist inspired by
public incident, yet one who can adapt the contemporaneous European
expressionist palette to a local situation.

Continental Europe has only occasionally featured in this account
of the visual arts in Ireland since 1800. In the nineteenth century, the
ocus of very many artists was on London and wider patronage. Yet,
3arry and in time Maclise were well versed in Italian and German art
espectively. Later nineteenth-century artists from Nathaniel Hone to
Roderic O'Conor lived and worked in France, and are part of the trans-
European preoccupation with *plein air* painting that continued well into

the twentieth century. Mainie Jellett's championing of new forms led
eventually to the setting up in 1943 of a Parisian style Salon des Refusé
in Dublin, called the Exhibition of Irish Living Art.

Post-Second World War

In the second half of the twentieth century, the status of the visual art
in Ireland was transformed. Ignored and underfunded for much of the
preceding 150 years, the role of the visual arts in post-Second World War
Ireland is one of public presence and official patronage. The setting up of
the Arts Council in 1951 and the slow growth in gallery spaces and loan
exhibitions has meant that art is now visible throughout the country in
a way unknown to previous generations. The restructuring of art education combined with student unrest in 1968, as well as the growth in the
number of art colleges, has given Ireland a greater opportunity to teach
and maintain its own graduates.

The establishment of the occasional Rosc (poetry of vision) exhibitions in 1967 is often seen as an important moment in the internation-
alisation of the Irish art world. The display of large works from the USA
and from across Europe had a considerable impact on those concerned
with the status of the visual in Ireland. Although Rosc can be criticised
for its preoccupations with form over content and internationalism for
its own sake, these exhibitions did set a conceptual agenda and they
asked Irish people to reassess their need for a visual culture. The exhibitions continued until 1988 and were varied in the extreme. On the
one hand, there was the up-to-date amalgam of current work produced
across the world, often interspersed with exhibits by such Irish artists as
James Coleman (1977), Louis le Brocquy (1980) and in the last Rosc, Mary
FitzGerald (1988). At the same time the Rosc organisers offered alternative exhibitions (often in non-Dublin venues) on historical themes: pre-
twelfth-century Irish stone carvings (Dublin, 1967); pre-800 CE Animal
Art (Dublin, 1977); 'Irish Art in the Nineteenth Century' (Cork, 1971);
'Jack B. Yeats and his Family' (Sligo, 1971). Such displays revolutionised
an awareness of a visual tradition. Concurrent with these events was an
expanding buying policy for historical Irish works by institutions such
as the National Gallery of Ireland in Dublin and the Ulster Museum in
Belfast. Gradually a visual history was beginning to be articulated with
the establishment of art history departments in both Trinity College
Dublin and University College Dublin.

With the growing numbers of private art galleries in many Irish cities, nd the creation of publicly funded contemporary art spaces such as the ouglas Hyde Galley and eventually the Irish Museum of Modern Art 1 1991, the story of Ireland's attitude to the visual arts is very differnt today from that in 1801. In that year of Union with Britain, apart om a month-long exhibition in the old Parliament House which consted mainly of portraits, the only other form of recorded visual display a Dublin was Robert Ker Porter's panorama of imperial success in the ooden rotunda. Two hundred years later Ireland boasts one of the most acrative art prizes in the world (Glen Dimplex Artists Award, since 1994), hile the nation's leading visual arts magazine, *Circa*, is hard pressed to arry reports on all the art shows that come and go in the capital city and roughout the island.

Although commercially viable and promoted by national agencies, ish art from the 1960s onwards still raises problems regarding the ongog relationship between Ireland and the outside world. Artists active om the 1950s to the 1970s, such as Patrick Collins and Camille Souter, ave been discussed in terms of how their work exhibits a 'Celtic' imagiation. Many artists of the period, it has been argued, focused on landcape and on the vicissitudes of Irish light, which, according to Brian 'Doherty, gave Irish art an independence that it rarely exhibited under olonial rule. Such praise, especially as it came from a New York based ritic (albeit an Irish émigré), was indeed welcome in an Ireland that was rying to turn itself into a modern nation, and that had in 1972 signed he treaty of accession to the European Economic Community. Yet such focus on a Celtic mystique can also be read as a retrogressive development. O'Doherty has celebrated Irish localism as opposed to international dependency. The argument suggests that Ireland's overwhelming ural environment can only sustain an art that is driven by an organic mpulse:

> The best works . . . have an independence that is not obtuse, avoiding
> the provincialism of the right (nationalism) and the provincialism of
> the left (modernism), They show that the successful local artist has to
> be as intelligent as any modernist, and perhaps even more self-
> conscious, since he has more to think about.[9]

et such an argument, as Tom Duddy has eloquently argued, lessens Irish rtistic output and turns it into a weak and somewhat unimaginative isual tradition. It maintains an aura of mystification and throws a Celtic

haze over Irish art that denies economic reality and the growth of a com
mercially viable artistic world from the 1960s onwards.[10]

Irish art production has rarely thrived on localism. It has either sat
isfied London fashions as in the nineteenth century or it has kept ar
intelligent eye on international developments and responded accord
ingly. Irish art after the 1980s is produced in a confident and financially
assured world. The artists are better trained, enjoy a world outlook and
are concerned with contemporary issues. A striking feature of recent ar
production has been the pre-eminence of women artists. This is not a
novel phenomenon but it has taken on a new dynamism in the work o
Kathy Prendergast, Alice Maher and Dorothy Cross. From Mainie Jellet
in the 1920s to 1940s and Norah McGuinness and Nano Reid in the 1950s
Ireland has not been short of female art producers, but today's generation
offers a more confrontational approach in their focus on gender imagery
All of these artists, Prendergast, Maher and Cross, have represented
Ireland at prestigious international exhibitions and have enjoyed continued success.

A concern with contemporary issues is equally striking in the work
of artists coming out of Northern Ireland. In *Segregation*, of 1989 (Fig. 17.3
Rita Duffy uses portrait-like forms to drive home her message about division. Education in Northern Ireland is seen as being dominated by stern
faces that refuse to contemplate integration. Duffy's work is often severe
and harsh, yet she revels in differences. By contrast, humour tends to be
the dominant aspect of the work of John Kindness who works in many
media. *Sectarian Armour* (Fig. 17.4) is just one example of his abiding focus
on the divisions within the Irish story. Using sheets of gilded steel he
has etched images from Ireland's two cultural groups to create a decorated, denim-like jacket that asks us to realise the futility of abiding shib-
boleths. On the front we see the bank-note effigy of Queen Elizabeth II
confronted by a haloed Madonna and Child. A British bull-dog faces an
Irish pig, while on the rear Gerry Adams, President of Sinn Féin, turns
his back on Ian Paisley, leader of the Democratic Unionist Party, both
associated (in the past at any rate) with republican and loyalist paramilitaries, respectively. 'In a parody', as Kindness himself has written, 'of the
famous Levis' logo', Adams and Paisley lead a horse each but are in fact
pulling 'the whole garment apart at the seams'.[11] Duffy's individuals are
mothers and children as well as ideologues, while Kindness creates his
visual juxtapositions on the sartorial emblem of the working-class youth
the denim jacket. In an important development in Irish visual arts, both
artists offer serious political comment about life as lived on the street.

7.3 Rita Duffy, *Segregation*, 1989, oil on gesso panel, Crawford Municipal Art Gallery, Cork © Rita Duffy

Conclusion

In the early years of the twentieth-first century, Irish art is in a healthy state. Young artists from both the Republic and Northern Ireland take up PS1 awards (sponsored by the Arts Councils of the Republic of Ireland and Northern Ireland in association with the Irish American Cultural Institute) which provide a year's studio space in New York,

17.4 John Kindness, *Sectarian Armour*, 1995, etched gilded steel, Imperial War Museum, London © John Kindness

.5 Louis le Brocquy, *A Family*, 1951, oil on canvas, National Gallery of Ireland,
ublin © Louis le Brocquy

hile more seasoned artists are now a regular feature at the Venice Bien-
ale. Kathy Prendergast won the Premio in 2000, an indicator if any is
eeded that localism has not dominated recent Irish art. More recently,
Villie Doherty was nominated for the Turner Prize 2003, the second time
e has been short-listed for this prestigious contemporary art award.
oherty, whose work hovers between the safety and danger of life in
Iorthern Ireland, has also been the subject of a major international one-
aan retrospective that originated in the Irish Museum of Modern Art
2001). Working mainly in photography, video and film, some of his most
cent photographs have seen him move beyond the divided world of
Iorthern Ireland to a period of time in Berlin, that other great divided
pace of recent European history.

That need to look beyond the confines of Ireland, yet still be deeply
nvolved in the nation, has in fact been a key aspect in the life and works of
ouis le Brocquy, whose group nude painting *A Family* of 1951 (Fig. 17.5)
lso won a Venice Biennale prize back in 1956. Le Brocquy's large paint-
ng has only recently returned to Ireland after a half century of exile
n Milan. The reason for such a long delay was due to the fact that its

bequest in the early 1950s to the artist's native city was turned down. The nervous Advisory Committee of Dublin Corporation's Municipal Gallery of Modern Art blanched at the unflinching nudity and Cold War pessimism of the image. But now Le Brocquy's sombre canvas with its urban greys and blacks is the centrepiece of the National Gallery of Ireland's Millennium wing, and can be ironically interpreted as a visual symbol of Ireland's preoccupation with its European role and its status as a liberal democracy.

Notes

1. Letter from Treasury to Henry Doyle, 30 December 1872 (Dublin: National Gallery of Ireland Archives).
2. Tim Barringer, *The Pre-Raphaelites* (London: Everyman Art Library, 1998), p. 127.
3. Margaret MacCurtain, 'The real Molly Macree', in *Visualizing Ireland: National Identity and the Pictorial Tradition*, ed. Adele M. Dalsimer (Boston and London: Faber and Faber, 1983), p. 20.
4. The Friends of the National Collections of Ireland, *The City's Art – the Original Municipal Collection. Catalogue* (Dublin: Hugh Lane Municipal Gallery of Modern Art, 1984), pp. 17–19.
5. Cyril Barrett, 'Irish nationalism and art 1800–1921', *Studies* 64, 256 (Winter 1975), 408.
6. David Lloyd, *Anomalous States: Irish Writing and the Post-Colonial Moment* (Dublin: The Lilliput Press, 1993), pp. 136–44.
7. I am grateful to Mary Clark of Dublin City Archives for this information.
8. Ernie O'Malley, 'The paintings of Jack B. Yeats', 1945, in *Sources in Irish Art: A Reader*, ed. Fintan Cullen (Cork: Cork University Press, 2000), pp. 138–9.
9. Brian O'Doherty, 'The native heritage', in *The Irish Imagination, 1959–1971* (Dublin: Rosc, 1971), p. 20.
10. Tom Duddy, 'Irish art criticism – a provincialism of the right?', in Cullen (ed.) *Sources*, pp. 91–100.
11. John Kindness, *Circa* 76 (1996), 6; Kindness was responding to Fintan Cullen, 'Confronting multiculturalism', *Circa* 75 (1996), 22.

Further reading

Circa Art Magazine (Belfast and Dublin, 1981); ongoing, see www.recirca.com
Anne Crookshank and the Knight of Glin, *Ireland's Painters 1600–1940* (New Haven and London: Yale University Press, 2002)
Fintan Cullen, *Visual Politics. The Representation of Ireland, 1750–1930* (Cork: Cork University Press, 1997)
    Sources in Irish Art: A Reader (Cork: Cork University Press, 2000)
    'Union and display in nineteenth-century Ireland', in *Cultural Identities and the Aesthetics of Britishness*, ed. Dana Arnold (Manchester: Manchester University Press, 2004)

dele M. Dalsimer (ed.), *Visualizing Ireland. National Identity and the Pictorial Tradition* (Boston and London: Faber and Faber, 1993)

om Dunne, '"One of the tests of national character": Britishness and Irishness in paintings by Barry and Maclise', in *Hearts and Minds: Irish Culture and Society Under the Act of Union*, ed. Bruce Stewart (Gerrards Cross: Colin Smythe, 2002), pp. 260–290

licola Figgis and Brendan Rooney, *Irish Paintings in the National Gallery of Ireland*, vol. I (Dublin: National Gallery of Ireland, 2001)

nnifer Grinnell and Alison Conley (eds.), *Re/Dressing Cathleen: Contemporary Works from Irish Women Artists* (Boston: McMullen Museum of Art, Boston College, 1997)

iam Kelly, *Thinking Long: Contemporary Art in the North of Ireland* (Kinsale: Gandon Editions, 1996)

. B. Kennedy, *Irish Art and Modernism, 1880–1950* (Belfast: Institute of Irish Studies at Queen's University Belfast, 1991)

aul Larmour, *The Arts and Crafts Movement in Ireland* (Belfast: Friar's Bush Press, 1992)

eanne Sheehy, *The Rediscovery of Ireland's Past: The Celtic Revival, 1830–1920* (London: Thames and Hudson, 1980)

heo Snoddy, *Dictionary of Irish Artists, Twentieth Century* (Dublin: Wolfhound Press, 1996)

ames Christen Steward (ed.), *When Time Began to Rant and Rage: Figurative Painting from Twentieth-Century Ireland* (London: Merrell Holberton, 1998)

)orothy Walker, *Modern Art in Ireland* (Dublin: Lilliput Press, 1997)

18

Irish theatre

Considered from the perspective of the early twenty-first century, when plays by Irish writers can be seen on stages from Los Angeles to Warsaw, it is difficult to imagine Irish culture without the theatre. However, if we turn back to the first major histories of the Irish theatre, published in the closing decades of the eighteenth century, we find them troubled by an awareness that the theatre does not fit easily into the prevailing definitions of Irish culture.

This problem is best defined by one of the foundational works of Irish theatre history, Joseph Cooper Walker's 'An Historical Essay on the Irish Stage', published by the Royal Irish Academy in 1788. Walker was a respected antiquarian who had published his 'Historical Memoirs of the Irish Bards' two years earlier. He was one of a number of antiquarians and historians of the period who sought to recover indigenous forms of Irish architecture, music, poetry, graphic design, sports, clothing and civil law. In all of these areas, the ancient Irish past seemed to be an almost inexhaustible source, connecting the emerging modern nation with an authenticating history. 'Can that nation be deemed barbarous in which learning shared the honours next to royalty?' asks Walker in one of the more passionate moments in his 'Memoirs of the Irish Bards'. 'Read this, ye polished nations of the earth, and blush!'[1] However, when Walker and his contemporaries looked for traces of theatre in Irish antiquity, they found nothing. 'It is very extraordinary that we cannot discover any vestiges of the Drama amongst the remains of the Irish Bards', comments Walker. 'If the Stage ever existed in Ireland previous to the middle ages, like the "baseless fabric of a vision" it has melted into air, leaving not a trace behind.'[2]

As Alan Fletcher has recently shown, while there were many forms of
erformance in medieval Ireland – from bards capable of reciting long,
ɔmplex poems, to contortionists and acrobats – there was not really the-
ɹre, as such. Indeed, the first public theatre in Ireland was opened in
ublin's Werburgh Street, probably in 1635,[3] by the lord lieutenant of
ɪe time, Thomas Wentworth, as an appurtenance of the viceregal court.
his close link between the theatre and Dublin Castle was to continue
ter the Restoration, and into the eighteenth and nineteenth centuries.
'riting of the commercial necessity of viceregal visits to the theatre in
ɪe early nineteenth century, the playwright John O'Keeffe noted that
hen the 'vice-regal presence fills the boxes, all other parts must then
ɹ full'.[4] Consequently, while almost every other aspect of Irish culture
ɔuld claim an authenticating, pre-Conquest genealogy, the theatre in
'eland was not only lacking in antiquity, it was a cultural form intro-
ɹced – and, to a certain extent, maintained – by the colonial adminis-
ation in Ireland. No matter how Irish its subject matter (and through-
ɹt the eighteenth century there were attempts to write plays based on
ish history and mythology), the theatre, *as a form*, was never going to
t a comfortably into a definition of Irishness that demanded an ancient
aelic pedigree.

Contrary to what one might think, however, the absence of an authen-
cating past for Irish theatre was not necessarily disabling for theatre
ractitioners; on the contrary, the blatant modernity of the theatre in
'eland could be liberating. While unwary Irish poets, or musicians,
r architects in the early nineteenth century could find themselves
ɪsnarled in scholastic debates over their fidelity to tradition, Irish play-
'rights and theatre managers had no such worries. Although there had
een Irish characters on the stage since the late sixteenth century, they
ɛre theatrical conventions, and recognised as such from the outset. This
ɪeant that by the time John O'Keeffe, for instance, began writing plays
'ith Irish settings in the late eighteenth century – notably *The Poor Soldier*
782) or *The Wicklow Mountains* (1795) – he could draw from a set of recog-
isable Irish character types: the full spectrum of blundering-but-canny
:age Irishmen and comely colleens, the kindly landlord (usually with a
assion for hunting), the hot-headed Irish duellist, the *raisonneur* priest,
ɪe good-hearted British soldier. To these would be added others: the
illainous land agent, the villainous rapparee, the noble rapparee, and
ɪe informer.

For much of the eighteenth century, these characters had made individual cameo appearances in plays set outside of Ireland, usually as servants or comic relief: Sir Lucius O'Trigger in Richard Brinsley Sheridan's *The Rivals* (1775) is a well-known example. However, in the plays of O'Keeffe, they all come together, and we are reminded of Umberto Eco's famous comment on *Casablanca*: 'Two clichés make us laugh but a hundred clichés move us.'[5] Although O'Keeffe's plays date from the late eighteenth century, they point the way to a nineteenth-century theatre in which conventional characters and plots could be combined in ways that facilitated the new stage technology that was transforming what had been an actor's theatre into a theatre of spectacle. Ireland, of course, was handsomely endowed with a spectacular, indeed sublime, landscape, and the theatres of the nineteenth century were perfectly suited to creating sets in which ruined abbeys shimmered in gas-lit moonlight against a painted backcloth of gorse-covered hills or sea-cliffs. Similarly, as music became increasingly important in nineteenth-century theatre (the word 'melo-drama', first appeared in 1802 to describe plays which had musical accompaniment throughout), Ireland was once again conveniently well stocked with 'airs' that could be adapted to a variety of dramatic situations by a theatre orchestra. When all of these elements combined – as they did in O'Keeffe's *The Poor Soldier* – what became known simply as 'the Irish play' was born.

By the time the English playwright John Baldwin Buckstone's Irish play, *The Green Bushes*, was staged at London's Adelphi Theatre on 27 January 1845, it was no longer necessary to be Irish to write an Irish play, and *Green Bushes* was simply one genre piece among the more than two hundred Buckstone wrote in his lifetime. The elements of which a play such as *Green Bushes* is composed are all entirely conventional. It opens thus:

> An Irish Fair. Tents discovered, composed of old blankets and tattered canvas – over the largest booth is a board, on which is written – 'Paddy Kelly, Dealer in all sorts of Liquors'. Paddy Kelly discovered in his tent serving liquor to three or four peasants. A loud shot and laughter.

We later meet characters such as colleen Nelly O'Neil (dressed in 'dark blue stockings, thick shoes with large silver buckles, short red cloth petticoat') and the stage Irishman, Murtogh ('old coloured stockings, one down . . . velveteen breeches, grey great coat, coarse ragged shirt, three cornered torn hat, rough wig').[6] With minor variations, these characters

nd settings reappear in dozens of Irish plays from the period, where they
ere recognised and welcomed by audiences as late as the mid 1920s. As
he most successful writer of Irish plays, Dion Boucicault, was later to put
:: 'Playmaking is a trade like carpentering. Originality, speaking by the
ard, is a quality that never existed.'[7]

Freed from the constraints of originality and representation, the
rish play in the nineteenth century proliferated, and became a global-
sed form. Probably the most successful Irish play of the century, Dion
oucicault's *The Colleen Bawn*, was written and premiered in New York,
as a hit in London, applauded in Dublin as heralding a 'new era in
rish character',[8] and later toured to Canada, Australia and New Zealand.
n this it was not unusual at a time when the theatrical world was
ominated by global touring circuits.

The effects of globalisation on the Irish play were to be complex.
)n one hand, if it was to reach as wide an audience as possible, the
rish play had to avoid extreme political perspectives, with the conse-
uence that most moved towards the conciliatory endings common in the
iction of the period, in which Anglo-Irish relations achieve a symbolic
esolution in the marriage of an Irish colleen and a well-intentioned
Englishman. At the same time, as the Irish diaspora made its presence
elt in theatres from Broadway to Melbourne, there was growing demand
or more overtly nationalistic material, which could be highlighted or cut
s the venue demanded. For instance, when Boucicault's *Arrah-na-Pogue*
set during the United Irishmen's rising of 1798) was played in Dublin
s a command performance for the Lord Lieutenant on 25 November
864, a rebel song originally included in the script – 'The Wearing of the
sreen' – was judiciously omitted, and replaced by a long speech in which
he kindly landlord, Colonel O'Grady, acquits Shaun the Post (played by
Boucicault) of a robbery of which he had been falsely accused.[9]

In the wake of the Fenian rising a few years later, however, Irish
udiences – whether in Manhattan, Liverpool or Dublin's Theatre Royal –
vere becoming less happy with reconciliatory endings, and a later
seneration of playwrights and theatre managers, including Edmund
'alconer, Hubert O'Grady, J. W. Whitbread and (in the twentieth cen-
ury), P. J. Bourke would take the Irish play in more militant direc-
ions. From the 1880s onwards, plays such as O'Grady's *The Fenian* (1888),
r Whitbread's *Theobald Wolfe Tone* (1898) were performed at Dublin's
Jueen's Royal Theatre ('The Home of Irish Drama'), before being toured
round the world. Unlike *Green Bushes*, the pleasures of these plays were

not to be found in a fictionalised reconciliation between England and Ireland, but in the exposure (and often execution) of a traitor against Ireland, almost invariably an informer.

As the Irish play moved closer to the culture of militant Irish nationalism, its overt conventionality, its globalised networks of production and reception and its disabling lack of an authenticating ancient genealogy became increasingly problematic. 'Though we are not prepared to accept *Lord Edward* or *Wolfe Tone* as ideal Irish plays', commented Arthur Griffith's *United Irishman* in March of 1899, 'they are certainly steps in the right direction.'[10] Two months after Griffith's newspaper made these comments, the Irish Literary Theatre staged its first production – *The Countess Cathleen*, by W. B. Yeats and Lady Gregory – and there is a sense in which the project of the Irish Literary Theatre can be understood as an assault on precisely the conditions in which the Irish play of the nineteenth century had thrived.

If the Irish play of the nineteenth century had been a globalised form with an industrial mode of production, the Irish Literary Theatre, by contrast, was to be a local theatre, produced in an artisanal mode. 'We hope to find in Ireland an uncorrupted and imaginative audience trained to listen by its passion for oratory', wrote the theatre's founders, W. B. Yeats, Lady Gregory and Edward Martyn, in 1897. 'We will show that Ireland is not the home of buffoonery or of easy sentiment, as it has been represented, but the home of an ancient idealism.'[11] By first of all conjuring up 'an uncorrupted and imaginative audience' (and thereby nullifying three centuries of theatre-going), and then accusing the nineteenth-century play of 'misrepresentation' (even though it had proliferated precisely because it had never seriously concerned itself with representation), the manifesto also signals an attack on the Irish theatre's lack of authenticity. In its next phrase, however, this key document proposes a solution to the problems it identifies: if the theatre in Ireland could not be genuinely ancient, it could at least be 'the home of an ancient idealism'.

Throughout its first decade, the Irish Literary Theatre (which later became the Irish National Theatre Society, Ltd., known as the Abbey Theatre), addressed these fundamental problems posed by Irish theatre history in a number of different ways. Yeats, working with the actors Frank and Willie Fay, quickly developed a performance style whose keynote was simplicity. Working on sparse sets composed in only two or three colours, the actors of the early Abbey developed an acting

yle which eschewed the gestures and vocal acrobatics of an earlier
eneration for stillness and clear, rhythmic attention to language. Apart
om any aesthetic attraction this may have held, it moved theatrical
roduction back into an artisanal mode. No theatre producer faced with
ie expensive set-pieces of a play like *The Colleen Bawn* (whose highlight
ivolves a rescue in the Lakes of Killarney) was going to take a chance
ı an unknown writer or actor; on the other hand, amateurs work-
ıg in a hired room with a homemade set could afford to try out new
riters or actors. Consequently, the Abbey (and its precursors) staged
ıore than sixty original plays in its first decade, and the theatre would
ıntinue to receive hundreds of unsolicited scripts for many years to
ıme. It also launched the careers of some of the most important Irish
:tors of the first half of the twentieth century, including Sara All-
ıod, the Fays, and later F. J. McCormick and Barry Fitzgerald. Equally,
ıe simplicity of this model of theatrical production inspired parallel
ramatic movements in Cork (the Cork Dramatic Society) and in Belfast
ıe Ulster Literary Theatre), both of which were to produce their own
:gional bodies of dramatic writing.

Yeats and his colleagues tackled the problem of the absence of
ı authenticating past for the Irish theatre with equal vigour. At a
me when Irish poetry, music and sport were being reinvigorated
y a rediscovered Gaelic past, the lack of a Gaelic past to be rediscovered
ır the theatre was dealt with through a simple, if bold, expedient: invent
ne in the present. So, the third season of the Irish Literary Theatre,
ı October 1901, included the first professionally produced play in the
ish language, Douglas Hyde's *Casadh an tSúgáin*. In most forms of Irish
ıltural history, Irish-language culture is seen as preceding English-
ınguage culture. If this relation of precedence was not possible in Irish
ıeatre history, it was still possible to deal with an inconvenient lacuna
y filling it retrospectively. Similarly, if the Irish theatre lacked a usable
ıedieval theatre, there was no reason that one could not be supplied
ı 1900, and so Douglas Hyde, Lady Gregory, Yeats, and later Patrick
earse, frequently took medieval mystery and morality plays as their
ramaturgical models. By the same token, if there was no theatrical
quivalent to *The Táin*, there was no reason not to make up the deficiency
ith a genre of mythological plays, such as Alice Milligan's *Last Feast of
ıe Fianna* (1900). 'It is possible we may hear on the stage, not merely the
ıimicry of human speech', announced George Russell in 1902, 'but the
ıd forgotten music which was heard in the duns of kings, which made

revellers grow silent and great warriors to bow low their faces in their hands.'[12]

None of these attempts to forge an authenticating theatrical tradition was to develop in quite the way that their proponents had imagined. For instance, the amount of Irish language theatre performed in Ireland – particularly at the Abbey – would be negligible for several decades, in spite of the efforts of individuals such as Piaras Béaslaí who formed his own Irish-language theatre touring company in 1913. Similarly, the mythological play would be something of a dramaturgical cul-de-sac for everyone other than Yeats, who would cross-fertilise it with Japanese Nōh to produce his distinctive later plays, including The Only Jealousy of Emer (1919) and the posthumous Death of Cuchulain (1939), neither of which would be popular successes with Irish theatre audiences. Indeed, the form was being heartily parodied by the Ulster Literary Theatre as early as 1912, in Gerald Macnamara's popular farce Thompson in Tir-na-nÓg, in which a common-sense Orangeman inexplicably finds himself in the company of figures from Irish mythology. Instead, the most effective strategy for linking the Irish theatre with tradition was to set plays in an Irish countryside where markers of temporality could be blurred, thereby creating the genre that was to dominate the Irish theatre for more than half a century: the peasant play.

The attractions of the peasant play were many, largely because it was less a formal genre than a milieu in which pre-existing genres could be reconfigured. Again, Hyde's Casadh an tSúgáin, with its cottage kitchen set, is a defining text (regardless of its language). Not only does it establish scenographic conventions, but its basic narrative of a rural family, disrupted by an outsider, would be reworked many times, in a trope that Nicholas Grene has aptly called 'the stranger in the house' motif.[13] Yeats's revolutionary parable, Cathleen ni Houlihan (1902), is in many respects very different from Casadh an tSúgáin, particularly in its emblematic title character, who lures a young man away from a wedding to die for Ireland; and yet, the play uses the same narrative trope, and could be staged on more or less the same set and with the same costumes as Hyde's comedy, as could T. C. Murray's sombre rural drama, Birthright (1910), or one of the most popular comedies in the Abbey's history, George Shiels's Professor Tim (1925). The same is also true of the major plays of John Millington Synge.

Synge's Playboy of the Western World (1907) made audiences aware of the pitfalls inherent in attempting to read a living culture as the embodiment f a past tradition. When the rural community in Synge's play welcomes a murderer, it exposes the dangerous malleability of a recently reconstructed history, with the result that the play was met with riots during its first week, in which there were calls of 'that's not the West'. However, while the riots are well known, it is often forgotten how quickly afterwards the play settled into the Abbey repertoire, becoming, (after a few more riots while on an American tour in 1911) the most frequently performed full-length play in the theatre's history. If nothing else, this suggests that most audiences shared with earlier writers like Boucicault an ability to accept the play's fictiveness; in the long term, whether or not Synge's *Playboy* accurately represented 'the West' as a living embodiment of history was less important for urban audiences than its effectiveness as a play.

The *Playboy* riots were also part of the final working out of the Irish theatre's relationship with Dublin Castle. The Irish National Theatre Society existed in the first place because an amendment to the Local Government Act of 1898 (61 & 62 Vict.) allowed the Lord Lieutenant to grant occasional performance licences to charitable organizations – and consequently the Lord Lieutenant's signature authorised every performance of the early Abbey. Lionel Pilkington has argued convincingly that when the Abbey directorate defied the predominantly nationalist protestors who objected to Synge's *Playboy*, it was part of a complex negotiation with Dublin Castle to define the place of Ascendancy culture in a changing political situation. 'You have earned the gratitude of the whole community' a prominent unionist judge wrote to Lady Gregory: 'You are the only people with the pluck to stand up against this organized intimidation in Dublin.'[14] Conversely, when the Abbey deliberately embarrassed the Lord Lieutenant, Lord Aberdeen, in 1909, by staging George Bernard Shaw's *The Shewing up of Blanco Posnet* (which the Lord Chamberlain's Office in England had banned), the Abbey directors were sending a clear message that they were not to be taken for granted, while simultaneously courting any potential Home Rule administration-in-waiting.

Underlying all of this manoeuvring was an awareness that had existed in Ireland since the eighteenth century: that a producing theatre could not exist without some form of subsidy, whether in the form of patronage or direct financial intervention. Consequently, when the Irish theatre's relationship with Dublin Castle was abruptly terminated by the establishment of the Irish Free State in 1922, it was entirely consistent that the Abbey would court the new administration, leading to the grant of an annual subsidy of £850 in 1925. While it is arguable that the granting of a subsidy saved the Abbey from complete collapse, its new status as state theatre was to limit its scope for formal experimentation and social critique. Indeed, the problems that were to face the Abbey over the next two and a half decades were made clear in 1926, when the final play in Sean O'Casey's Dublin Trilogy was premiered at the Abbey. The first two plays in the Trilogy – *The Shadow of the Gunman* (1923), *Juno and the Paycock* (1924) – dealing with the War of Independence and the Civil War, had had a powerful effect on Irish audiences in the 1920s, by 'making palpable the atmosphere of modern warfare when ordinary people's lives are invaded by violence and terrorism', as Christopher Murray puts it. At the same time, their caustic, uncompromising, humanist critique of political violence was to pose difficulties for the Abbey at a time when it was attempting to establish itself as the state theatre of a state founded on all-too-recent violence. So, when *The Plough and the Stars* – which is set during the 1916 Rising – was first performed, it was met with protest from anti-Free State republicans. Nonetheless, like Synge's *Playboy* before it, O'Casey's Dublin plays quickly established themselves as core part of the Abbey's repertoire, where they were to provide the dramaturgical models for a genre of plays dealing with the conflict in Northern Ireland forty-five years later.

The controversy over *The Plough and the Stars* exemplifies the difficulties faced by a state theatre in staging plays that were in any way critical of the state or its founding myths. Occasionally, however, a voice of dissent broke through. For instance, Teresa Deevey began writing for the Abbey in the early 1930s, and in plays such as *A Disciple* (1931) and *Katie Roche* (1936), she creates a series of female protagonists caught in a post-Independence Ireland which seems designed to rob them of their freedom as women. Indeed, in *The King of Spain's Daughter* (1935), she finds a vivid theatrical metaphor for the restrictive life led by so many Irish women in the period, setting her play on a barricaded road, the stage dominated by a large sign reading 'Road Closed'. However, in spite of her growing posthumous reputation, her final work for the stage – *Wife to James Whelan* – was rejected by the Abbey in 1937, and she turned to writing for radio.

The theatre history of the mid-twentieth century in Ireland is filled with such false starts, often the product of revolutionary ideals calcified into orthodoxies. This was particularly true of the period from 1941 until

e early 1960s, when the Abbey was managed by Ernest Blythe, who
w the national theatre as an instrument of state policy. Blythe was a
mmitted supporter of the Irish language, who made strenuous efforts
pick up the unfulfilled promise of an Irish-language theatre, introduc-
g a policy that required all members of the Abbey company to be fluent
ish-speakers, and encouraging the development of an Irish-language
pertoire. While few people would have questioned the value of creat-
g a theatre in Irish, Blythe's efforts are still recalled with rancour, and
en the most ardent language activists were wary of the Abbey's annual
ish-language Christmas pantomime, in which audiences were regaled
ith Irish translations of popular songs such as 'Chatanooga-Choo-
hoo'.

Consequently, from the late 1920s onwards, the energies of the
ish theatre spread beyond the Abbey. In the case of Irish-language
eatre, the focus moved westward, with the founding of An Taibhdhearc
Galway by Micheál Mac Líammóir, Hilton Edwards and Liam Ó
riain. Opening with Mac Líammóir's *Diarmuid agus Gráinne* in 1928, An
aibhdhearc developed an extensive repertoire of Irish-language theatre,
erforming both translations and original works, and introducing writ-
rs such as Máiréad Ní Ghráda, who was to be active until the mid-1960s.
rom 1923 to 1942, the Galway theatre was joined by the Dublin-based
n Comhar Drámuíochta, who made use of the Abbey's second stage, the
eacock; and from 1955 to 1970, by An Chulb Drámaíochta, working from
e Damer Theatre in Dublin, where they premièred Brendan Behan's *An
iall* (*The Hostage*) in 1958.

Similarly, in terms of theatre technique, the most innovative exper-
nents in staging were to be found not at the Abbey, but at Dublin's
ate Theatre, founded in the same year as An Taibhdhearc by the same
air of actors, Hilton Edwards and Micheál Mac Líammóir. Reviving
orks such as Oscar Wilde's *Salomé* (Gate production 1928), which had
ever been staged in Ireland during Wilde's lifetime, the Gate not only
rovided a venue for exploring theatrical form, it also opened up issues
f gender and sexuality that the increasingly orthodox administration of
e Abbey dared not consider.

As part of this same drift away from the institutionalised centre,
om the early 1930s onward there was a burgeoning of amateur com-
anies throughout the island, leading to the creation of an All Ireland
rama Festival in 1953. While many of these companies relied on the
easant comedies that had become staple fare at the Abbey, others were

more adventurous, and many of the period's leading actors, and at least two important writers of the 1950s – M. J. Molloy and John B. Keane – were largely reliant on amateur productions at key moments in their careers.

Indeed, for many years the distinction between amateurs and professionals in the Irish theatre world was hazy, and the flourishing of the amateur movement was accompanied by a growing number of small professional and semi-professional companies. In Belfast, the Lyric Theatre (founded in 1951) was to develop from a tiny amateur company with a special commitment to verse plays, into something approaching a state theatre for Northern Ireland, with all of the difficulties that would come with such a situation. In Dublin, a number of small theatres appeared in the 1950s, including the Pike Theatre, which staged Brendan Behan's first major English-language work, *The Quare Fellow* (1954), and gave Samuel Beckett's *Waiting for Godot* its Irish première in 1955.

Anthony Roche has argued that Beckett is 'the presiding genius of contemporary Irish drama, the ghostly founding father',[16] and there is a very real sense in which *Waiting for Godot* defines the territory (if not the theatrical language) of much that would follow on the Irish stage. Opening only a few years before the Industrial Development Act of 1958, *Godot* appeared in an Ireland about to enter several decades of quick-step modernisation. Increasingly anxious to forget (or, at least, sanitise) its fractured past, particularly in relation to Partition, and fretfully trying to imagine its future, the Ireland that stepped into the 1960s bore more than a little resemblance to two tramps, alone on an empty road, uncertain about what had happened yesterday, contemplating an equally uncertain tomorrow.

In more than one way, Beckett's play is emblematic of its time. *Godot* is pre-eminently a play about one of the formal properties of theatre in performance: its existence in a perpetual present. 'On the stage it is always *now*', theatre semiotician Keir Elam reminds us.[17] As such, the theatre provides an ideal form in which to explore the weightless modernity into which Ireland entered in the early 1960s, suspended in a seemingly perpetual present between past and future. Where the lack of an ancient Gaelic pedigree had been so troubling to the founders of the Abbey at the beginning of the twentieth century, by the early 1960s Irish theatre practitioners had the opposite problem. As early as 1936, critic Gabriel Fallon had noted that people are beginning 'to speak of the Abbey *tradition*. One day someone asked the awkward question: "Is the present

ompany as good as the old one?" And then it was discovered for the
first time that the Abbey had a *past*.'[18] Constant comparisons with a
sepia-tinged past generated a growing impatience with the theatrical
heritage created in the early years of the Irish Literary Theatre. The visible
sign of this dissatisfaction was the opening in 1966 of the new Abbey
Theatre building designed in a pure modernist style by Michael Scott.
This belatedly replaced the original structure, which had burned in 1951.
Moving into a new building, suggested director Tomás Mac Anna, would
provide 'an opportunity of breaking with a certain tradition of writing.'[19]
Equally important was the founding of the Dublin Theatre Festival in
1957, which brought an awareness of international trends to a hitherto
relatively insular theatre community.

The sense of cutting free from tradition was evident in the energy
of Irish-language theatre in the 1960s, which increasingly disentangled
itself from its association with a folk tradition to address contemporary
issues in plays such as Máiréad Ní Ghráda's *An Triail* (1964) or Criostóir
Ó Floinn's *Aggioramento* (1968), a satire about the effects of Vatican II.
Equally, in English-language theatre, the early 1960s saw the emergence
of a generation of playwrights whose attitude to tradition differed
sharply from their predecessors, in that they found it oppressive (Tom
Murphy, in *A Whistle in the Dark*, 1961; John B. Keane, *Sive*, 1959), unknow-
able (Brian Friel, *Philadelphia, Here I Come!*, 1964), or farcically irrelevant to
the present (Hugh Leonard, *Patrick Pearse Motel*, 1971).

Each of these four major playwrights, whose work was to dominate
Irish theatre into the twenty-first century, began writing in the late 1950s,
and collectively their work charts the dialectic of tradition and modernity that was at the core of so many debates over Irish culture in the final
decades of the twentieth century. For John B. Keane, in plays like *Sive*, or
The Field (1965), writing from within the rural communities of the West
of Ireland that had been idealised at the turn of the century, the conflict of two sets of values is often tragic. The Bull McCabe, protagonist
of *The Field*, is a struggling small farmer who is the victim of both an
oppressive past and an emerging modernity that has no place for him;
at the same time, he is also a violent bully and a murderer – a tension that
creates an almost neoclassical tragic scenario. For Hugh Leonard, on the
other hand, writing in an urban setting, the transition between past and
present is usually gentler, more comic and tinged with nostalgia, as in his
best-known play, *Da* (1973), where the character of Charlie shares the perpetual present of the stage with his recently deceased father, the living

manifestation of an irrepressibly lively – and entertaining – past that
far from dead.

In the plays of Ireland's most successful dramatist since the 1960
Brian Friel, the condition of being suspended between past and presen
provides the occasion for a series of theatrical meditations on the exten
to which the past can be known. Usually presented in the contex
of apparently naturalistic plays (which owe an acknowledged debt t
Chekhov), Friel's characters typically find that only the living presen
is knowable and solid, while the past, mediated by the vagaries of lan
guage, is shifting and constantly revised. Friel would eventually crys
tallise his concerns with the ontology of the past in what is arguabl
his best play, *Faith Healer* (1979), composed entirely of monologues i
which three characters present conflicting versions of the same set c
events.

Tom Murphy's characters, by contrast, wear the scars of the pas
visibly on their bodies. In his plays of the 1960s, such as *A Whistle in th
Dark* (1961) and *Famine* (1968), they are overcome by the circumstances the
inherit. However, in the 1970s he began writing a series of plays that are
as Fintan O'Toole puts it, 'images of transformation rather than men
reflections of reality'.[20] In what is often considered to be Murphy's bes
play, *Bailegangaire* (1985), the audience find themselves facing a cottag
kitchen set, of the sort that had dominated the Abbey stage for much o
the century. Here, an old woman, Mommo, tells what appears to be a fol
tale, which initially seems to have no connection to the offstage worl
of foreign investment, electronics factories and motorcycles to whicl
her daughters belong. As the story unfolds, however, Murphy weaves
healing connection between a traumatic past and a maimed present
culminating in a tentative – yet clearly stated – moment of recognition
between mother and daughter, past and present.

This renegotiation of the past was given an added urgency in the 1970
and 1980s by the conflict in Northern Ireland. In an influential article in
Threshold, the journal published by the Lyric Theatre in Belfast, Seamu
Deane noted in 1982: 'After thirteen years of violence, Northern Ireland i
further from a solution and closer to disaster than it ever was. The mor
intractable the problem seems, the more we consign it to the realm of th
irrational, the purblind, the atavistic.'[21] Indeed, by the mid-1970s, it wa
possible to identify a distinct genre of play dealing with political violenc
in Northern Ireland, known as 'the Troubles play'. While owing mucl
structurally to O'Casey, this genre goes back to St John Ervine's *Mixe*

arriage in 1913, developing through plays such as Sam Thompson's *Over
e Bridge (1960), and emerging in its fully developed form in John Boyd's
he Flats, staged at the Lyric in 1971. However, as Deane and others argued,
.ther than confronting the causes of violence, the typical 'Troubles play'
.cused on the effects of violence, usually on a family, while the political
.ots of the problem remained offstage.

Moreover, there was dissatisfaction among many people in the theatre
.mmunity in Northern Ireland that their society should be defined
.lely by plays dealing with paramilitary conflict. Unfortunately, how-
.er, there was an infrastructural obstacle to theatrical exploration in the
.70s, in that all but a fraction of the theatre budgets of the Arts Councils
. the Republic and Northern Ireland went to three institutions in two
.ties – the Abbey and Gate in Dublin, and the Lyric in Belfast – and to a
.uring group, the Irish Theatre Company. This situation was to change
. the early 1980s, however, when the two Arts Councils made funds
.vailable for smaller companies, particularly outside the traditional
.eatre centres of Dublin and Belfast. The Druid Theatre Company in
.alway – who premièred Murphy's *Bailegangaire* – was one early benefi-
.ary of this policy; another was the Field Day Theatre company, founded
. Derry by Brian Friel and actor Stephen Rea.

Field Day's first production, Friel's *Translations* (1980), set at a moment
. transition from Irish to English in the 1830s, would continue the
.aywright's exploration of language as a medium that shapes (rather
.an passively records) experience. Later, branching out into publish-
.g, producing an influential series of pamphlets, Field Day was very
.uch situated in the North; however, beginning with *Translations*, the
.ompany's approach to the situation in Northern Ireland usually avoided
.e direct – if limited – representational strategies of the standard
'roubles play'. Instead, the company approached inter-community
.onflict from a series of oblique angles, in plays such as Thomas Kilroy's
.ouble Cross (1986). 'To base one's identity, exclusively, on a mystical sense
. place rather than in personal character where it properly resides seems
. me a dangerous absurdity', wrote Kilroy in the introduction to his
.ouble Cross. 'To dedicate one's life to the systematic betrayal of that
.leal seems to me equally absurd.'[22] This same attempt to balance
.e competing claims of communal and personal identity provides
.e driving force for a play originally intended for Field Day, Frank
.cGuinness's *Observe the Sons of Ulster Marching Towards the Somme*
.985), which is equally about the formative crucible of the First World

War for Ulster loyalist identity, and about personal relationships among
a group of men divided by class and sexual orientation.

Although there is no doubting the importance of Field Day in the
theatre culture of the 1980s, there is also a sense in which it belonged to
an earlier cultural formation; for, while it was based in Derry, it was a
touring company, whose work bore all the traces of attempting to bear
the burden of representing an entire nation, much as the Abbey had
done before it. Even while Field Day was at its peak, Irish theatre culture was diversifying, with theatre companies and practitioners opting
to explore particular theatrical forms or ideas in an Irish context, rather
than with defining Irishness *per se*. For instance, among the new theatre
companies formed in the early 1980s, the Belfast-based Charabanc was
founded by a group of women tired of 'playing Noras and Cathleens', as
one of their founders, Eleanor Methven, put it. Less interested in interpreting the Northern conflict than with providing good female roles in a
theatre culture which had long endured a dearth of women writers, the
company was to nurture at least two new writers in Christina Reid and
Marie Jones.

Hence, if there is any one dominant trend that can be identified
in Irish theatre since the beginning of the 1990s, it is that the expansion and diversification of theatre culture has lifted from any one writer
or company the burden of representing the entire nation, a responsibility felt so heavily by the Abbey theatre throughout the twentieth
century. Admittedly, some writers still continue to tackle big, culture-
defining topics, such as Frank McGuinness with *Mutabilitie* (1997), or
Marina Carr with *Ariel* (2002). However, much more common (and, in
some senses, successful), have been chamber pieces such as McGuinness's
Someone Who'll Watch Over Me (1992), Carr's *The Mai* (1994), or the monologues of Conor McPherson's characters, most notably in *The Weir*
(1997).

The diversification of the Irish theatre community is a tangible
physical phenomenon, with more than forty theatre companies scattered
throughout the island now receiving Arts Council funding, including
two dedicated Irish-language theatre companies, Amharclann de híde
in Dublin, and Aisling Ghéar in Belfast. Equally, however, the establishment of formal theatre training, particularly in third-level education,
is creating a generation of theatre practitioners for whom the most recent
international developments in multimedia or performance theory are
more familiar than stale quarrels over the true legacy of the Abbey. In

is freedom from the dictates of the past, and sense of their own place
a global theatre community, Irish theatre practitioners in the early
venty-first century resemble their ancestors at the beginning of the
ineteenth century, who created theatre in the absence of an authenticat-
g tradition – an absence which troubled early theatre historians such as
seph Cooper Walker. However, unlike those nineteenth-century actors
nd playwrights, Irish theatre workers today can choose, if they wish,
 draw upon aspects of a theatre tradition that was forged in the early
ears of the twentieth century, and which has now matured to the point at
hich it can accommodate diversity and formal change. The Irish theatre
as thus entered the new millennium neither fully obsessed with its own
ast, nor forgetful of its beginnings.

Notes

1. Joseph Cooper Walker, 'Memoirs of the Irish bards', quoted in Joep Leerssen, *Mere Irish and Fíor Ghael: Studies in the Idea of Irish Nationality, its Development and Literary Expression Prior to the Nineteenth Century* (Cork: Cork University Press, 1996), pp. 365, 374.

2. Joseph Cooper Walker, 'An historical essay on the Irish stage', *Transactions of the Royal Irish Academy* 2 (1788), 75.

3. There is controversy regarding this date: see Alan J. Fletcher, *Drama, Performance and Polity in Pre-Cromwellian Ireland* (Cork: Cork University Press, 2000), pp. 263–4.

4. John O'Keeffe, *Recollections of the Life of John O'Keeffe, Written by Himself*, 2 vols. (London: Henry Colburn, 1826), vol. I, pp. 289–90.

5. Umberto Eco, *Travels in Hyperreality: Essays*, translated William Weaver (London: Harcourt Brace Jovanovich, 1983), p. 209.

6. John Baldwin Buckstone. *The Green Bushes: Or, a Hundred Years Ago: A Drama in Three Acts.* (London: National Acting Drama Office, n.d. [1845]), pp. iv, v.

7. Cited in Richard Fawkes, *Dion Boucicault: A Biography* (London: Quartet, 1979), p. 81.

8. *The Catholic Telegraph*, 30 March (1861) and 6 April (1861).

9. Dion Boucicault, *Arrah-na-Pogue: Or the Wicklow Wedding: An Irish Drama in Three Acts.* Promptbook (Dublin: Theatre Royal, 1864), Harvard Theatre Collection, Houghton Library, TS 3055 45, p. 43.

10. 'The Dublin Stage', *United Irishman* 2:1 (4 March 1899), 3.

11. Lady Gregory, *Our Irish Theatre: A Chapter of Autobiography* (Gerrards Cross, 1972), p. 20.

12. Æ [George Russell], 'The dramatic treatment of heroic literature', *United Irishman* 7:166 (3 May 1902), 3.

13. Nicholas Grene, *The Politics of Irish Drama: Plays in Context from Boucicault to Friel* (Cambridge: Cambridge University Press, 1999), pp. 51–76.

14. Cited in Lionel Pilkington, *Theatre and the State in Twentieth-Century Ireland: Cultivating the People* (London: Routledge, 2001), p. 60.

15. Christopher Murray, *Twentieth-Century Irish Drama: Mirror Up to Nation* (Manchester: Manchester University Press, 1997), p. 101.
16. Anthony Roche, *Contemporary Irish Dramatists: From Beckett to McGuinness* (Dublin: Macmillan, 1994), p. 5.
17. Keir Elam, *The Semiotics of Theatre and Drama* (London: Methuen, 1980), p. 117.
18. Gabriel Fallon, 'Yellow moons and purple cathedrals', *Irish Monthly* 64, 75 (July 1936), p. 455.
19. Fergus Linehan, 'The Abbey and the future', *Irish Times*, 18 July 1966.
20. Fintan O'Toole, *Tom Murphy: The Politics of Magic* (Dublin: New Island, 1994), p. 207.
21. Seamus Deane, 'The longing for modernity', *Threshold* 32 (Winter 1982), 1.
22. Thomas Kilroy, *Double Cross* (London: Faber, 1986), p. 7.

Further reading

William M. Demastes and Bernice Schrank (eds.), *Irish Playwrights, 1880–1995: A Research and Production Sourcebook* (Westport, CT: Greenwood Press, 1997)

Alan J. Fletcher, *Drama, Performance and Polity in Pre-Cromwellian Ireland* (Cork: Cork University Press, 2000)

Adrian Frazier, *Behind the Scenes: Yeats, Horniman and the Struggle for the Abbey Theatre* (Berkeley: University of California Press, 1990)

Nicholas Grene, *The Politics of Irish Drama: Plays in Context from Boucicault to Friel* (Cambridge: Cambridge University Press, 1999)

John P. Harrington, *The Irish Play on the New York Stage, 1874–1966* (Lexington, KY: Kentucky University Press, 1997)

Eamonn Jordan (ed.), *Theatre Stuff: Critical Essays on Contemporary Irish Drama* (Dublin: Carysfort Press, 2000)

D. E. S. Maxwell, *Modern Irish Drama 1891–1980* (Cambridge: Cambridge University Press, 1984)

Christopher Morash, *A History of Irish Theatre: 1601–2000* (Cambridge: Cambridge University Press, 2002)

Christopher Murray, *Twentieth-Century Irish Drama: Mirror up to Nation* (Manchester: Manchester University Press, 1997)

Lionel Pilkington, *Theatre and the State in Twentieth-Century Ireland: Cultivating the People* (London: Routledge, 2001)

Marilyn Richtarik, *Acting Between the Lines: Field Day Theatre Company and Irish Cultural Politics, 1980–84* (Oxford: Oxford University Press, 1995)

Anthony Roche, *Contemporary Irish Dramatists: From Beckett to McGuiness* (Dublin: Macmillan, 1994)

Stephen Watt, *Joyce, O'Casey and the Irish Popular Theatre* (Syracuse, NY: Syracuse University Press, 1991)

Robert Welch, *The Abbey Theatre 1899–1999: Form and Pressure* (Oxford: Oxford University Press, 1999)

Index

Printed in the United States
75933LV00002B/246

9 780521 82